JOHN CATT'S
Preparatory Schools 2022

25th Edition
Editor: Jonathan Barnes

Published in 2022 by
John Catt Educational Ltd,
15 Riduna Park, Melton
Woodbridge, Suffolk IP12 1BL UK
Tel: 01394 389850   Fax: 01394 386893
Email: enquiries@johncatt.com
Website: www.johncatt.com
© 2022 John Catt Educational Ltd

All rights reserved. No part of this publication may be reproduced, stored in a retrieval system, transmitted in any form or by any means, electronic, mechanical, photocopying, recording, or otherwise, without the prior permission of the publishers.
Database right John Catt Educational Limited (maker). Extraction or reuse of the contents of this publication other than for private non-commercial purposes expressly permitted by law is strictly prohibited. Opinions expressed in this publication are those of the contributors, and are not necessarily those of the publishers or the sponsors. We cannot accept responsibility for any errors or omissions.
Designed and typeset by John Catt Educational Limited.

A CIP catalogue record for this book is available from the British Library.

ISBN: 978 1 915261 07 6

Cover images courtesy of Greenfield School, St Catherine's Prep and Eagle House School

Contacts
Editor
Jonathan Barnes

Advertising & School Profiles
Tel: +44 (0) 1394 389850
Email: sales@johncatt.com

Distribution/Book Sales
Tel: +44 (0) 1394 389863
Email: booksales@johncatt.com

Contents

Editorial
Foreword – Pride in our schools today – and plenty of optimism for the future, *Christopher King, IAPS* 5
How to use this guidebook 9
Choosing a school - what to consider 10
Levelling up, *Charlie Minogue, Moor Park* 12
Can I ask a silly question?, *Ipswich Prep School* 14
Forging habits through a soft skills revolution, *James Featherstone, Exeter Cathedral School* 16
'Play is the highest form of research', *Danielle Armstrong, Bridgewater School* 18
Paved paradise in a parking lot, *Regan Schreiber, Hazlegrove Prep School* 20
A guide to choosing your child's primary school, *Samantha Scott, Heathcote Preparatory School* 22
Why scholarships are such a win-win, *Highfield and Brookham Schools* 24
The real-world benefits of a broad education, *Tania Botting, Greenfield School* 26
The opportunity to shine, *Ballard School* 28
A focus on happiness, wellbeing and integrity, *Merchiston* 30
Selecting senior schools, *Richard Berlie, St. Anthony's School for Boys* 32
Initial advice 34
Help in finding the fees, *Chris Procter* 42

Profiles
Schools in the UK
England Central & West 46
         East 55
         East Midlands 72
         Greater London 73
         London 80
         North-West 94
         South-East 96
         South-West 115
         West Midlands 122
         Yorkshire & Humberside 131
Scotland 137
Wales 143

continued...

Geographical directory of schools in the United Kingdom D147
Channel Islands D149
England   Central & West D151
          East D157
          East Midlands D165
          Greater London D169
          London D175
          North-East D185
          North-West (including Isle of Man) D187
          South-East D193
          South-West D205
          West Midlands D211
          Yorkshire & Humberside D217
Northern Ireland D221
Scotland D223
Wales D227

Index 231

Pride in our schools today – and plenty of optimism for the future

Christopher King, CEO of IAPS, writes the foreword to the 2022 edition

"So how are your schools?" is pretty much the standard way people I meet professionally open a conversation with me. I'm not entirely sure what response is anticipated by those who ask this question but I certainly know how I frame my answer. Essentially the questioner can expect a response from me along the lines of, "They're upbeat, optimistic and pushing ahead, thank you".

The truth is the first lockdown and subsequent Covid-19 related setbacks, operationally speaking, were hugely difficult and there was a negative impact on finances. However, apart from a few stand out cases where governors were overly aggressive when demanding fees be paid in full, the schools played it fair with parents, set out the financial situation they found themselves in and discovered there was, and indeed is, tremendous levels of inbuilt support for our schools. No doubt helped by the very successful roll-out of an online learning experience; few, if any, schools are reporting a knowledge deficit amongst their pupils as a result of Covid-19. The vast majority of parents have paid their fees bill, with remarkable good grace, and confidence within our schools rapidly returned. The doomsayers who predicted the closure of vast numbers of independent schools as a direct result of the pandemic are left looking rather silly, as their dire gloomy predictions proved a million miles from the reality.

The reality is one where pupil rolls have risen right across the IAPS membership, no matter in which geographical area they are located. There are challenges, with some schools reporting a particularly competitive recruitment situation with regards to the nursery and early years. However, the perspective switches very rapidly to a far more positive picture in the older age groups and the buoyant nature of recruitment has become a feature of our schools.

All this has had knock-on effects as confidence has grown throughout IAPS membership. Capital projects, which were put on hold for 12 months, are now underway and, as I travel around the country, I see new investment manifested in construction sites as buildings come out of the ground. It is interesting to note that schools are investing in new classrooms to support the delivery of the core curriculum. The statement being made is one around the importance of the main activity of any school being, of course, the delivery of knowledge and skills associated with the school's curriculum.

Just two examples of this would be the investment Westonbirt School is making in classroom facilities on a site which has to be sensitively considered given the Grade 1 listed buildings in close proximity to the new build. Belmont School, located at Holmbury St. Mary near Dorking has seen a growth in demand as it took the decision to educate through to 16 and offer GCSEs. This positive move for the schools has allowed the cranes to move onto the school site as their new facilities begin to take shape. Here again, the emphasis is on classrooms to support the delivery of the curriculum.

The whole experience of managing the day-to-day ever-changing situation associated with the time of the coronavirus has taken some toll on the heads and leaders of our schools. The changing advice from the government made for the most difficult of times. Nobody but a fool would want to openly declare that they are feeling so confident that they can say the worst is behind us but a more positive mood has started to wash over the leadership of our schools and, be it plans for a new school,

> The doomsayers who predicted the closure of vast numbers of independent schools as a direct result of the pandemic are left looking rather silly, as their dire gloomy predictions proved a million miles from the reality.

WWW.STORAGETRUNKS.CO.UK

UK MANUFACTURER OF BOARDING, SHIPPING AND STORAGE TRUNKS
20 SIZES IN OVER 100 STYLES AND TRIMS

LARGE BOARDING TRUNKS

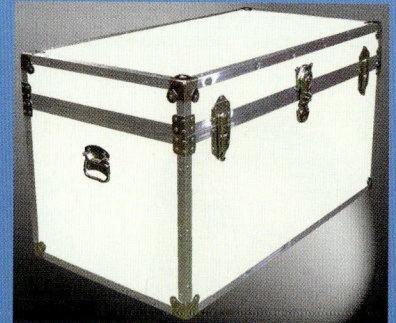

MEDIUM BOARDING TRUNKS

SCHOOL TUCK BOXES

Info@storagetrunks.co.uk

Trunks direct from the factory with a lifetime guarantee

Sales office hours: 01702 216 222 - Outside office hours: 07768 364 726

Logicline Trunks Ltd, Unit 3 High House Farm, Barling Road, Barling, Essex SS3 0LZ

Foreword

Ballard School – see editorial on page 28

a new library or Astro turf, our heads are undoubtedly looking forward, more than back, on very gloomy times.

Those of us who have leadership roles in the independent sector have also started to push ahead with plans to support the current and future membership. In supporting the membership, IAPS is working to help the pathway into headship and during the time in post. A new, demanding coaching course, supported fully in financial terms, is producing a qualified support team who can work with added authority to support newly appointed heads. Before achieving the post of head, IAPS is offering a comprehensive training pathway for those who aspire to senior leadership roles. Targeted, online training offers support with comprehensive, current INSET through the 'ilearning' programme. One head, commenting on ilearning, said that his staff had accessed the training over 1650 times at a cost of about 55p per person. If that's not great value then what is?

It was not so long ago that the IAPS professional development programme ran about 40 courses but that number is now pushing towards 70 and, when collaborations with other organisations are taken into account, the number is higher. The summary of the situation in this regard would be that IAPS members are being provided with an ever-increasing range of services and support delivered in a more professional way.

There are times when heads feel they need additional support for an independent and qualified source. To date, though, it has been only the wealthier schools who could afford external consultants so, to bridge the gap between demand and affordability, IAPS has started its own consultancy arm; Consultancy@IAPS. This new offer can match experience in a wide range of topics to member schools in a very cost-effective manner. It has already helped with staff appointments, staff appraisals or advised in-depth on curriculum development. It is hoped that as awareness grows of this service it will be widely adopted by IAPS heads.

IAPS as an organisation has been around for approaching 130 years. It would not have endured unless it and the schools in membership were innovators and progressive in outlook. We can see this continues to be the case today and, as a result, there is a lot of well-placed optimism now and for the future.

For more information about IAPS, see page 37

How to use this guidebook

Are you looking for...

Help and advice?
If so, take a look at our editorial section (pages 5 to 43). Here you will find articles written by experts in their field covering issues you may well come across when choosing a school for your child.

A school or college in a certain geographical region?
Then you need to go to the map on D148 to find the directory page reference to a particular region. We suggest that you look first in the directory for basic information about all the schools in each region, complete with contact details, so that you will be better informed about the choices available to you. From this section you will be directed to more detailed information in the profile section, where this is available.

A certain type of school or college in a particular area?
Look in the directories for the area you want (again, you can find a directory page reference from the regional map on D148). Underneath each school listed you will find icons that denote different types of schools or qualifications that they offer. You can find a key to these icons on the following page; this key is repeated at the front of each section of the directory.

A specific school or college?
If you know the name of the school or college but are unsure of its location, simply go to the index at the back of the guide where you will find all the schools listed alphabetically. You will find that some page numbers are prefixed with the letter D, this denotes that the school appears in the directory section. Page numbers not prefixed by the letter D denote schools that have chosen to include a fuller school profile, which will provide you with much more extensive information.

More information on relevant educational organisations and examinations?
In the editorial section you will find 'Initial advice', a helpful explanation of the various educational organisations relevant to preparatory schools. There are articles from the Boarding Schools Association (BSA), Girls' Schools Association (GSA), Headmasters' and Headmistresses' Conference (HMC), Independent Association of Preparatory Schools (IAPS), Independent Schools Association (ISA), Independent Schools Council (ISC) and the Society of Heads.

Keys to directory information
The diagrams below explain what the different icons used in the directory mean, and indicate the type of information given for each school in the directory.

Key to directory

- County
- Name of school or college
- Address and contact number
- Head's name
- Age range
- Number of pupils. B = boys G = girls
- Fees per annum.
  Day = fees for day pupils.
  WB = fees for weekly boarders.
  FB = fees for full boarders.

Wherefordshire

College Academy

For further details see p. 00

Which Street, Whosville,
Wherefordshire AB12 3CD

Tel: 01000 000000

Head Master: Dr A Person

Age range: 11–18

No. of pupils: 660 B330 G330

Fees: Day £11,000 WB £16,000 FB £20,000

Key to icons (abridged)

Key to symbols:
- Boys' school
- Girls' school
- International school

Schools offering:
- Boarding accommodation
- Bursaries
- A levels
- International Baccalaureate
- Learning support

Choosing a school – what to consider

However much a school may appeal at first sight, you still need sound information to form your judgement

Schools attract pupils by their reputations, so most go to considerable lengths to ensure that parents are presented with an attractive image. Modern marketing techniques try to promote good points and play down (without totally obscuring) bad ones. But every Head knows that, however good the school prospectus is, it only serves to attract parents through the school gates. Thereafter the decision depends on what they see and hear. Research we have carried out over the years suggests that in many cases the most important factor in choosing a school is the impression given by the Head. As well as finding out what goes on in a school, parents need to be reassured by the aura of confidence that they expect from a Head. How they judge the latter may help them form their opinion of the former. In other words, how a Head answers questions is important in itself and, to get you started, we have drawn up a list of points that you may like to consider. Some can be posed as questions and some are points you'll only want to check in your mind. They are not listed in any particular order and their significance will vary from family to family, but they should be useful in helping you to form an opinion.

Before visiting and asking questions, **check the facts** – such as which association the school belongs to, how big it is, how many staff *etc*. Is there any form of financial pie chart showing how the school's resources are used? The answers to questions like these should be in the promotional material you've been sent. If they aren't, you've already got a good question to ask!

Check the website. Is it up-to-date? Look at the school's social media feeds and videos. What type of tone do they set? That first impression is very important.

When you get to the school you will want to judge the overall atmosphere and decide whether it will suit you and your child. Are any other members of the family going to

Greenfield School – see editorial on page 26

help to pay the fees? If so, their views are important and the school's attitude towards them may be instructive.

When you make it to the inner sanctum, **what do you make of the Head as a person?** Age? Family? Staying? Moving on? Retiring? Busted flush? Accessible to children, parents and staff? If you never get to see the Head, but deal with an admissions person of some sort, it may not mean you should rule the school out, but it certainly tells you something about the school's view of pupil recruitment.

Academic priorities – attitude towards league tables? This is a forked question. If the answer is 'We're most concerned with doing the best for the child', you pitch them a late-developer; if the answer is, 'Well, frankly, we have a very high entry threshold', then you say 'So we have to give you a foolproof academic winner, do we?'

Supplementary questions:

- What is the ratio of teachers to pupils?
- What are the professional qualifications of the teaching staff?
- What is the school's retention rate? In prep schools this means how many pupils do they lose at 11 when the school goes on to 13.
- How long is the school day – and week?
- What are the school's exam results?
- What are the criteria for presenting them?
- Were they consistent over the years?
- Is progress accelerated for the academically bright?
- How does the school cope with pupils who do not work?
- Where do pupils go when they leave?
- How important and well resourced are sports, extra-curricular and after school activities, music and drama?
- What cultural or other visits are arranged away from the school?

Other topics to cover:

- What is the school's mission?
- What is its attitude to religion?
- How well is the school integrated into the local community?
- How have they responded to the Charities Act initiatives?
- What are the responsibilities and obligations at weekends for parents, pupils and the school?
- Does the school keep a watching brief or reserve the option to get involved after a weekend incident?
- What is the school's attitude to discipline?
- Have there been problems with drugs, drink or sex? How have they been dealt with?
- What is the school's policy on bullying?
- How does the school cope with pupils' problems?
- What sort of academic and pastoral advice is available?
- What positive steps are taken to encourage good manners, behaviour and sportsmanship?
- What is the uniform?
- What steps are taken to ensure that pupils take pride in their personal appearance?
- How often does the school communicate with parents through reports, parent/teacher meetings or other visits?
- What level of parental involvement is encouraged both in terms of keeping in touch with staff about your own child and more generally, *eg* a Parents' Association?

And finally – and perhaps most importantly – what does your child make of the school, the adults met, the other children met, pupils at the school in other contexts, and the website?

Levelling up

Charlie Minogue, Headmaster of Moor Park in Shropshire, explains the transformative power of bursaries and how we might level up rather than dumb down

If a random sample of British adults were to play a game of word association when the chosen words were 'prep', 'independent' or 'private school', the results would be predictable. 'Posh', 'exclusive' and 'expensive' might make an appearance, although so might 'excellence', 'results' and 'success'. Placed against these preconceptions of independent education, it is easy to see why some politicians feel the days of independent schools' charitable status to be numbered.

Even as a Headmaster of an independent prep school, I sometimes struggle, morally, to reconcile the opportunities that we can create with the reality for many children across the country, despite the best efforts of so many fellow professionals in maintained schools. Having started my career in the state sector, I only made the switch because I felt I would have the freedom to design an education that worked in the fullest sense and the ability to create something unique and bespoke for every child is a joy. The moral tension comes from considering why this is only available for those who can afford it, although surely it can never be right to knock excellence and reduce everything to the lowest common denominator in the quest for equality.

The charitable status of most independent schools hides, from some, our need to balance the books. This is particularly challenging in prep schools where the fees are lower and the margins tighter: the preconceptions of wealth held by many are simply incorrect in most cases. Competition between prep schools can be fierce and the need to demonstrate relative strength and quality over rival schools is essential. This need creates a tension between the school as a business and the school as a charity, and it would be easy for Heads and Bursars to prioritise the former at the expense of the latter. Not only would this be morally wrong, it is also a short-term and blinkered course of action and schools, even small prep schools, need to factor creating inclusivity into their business plans so that they are a charity in action as well as in name.

I can't describe the satisfaction to be gained from watching a child benefit from support from the school as a charity. It feels right, is transformative for those involved, and justifies the charitable status of the school. All involved benefit. Given appropriate levels of financial and strategic planning, it is possible, even for small independent schools, to provide their brand of education to a wider cross-section of society and this broadening of access to the best of British education is something to be celebrated. In senior schools, the level of bursary support is greater again, with many schools actively seeking to broaden access with bursaries of up to 100% of the fees and some even work with prep schools to create a pathway from prep school entry through to the end of their secondary education.

The provision of bursaries demonstrably levels up society in some small way but the scale of what is possible is, of course, not enough. There is no philosophical barrier to opening our doors to the whole of society. I know of no Head of an independent school who would not leap at the chance to open their doors and provide an education for free, and any blockage to this is caused by pure economics.

What is the answer? Well, we can look to the rest of the world for examples of how state and private education co-exist far more equitably than they do in the UK. In this country, all taxpayers fund state education but only some are using it, the others choosing to pay extra for their children to be educated privately. In other countries, the money follows the child and parents may choose to top this sum up to have their child attend an independent school. This broadens access, meaning that there is no need for charitable status tax perks and the gap between private and state is much narrower.

I can't think of an argument against making this a reality, other than it may be politically inconvenient to do so. We need to find ways of providing the best possible education to all children in the UK and, whilst there is a moral imperative on schools to offer bursaries and broaden access, there must surely also be a duty for government to be more creative and forward-thinking in finding ways to level up without dumbing down.

For more information about Moor Park, see page 123

Can I ask a silly question?

How to get the most out of a school tour – insights from staff at Ipswich Prep

Looking around the schools you are considering plays perhaps one of the most important parts in the decision making process. Schools, trying their best to make a good impression, will focus on the positives, downplay any potentially weaker areas and be prepared for your visit. So how can you make the most of a tour, what should you be looking out for and what are some of the best questions to ask? Here, a number of Ipswich Prep staff give an insiders' viewpoint.

Pastoral care

James McCaughran, Deputy Head and Pastoral Lead, says that wellbeing has deservedly become even more of a focus for parents during the pandemic as we have come to appreciate more than ever the value of human connection. It's essential to really understand how a school supports pupils and families during difficult times and how it promotes positive mental health more generally. Good Prep schools will have established pastoral programmes and you should expect confident and detailed answers.

Talk directly with pupils and staff when you get a chance. Enthusiastic pupils and staff are a good indicator of a strong pastoral care system. A strong pupil voice promotes confidence in children when sharing their experiences at school with someone they have just met. Likewise, caring staff will be welcoming to families looking at their school and proud to showcase their lessons. Watching the interactions between staff and pupils will give you the best feel for how your child will settle into this school environment as well as show how these relationships are valued by both pupil and teacher.

Learning environments should highlight the achievements of the children and be a strong record of the abilities and hard work that they have put into their outcomes. Classes should be colourful, creative and vibrant places where there is a strong sense of purpose aligned with a tingling feel of excitement and fun. Good schools are child-centred and should feel like a place where children can have fun, be creative and express themselves whilst feeling supported and confident whatever the task.

Life outside the classroom

Parents should ask about the range of activities outside of the core curriculum – clubs, wraparound care and school trips. A wide range of choice is important here so that a child can discover new passions, meet different children and learn how to enjoy something they may not necessarily excel at. James McCaughan explains that a broad co-curricular programme is about teamwork, opportunity and taking a risk by trying something new. The aim is to nurture different skill sets to those developed in the classroom and perhaps instil passions for activities that will last a lifetime. We are fortunate to have a wide range of skills in our staff so that we can offer a wonderfully diverse programme of activities and clubs. What might you expect in terms of clubs available? Anything from bushcraft, bingo and gardening all the way through to fives, skiing and robotics.

Behaviour and wellbeing

Don't be embarrassed to ask some hard-hitting questions, particularly around discipline, bullying and if the children feel safe at school. All schools will have issues with behaviour and if a school brushes this question off that should send warning signals.

Rachel Bryanton, Prep Director of Studies Curriculum, explains that teaching children to behave responsibly and with kindness involves continuous dialogue and an interactive approach. Fostering a caring environment by taking time to talk to pupils is important so that they feel happy and safe in and out of school. We teach children that every single one of us has a part to play in ensuring our school remains a happy and safe place to learn.

Ask schools to explain how their anti-bullying policies are addressed – what does this look like in lessons and rewards systems? Recent examples at Ipswich Prep include a 'Kindness Tree' with leaves made by the children to highlight acts of kindness they have experienced or performed. Pupils also took on the role of 'Agony Aunts' and considered what advice they themselves would give to other children experiencing problems. Rachel explains that these activities teach children how to recognise issues and give them the tools and confidence to speak out if anything happens to potentially affect their wellbeing.

There is no such thing as a silly question

It's well worth spending time with the Admissions Manager who will know all about availability of places, assessments and follow-on schools. Make sure you ask the questions that are important to you. Kate Frankland, Ipswich Prep Admissions Manager is adamant that no question is a

silly question! If it matters to you then the answer should matter to the school whether it be a simple question such as what can children bring for a snack, or how much homework do they get, to more difficult questions like how do you deal with friendship niggles or discipline.

We often talk about the most stressful things you do in life being buying a house and getting married but choosing a school for your child is equally as important as one of these big life choices. It is a financial commitment. It is a decision that hopefully you only make once. So it is important to feel completely confident in your choice. Don't allow a school to put undue pressure on you through unrealistic deadlines. There are timelines for the admissions process obviously, but we also appreciate that family lives can be busy.

We always recommend visiting on a normal school day. Open events are great and showcase lots of lovely 'wow moments' but, does the school really do what it says on the tin? You can see first hand the enthusiasm in pupils and staff, get honest answers to the questions that matter to you and see the interactions between teachers and pupils. This really will give you the best feel for how your child would settle into the school.

For more information about Ipswich Prep School, see page 60

Forging habits through a soft skills revolution

James Featherstone, Headmaster of Exeter Cathedral School, advocates for character education

'We cannot live life well or create a good society apart from acquiring and practising virtue': Aristotle

Dennis Silk, celebrated former Warden of Radley College and sometime President of the MCC, says in the BBC documentary 'Public School' that a school's main purpose is to help its pupils acquire 'the right habits for life'. That was in 1979. 40-plus years later, most of modern educational thinking seems to be agreeing with him. Most months there's something in the press about the increased importance that employers are placing on 'soft skills' (terminology which, with one bullishly ill-advised adjective, undermines and undervalues the very point these articles – and employers – are making); Dr Anthony Seldon, whilst (iconic) Head of Wellington College, made the headlines with the rolling-out of his Wellbeing lessons, his insistence on 'service', and his school's sector-leading focus on Character, Grit, and Resilience; the founding of the UK-wide Jubilee Centre for Character and Virtues; and the rapid rise in in-house initiatives across the country such as Failure Weeks, Silent Retreats, Random Acts of Kindness Weeks; and our own daily periods of stillness and reflection in the Cathedral as part of our programme called 'Mind, Body & Soul', all suggest pretty strongly that we are, as a nation and as a sector, becoming slightly less hesitant to agree with Professor James Arthur's assertion (2013) that 'character matters more than attainment'.

Heads are afforded various soap-box moments during term time, and one of the consistent messages that I try to give during mine (Newsletters, Head's Assemblies, Speech Days and the like) is that it matters very much to me that children be recognised and rewarded not just for what they achieve, but for the way in which they go about trying to achieve it. In other words: attainment matters, but character matters more. In other words: those 'soft' skills are the ones that count the most. In other words: those 'habits for life' are what we really prize. The development and promotion of good character, the upholding and embedding of core values, the modelling and nurturing of the right habits, and the acquiring and practising of key skills are at the heart of what we try to do as a staff team at Exeter Cathedral School.

There is a great deal of talk across the educational sectors about the quasi-impossible task facing schools

Exeter Cathedral School

today: as Richard Riley (US Secretary of Education under Bill Clinton) once put it, 'We are currently preparing students for jobs that don't yet exist…using technologies that haven't yet been invented…in order to solve problems we don't even know are problems yet'. Terrific emphasis continues to be placed on the importance of STEM (Sciences, Technology, Engineering, Maths): the future is computer-based; educate children for that future.

And yet Andrew Pinsent, Research Director at the Ian Ramsey Centre for Science and Religion, University of Oxford, makes the point that from here-on-in anything that can be automated will be; anything that can be run by/done by computers will be; and so what's left for people at that point? His answer: all the important stuff. To think on that a little longer: in a world increasingly governed by and served by machines, the 'soft skills' (empathy, emotional intelligence, manners, social intelligence, nuance, persuasion, kindness, subtlety of expression, interpretation of information, team work, leadership, self-reflection, self-awareness, perspective, gentleness: in short, awareness) are going to be more important than ever as today's young adults head out into the world seeking employment and meaningful relationships. Will Gompertz, the BBC's Arts Editor, takes this to its logical conclusion and makes the case for every school being an arts school, because everything else will end up being done by computers.

There is, as is usually the case with these things, a balance to be struck. Schools must embrace the use of technology as a learning tool and recognise the importance of digital literacy in the lives and futures of pupils. Which is why we were so pleased when our lockdown remote learning package – ECS@Home (and its spin-off, Choristers@Home) – received acclaim from Microsoft Education who branded us an 'Industry Leader for Remote Learning'.

But good schools must also be environments where 'soft skills' are highly-valued, modelled, promoted and prized. As I have said before during my soap-box moments, the primary role of an outstanding school is to work with families to help pupils acquire the right values, habits, and skills for life. Our 9 ECS Habits (child-friendly value concepts) underpin everything we do; all of our interactions and all of our decision-making. Awareness – of self, of others, and of one's own impact – is key: we encourage children to be mindful of, and grateful for, those around them, and, through faith or a broader sense of spirituality borne out of the daily presence of the cathedral's gentle majesty in their lives, appreciate that they are part of something greater and more timeless than themselves.

Silk, Seldon, Pinsent, Gompertz and Featherstone (audacity fully acknowledged) may all agree on what matters most, but none of these can claim to be the first to have thought of it: I suspect that we ought to hand that one to Aristotle, too – 'It is not unimportant, then, to acquire one sort of habit or another right from our youth; rather it is very important, indeed all important'.

For more information about Exeter Cathedral School, see page 115

'Play is the highest form of research'

The benefits of attending preschool, by Danielle Armstrong, Early Years Teacher at Bridgewater School, Worsley

As an Early Years teacher, I am a huge advocate of young children attending preschool and formal nursery settings. I believe that doing so allows children to develop in various ways, both earlier and more successfully than they would if they only began their journey through education from compulsory school age. There is a lot of research around this subject that serves to back up these thoughts and shows the many benefits of beginning education at an early age.

Melhuish, Gardner and Morris (2017) reported that the use of formal early childcare settings was linked to more prosocial behaviour, better verbal ability and better behavioural self-regulation. This is something that we see first-hand in our setting. Bridgewater School is a 3-18 school and many pupils begin their journey in Kindergarten and continue right through to Sixth Form. We are able to see their growth and development right the way through their education and celebrate their successes throughout.

Preschool settings have a plethora of opportunities, designed to develop and support children to progress in all 'Areas of Learning'. Many of these activities, in addition to resources, are not available in more informal or childminder settings. Children who attend preschools settle into routines quickly and are able to enjoy and benefit from the slight formality of structure. I find that the children in our care thrive on the security of the routine of our day. They settle into it quickly and soon learn that we are part of a whole school environment.

During the first national lockdown in 2020, children were unable to attend their preschool settings. This has had a noticeable effect on key skills for young children, especially with regards to their communication and social skills. Although subsequent lockdowns saw nursery and preschool settings reopening to all children, and not just those that were deemed to be vulnerable or the children of keyworkers, many parents chose to keep their children at home. As more normality returns, class sizes in preschools are rising and are closer now to 'pre-Covid' levels. Many of these children are coming into settings having never been exposed to the language and opportunities that they would otherwise have had. As a result of this, a stronger emphasis has been placed upon the importance of Communication and Language (C&L) as well as Personal, Social and Emotional Development (PSED) within the Early Years Framework.

When Covid-19 hit and lockdowns were implemented, children's worlds became considerably smaller. They were contained to their homes and gardens, many only saw their extended families over Zoom, they missed out on important and integral interactions with their peers and they were unable to engage in normal life experiences. Sadly, this has had a detrimental effect on the confidence and emotional stability of young children. A recent study, by Davis, Hendry, Gliga and McGillion (2021), found that children who did attend nursery and preschool during the pandemic displayed a greater growth in receptive vocabulary and executive function. It is imperative that we, as Early Years practitioners, work hard in order to repair the damage that lockdown and the pandemic has had upon the children who missed out on early opportunities. We must support children as they separate from their parents and carers, guide them as they begin to interact with their peers and encourage them to talk and listen.

As we know, the early years of a child's life are crucial to their development. The experiences that they have and the neurological pathways that are created during this time, are the same pathways that they will use for a variety of tasks throughout their whole lives. Preschools are essential to ensure that children are 'school ready' and have had the chance to create a solid foundation. This has been seen to have a knock on effect throughout their education, both primary and secondary, as well as having an impact upon employment and income in their adult lives. The Effective Pre-School, Primary and Secondary Education Project (EPPSE) showed that children who attended preschools had better educational and social outcomes at the end of Key Stage 1, at the end of primary school and at the end of secondary school (Sylva et al, 2004). It was reported that this was particularly true when children had attended preschool at an early age and in settings with highly qualified staff (Sylva et al. 2004). There has been additional research that suggests that children who attended preschool would go on to experience financial benefits in terms of higher estimated earnings (Goodman & Sianesi 2005; Taggert et al., 2005).

Government funding schemes have allowed more children to attend preschools and nurseries where they are able to benefit from the rich and stimulating environments that these settings provide. This, in turn, means that more children in the country are being given the best start in life and are being encouraged and supported to develop across all 'Areas of Learning', in particular, in C&L and PSED. They have the advantage of being scaffolded by highly trained early years practitioners who know how to encourage children to meet their full potential. This is something that we continually strive to do here at Bridgewater School.

Hopefully, as we begin to look towards putting the turbulent events of the last couple of years behind us, we can concentrate on ensuring that the current and future generations continue to have full and enriched experiences throughout their crucial early years.

References
Davies, C., Hendry, A., Gibson, S. P., Gliga, T., McGillion, M., & Gonzalez-Gomez, N. (2021). Early childhood education and care (ECEC) during COVID-19 boosts growth in language and executive function. Infant and Child Development, 30(4), e2241.
Goodman, A., & Sianesi, B. (2005). Early Education and Children's Outcomes: How Long Do the Impacts Last? Fiscal Studies, 26, 513-548.
Melhuish, E., Gardiner, J. & Morris, S. (DfE) (2017). Study of Early Education and Development (SEED): Impact Study on Early Education Use and Child Outcomes up to Age Three. DFE-RR706. London: DfE.
Sylva, K., Melhuish, E., Sammons, P., Siraj-Blatchford, I. and Taggart, B. (2004b), The Effective Provision of Pre-School Education (EPPE) Project: Final report. London: SureStart DfES Publications Ref SSu/FR/2004/01

For more information about Bridgewater School, see page 94

Paved paradise in a parking lot

(With apologies to Joni Mitchell and her Big Yellow Taxi), Regan Schreiber, Head of Boarding at Hazlegrove Prep School, considers the importance of the school car park

Ignore the website, forget the shiny brochure, and don't even bother with the front hall – go no further than the school parking lot!

Word of mouth is everything in this game, and where is this more evident and truthful than in the car park? The gravel serves as a natural truth serum – all is revealed. Everything from life hacks and the frustrations and tribulations of being a parent to the best deals and bargains to be bought are discussed in this arena of mothers and fathers. Drop-off and collection serve as the touchpoints – the chance to engage and connect, to find out the truth. "Have you heard about...? Is it true? Apparently..." All is revealed in the school car park. Like children in classrooms, sharing anecdotes about their parents, parents solve the world's problems and spill the beans whilst pausing and chatting in this, the real and very honest entrance to the school.

What does the car park say about the school? What can you learn about the school from the gravel quadrangle where all roads meet?

The humble car park – gravel or tarmac, with the obligatory muddy puddle for little wellies, all look similar. The gravel may even put you at ease as children bounce through it like bathers on Durdle Door's stony shores. But step back, if you dare, and you may see the start of the magic of the school, as it unfolds right before your very eyes.

Teachers will greet you and your children by name. They will smile and more than likely (and we, teachers, make no apologies for this), crack a "dad joke"; all adding to the richness and promise of a new school day. The children will make their way down the path – cobbled, brightly-coloured mosaic or grassy, on their own – with their heads held high, embracing independence as they start writing their own story.

In the depths of winter, warm lights will illuminate their path as they skip along to school, bag in hand – while the sport's bag, music instrument or ballet shoes, are left in the car for you to take to the front hall...after all, they too want you to experience the warm welcome!

In the evenings, teachers will tick the register and "insist" on a polite and proper "Good evening and good-bye", similar to Jim Carrey's character, in the Truman Show. At Christmas time, your conversation will be soaked in the glow of a Christmas tree and fairy lights, as you talk about the Pre-Prep Nativity and the school's delicious home-made mince pies...and hopefully, the generous glass of mulled wine on offer!

In the summer, you'll fill your shopping bag with fresh produce and baked goodies from the stalls of the school fete, as the children do their bit for charity; and you may even find yourself tempted to "bust some moves" or "sing along" to budding young musicians busking.

And just maybe, if the entertainment and chauffeur duties allow, you could also find yourself earwigging on the conversation a car down from you. You will hear stories filling the air – stories of fun lessons, the latest antics on the playground or awards won in assembly.

Schools shouldn't shy away from the car park; they should stride along to it, happy to share and meet-and-greet. Word-of-mouth is so important in this business but word-of-mouth, to schools, also means connecting,

> Word of mouth is everything in this game, and where is this more evident and truthful than in the car park? The gravel serves as a natural truth serum – all is revealed.

engaging and listening to our children and parents, in this, the coliseum of truth, the car park.

So, before you lean over and check the rear-view mirror or lick your hand to tease your child's bed-hair, wind your window down and allow the natter of the car park to fill your car. And then bravely crunch into the gravel and soak it all up – your child's journey starts here, in the car park – on the paved paradise.

For more information about Hazlegrove Prep School, see page 116

A guide to choosing your child's primary school

Samantha Scott, Headteacher of Heathcote Preparatory School, considers the most important factors

It seems unbelievable to me, that over a decade ago my husband and I were starting to consider which primary school would be best for our daughter. As an experienced educator, I felt certain I would know the perfect school just by looking at its website and reading through their most recent inspection report. However, this did not prove to be the case and as we delved more deeply into the plethora of choices in our local area I started to become increasingly anxious. I wanted a school that would challenge my child academically of course but I also wanted it to be nurturing, kind and caring and provide creative and sporting opportunities to ensure my little girl grew to be an all-rounder. Of course, I did scrutinise the inspection reports and when looking at independent schools I considered if they had elements of the school that had won awards, such as our recent ISA 'Junior School of the Year' national award and our Science teacher being a finalist for Pearson 'Outstanding New Teacher of the Year'. Not the only things to consider, however they show the recognition of school achievements, provision and talent alongside the fact that the school clearly strives exceptionally hard to be the best. No mean feat I can assure you!

Primary school choices basically split into two categories: independent schools (fee paying) and state schools (maintained e.g. faith schools, free schools (non-government), academies and special educational needs schools). With independent schools, the parents are able to choose from a wider catchment usually as there isn't a geographical restriction placed upon the school, the family chooses the school based upon the opportunities it offers their child, usually the child has taster sessions and settling periods and then hopefully a place will be offered for the child by the Headteacher. Often these schools have nurseries as part of the school and this allows for early, accelerated opportunities of learning and an ease of transition. Often, as with Heathcote, they accept nursery vouchers for this part of the child's start at school. With regard to state schools, the parents look at local schools, considering their likelihood of being offered a place with regard to the numbers in that cohort, the number of places per year group and their locality to their desired 'first place' school.

Primary/Preparatory schools often follow a similar curriculum (the National Curriculum) and offer similar subjects for lessons, although independent schools may follow this curriculum at an accelerated rate due to lower pupil numbers in class and offer specialist subject provision (e.g. specialist language, PE, IT, Music teachers etc with additional rooms/science labs etc). Independent school classes are usually straight cohorts e.g. year 2 not year 1/2 and much smaller in pupil numbers per class. I believe this allows for more teacher/pupil time and for the staff to get to know your child more fully and therefore provision for the pupils is more individualised. Sadly, at this time we need to consider the school's response to the pandemic – did they go straight to live, online lessons as Heathcote did, training all staff to be Microsoft Innovative Educators (MIEs) and an IT lead who is an MIEE, an expert able to support staff at other schools. We were fortunate as our class sizes were smaller than large, state schools that we could safely return to the school site before many others, ensuring our learning provision could continue, intervention programs could be updated and accelerated and our pupil wellbeing was supported through staff MHFAs.

Therefore, with these issues in mind it is important to spend time considering the schools on your short list and think through the following questions, deciding which are your own priorities for your child's educational provision:

- What do I think of their website/recent inspection report?
- What is the transition like to school from Nursery/Preschool?
- What is the provision for learning in the classes? Does it seem a rich, varied curriculum?
- Is there wrap around care? What form does this take and will my child have to travel off site for this? Does this include before and after school and during the holidays? Who supervises the children and are they qualified/first aid trained/will know my child?
- What are the opportunities for my child alongside the curriculum e.g. clubs, co-curricular provision, trips?
- What homework provision is there? Is this part of a pre-planned program that progresses year on year?
- Will my child be supported/extended for their learning to meet their needs?
- Is there a program for individualised learning to promote their understanding/attainment?
- What is the opportunity for assessment and how will this information be shared with parents? Reports? Parents' evenings and are these regularly held?
- Does the school have an active parents' association?
- How is school information shared with parents? Is there a termly/weekly newsletter?
- Will this school meet my child's needs beyond their EYFS experience e.g. sporting opportunities in year 6, 11+ provision for grammar entrances in year 5, academic success in KS2, secondary scholarship support…

Following a call and visit to the school; question if you had access to meet leadership team members – did the Headteacher make time to meet with you if possible? Are the staff welcoming and friendly? Most importantly, can I envisage my child here? Will this school enable them to engage, achieve, flourish and thrive?

Finally, I can't emphasise enough how important it is to look at the school's website as this will give you so much information and showcase how they value their school community. Is there a warmth beyond the information? Is there recent, relevant information? Is it accessible to the school's family that use it? Does it show pupils learning and engaged? Sometimes your personal instincts are more valuable than any written information and you know your child best. Good luck!

Samantha Scott is Headteacher of Heathcote Preparatory School and Nursery, Danbury, Essex currently the ISA's 'Junior School of the Year'.

For more information about Heathcote Preparatory School, see page 58

Why scholarships are such a win-win

Highfield and Brookham Schools are no strangers to scholarship success

The Oxford English dictionary defines a scholarship as 'an amount of money given to somebody by an organisation to help pay for their education'.

Like bursaries, with which they are occasionally confused, scholarships are invariably a mainstay of the private school sector, but while bursaries cover educational expenses based primarily on financial need, scholarships are awarded to pupils based on academic performance.

And that's where their true value really shines through.

Scholarships are a prized asset and have wide-ranging benefits all round – not just to a particular pupil but also to their existing school (which has placed them on a scholarship programme) and their prospective school (which has made the offer of a scholarship).

For the pupil, receiving a scholarship offers easier access to education, access to extensive support and guidance in their specialist pursuit, looks impressive on their CV, and not needing to get a part-time job to fund their education frees up more time to study. The pursuit of a scholarship also helps pupils grow intellectually and emotionally.

For the child's existing prep school, knowing that their pupils have the ability to pick up senior school scholarships is a huge selling point when attempting to attract parents of prospective pupils and is a matter of prestige. It underlines both the quality of teaching and leadership and the calibre of pupils at the school.

And for the senior school, they can gain an advantage over their rivals in the fierce battle for students and breathe easy in the knowledge that their future pupils

Highfield and Brookham Schools

are of sufficient educational standing and ability that their reputation as a leading light in private education will in no way be tarnished.

Highfield and Brookham Schools, respected pre-prep and prep schools in a beautiful rural setting in Liphook, Hampshire, in the heart of the South Downs National Park, are no strangers to the world of scholarship successes.

In the last seven years alone, more than one hundred scholarships have been awarded to children in Year 8, the final year the children spend at Highfield before moving on to some of the top senior schools in the country, such as Wellington, Eton, Marlborough, Charterhouse and Cranleigh.

These scholarships have been awarded across a variety of disciplines – namely academic, dance and drama, art and sport – and bear great testament not only to the regard in which scholarships are held by the school but to the ability and character of the pupils too.

"Children need to show real love and enthusiasm for their subject," said John Muhlemann, who has been Head of Scholarships at Highfield for the past three years.

"Senior schools look at the potential of a pupil and want to know that a pupil is of a certain standard academically, but they also want students who can make a real contribution and play a busy role in school life."

Life in a prep school is always busy and curricular and extra-curricular opportunities plentiful, giving willing children ample chance to gain, foster and harness the skills necessary to impress potential senior schools.

"Prep schools like ours play a huge part in readying children for life at senior school," said Mr Muhlemann.

"Through expert teaching, a high level of pastoral care and a strong and far-reaching range of extra-curricular opportunities, the scholars leave our programme more confident, resilient and ready to take on any challenge that awaits them at senior school.

"The children are routinely challenged and taken out of their comfort zones. You have to be brave to sit a scholarship. These children are constantly pushing the boundaries of what is possible for their age."

As well as receiving the very best direction possible in the classroom, scholars are presented with a wealth of life-enriching, eye-opening and educational trips, discussions, workshops and presentations relevant to their particular specialist subject.

For academic scholars at Highfield, for example, that included a trip to the Houses of Parliament to meet Chichester MP Gillian Keegan (whose constituency includes the Liphook school) and a cultural exchange trip to Fontanellato in Italy.

And the maturity and dedication with which the scholars approached their work left a lasting impression on Jane Hamilton, Mr Muhlemann's predecessor at Highfield, and reinforced the value of scholarship programmes.

"The children were a joy to spend time with. They challenged my thinking, were open to new ideas, and approached everything with enthusiasm and determination. We truly learnt from each other," she said.

The hard work, commitment and resolve shown by all concerned on all sides of the scholarship programme at Highfield, for one, repeatedly make it a win-win situation for the pupils, staff and school alike. There's a lesson to be learned there.

For more about Highfield and Brookham Schools, see page 105

The real-world benefits of a broad education

Tania Botting, Headmistress at Greenfield School, wants to empower her pupils to achieve great things

One of the biggest appeals of an independent education is surely the breadth of the curriculum and opportunities on offer. But what does this breadth offer to our children in real terms?

In pursuit of passion

Everyone should have a passion; something that they adore above all else; something they return to as a source of comfort, pleasure and inspiration. At Greenfield School, we are passionate about providing our pupils with as many opportunities as possible, in order for each child to discover what makes them tick. Be it reading a beloved author's novels, tinkering with mechanical bits and bobs or playing a game that continues to challenge and surprise us, we endeavour to unite each of our pupils with an interest that they will turn to time and time again.

Self-belief

Lots of schools speak of instilling confidence in their pupils, but the root of confidence is found in self-belief and this is something that often has to be nurtured. A school with a broad curriculum offers greater opportunities for cultivating self-belief, particularly in young children. If Art isn't for you, perhaps you'll prefer the Sciences? Or if you find words tricky, maybe you'll feel more secure working with the certainty of number? If numbers make you feel confident then you'll probably enjoy working from a recipe in cookery lessons, or find that you really fly when you are let loose on a STEAM project. Without variety, children miss out on the chance to really identify their strengths and build their self-belief and confidence.

Humility

There is something to be said for recognising that we all encounter things we are less naturally aligned to. Cultivating a genuine sense of humility in the most able children can be a challenge for schools. Recognising that another person has a more natural aptitude or skill for a particular pursuit is an important lesson to learn. An opportunity-focussed education can be academically and intellectually challenging, but it can also help to breed humility amongst children who would otherwise believe themselves to be 'the best' at absolutely everything.

Bravery-building

Learning in an environment where we are all encouraged to try new things lets each child know that success takes work and that it's perfectly acceptable to enjoy some subjects more than others. Developing skills such as determination and perseverance, there is a lot to be said for participating in activities that we find challenging in one way or another. One of the most rewarding sights at Greenfield is watching a child who is yet to find their niche, and perhaps finding school quite challenging, discover that they are the most naturally adept at computer programming, or engineering, or dodgeball, or pottery. One lesson where a child feels emboldened can have the most remarkable ripple-effect on their day, their week or even their year and this is why variety and opportunity is so important.

Real-world skills

Maths, English and Science are an essential foundation for us all, regardless of where we end up. Those who excel in these subjects could do very well right through their educational journey, passing through prep, senior, sixth form and onto a Russell Group University. But what then? Exam results are the currency of education, but once we graduate how do these results translate and what will it be that allows us, or our child, to stand out from the crowd? One of the greatest benefits of a broad curriculum is the skill-building and real-world experiences it can offer. At Greenfield, we work hard to translate every activity, project and skill into a real-world benefit to highlight to the children why public speaking competitions are important, how adapting play during a football game will make them more employable and the impact that tucking your shirt in can have on a first impression.

Intellectual challenge

Some may mistakenly believe that a broad curriculum has a negative impact on academic results due to diminished attention and lesson-time dedicated to Maths, English and Science. Greenfield School had a full curriculum overhaul in 2014 and took the decision to focus on breadth and opportunity. In 2022, we are proud to say that results across the board have soared since then and happily debunk the myth that outstanding academic results can only be achieved from behind a school desk. Practical application of mathematical knowledge, opportunities to conduct experiments outside of the lab and use of English language and literature through drama and dance are just some of the ways in which our children broaden their understanding and elevate their thinking, with astonishing results.

Understanding our place in the world

Schools with truly broad curriculums will cover more than just the anticipated subjects such as Art or Drama. Some schools will even go so far as to invent their own subject in order to tackle issues not otherwise covered in great detail. At Greenfield, the subject Understanding the World was created back in 2014 to address a need to develop a greater understanding of global issues, societal norms, historical movements and modern-day politics amongst the children. This subject is universally loved due to the opportunity it provides for open-ended discussions and debates. As a by-product, the subject boosts pupil involvement, improves negotiation, listening and debating skills and allows our most able children to do some very high-order thinking, which in turn has improved their interview skills when applying to senior school.

Greenfield also has a strong Social Responsibility scheme, which further enforces the impact and influence each individual can have on the world around them. Children who are given the opportunity to participate in democratic voting, debating and discussing ethical issues have a much greater understanding of the impact one individual can have. As an example, it was a pupil at Greenfield who wrote to the Headmistress expressing her desire to wear trousers and presenting her argument in a fair and articulate manner. Needless to say, separate boys' and girls' uniform is a thing of the past! A group of Year 6 children are petitioning the Head of Sport to increase girls' football lessons so that they are equal to those for boys and it is these sorts of spontaneous manifestations that evidence the impact of empowering young children. The effects of a broad curriculum are clear to see as these children continue to effectively express their views and get results. What better way to set a person up for a successful future? Surely, that is the true value of an independent education.

For more information about Greenfield School, see page 104

The opportunity to shine

The co-curricular programme at Ballard School has the highest priority

One of the key benefits of an independent school education is the access to a wide range of co-curricular opportunities. In their study, 'An Unequal Playing Field' (2019), the Social Mobility Commission Chair, Dame Martina Milburn, found that co-curricular activities led to a number of "…important benefits – a sense of belonging, increased confidence and social skills, which are invaluable to employers."

At Ballard, we have underlined the importance of co-curricular activities by creating a new role, Director of Co-curricular, within our Leadership Team, putting it alongside pastoral and academic as the third pillar of our successful holistic education.

"At Ballard, we have a passion for developing the 'whole child'. We believe that in addition to providing a vigorous and challenging academic programme, education must also extend well beyond this, opening up experiences and opportunities that allow all our pupils to develop skills including creativity, independence, teamwork and critical thinking: we prepare them for work and life in a rapidly changing world," said Mrs Victoria Gray, Director of Co-curricular and Director of Performing Arts.

With 120+ activities and GCSE 'Raising Attainment' sessions a week, Ballard's co-curricular programme is designed to give pupils of all ages a breadth of opportunities, from Archaeology to Zumba! Whether it be to develop a passion, focus on a talent, or try something completely new, activities are categorised to help pupils choose appropriately. Whatever their individual strengths or curiosities, there is something for everyone.

Categories include:

- Academic Ambition – broadening our pupils' minds with enrichment beyond the curriculum e.g. chess club and the Townsend Warner History prize.

- Young Entrepreneur – pupils starting their own business through the Young Enterprise scheme or helping to create and edit a podcast or magazine.
- Health and Wellbeing – encouraging pupils to take up a new sport for leisure or enjoy some relaxing mindfulness colouring.
- Technology – our pupils can get involved with CADCAM in the DT department, help in our sound and lighting box, or join the Coding Club.
- Creative Arts – our pupils can take part in one of our productions on stage or behind the scenes; experience working with varied materials in the Art Department, join our Visions Dance company, or become a member of one of our choirs and bands, working towards the next European tour.
- Accreditation – Ballard has a strong record with the Duke of Edinburgh Award and Arts Award scheme.
- Community and Campaigning – our pupils are community focused with many raising money for an array of charities. Our Eco Ambassadors and Climate Change clubs have shaped Ballard's green credentials, including the introduction of bees, chickens and allotments. Recently, three of our ten-year-old girls asked for donations to their fundraising page, rather than birthday presents, raising over £1,000 for a local hospice.

We have also embraced traditional extra-curricular activities within our curriculum including: from Nursery, regular Nature Walks; from Kindergarten the addition of Forest School and Beach School. In Lower Prep (Years 3 to 5), we have included three strands of Life Skills within our curriculum, introducing all our pupils to charity work, housekeeping and emotional intelligence. In the Autumn Term, our Year 3 pupils have learnt: what is the purpose of a charity, working effectively in a team, planning and running a bake sale; in the Spring Term they learn how to follow a recipe, use and select a screwdriver, use a microwave and dishwasher; in the Summer Term they learn the difference between wants and needs, recognising our feelings and overcoming a disagreement. These are all excellent skills for pupils to learn.

Trips are an excellent source of enrichment too and it is always worth asking your potential schools what trips they arrange. At Ballard we are lucky enough to have many day-trips: from the Titanic story at SeaCity to coasteering off the Dorset coast; from playing hockey at the Olympic Stadium to singing at the Royal Albert Hall. Pupils in Years 5 to 11 also have at least one residential trip each year, with many wonderful memories being made. Additional opportunities include ski trips, cultural trips and music and sports tours.

"I started Ballard in Nursery and have loved every moment. I love Forest School: playing with my friends; making fairy houses; weaving sticks together and going in the stream with my wellies on. I love Expressive Arts too – music, dancing and acting; singing in the concerts and at the Priory is really special." Lorelei (Year 4)

"There are lots of opportunities at Ballard. Highlights for me include our: team building days; weekly 'Apprentice Challenge' (Year 5); Leadership and Gifted & Talented days and pitching in the Dragons' Den. I loved Harp Club and I'm now studying Grade 5 cello; I was Narla in the 'Lion King' and then Wendy in 'Peter Pan'. I'm a big fan of all the extra-curricular activities; jewellery making, volleyball, pop orchestra and DofE. I love all the trips: from learning the physics of rides at Paulton's Park in Year 4 to speaking French throughout our Year 6 Normandy trip. My favourite, so far, was the Bude activities trip – it was incredible and our year group got even closer." Ella (Year 8)

"Opportunities at Ballard are countless; the amount of activities are awe-inspiring. Pupils can start at 7:30am and leave at 5.00pm or 6.00pm, having done breakfast, break, lunch and after-school activities or clinics. There's an extensive range of trips to cater for all interests, both locally and abroad; creating lasting memories. I particularly loved the Tuscany music trip. Singing in a sacred Florentine church and on top of the Leaning Tower to applause from below; we cheered with locals and danced as the band belted out 'Wonderland' at our final gig. These trips shape you, increasing knowledge and encouraging independence." Amy (Year 11)

So, when selecting your school, make sure that you ask about their enrichment programme and the opportunities afforded to your children, it will not only help your child's studies but also their wellbeing and individuality; most of all, it will help with their happiness.

"It goes without saying how happy both of our children are at Ballard and we love the nurturing and building up of their character that is given." (Lower Prep parent)

For more information about Ballard School, see page 98

A focus on happiness, wellbeing and integrity

How Merchiston supports individuals' wellbeing to benefit the whole community

Wellbeing underpins everything we do at Merchiston. It is what makes for meaningful and connected conversations. It is how we get to know our students really well, how we can support and motivate them, to enable them to thrive because they are understood, valued, and supported in everything they do.

Our Rights Respecting Schools work informs the whole School and leads to a focus on children's rights and wellbeing, encouraging us to advocate for global justice and sustainable living.

Merchiston's pupils hold strong feelings about how we can all take action to slow the impact of climate change and the School is very excited to have launched its new Sustainability Committee. It is co-ordinated by pupils in all year groups with support from the Geography Department and involves the whole school, from ground staff, kitchen and domestic staff to support staff and teachers. The pupils are undertaking research and proposing improvements, ensuring sustainable practices across the School. These younger generations are determined to make a difference. Overall, the motivation for all is knowing that, "There is no Planet B!".

Students and staff are thrilled to have the opportunity to continue their work to promote sustainability by supporting Edinburgh Zoo and RZSS in their vital efforts to protect animals that are at risk from extinction. To this end, we will soon invite our local Preparatory Schools to get involved in our new art competition in collaboration with the Zoo. We will welcome children to submit designs showing how they would paint and decorate one of the

Zoo's 4-foot giraffe sculptures. The winners will work with our Art Department's staff and students to turn their plan into a reality. After the project is complete, the young artists will take their giraffe back to their school, complete with resources for their friends to learn about these beautiful animals and with a plan to create a habitat for their giraffe as a creative continuation of their work.

We always make sure there is time for creativity and playfulness here at Merchiston. In fact, in order to promote student wellbeing we are currently focusing on the 12 Happiness Habits, of which 'Learning to Play' is just one. Our Deputy Head Wellbeing, Mr Danny Rowlands, writes:

"Happiness is something which needs to be actively pursued, and those who enjoy happiness often do not do so simply through good fortune. Helpfully, various studies have observed that there are common behavioural traits amongst happy people and these have been enshrined in 'The 12 Happiness Habits':

Learn to play
Express gratitude
Savour the positive
Harness your strengths
Live with meaning
Learn optimism
Value relationships
Practice kindness
Get physical
Turn to nature
Practise mindfulness
Strive for success.

During our first term of the academic year we celebrated one habit each week in order to instil these amongst our boys. We have enjoyed assemblies at all levels highlighting individual happiness habits; encouraged play with wild outdoor camps and water sports trips; displayed gratitude towards our friends and staff across the school. With a plethora of outlets for these goals, and by making good practice a habit, there is a real buzz around Merchiston with huge excitement about the opportunities for learning the coming months will bring.

Our exam results show both the consistency and excellence of an education at Merchiston, which place us annually at the top of the league tables of Scottish schools. Not only do our students achieve the highest level of personal academic success, but they have a strong sense of who they are, with respect for others, having learnt what it means to have true integrity.

Now, there's another all-important word: Integrity.

So many of those who have been part of the Merchiston community will often comment that ours is a school with something very special to it that is incredibly hard to articulate. This intangible 'something' that gives a school its identity – far beyond bricks, mortar, and open space – is the most precious asset we have; but how to authentically express it has, for many years, been an unresolved challenge.

We are soon to launch our new 'statement of self' – 'Young Men of Integrity' – both to our own community and the world beyond our walls. In these four words we feel we have honed in on what truly distinguishes Merchiston. It is not our results, as enviable as they may be; nor is it our setting, as stirring and unforgettable as that may remain. It is the young men we are so proud to call our own. In those 'boys' – those young men of integrity - are imbued all the qualities that make a parent proud of their son. Honesty, empathy, determination, commitment, and manners that some might dismiss as 'old fashioned', yet to us mean so much. As part of our new brand 'narrative' extolls:

"To hold that door an extra beat,
To get to your feet,
When the moment calls.
To shake a hand like you mean it,
To take your leave or say your bit.
Means something in these walls."

Through this new expression of ourselves we are now able to confidently return to a single idea that will underpin everything we do as a community. Our mission is as simple as it is profound; to develop young men of integrity. If we can cement that integrity in each and every young man in our care, we have achieved our most fundamental of goals. Examination grades and achievements of all kinds will provide opportunities, but young men of integrity will walk out of our doors and through those that will matter most in the future of our world.

We would enjoy nothing more than to welcome you into our community and to share our beautiful School and grounds with you. Please join us for an in-person visit during which you will be able to meet our students and staff. To find out more, please get in touch with our Director of Admissions, Mrs Kay Wilson on 0131 312 2201 or admissions@merchiston.co.uk. A warm welcome awaits.

For more information about Merchiston, see page 138

Selecting senior schools

Planning the next stage in your child's education needn't be stressful, says Richard Berlie, Headmaster at St. Anthony's School for Boys, London

St. Anthony's School for Boys is an ISI Excellent school in Hampstead, where academic endeavour is nurtured in a safe, familiar community. Thanks to the school's unique ethos, from the time when they start at the school in Reception, all the way through to when they leave at the end of Year 6 or Year 8, every boy is recognised as an individual, with their own personal talents and interests. A rigorous academic curriculum, overseen by the Heads of Faculty, has been put in place to foster inquiry and build knowledge and understanding. Furthermore, a huge array of co-curricular activities – including drama, music-making, singing, art, debating, coding and many more – capture the interest and enthusiasm of young minds.

Pastoral care is of utmost importance throughout the boys' time at the school, but perhaps never more so than as they come to the end of their time there, when the role played by the form tutor enables helpful conversations between home and school regarding selecting secondary schools. The approach is to put the child's needs first, identifying suitable schools where they will be happy and will continue to fulfil their potential.

"My constant refrain to parents is to 'cast the net wide' when it comes to senior school applications," Richard Berlie, Headmaster, explains. "A number of senior staff at St. Anthony's have experience working at ISI Excellent – the highest category – independent boarding and day schools (in my case at Ampleforth, Emanuel and Dulwich), and we have great success in sending

St. Anthony's School for Boys

boys to the 'big and famous' schools. For some boys a highly competitive and academic environment is just the ticket; for others, who are no less bright academically, a more nurturing, less-imposing institution will be more appropriate."

Richard advises that now boys can, they should visit schools on open days. "It is always a good sign when a child waxes lyrical about sporting provision, an experiment seen in the laboratory, or, perhaps most important of all, having felt welcomed and looked after by their hosts," he says. "There is no exact science behind a decision to apply to a particular school and it can be counter-productive to over think the process. Trusting one's instincts, and those of the child himself does require a leap of faith, but at St. Anthony's we can help parents to reach informed decisions."

St. Anthony's advise their families to apply for around six schools, including some competitive options alongside 'safer' choices. Boys going through the 11+ process will be judged on their performance on the day they sit their entrance exams. This is very much a data driven process, with perhaps only the top third of candidates making it through to interview. The 13+ process is more nuanced, with schools paying a little more attention to factors such as co-curricular involvement. Not surprisingly, many parents hedge their bets and apply for a mix of 11+ and 13+ schools.

The school offers comprehensive support to boys preparing for senior school entrance tests. This coming academic year, all Year 6 boys will be allocated an individual laptop that will assist in their preparation for reasoning tests, as well as helping with digital learning in general. A detailed 'Guide to Senior Schools' is updated each year and shared with Year 5 families, and meetings are scheduled to explain the process, dispel myths and steady nerves. Individual interview practice is also arranged for boys. "At St. Anthony's, the individual child is at the centre of our mission, and this informs the bespoke approach we take to senior school applications, and our wider philosophy of education," Richard says.

For admission enquiries, call 020 7435 0316 (stanthonysprep.org.uk)

For more infomation about St Anthony's School for Boys, see page 90

Initial advice

Educational institutions often belong to organisations that encourage high standards. Here we give a brief guide to what some of the initials mean.

BSA

The Boarding Schools' Association

Since its foundation in 1966, the Boarding Schools' Association (BSA) has had the twin objectives of promoting boarding education and the development of quality boarding through high standards of pastoral care and boarding accommodation. Parents and prospective pupils choosing a boarding school can, therefore, be assured that more than 600 schools in nearly 40 countries worldwide that make up the membership of the BSA are committed to providing the best possible boarding environment for their pupils.

A UK boarding school can only be a full member of the BSA if it is also a member of one of the Independent Schools Council (ISC) constituent associations, or in membership of the State Boarding Forum (SBF). These two bodies require member schools to be regularly inspected by the Independent Schools' Inspectorate (ISI) or Ofsted. Other boarding schools who are not members of these organisations can apply to be affiliate members. Similar arrangements are in place for overseas members. Boarding inspection of ISC accredited independent schools has been conducted by ISI since September 2012. Ofsted retains responsibility for the inspection of boarding in state schools and non-association independent schools.

Boarding inspections must be conducted every three years. Boarding is judged against the National Minimum Standards for Boarding Schools which are due to be updated in the next few months.

Relationship with government

The BSA is in regular communication with the Department for Education (DfE) on all boarding matters. The Children Act (1989) and the Care Standards Act (2001) require boarding schools to conform to national legislation and the promotion of this legislation and the training required to carry it out are matters on which the DfE and BSA work together. BSA has worked especially closely with the DfE and other government departments during the coronavirus pandemic over the past 18 months, support the safety and continuity of education for its member schools' pupils and staff, both domestically and internationally.

Boarding training

BSA delivers the world's largest professional development programme for boarding staff. It offers:

- Two-year courses for graduate and non-graduate boarding staff– these involve eight study days and two assignments, each about 4,000 words long. This is the flagship training opportunity for staff seriously interested in boarding excellence

- A Diploma course for senior experienced boarding staff, involving three study days and two assignments spread between March and October

- A broad range of day seminars on topics of particular interest to boarding/pastoral staff – e.g. Essentials of Boarding, Leading the Boarding Team, Meeting the Needs of Overseas Boarders

- Specialists one or two-day conferences for Boarding Staff, Heads, Health & Wellbeing staff**, Marketing and Admissions staff* and State Boarding Schools staff and Safeguarding Leads**& Basic training online, for those very new to boarding.

* With Sacpa (Safeguarding and Child Protection Association), part of the BSA Group
**With Hieda (Heath in Education Association) part of the BSA Group
**With BAISIS (British Association of Independent Schools with International Students), part of the BSA Group

State Boarding Forum (SBF)

BSA issues information with regards to its state boarding school members and BSA should be contacted for details of these schools. In these schools, parents pay for boarding but not for education, so fees are

substantially lower than in an independent boarding school.

Chief Executive: Robin Fletcher
Chief Operating Officer: Aileen Kane

The Boarding Schools' Association
First Floor
27 Queen Anne's Gate
London, SW1H 9BU.
Tel: 020 7798 1580
Email: bsa@boarding.org.uk
Website: www.boarding.org.uk

GSA

The Girls' Schools Association, to which Heads of independent girls' schools belong

The Girls' Schools Association is the 'expert voice of girls' education', helping girls and their teachers to flourish. They represent the Heads of a diverse range of largely independent girls' schools, among which are some of the top-performing schools in the UK.

GSA schools are experts in educating girls. They encourage the highest standards of education, pastoral care and co-curricular activity, with a wealth of extra-curricular opportunity in art, music, drama, science, sport and more. A lack of gender stereotyping and high-quality teaching enable students to develop the resilience, skills and confidence to lead a healthy, fulfilling life, with their mental and physical well-being a top priority.

The innovative practice and academic rigour of GSA schools attract pupils from around the world. Students thrive in the humanities and do disproportionately well in 'difficult' modern languages and STEM (science, technology, engineering, maths) subjects. The overwhelming majority continue their studies at top universities in the UK, the US and elsewhere, and there is a growing interest in higher and degree apprenticeships.

GSA schools share experience, specialisms, events and facilities in a variety of inter-school partnerships, and some schools offer means-tested bursaries for families of limited means.

GSA highlights the benefits of being taught in a predominantly girls-only environment, helping to inform and influence the national education debate and enabling continual professional development through a wide range of collaborative conferences and courses.

They work closely with the Association of School and College Leaders, are a member of the Independent Schools Council, and join hands with organisations in the UK and internationally – such as the Association of State Girls' Schools (UK), the National Coalition of Girls' Schools (USA) and the Alliance of Girls' Schools Australasia – in the interests of girls' education worldwide.

Twenty first century girls' schools come in many different shapes and sizes. Some cater for 100% girls, others provide a predominantly girls-only environment with boys in the nursery and/or sixth form. Some follow a diamond model, with equal numbers of boys but separate classrooms between the ages of 11 to 16. Educational provision across the Association offers a choice of day, boarding, weekly, and flexi-boarding education. Schools range in type from large urban schools to small rural schools. Many schools have junior and pre-prep departments and can offer a complete education from age 3/4 to 18. Some have religious affiliations. Heads of schools in the Girls' Day School Trust (GDST) are members of the GSA.

As the GSA is one of the constituent bodies that make up the Independent Schools' Council (ISC), schools whose Heads are full GSA members are required to undergo a regular cycle of inspections to ensure that rigorous standards are maintained.

The Association's secretariat is based in Leicester.

Suite 105, 108 New Walk, Leicester LE1 7EA
Tel: 0116 254 1619
Email: office@gsa.uk.com
Website: www.gsa.uk.com
Twitter: @GSAUK

President 2021/22: Samantha Price, Benenden School
President 2022/23: Heather Hanbury, Lady Eleanor Holles School
Chief Executive: Donna Stevens

Initial advice

HMC

The Headmasters' and Headmistresses' Conference, to which the Heads of leading independent schools belong

Founded in 1869 the HMC exists to enable members to discuss matters of common interest and to influence important developments in education. It looks after the professional interests of members, central to which is their wish to provide the best possible educational opportunities for their pupils.

The Heads of some 296 leading independent schools are members of The Headmasters' and Headmistresses' Conference, whose membership now includes Heads of boys', girls' and coeducational schools. International membership includes the Heads of around 56 schools throughout the world.

The great variety of these schools is one of the strengths of HMC but all must exhibit high quality in the education provided. While day schools are the largest group, about a quarter of HMC schools consist mainly of boarders and others have a smaller boarding element including weekly and flexible boarders.

All schools are noted for their academic excellence and achieve good results, including those with pupils from a broad ability band. Members believe that good education consists of more than academic results and schools provide pupils with a wide range of educational co-curricular activities and with strong pastoral support.

Only those schools that meet with the rigorous membership criteria are admitted and this helps ensure that HMC is synonymous with high quality in education. There is a set of membership requirements and a Code of Practice to which members must subscribe. Those who want the intimate atmosphere of a small school will find some with around 350 pupils. Others who want a wide range of facilities and specialisations will find these offered in large day or boarding schools. Many have over 1000 pupils. 32 schools are for boys only, others are coeducational throughout or only in the sixth form. The first girls-only schools joined HMC in 2006. There are now 39 girls-only schools.

Within HMC there are schools with continuous histories as long as any in the world and many others trace their origins to Tudor times, but HMC continues to admit to membership recently-founded schools that have achieved great success. The facilities in all HMC schools will be good but some have magnificent buildings and grounds that are the result of the generosity of benefactors over many years. Some have attractive rural settings, others are sited in the centres of cities.

Pupils come from all sorts of backgrounds. Bursaries and scholarships provided by the schools give about a third of the 240,000 pupils in HMC schools help with their fees. These average about £35,000 per annum for boarding schools and £15,000 for day schools. About 190,000 are day pupils and 45,000 boarders.

Entry into some schools is highly selective but others are well-suited to a wide ability range. Senior boarding schools usually admit pupils after the Common Entrance examination taken when they are 13.

Most day schools select their pupils by 11+ examination. Many HMC schools have junior schools, some with nursery and pre-prep departments. The growing number of boarders from overseas is evidence of the high reputation of the schools worldwide.

The independent sector has always been fortunate in attracting very good teachers. Higher salary scales, excellent conditions of employment, exciting educational opportunities and good pupil/teacher ratios bring rewards commensurate with the demanding expectations. Schools expect teachers to have a good education culminating in a good honours degree and a professional qualification, though some do not insist on the latter especially if relevant experience is offered. Willingness to participate in the whole life of the school is essential.

Parents expect the school to provide not only good teaching that helps their children achieve the best possible examination results, but also the dedicated pastoral care and valuable educational experiences outside the classroom in music, drama, games, outdoor pursuits and community service. Over 89% of pupils go on to higher education, many of them winning places on the most highly-subscribed university courses.

All members attend the Annual Conference, usually held in a large conference centre in September/October. There are ten divisions covering England, Wales, Scotland and Ireland where members meet once a term on a regional basis, and a distinctive international division.

Initial advice

The chair and committee, with the advice of the general secretary and membership secretary, make decisions on matters referred by membership-led sub-committees, steering groups and working parties. Close links are maintained with other professional associations in membership of the Independent Schools Council and with the Association of School and College Leaders.

Membership Secretary: Dr Simon Hyde
Tel: 01858 469059

12 The Point, Rockingham Road
Market Harborough, Leicestershire LE16 7QU
Email: gensec@hmc.org.uk
Website: www.hmc.org.uk

IAPS

The Independent Association of Prep Schools (IAPS) is a membership association representing leading headteachers and their prep schools in the UK and overseas

With around 660 members, IAPS schools represent a multi-billion pound enterprise, educating more than 170,000 children and employing more than 15,000 staff. As the voice of independent prep school education, IAPS actively defends and promotes the interests of its members.

IAPS schools must reach a very high standard to be eligible for membership, with strict criteria on teaching a broad curriculum, maintain excellent standards of pastoral care and keeping staff members' professional development training up-to-date. The head must be suitably qualified and schools must be accredited through a satisfactory inspection. IAPS offers its members and their staff a comprehensive and up-to-date programme of professional development courses to ensure that these high professional standards are maintained.

Member schools offer an all-round, values-led broad education which produces confident, adaptable, motivated children with a passion for learning. The targets of the National Curriculum are regarded as a basic foundation which is greatly extended by the wider programmes of study offered. Specialist teaching begins at an early age and pupils are offered a range of cultural and sporting opportunities.

IAPS organises a successful sports programme where member schools compete against each other in a variety of sports. In 2019-20, over 17,000 competitors took part in 119 events across 7 sports.

Our schools are spread throughout cities, towns and the countryside and offer pupils the choice of day, boarding, weekly and flexible boarding, in both singe sex and co-educational schools. Most schools are charitable trusts, some are limited companies and a few are proprietary. There are also junior schools attached to senior schools, choir schools, those with a particular religious affiliation and those that offer specialist provision as well as some schools with an age range extending to age 16 or above.

Although each member school is independent and has its own ethos, they are all committed to delivering an excellent, well-rounded education to the pupils in their care, preparing them for their future.

IAPS
Bishop's House
Artemis Drive
Tachbrook Park
CV34 6UD
Tel: 01926 887833
Email: iaps@iaps.uk
Website: iaps.uk

Initial advice

ISA

The Independent Schools Association, with membership across all types of school

The Independent Schools Association (ISA), established in 1879, is one of the oldest of the Headteachers' associations of independent schools that make up the Independent Schools' Council (ISC). It began life as the Association of Principals of Private Schools, which was created to encourage high standards and foster friendliness and cooperation among Heads who had previously worked in isolation. In 1895 it was incorporated as The Private Schools Association and in 1927 the word 'private' was replaced by 'independent'. The recently published history of the association, *Pro Liberis*, demonstrates the strong links ISA has with proprietorial schools, which is still the case today, even though boards of governors now run the majority of schools.

Membership is open to any Head or Proprietor, provided they meet the necessary accreditation criteria, including inspection of their school by a government-approved inspectorate. ISA's Executive Council is elected by members and supports all developments of the Association through its committee structure and the strong regional network of co-ordinators and area committees. Each of ISA's seven areas in turn supports members through regular training events and meetings.

ISA celebrates a wide-ranging membership, not confined to any one type of school, but including all: nursery, pre-preparatory, junior and senior, all-through schools, coeducational, single-sex, boarding, day and performing arts and special schools.

Promoting best practice and fellowship remains at the core of the ISA, as it did when it began 140 years ago. The association is growing, and its 569 members and their schools enjoy high quality national conferences and courses that foster excellence in independent education. ISA's central office also supports members and provides advice, and represents the views of its membership at national and governmental levels. Pupils in ISA schools enjoy a wide variety of competitions, in particular the wealth of sporting, artistic and academic activities at area and national level.

President: Lord Lexden
Chief Executive: Rudolf Eliott Lockhart

ISA House, 5-7 Great Chesterford Court, Great Chesterford, Essex CB10 1PF
Tel: 01799 523619
Email: isa@isaschools.org.uk
Website: www.isaschools.org.uk

ISA celebrates a wide-ranging membership, not confined to any one type of school, but including all: nursery, pre-preparatory, junior and senior, all-through schools, coeducational, single-sex, boarding, day and performing arts and special schools

Initial advice

The Society of Heads

The Society of Heads represents the interests of independent secondary schools

The Society of Heads represents the interests of independent, secondary schools. Established in 1961, The Society has as its members 125 Heads of well-established secondary schools, many with a boarding element, meeting a wide range of educational needs. All member schools provide education up to 18, with sixth forms offering both A and AS levels and/or the International Baccalaureate. Also some offer vocational courses. Many have junior schools attached to their foundation. A number cater for pupils with special educational needs, whilst others offer places to gifted dancers and musicians. All the schools provide education appropriate to their pupils' individual requirements together with the best in pastoral care.

The average size of the schools is about 350, and all aim to provide small classes ensuring favourable pupil:teacher ratios. The majority are coeducational and offer facilities for both boarding and day pupils. Many of the schools are non-denominational, whilst others have specific religious foundations.

The Society believes that independent schools are an important part of Britain's national education system. Given their independence, the schools can either introduce new developments ahead of the maintained sector or offer certain courses specifically appropriate to the pupils in their schools. They are able to respond quickly to the needs of parents and pupils alike.

Schools are admitted to membership of the Society only after a strict inspection procedure carried out by the Independent Schools Inspectorate. Regular inspection visits thereafter ensure that standards are maintained.

The Society is a constituent member of the Independent Schools Council and every full member in the Society has been accredited to it. All the Society's Heads belong to the Association of School and College Leaders (ASCL) (or another recognised union for school leaders) and their schools are members of AGBIS.

The Society's policy is: to maintain high standards of education, acting as a guarantee of quality to parents who choose a Society school for their children; to ensure the genuine independence of member schools; to provide an opportunity for Heads to share ideas and common concerns for the benefit of the children in their care; to provide training opportunities for Heads and staff in order to keep them abreast of new educational initiatives; to promote links with higher and further education and the professions, so that pupils leaving the Society's schools are given the best advice and opportunities for their future careers; and to help Heads strengthen relations with their local communities.

> The average size of the schools is about 350, and all aim to provide small classes ensuring favourable pupil: teacher ratios. The majority are coeducational and offer facilities for both boarding and day pupils. Many of the schools are non-denominational, whilst others have specific religious foundations

The Society of Heads Office,
12 The Point, Rockingham Road, Market Harborough, Leicestershire LE16 7QU
Tel: 01858 433760
Email: info@thesocietyofheads.org.uk
Website: www.thesocietyofheads.org.uk

Initial advice

The Independent Schools Council

The Independent Schools Council (ISC) works with its members to promote and preserve the quality, diversity and excellence of UK independent education both at home and abroad

What is the ISC?
The ISC brings together seven associations of independent schools, their heads, bursars and governors. Through our member associations we represent more than 1,350 independent schools in the UK and overseas. These schools are among the best in the world and educate more than half a million children each year.

The ISC's work is carried out by a small team of dedicated professionals in an office in central London. We are assisted by contributions from expert advisory groups in specialist areas. Our priorities are set by the board of directors led by our chairman, Barnaby Lenon. We are tasked by our members to protect and promote the sector in everything we do.

ISC schools
Schools in UK membership of the ISC's constituent associations offer a high quality, rounded education. Whilst our schools are very academically successful, their strength also lies in the extra-curricular activities offered – helping to nurture pupils' soft skills and encourage them to be self-disciplined, ambitious and curious. There are independent schools to suit every need, whether you want a day or boarding school, single sex or co-education, a large or a small school, or schools offering specialisms, such as in the arts.

Our schools are very diverse: some are selective and highly academic, while others have very strong drama or music departments full of creative opportunities in plays, orchestras and choirs. For children with special needs such as dyslexia or autism there are many outstanding independent schools that offer some of the best provision in the country.

Academic results
Typically, the ISC publishes a sector-wide analysis of Year 11 and Year 13 exam results for independent schools every August. However, due to the coronavirus pandemic, there was no sector-wide publication of results in 2020 or 2021 because exams were temporarily replaced by different assessment processes that Ofqual had to create in response to the crisis. Schools provided students with their grades in August as they normally would in both 2020 and 2021.

Looking back at 2019, when exam results were last published, 45.7% of Year 13 exam entries at independent schools were graded A*/A, compared to the national average of 25.5%. That year also saw 95.6% of Year 11 exams at independent schools graded C/4 or higher, compared to the national average of 67.3%. Figures recorded in 2019 also demonstrated more students were following different pathways post-GCSE.

Fee assistance
Schools take issues around affordability very seriously and are acutely aware of the sacrifices families make when choosing an independent education. Schools work hard to remain competitive whilst facing pressures on salaries, pensions and maintenance and utility costs. They are strongly committed to widening access and have made strenuous efforts to increase the amount they can offer in bursaries. Despite the financial strain brought about by the pandemic, many schools have extended their bursary provision – this year, £455m was provided in means-tested fee assistance, an increase of £15m from last year. Almost 180,000 pupils currently benefit from reduced fees, representing over a third of pupils at our schools.

> Our schools are very diverse: some are selective and highly academic, while others have very strong drama or music departments full of creative opportunities in plays, orchestras and choirs.

Initial advice

School partnerships
Independent and state schools have been engaged in partnership activity for many years, with the majority of ISC schools currently involved in important cross-sector initiatives. These collaborations involve the sharing of expertise, best practise and facilities, and unlock exciting new opportunities for all involved. To learn more about the partnership work taking place between state and independent schools, visit the Schools Together website: www.schoolstogether.org/

ISC Associations
There are seven member associations of the ISC, each with a distinctive ethos in their respective entrance criteria and quality assurance: Girls' Schools Association (GSA), Headmasters' and Headmistresses' Conference (HMC), Independent Association of Prep Schools (IAPS) Independent Schools Association (ISA), The Society of Heads, Association of Governing Bodies of Independent Schools (AGBIS), and the Independent Schools' Bursars Association (ISBA).

Further organisations who are affiliated to the ISC: Boarding Schools Association (BSA), Council of British International Schools (COBIS), Scottish Council of Independent Schools (SCIS) and Welsh Independent Schools Council (WISC).

The Independent Schools Council can be contacted at:
First Floor,
27 Queen Anne's Gate,
London,
SW1H 9BU
Telephone: 020 7766 7070
Website: www.isc.co.uk

independent schools council

Help in finding the fees

Chris Procter, joint managing director of SFIA, outlines a planned approach to funding your child's school fees

Average school fee increases between the last year 2 school years, according to the ISC census, were 4.1%. This is lower than expected given the increased cost of Teachers Pension Scheme which came in last year. There appears to have been a conscious effort by schools over the last 10 years to control fees. Since 2010 fee increases have averaged 3.9%. Between 2000 and 2010 they averaged 6.6%.

The latest Independent Schools Council (ISC) survey, conducted in January 2020 and completed by all 1,374 schools in UK membership, indicate that there are now a record 537,315 pupils being educated privately, the highest number since records began in 1974, rising 0.22% since 2019.

Pupils registered to board stands at 13.0% with weekly and flexi boarding becoming increasingly popular. The percentage of pupils attending single sex schools stands at 24.5%, marginally lower than last year.

The overall average boarding fee is £11,763 per term and the overall average day fee is £4,980 per term.

However, fees charged by schools vary by region – for example, the average boarding fee ranges from £9,292 per term in the North East to £13,372 per term in Greater London; the average day fee ranges from £3,725 per term in the North West to £5,993 per term in Greater London.

The overall cost (including university fees) might seem daunting: the cost of educating one child privately could well be very similar to that of buying a house but, as with house buying, the school fees commitment for the majority of parents can be made possible by spreading it over a long period rather than funding it all from current resources.

It is vital that parents do their financial homework, plan ahead, start to save early and regularly.

Grandparents who have access to capital could help out; by contributing to school fees they could also help to reduce any potential future inheritance tax liability.

Parents would be well-advised to consult a specialist financial adviser as early as possible, since a long-term plan for the payment of fees – possibly university as well – can prove very advantageous from a financial point of view and offer greater peace of mind. Funding fees is neither science, nor magic, nor is there any panacea. It is quite simply a question of planning and using whatever resources are available, such as income, capital, or tax planning opportunities.

The fundamental point to recognise is that you, your circumstances and your wishes or ambitions, for your children, or grandchildren are unique. They might well appear similar to those of other people but they will still be uniquely different. There will be no single solution to your problem. In fact, after a review of all your circumstances, there might not be a problem at all.

So, what are the reasons for seeking advice about education expenses?

- To reduce the overall cost
- To get some tax benefit
- To reduce your cash outflow
- To invest capital to ensure that future fees are paid
- To set aside money now for future fees
- To provide protection for school fees
- Or just to make sure that, as well as educating your children, you can still have a life

Any, some, or all of the above – or others not listed – could be on your agenda, the important thing is to develop a strategy.

At this stage, it really does not help to get hung up on which financial 'product' is the most suitable. The composition of a school fees plan will differ for each family depending on a number of factors. That is why there is no one school fees plan on offer.

The simplest strategy but in most cases, the most expensive option, is to write out a cheque for the whole bill when it arrives and post it back to the school. Like most simple plans, that can work well, if you have the money. Even if you do have the money, is that really the best way of doing things? Do you know that to fund £1,000 of school fees as a higher rate taxpayer paying 40% income tax, you currently need to earn £1,667, this rises to £1,818 if you are an additional rate taxpayer where the rate is 45%.

How then do you start to develop your strategy? As with most things in life, if you can define your objective, then you will know what you are aiming at. Your objective in this case will be to determine how much money is needed and when.

You need to draw up a school fees schedule or what others may term a cash flow forecast. So, you need to identify:

- How many children?
- Which schools and therefore what are the fees? (or you could use an average school fee)
- When are they due?
- Any special educational needs?
- Inflation estimate?
- Include university costs?

Finding the fees

With this basic information, the school fees schedule/cash flow forecast can be prepared and you will have defined what it is you are trying to achieve.

Remember though, that senior school fees are typically more than prep school fees – this needs to be factored in. Also, be aware that the cost of university is not restricted to the fees alone; there are a lot of maintenance and other costs involved: accommodation, books, food, to name a few. Don't forget to build in inflation, I refer you back to the data at the beginning of this article.

You now have one element of the equation, the relatively simple element. The other side is the resources you have available to achieve the objective. This also needs to be identified, but this is a much more difficult exercise. The reason that it is more difficult, of course, is that school fees are not the only drain on your resources. You probably have a mortgage, you want to have holidays, you need to buy food and clothes, you may be concerned that you should be funding a pension.

This is a key area of expertise, since your financial commitments are unique. A specialist in the area of school fees planning can help identify these commitments, to record them and help you to distribute your resources according to your priorities.

The options open to you as parents depend completely upon your adviser's knowledge of these complex personal financial issues. (Did I forget to mention your tax position, capital gains tax allowance, other tax allowances, including those of your children and a lower or zero rate tax paying spouse or partner? These could well be used to your advantage.)

A typical school fees plan can incorporate many elements to fund short, medium and long-term fees.

Each plan is designed according to individual circumstances and usually there is a special emphasis on what parents are looking to achieve, for example, to maximise overall savings and to minimise the outflow of cash.

Additionally, it is possible to protect the payment of the fees in the event of unforeseen circumstances that could lead to a significant or total loss of earnings.

Short-term fees
Short-term fees are typically the termly amounts needed within five years: these are usually funded from such things as guaranteed investments, liquid capital, loan plans (if no savings are available) or maturing insurance policies, investments etc. Alternatively, they can be funded from disposable income.

Medium-term fees
Once the short-term plan expires, the medium-term funding is invoked to fund the education costs for a further five to ten years. Monthly amounts can be invested in a low-risk, regular premium investment ranging from a building society account to a friendly society savings plan to equity ISAs. It is important to understand the pattern of the future fees and to be aware of the timing of withdrawals.

Long-term fees
Longer term funding can incorporate a higher element of risk (as long as this is acceptable to the investor), which will offer higher potential returns. Investing in UK and overseas equities could be considered. Solutions may be the same as those for medium-term fees, but will have the flexibility to utilise investments that may have an increased 'equity based' content.

Finally, it is important to remember that most investments, or financial products either mature with a single payment or provide for regular withdrawals; rarely do they provide timed termly payments.

Additionally, the overall risk profile of the portfolio should lean towards the side of caution (for obvious reasons).

There are any number of advisers in the country, but few who specialise in the area of planning to meet school and university fees. SFIA is the largest organisation specialising in school fees planning in the UK.

This article has been contributed by SFIA and edited by Chris Procter, Managing Director.
Chris can be contacted at: SFIA, 29 High Street, Marlow, Buckinghamshire, SL7 1AU
Tel: 01628 566777
Fax: 0333 444 1550
Email: enquiries@sfia.co.uk
Web: www.schoolfeesadvice.org

UK region map – Profiles

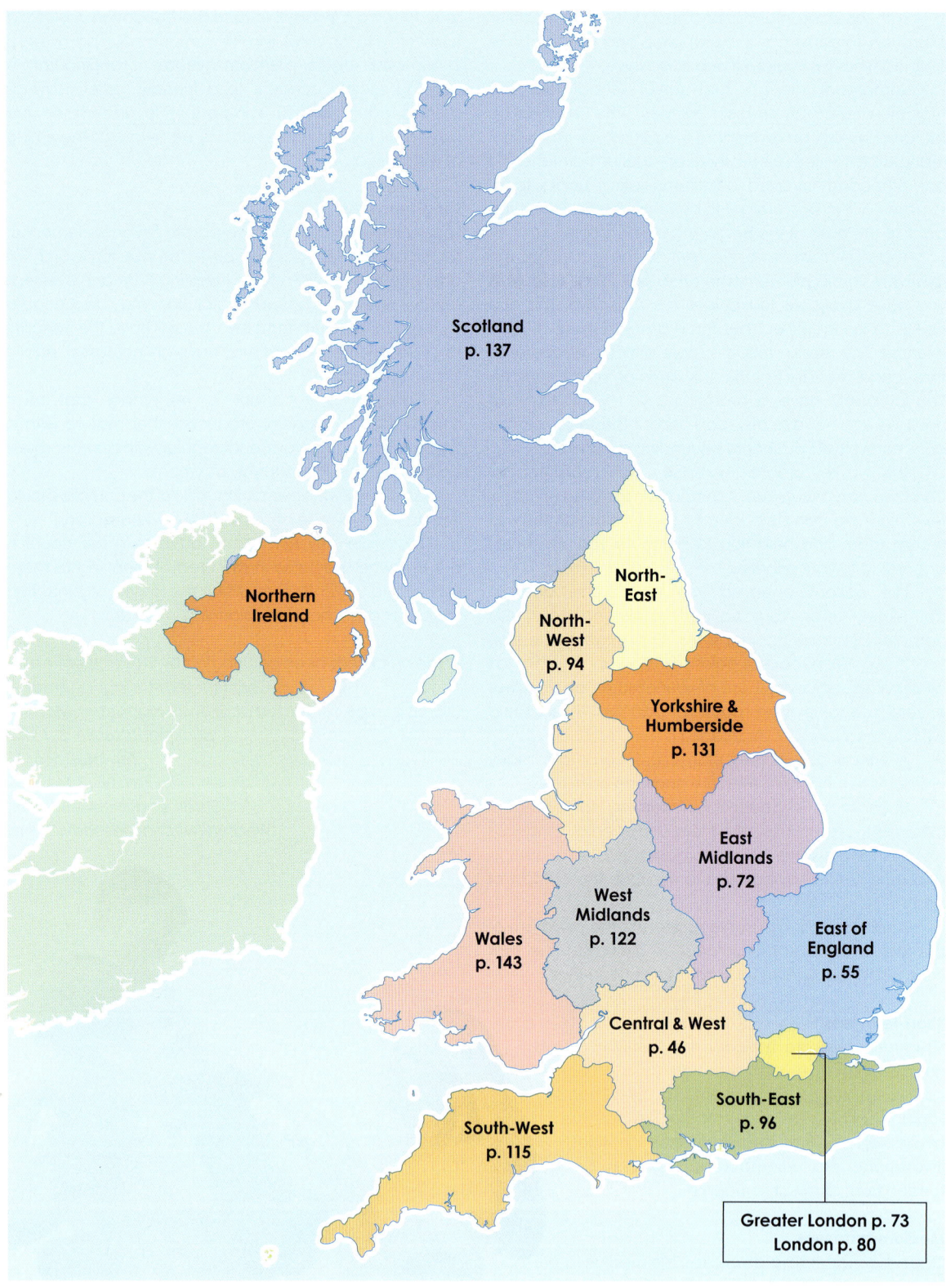

Prep schools in England

Please note that, to facilitate the use of this guide, we have introduced the geographical region 'Central & West' (see map opposite). This is not an officially designated region, and has been created solely for the purposes of this publication.

England – Central & West

Berkhampstead School

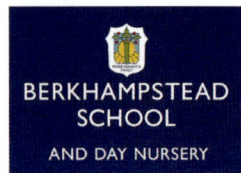

(Founded 1945)
Pittville Circus Road, Cheltenham,
Gloucestershire GL52 2QA
Tel: 01242 523263
Email: office@berkhampsteadschool.co.uk
Website: www.berkhampsteadschool.co.uk
Headmaster: Richard Cross
Appointed: September 2010

School type: Co-educational Day Preparatory & Nursery
Age range of pupils: 3 months–11 years
No. of pupils enrolled as at 01/01/2022: 254
Fees per term as at 01/01/2022:
Day: £2,820–£4,045
Average class size: 17
Teacher/pupil ratio: 1:8

Exceptional school with a happy, close-knit community

Berkhampstead is an independent, co-educational School and Day Nursery for children aged 3 months to 11 years, and is located in pretty, tree-lined Pittville Circus Road, Cheltenham. We pride ourselves on our atmosphere of warmth, happiness and encouragement, which we believe is fundamental to each child's achievement, and our fantastic results are testament to this. Our last ISI inspection affirmed that we offer a superb education and fantastic care. We were awarded 'Outstanding' in all areas - the finest possible outcome - and a huge accolade to the wonderful staff and strong leadership that we have here at the School and Day Nursery.

According to the report's key findings, pupils have "extremely strong literacy and reading skills" and are "extremely confident at handling numbers and calculations." The School's emphasis on the value of creativity means that pupils also achieve "high standards in music and creative arts." We are proud that the inspectors recognised that pupils are confident, have strong self-esteem and treat each other with consideration and respect. The staff throughout the Day Nursery and School work hard to encourage these all-important qualities.

The life in the school is based on the following aims:

- To provide a happy, caring and fun environment, which encourages effort and achievement.
- To foster a genuine feeling of community based on strong family and Christian values.
- To provide a learning environment that is stimulating, exciting and varied where all pupils and staff feel respected and valued and will strive for excellence.
- To focus on pupils' individual strengths and support their weaknesses, to celebrate their achievements and to encourage the growth of self-confidence and the development of social skills.
- To foster a 'can do' attitude to all aspects of school and encourage participation and enjoyment of music, art, drama and competitive sport.
- To prepare all pupils in such ways that they are able to transfer confidently to the next stage of their education and ultimately to the senior school of their choice.

We take great pride that our pupils leave us confident and able learners, and ready to embrace the challenges ahead.

We offer private tours along with our regular schedule of Open Days throughout the year. Please call 01242 523263 or email admissions@berkhampsteadschool.co.uk We look forward to welcoming you!

England – Central & West

Cranford House School

(Founded 1931)

Moulsford, Wallingford, Oxfordshire OX10 9HT
Tel: 01491 651218
Email: admissions@cranfordhouse.net
Website: www.cranfordhouse.net
Headmaster: Dr James Raymond

Appointed: 2014
School type: Co-educational Day
Age range of pupils: 3–18 years
No. of pupils enrolled as at 01/01/2022: 525
Fees per term as at 01/01/2022:
Day: £3,650–£6,175

Cranford House is a leading co-educational independent day school for boys and girls aged 3-18 years. It has an excellent reputation for providing pupils with a balanced, all-round education within a warmly nurturing environment. Set in over 14 acres of rural South Oxfordshire in the heart of Moulsford village, the small class sizes, close community and committed staff ensure each pupil is ably supported and challenged to achieve their full potential. The school was rated as 'Excellent' in all categories in its ISI Inspection of November 2014. The Early Years Foundation Stage was rated as 'Outstanding'. In September 2020, the school opened a new co-ed Sixth Form, with more than 20 A-level option choices and an extensive co-curricular programme.

At Cranford House, the aim is to encourage pupils to achieve their full potential, becoming motivated, confident and happy individuals, recognising the importance of respect and support for others, but ready to seize life's opportunities.

Academic attainment at Cranford House is outstanding. The school has been ranked 2nd nationally in the Sunday Times Parent Power League Table 2022, based on their GCSE results. Value-added scores are more impressive than ever with pupils achieving an average 1.5 of a grade higher per subject than predicted elsewhere.

Pupils benefit from an excellent pastoral offering, key to which is a vibrant House system which encourages both a sense of community and leadership. The school has extensive recreational and games fields. In winter, hockey, football and netball are played, and in summer, tennis, rounders, cricket and athletics. Swimming takes place on site. Dramatic, musical and dance productions are an important aspect of school life and all are encouraged to take part.

In addition to the extensive range of enrichment activities offered throughout the school, all pupils have the opportunity to join educational trips and excursions. For Senior School pupils, Bronze and Silver levels of The Duke of Edinburgh's Award scheme are offered, in addition to far-flung expeditions with World Challenge. Opportunities for overseas travel are also offered through exchanges, ski and sports trips and choir tours. School transport operates over a wide area throughout both Berkshire and Oxfordshire.

To discover all that a Cranford education could offer your child, open events and personal tours are available throughout the year. Please contact our Admissions Department on 01491 651218.

England – Central & West

Crown House Preparatory School

Bassetsbury Manor,
Bassetsbury Lane, High Wycombe,
Buckinghamshire HP11 1QX
Tel: 01494 529927
Email: office@crownhouseschool.co.uk

Website: www.crownhouseschool.co.uk
Headteacher: Mrs Sarah Hobby
School type:
Co-educational Day Preparatory
Age range of pupils: 3–11 years

Crown House Preparatory School in High Wycombe provides an outstanding education for girls and boys age 3-11 and prides itself on its close-knit community and nurturing environment. The school, named by the Sunday Times as the best performing independent co-educational school in Buckinghamshire in 2021, encourages all pupils to develop a lifelong love of learning through a rich and broad curriculum where activities are characterised by a sense of fun and challenge to ensure that all pupils flourish.

Crown House, part of the Chatsworth Schools family of schools, has a reputation for dedicated and passionate staff who nurture and inspire the pupils in their care, not only academically but socially and emotionally too. The school knows that confidence and a sense of security and warmth is fundamental to success, so teachers work hard to create a secure and welcoming environment. At Crown House, every child is supported with individual attention throughout their journey at the school.

The school's curriculum is designed around children's interests and from an early age teachers harness children's love of asking questions allowing them to become independent learners. As children progress throughout the school, Crown House continues to hold the development of the learner as well as the pursuit of academic excellence in equally high regard. Pupils enjoy a weekly timetable that emphasises the core subjects of English, mathematics and science as well as the foundation subjects of humanities, sport, art and languages alongside extra-curricular and wellbeing opportunities.

Crown House pupils are encouraged to question, discuss and reason across all areas of the curriculum. Experienced staff encourage curiosity and perseverance to develop enquiring minds and this approach along with a challenging curriculum and small class sizes ensures Crown House pupils achieve consistently high results.

Sport is an integral part of school life at Crown House and children enjoy playing different games with each other, learning the meaning of teamwork, patience, fair play and resilience. The school has timetabled PE and Games lessons that start in Reception and in the Prep School all pupils participate and represent the school in a wide range of sports including Cross-Country, Tag-Rugby, Netball, Football, Hockey, Rounders, Cricket and Athletics. The school also takes part in many regional and national tournaments.

Every child has a creative side and this is developed at Crown House where the school's Creative Arts room and specialist teaching generates a vibrant and dynamic environment where exciting, innovative work takes place alongside reflective thinking. Drawing underpins all projects and each child from Year 2 to Year 6 has their own sketchbook to explore ideas and techniques. Pupils at all levels throughout the school are also encouraged to acquire a passion for music and the world of wonder that is drama. At the end of summer term, all

England – Central & West

children from Reception upwards take part in the school's Summer Production at the Swan Theatre in Wycombe.

Crown House consistently achieves a 90% 11+ pass rate and Year 6 leavers go on to a range of local grammar and independent schools including Wycombe High School, Beaconsfield School and Dr Challoners School. The Headteacher and Senior Leadership Team start to meet with parents from Years 4 and 5 to discuss the best options and fit for the next stage in their child's education and this approach coupled with teachers' excellent knowledge of the 11+ means that Year 6 pupils achieve excellent results and usually get into their first-choice school.

Pupils' happiness and wellbeing are at the heart of the Crown House ethos and this combined with small class sizes and an individualised learning environment ensures that children are given the attention and support they deserve to excel and have an exceptional education. Crown House children find their passion and reach their full potential.

England – Central & West

Griffin House Preparatory School

(Founded 1939)
Little Kimble, Aylesbury,
Buckinghamshire HP17 0XP
Tel: 01844 346154
Email: secretary@griffinhouseschool.co.uk

Website: www.griffinhouseschool.co.uk
Headmaster: Mr Tim Walford
School type: Co-educational Day Preparatory
Age range of pupils: 3–11 years

Set within 5 acres of grounds nestled in the Chiltern Hills, Griffin House School provides an outstanding education for boys and girls aged 3 - 11 in a happy and nurturing environment. The school's small class sizes and individualised learning environment ensures that children are given the attention and support they deserve to excel as well as being exceptionally well cared for. This is reflected in excellent 11+ results and inclusion in the Sunday Times Top 100 Independent Schools list (based on SATs results) for the past five years.

Learning at Griffin House School, part of Chatsworth Schools, is brought to life in all subjects through the passion and knowledge of dedicated teachers. Committed staff team have high expectations of pupils inspiring them to believe anything is possible and there is a calm and purposeful learning environment that encourages mutual respect and enables children to reach their full potential. The personalised approach to teaching ensures that learners of all abilities are stretched and challenged or supported and encouraged. Furthermore, creative subjects of sport, art, music and drama enhance the academic curriculum to develop fully rounded and adventurous young people who engage joyfully in their learning.

Griffin House School encourages pupils to grow as a whole person, ensuring they develop self-confidence and become thoughtful and valuable members of the community. As part of the school's pastoral care, younger pupils are encouraged to look up to the older children, whilst the older children in turn are taught responsibility and compassion. Every member of the school community has an important role in creating the distinct ethos of value and respect and the Head, Tim Walford, plays a part in each child's day, welcoming them through the school gate every morning and taking opportunities to interact with the pupils through celebration assemblies and regular timetabling.

With 5 acres of grounds, Griffin House School boasts a unique opportunity to learn outside of the classroom. Each Early Years class has a specific, designated outdoor space and across the school the timetable includes outdoor learning opportunities. The school grounds host wonderful locations for den building, campfires and unearthing minibeasts as well as the chance to positively encourage children to look after their natural environment and to be part of the force for taking care of the planet and improving it for their future. The grounds are also home to an abundance of wildlife including red kites, rabbits, deer as well as local sheep and neighbourly ducks.

At Griffin House School, sport is an integral part of school life. All children enjoy playing different games with each other, learning the meaning of teamwork, patience, fair play and resilience. Through specialist taught, timetabled PE and Games lessons, weekly swimming lessons that start in Reception and after school activities, pupils are encouraged to lead a healthy and active lifestyle. In the Prep School all pupils (boys and girls) participate and represent the school in a wide range of sports including cross-country, tag-rugby, netball, football, hockey, rounders, cricket and athletics. The school also takes part in many

Independent Schools Association regional and national tournaments.

After lessons end, Griffin House's vibrant and diverse extra-curricular program kicks in with a termly timetable of sporting, artistic, educational and above all fun activities for children to choose from. The school runs a variety of exciting, interest-led and seasonal clubs each term, giving children the chance to form friendships and links with others across different form groups.

Griffin House School children achieve fantastic academic success with exceptional 11+ results and around 75% of children moving onto selective grammar and independent schools - including Wycombe High School, Aylesbury Grammar School and Abingdon School. These results are all the more impressive as Griffin House School is non-selective. The school has a range of extra support in place, such as one-to-one time with the Headteacher to prepare for interviews, to make the transition as successful and smooth as possible and to ensure children

fulfil their full potential. The school's pastoral focus and attention to each child ensures all Griffin House children are ready to flourish in any setting that they are moving on to.

Griffin House School provides an outstanding education in a nurturing environment. The school takes pride in Year 6 pupils leaving as capable and confident individuals ready to continue their educational journey and take on the world.

England – Central & West

Godstowe Preparatory School

(Founded 1900)
Shrubbery Road, High Wycombe,
Buckinghamshire HP13 6PR
Tel: 01494 529273
Email: schooloffice@godstowe.org
Website: www.godstowe.org

Headmistress: Ms Sophie Green
School type: Girls' Day & Boarding, Co-educational Nursery & Pre-Prep
Age range of boys: 3–7 years
Age range of girls: 3–13 years

"Something Special is happening at Godstowe"

Godstowe was founded by two strong, progressive women, originally in fact as a school whose purpose would be to prepare girls for the move down the hill to Wycombe Abbey School. Their vision was for an innovative, academic and broad education for girls and, without a doubt, this continues to live on in today's school.

Our ethos is simple. All we want is for our girls and boys to be Confident, Happy and Successful. Indeed, if the first two are true, the third will almost certainly follow. Success is defined in many ways, and we mean successful in the broadest sense: successfully kind, successfully courteous as well as successful in achieving a wide range of goals. We keep our pupils busy and engaged, we entertain and intrigue them, encourage them, and excite them.

Happy children are easy to teach. With outstanding, highly qualified teaching staff as well as a strong and experienced pastoral team, excellent facilities, wonderful surroundings, a non-selective intake policy and a more positive, exuberant and industrious atmosphere than you will find in other schools, it is likely that most of our children will be happy to learn, happy to stretch themselves, happy to support each other, and happy to do whatever they can to take an active part in their own education.

Why push children through the curriculum when they can be inspired to make their own journey, choose their own routes and arrive at their destination under their own steam?

Our pupils love their time at school. It never ceases to amaze me just how much highly motivated and enthusiastic people can willingly contribute, and we don't just mean the girls and boys, we mean the staff and the parents too!

Godstowe is alive with opportunity. Remember, to learn a lesson you need to live it.

England – Central & West

High March

23 Ledborough Lane, Beaconsfield, Buckinghamshire HP9 2PZ
Tel: 01494 675186
Email: office@highmarch.co.uk
Website: www.highmarch.co.uk
Head of School: Mrs Kate Gater
Appointed: September 2019

School type:
Girls' Day, Co-educational Nursery
Age range of boys: 3–4 years
Age range of girls: 3–11 years
No. of pupils enrolled as at 01/01/2022: 280
Fees per annum as at 01/01/2022:
Day: £5,850–£16,185
Average class size: Max 20

Since our foundation in 1926, we at High March have treasured our core values of kindness, friendship and educational excellence. We are proud of our broad and inspiring curriculum and of our happy and vibrant spirit.

High March is a community in which everyone is welcomed, known and valued. We appreciate each girl's individual strengths, support her growth and encourage her ambition and are dedicated to helping every girl make outstanding progress, to grow in self-confidence and to develop the skills which will be the foundation of her future successes.

Our commitment to educational excellence is far-reaching and we embrace a love of learning in the broadest sense - academics, sport, music and the creative arts all have room to thrive at High March. Our academic results are impressive with an excellent pass rate in the Buckinghamshire 11+ Secondary Transfer Tests and in entrance examinations to a wide range of the best senior independent schools, both locally and further afield. Moreover, our girls are often successful in securing scholarship awards of every variety.

We ensure there is an abundance of opportunities throughout the school for girls to take part in sporting events, perform in dramatic and musical productions and exhibit their artistic endeavours. We love to sing together and our choirs perform regular concerts in our local community as well as participating in local and national choral competitions. Our annual public Art Exhibition is an extraordinary showcase of the girls' artistic talents and industry.

Outside the classroom, High March girls enjoy an extensive extracurricular programme incorporating activities as diverse as judo, ballet, triathlon, coding and knitting, not to mention fencing and Mandarin! There is also an inclusive after-school care facility from 8am until 5.30pm, which is a welcome boon for many parents.

We work in close partnership with parents to explore the many senior school options available and to help them choose the best next step for their daughter when she leaves High March at the end of Year Six. Above all, our aim is for High March girls to leave us as happy, assured, balanced and compassionate individuals ready for success in their chosen senior school and beyond.

We believe that High March is an exceptional preparatory day school for girls, and our girls believe it too - as does the Independent Schools Inspectorate! In our recent school inspection in June 2019, we were graded 'excellent' in every category, a testament to the outstanding teaching and care on offer at High March.

We would be delighted to welcome you in person, so do come along to an open event or arrange a personal tour to experience our 'special something' for yourself.

England – Central & West

Moulsford Preparatory School

(Founded 1961)
Moulsford-on-Thames,
Oxfordshire OX10 9HR
Tel: 01491 651438

Email: admissions@moulsford.com
Website: www.moulsford.com
Headmaster: Mr B Beardmore-Gray
Appointed: September 2014
School type: Boys' Day & Boarding Preparatory
Age range of boys: 4–13 years

No. of pupils enrolled as at 01/01/2022: 372
Fees per term as at 01/01/2022:
Full Boarding: £7,850 per term
Prep Day Fee: £6,275 per term
Pre-Prep: £4,200 per term
Average class size: 16
Teacher/pupil ratio: 1:9

Moulsford is a thriving independent day and boarding Prep School for boys aged 4-13 years set on the banks of the River Thames in South Oxfordshire.

Moulsford offers boys superb opportunities for learning whilst having fun, with a restructured curriculum designed not only to prepare boys for senior schools, but also to ensure they have the skills for life beyond. The curriculum promotes intellectual agility, encourages them to think and analyse critically, makes connections across the subjects and gives plenty of opportunity for creativity and collaboration. The boys are encouraged to build resilience by having a go, taking a well-thought-out risk, and, on occasion, failing.

Through Moulsford's Activities programme, the school aims to offer opportunities to develop new skills and talents, whilst becoming a conscientious citizen. Working towards the Moulsford Award, boys can try magic tricks, bike maintenance, cookery, bushcraft, photography, climbing, drama, sailing, chess, pantomime, parkour, stand-up comedy, geocaching and many more activities covering the five key elements of performance and arts, community, self-development, adventure and healthy living.

Moulsford's reputation for sport remains extremely strong with all boys in teams A to F regularly playing competitive matches. Major sports are football, rugby, hockey, cricket and athletics. Minor sports have also seen significant successes in golf, skiing, fencing and judo. Music and drama remain popular with roughly three quarters of the boys from Years 3-8 playing an instrument.

Boys progress to the UK's leading independent day and boarding schools at 13+ including Abingdon, Eton, Harrow, Magdalen College School, Marlborough, Radley, St Edward's Oxford, and Wellington.

The riverside setting provides a different dimension to prep school life with kayaks, canoes, stand up paddleboards and sailing dinghies all put to use. At Forest School there are opportunities for fire building, whittling and making bows and arrows. It is something of a cliché, but boys really can be boys at Moulsford.

A new purpose-built Pre-Prep will open in September 2022, and includes a new Pre-School for children age 3+.

England – East

Abbot's Hill School

(Founded 1912)
Bunkers Lane, Hemel Hempstead,
Hertfordshire HP3 8RP
Tel: 01442 240333

Email: registrar@abbotshill.herts.sch.uk
Website: www.abbotshill.herts.sch.uk
Headmistress:
Mrs K Gorman BA, MEd (Cantab)
Appointed: January 2020
School type: Girls' Day
Age range of girls: 4–16 years

No. of pupils enrolled as at 01/01/2022: 482
Fees per term as at 01/01/2022:
Prep School: £3,863–£4,870 per term
Senior School (Years 7-11):
£6,651 –£6,691 per term
Average class size: 12–18

Abbot's Hill is a happy and thriving community in which pupils are encouraged to aim high, to grasp opportunities, enjoy learning and make lasting friendships.

The school offers an all-round education for girls aged 4-16 years, and the Day Nursery & Pre-School caters for girls and boys from 6 months. Abbot's Hill's historic campus offers modern and extensive facilities in a magnificent country setting, situated in over 70 acres of beautiful parkland.

Abbot's Hill has a strong record of academic success. Throughout the school, pupils are taught in genuinely small classes. Excellent teaching and personalised support ensure that everyone is inspired to exceed their potential and to shine.

The broad curriculum is enhanced by a wide range of trips and activities to stimulate learning. Extra-curricular clubs offer a lively balance of music, sports, languages, debating, drama and more. In short, there is something for everyone!

At Abbot's Hill, there is a great focus on pastoral care. We give individual attention to each girl so that she will develop as a person, but also to ensure she succeeds. The sense of being part of an extended family is frequently commented on by pupils, parents and staff alike.

In such a nurturing environment, children grow naturally in confidence, are happy to embrace new challenges and eagerly take on increasing responsibilities.

Abbot's Hill girls progress seamlessly from one stage of education to the next. They become fully equipped to take on the challenges and opportunities life has to offer.

"I feel happy sending my daughter to school knowing that she is being given every opportunity to develop into a confident, well-rounded individual." - Prep School Parent

England – East

Brentwood Preparatory School

(Founded 1892)
Shenfield Road, Brentwood,
Essex CM15 8BD

Tel: +44 (0)1277 243300
Email: prepadmissions@brentwood.essex.sch.uk
Website: www.brentwoodschool.co.uk
Headmaster: Mr Jason Whiskerd
Appointed: 2011
School type: Co-educational Day Preparatory

Religious Denomination: Church of England
Age range of pupils: 3–11 years
No. of pupils enrolled as at 01/01/2022: 591
Fees per annum as at 01/01/2022:
Nursery: pro rata
Prep: £15,735
Average class size: 18
Teacher/pupil ratio: 1:9

The simple truth is - happy children learn best - so at Brentwood Preparatory School we focus on giving our pupils a positive start in their education; a positive beginning that will influence the rest of their lives.

We are privileged to be with children as they embark on one of the greatest journeys in life: education. It is in these early years that they begin to investigate the world with great expectation, interest and energy. It is in these early years that we can show them the world is indeed a feast for the curious and full of opportunities.

From the age of three, we welcome children into a community that is small enough to feel secure, but large enough to offer a huge breadth of experiences. Pupils are encouraged to be enterprising and develop their own ideas. Whether they are taking part in the School Council, or joining in one of the many clubs, sports and drama activities, our pupils soon develop their own sense of responsibility. They learn to care about their work, to value their contribution to the wider school community and through many pupil-led fundraising initiatives, their eyes are opened to the world beyond school.

Our School has the kind of facilities one would expect to see at secondary level. What this means is that children who come here very quickly find aptitudes, gifts and talents that may have been missed elsewhere.

Work has just been completed on a multi-million pound development which puts the school at the forefront of cutting edge educational facilities.

Highlights include a Futures Room - a place for experimentation - which can be transformed from the solar system to the bottom of the ocean or the chaos of a battlefield by the switch of a button.

Eight specialist classrooms include a Music Room, with cutting-edge Music Technology, two Science Rooms, an IT Suite, a light and airy Art loft, a Design Technology classroom with Laser Cutter and 3D Printer, and a Food Technology suite with mini hotplates, ovens and child-height workstations and sinks.

Academically, our pupils are high achievers; they are consistently at the top of the field at age 11 and a large proportion achieve scholarships at the same age. We encourage all pupils to have the confidence to stretch themselves, to celebrate their own achievements and to be generous about the success of others.

Our staff teach with great energy, flair and sensitivity and because we keep class sizes small, our Form teachers get to know their pupils really well. Our Matron and the Chaplain play central roles in taking care of the children and the House system enables each pupil to build relationships with older peers.

Much has changed since we were founded in 1892, but our motto of Virtue, Learning & Manners remains and you will see that in droves when you visit us, so book a tour today.

England – East

Fairstead House School

FAIRSTEAD HOUSE

(Founded 1950)

Fairstead House, Fordham Road, Newmarket, Suffolk CB8 7AA
Tel: 01638 662318
Email: secretary@fairsteadhouse.co.uk
Website: www.fairsteadhouseschool.co.uk
Head of School: Mr Michael Radford

School type: Co-educational Day Preparatory
Age range of pupils: 3 months–11 years
No. of pupils enrolled as at 01/01/2022: 95
Fees per annum as at 01/01/2022:
Day: £10,704–£11,934
Average class size: 13

Fairstead House is conveniently located in the centre of Newmarket on the Suffolk/Cambridgeshire border. We are an excellent choice for parents looking for an independent Nursery and School in a rural setting but with the rich cultural resources of Bury St Edmunds, Cambridge and Ely a short distance away.

Fairstead House will provide your child with a unique introduction into the world of learning and discovery. We are extremely proud of our high academic standards, our superb pastoral care and the happy, enriching environment we provide for our children.

Physical Education plays a very important part in the life of the school, both curricular and extra-curricular. Children are encouraged to achieve their full potential, to understand what is involved in being part of a team, to appreciate fair play and to learn the values of good sportsmanship.

Residential Trips and Day Outings form a vital part of the broad, balanced and creative education that Fairstead House provides.

Music and Drama performance is a great strength and plays an important part in the life of the school under the direction of a specialist teacher. All children are given opportunities for singing, performing, composing and playing a selection of instruments. Specialist private tuition is available in a wide range of instruments.

A whole host of clubs and activities are available to children. These range from a wide selection such as; sports, arts, music, craft, drama, Russian, storytelling and many more. Children have the opportunity to choose their activities at the beginning of each term. A Breakfast Club is available each day from 7.30 a.m. and we have a well-established and very popular After-School Care Club until 6 p.m.

Please phone 01638 662318 or email registrar@fairsteadhouse.co.uk to arrange a visit.

England – East

Heathcote School

(Founded 1935)

Eves Corner, Danbury, Chelmsford, Essex CM3 4QB
Tel: 01245 223131
Email: enquiries@heathcoteschool.co.uk
Website: www.heathcoteschool.co.uk
Head of School: Mrs Samantha Scott

School type:
Co-educational Day Preparatory
Age range of pupils: 2–11 years
No. of pupils enrolled as at 01/01/2022: 105
Fees per annum as at 01/01/2022:
Day: £9,450

What it is to be a Heathcote pupil…
As a small rural Essex school, Heathcote knows that for an 'excellent' (ISI, 2019) academic foundation to remain in place, our pupils must be happy, healthy and engaged. Our school day is full of personalised learning, challenge, mastery and opportunities with termly enrichment days working collaboratively across key-stages and in a cross-curricular way. We use our nationally award-winning specialist teachers for all pupils to ensure quality-first provision across the full range of subjects. Termly gap-analysis and early-intervention programs support and extend pupils to ensure they strive for the stars. This attitude of 'excellence for all' clearly works: 88% of our pupils are above average for Reading and Maths (July 2021), 90% pass rate for 11+ pupils (2020/21) and 100% of our pupils progress onto first choice secondaries whether grammar, state or independent places (many with scholarships).

To enhance our diverse sporting curriculum, we hold wellbeing activities such as woodland-walking, community litter-picking and time with our gold-level school dog mentor. Our qualified mental health first-aiders focus on our pupils' and staff emotional and mental health. We value our families including them in regular events such as coffee-mornings, Friday whole school assemblies, prize-giving ceremony, sports day and sporting meets, Grandparents' afternoons, whole-school productions, performing-arts concerts, curriculum days and parent workshops. We are a whole-school community who value every stake-holder.

Our children are given a voice, they are responsible and socially mature. We have a full pupil-led team that organise events for fundraising, charity work and social activities. The school council, class leaders, wellbeing-ambassadors and ECO reps are democratically chosen from each class and hold valued positions alongside staff. The children have strength, autonomy and know they make a difference at Heathcote to our community.

Our children know that at Heathcote we are not just a place of education but we create a nurturing environment as if they were our own family, they feel valued, enriched and able to achieve.

England – East

Howe Green House School

Great Hallingbury, Bishop's Stortford, Hertfordshire CM22 7UF

Tel: 01279 657706
Email: schooloffice@howegreenhouse.essex.sch.uk
Website: www.howegreenhouseschool.co.uk
Headmistress: Ms Deborah Mills BA (Hons) Q.T.S

School type:
Co-educational Day Preparatory
Age range of pupils: 2–11 years
No. of pupils enrolled as at 01/01/2022: 177
Boys: 97 **Girls:** 80
Fees per term as at 01/01/2022:
Day: £433–£4,313

For a Life Less Ordinary…
Set in nearly 15 acres of grounds near to Hatfield Forest, Howe Green House School consists of a number of beautifully appointed buildings which help to create the feeling of a small and friendly community in which children thrive.

With bright and airy classrooms, well-equipped facilities and the variety of musical and sporting opportunities on offer, children are naturally motivated to succeed. Our single form entry throughout the school and exceptional staff:pupil ratio enables each child to be known and understood well. The school is non-selective and natural abilities may vary, but it achieves consistently excellent academic results with children going on to attend a wide variety of senior schools throughout the country, with many scholarships awarded.

At the heart of all that the school does is the emphatic belief that childhood should be a time filled with warmth, opportunity, awe and wonder.

The school's ambition is that children can learn about themselves and others within a supportive, liberating and stimulating environment to become eager, creative thinkers with a desire to contribute positively to the world around them.

Little Oaks Nursery is a sessional facility for 2 - 4 year olds which is designed specifically to meet the needs of each individual child, responding to their developmental readiness and tailor-making their educational experience according to their own profile.

Howe Green House School pupils make bold decisions, they are industrious and keen to succeed, they care for each other and revel in the success and happiness of their peers. It is an unusual blend of the most desirable qualities which can be attributed to the unique atmosphere and values driven ethos throughout the school.

Howe Green House School and Little Oaks Nursery is located just two miles from the centre of Bishop's Stortford and is easily accessible from Great Dunmow, Saffron Walden and surrounding villages.

England – East

Ipswich Prep School

(Founded 1878)

3 Ivry Street, Ipswich, Suffolk IP1 3QW
Tel: 01473 282800
Email: prepenquiries@ipswich.school
Website: www.ipswich.school
Headmistress: Amanda Childs

School type:
Co-educational Day Preparatory
Age range of pupils: 0–11 years
No. of pupils enrolled as at 01/01/2022: 353
Fees per annum as at 01/01/2022:
Day: £10,914–£13,410
Teacher/pupil ratio: 1:11

'Forward-thinking and committed to maintaining a high staff-to-pupil ratio, high teaching standards and a jam-packed list of clubs.' Good Schools Guide

Come and look around Ipswich Prep and you'll meet happy pupils and caring staff. Our ethos is based around the core values of care, passion, potential and communication and these values are evident in the tangible sense of excitement and fun that you'll notice when you visit.

You won't find our children cramming for SATs or worrying about their next assessment. Instead you'll find them bringing in a picture of a bee swarm they've spotted and explaining how it relates to their last biology lesson. You'll find them creating science experiments that fizz and bang with kitchen ingredients. Or you'll notice the beauty in their Hockney inspired Suffolk landscapes.

Our children achieve their full potential - this may be academic accolades, musical performances, representing the school in sport or by being recognised for helping others. Pupils develop a portfolio of interests that enables them to thrive as individuals and to be fully prepared for the next step. Whilst most children choose to move on to Ipswich School (ranked 6th in East Anglia by the Sunday Times) we ensure that the next school suits each individual child.

A strong pupil voice promotes confidence and enthusiasm in all our children. Good schools like ours are child-centred: they are places where children can have fun, be creative and express themselves whilst feeling supported and confident whatever the task. Our curriculum is extensive and includes many subjects now obsolete in the state system such as Drama. Specialist teaching starts right from Nursery with PE, Music and Library sessions. French starts from Reception and later on we teach a language carousel. In Upper Prep specialist teaching extends to include Art, DT and Science.

The co-curricular provision is deliberately jam-packed and covers anything from bushcraft, bingo and gardening all the way through to Fives, Skiing and Robotics. By encouraging the children to try new things they develop different skill sets to those formed in the classroom. This holistic approach to education enables our children to develop a growth mindset and prepares them brilliantly for their next steps.

England – East

King's Ely Junior

(Founded 970 AD)

Ely, Cambridgeshire CB7 4DB
Tel: 01353 660707
Email: admissions@kingsely.org
Website: www.kingsely.org
Head: Mr Richard Whymark
School type: Co-educational Day & Boarding Preparatory

Age range of pupils: 7–13 years
No. of pupils enrolled as at 01/01/2022: 374
Fees per annum as at 01/01/2022:
Day: £15,690–£17,121
Full Boarding: £25,017–£26,415
Average class size: 16-20
Teacher/pupil ratio: 1:9

"Within the first week of our sons joining King's Ely, we simply could not believe the change in both their happiness and their commitment to learning. King's Ely's reputation certainly precedes itself, but you don't really get a true feeling for the depth of those recommendations until you have visited the school yourself..." These are the words of Mr and Mrs Golding, whose sons, Benjamin and Edward, joined King's Ely Junior recently.

King's Ely is a leading independent day and boarding school which serves the academic and pastoral needs of around 1,000 boys and girls from the age of 2 through to 18, with boarders from 8 years old. Our prep school (ages 7-13) is filled with the same contagious excitement and energy that the whole of King's Ely is renowned for.

Our school is nestled in the picturesque cathedral city of Ely in Cambridgeshire, which is 15 minutes from Cambridge and 1 hour from London, with direct rail links to both. Our privately-run school buses stop at key locations around Cambridgeshire, Suffolk and Norfolk.

King's Ely is a vibrant, nurturing, inclusive and forward-looking community which has prepared children's futures for a millennium, making us one of the oldest schools in the world. We were delighted to be a finalist in the recent Independent Schools of the Year Awards, and our latest Independent Schools Inspectorate (ISI) inspection resulted in King's Ely achieving the highest grading possible in every single category.

Whether a student shines in a classroom, in a laboratory, on a stage, on a pitch or on a mountainside, our school promises an abundance of opportunity for personal development, both academically and socially. As reported in the Good Schools Guide, King's Ely *"turns out well rounded, likeable individuals who attain academically but who also realise there is more to life than just results."*

Only by visiting King's Ely and meeting our students and staff, can you feel the energy and warmth of our community. We look forward to welcoming you!

England – East

Kingshott

(Founded 1931)

Stevenage Road, St Ippolyts, Hitchin, Hertfordshire SG4 7JX
Tel: 01462 432009
Email: admissions@kingshottschool.com
Website: www.kingshottschool.com
Headmaster: Mr David Weston
Appointed: September 2020

School type:
Co-educational Day Preparatory
Age range of pupils: 3–13 years
No. of pupils enrolled as at 01/01/2022: 400
Fees per annum as at 01/01/2022:
Day: £6,555–£14,115
Average class size: 15
Teacher/pupil ratio: 1:9

Kingshott School is set on the outskirts of Hitchin, Hertfordshire, and provides an outstanding co-educational learning experience for boys and girls aged 3 to 13. At Kingshott, we embrace the whole child. Happy and secure pupils engage with all the opportunities presented to them, where all aspects of education are given equal footing whilst being underpinned by academic rigour.

Year on year, Kingshott continues to make major improvements to its facilities, embracing the idea that innovation and tradition go hand in hand. Most recently, we opened a multimillion pound Sports and Drama Hall to ensure that taking part in our varied Games and P.E. curriculum and our exciting performing arts programme, is an even more challenging and engaging experience. This was preceded by a modern, state of the art teaching block which offers a sizeable, bright and airy Art room, a dedicated Music room, Drama studio, Food Technology room, Science laboratory and nine teaching classrooms.

Kingshott School is thriving and is entering an exciting time where the developments in our curriculum and the investment in facilities to support the delivery of that curriculum are continuing to propel the school forward for the next generation. Senior schools compliment Kingshott pupils on their fine work ethic, outstanding manners, desire to achieve and their excellent academic foundations.

Our ambition is that our pupils leave us as confident and upstanding global citizens fully prepared to take their learning to the next level and engage in their respective communities as future leaders.

Please contact admissions@kingshottschool.com who will be delighted to make arrangements to meet.

England – East

Notre Dame Preparatory School

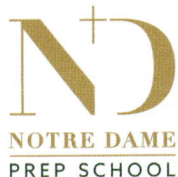

(Founded 1864)
147 Dereham Road, Norwich,
Norfolk NR2 3TA
Tel: 01603 625593
Email:
admissions@notredameprepschool.co.uk

Website:
www.notredameprepschool.co.uk
Headmaster: Mr Rob Thornton MA
School type: Co-educational Day Preparatory
Age range of pupils: 2–11 years

Located within easy reach of Norwich City Centre, Notre Dame Prep School is a leading Independent Catholic School for children aged 2 to 11. Academic results are excellent and we remain the top East Anglian Prep School (Sunday Times Parent Power) for Year 6 SATS. Children of all faiths (or none) are welcomed and class sizes do not exceed 23.

Notre Dame Prep provides families with a trusted learning environment where dedicated staff are committed to the academic, personal, social and emotional development of the children in our care, summarised in our school motto: 'Ahead in education, a heart in community.'

Children at Notre Dame Prep follow a broad, rich curriculum committed to both the development of skills and creativity. Subject specialists teach PE and Music to all our children, from Nursery age. Meanwhile, a wide range of extra-curricular clubs, ranging from Speech and Drama to Sports, Cookery and Arts and Crafts, continue after the school day is over to develop children's interests.

Achievement is not just evident in the classroom; at Notre Dame, we place a strong emphasis on developing the whole child through Music and the Arts. Children embrace the opportunity to experience a broad range of instruments for individual lessons, in addition to taking part in the school choir, while our annual Summer productions give them the opportunity to perform on the professional stage of Norwich Playhouse.

Pastoral support is central to Notre Dame's mission. Like a family, our staff support the social and emotional wellbeing of every child. Our small class sizes allow the children to build close, lasting friendships which grow as they move through this unique school.

An education at Notre Dame Prep provides children with a secure, nurturing foundation that enables them to progress to high school as confident, happy and caring individuals.

England – East

Old Buckenham Hall School

(Founded 1862)

Old Buckenham Hall, Brettenham Park, Ipswich, Suffolk IP7 7PH
Tel: 01449 740252
Email: admissions@obh.co.uk
Website: www.obh.co.uk
Headmaster: Mr David Griffiths
Appointed: September 2018

School type: Co-educational Day & Boarding Preparatory
Age range of pupils: 3–13 years
No. of pupils enrolled as at 01/01/2022: 242
Fees per term as at 01/01/2022:
Day: £6,947
Full Boarding: £9,052
Average class size: 15
Teacher/pupil ratio: 1:9

Old Buckenham Hall, near Lavenham, Suffolk, is one of the UK's leading independent co-educational preparatory schools for children aged 3-13, and has been educating children for over 150 years.

Old Buckenham Hall is a very special place for your child to begin their educational journey. Here, children remain just that. They experience, they learn, they grow, and they do so within one of the most idyllic environments imaginable. Every teacher at Old Buckenham Hall is committed to delivering the very best for every child. For us this means inspirational academic and co-curricular teaching, outstanding pastoral care and embracing risk and challenge. Children here feel happy and safe and they have a chance to explore their aspirations and develop their character.

We have three Boarding Houses and provide a range of boarding options; from two or three nights in school as a transitional boarder, to weekly boarding - enabling fuller involvement in evening activities and full boarding, which allows pupils to stay in for 11 nights and enjoy the exciting activities offered throughout the weekend.

Every child takes part in the Old Buckenham Explorer's - a bushcraft, survival, wilderness living, character and leadership development programme which is embedded into the school curriculum. Years 6, 7 and 8 work towards gaining their Level 1 and 2 NCFE Diploma in wilderness living and bushcraft skills, whilst also completing other modules in leadership training.

In May 2018, Old Buckenham Hall received the top rating of 'excellent' in all areas by ISI. Their report comments that pupils of all ages are energetic, enthusiastic, confident and happy learners who make excellent progress and achieve high levels of success in scholarships and senior school entrance examinations.

Headmaster, David Griffiths and his wife Becky live at the school with their three young children. They welcome visits to the school and virtual tours and look forward to meeting families at one of our regular open mornings or on an individual visit.

For further information about the school please contact the Registrar. Email: admissions@obh.co.uk or telephone 01449 740252.

England – East

St Cedd's School

(Founded 1931)

178a New London Road, Chelmsford, Essex CM2 0AR
Tel: 01245 392810
Email: info@stcedds.org.uk
Website: www.stcedds.org.uk
Head: Mr Matthew Clarke
Appointed: September 2018

School type:
Co-educational Day Preparatory
Age range of pupils: 3–11 years
No. of pupils enrolled as at 01/01/2022: 400
Boys: 200 **Girls:** 200
Fees per annum as at 01/01/2022:
Day: £9,240–£11,820
Average class size: Average 23; Max 24

St Cedd's School is a co-educational 3-11 IAPS Charitable Trust School offering pupils the opportunity to aspire and achieve in a caring environment that nurtures talent and supports individual endeavour. This is a school in which every child matters. We value and celebrate their many diverse talents and qualities and the grounded confidence the pupils develop results in great personal achievement.

Individual pupil progress
The progress of pupils, of all abilities, throughout the school is rapid. Our internal assessment results and 11+ scores far exceed national averages and annually we celebrate an unrivalled success rate to selective grammar and independent senior schools with an impressive track record of scholarship awards. This level of achievement is significant given that the school is academically non-selective. Assessments on entry are designed to capture the strengths and areas for development of each child so that the education is tailored to the needs of the individual.

Centre of excellence
The Independent Schools Inspectorate (ISI) put St Cedd's School at the top level in every category of inspection in February 2013 which places the school amongst the very best 3-11 preparatory schools in the country. The accolade confirms what we witness every day; high academic achievement, outstanding records of attainment in music, an inclusive sporting ethos and successes at national tournaments, a sense of purpose and ambition that shows itself in the attitude and actions of the pupils and staff, and a very effective pastoral care system.

In December 2021, the academic excellence of the school, and our provision for the most able, was recognised by the National Association for Able Children in Education in the awarding of the NACE Challenge Award for the second time.

Broad and balanced curriculum
With over 70 after-school activities to choose from, extra curricular opportunities are balanced with a firm focus on academic work. This synergy supports the development of confident, self-assured pupils ready for the challenges ahead. PE, music, art, French and science are taught by specialists with the teaching of PE, music and French starting in Pre-School. Acknowledging the breadth of talents of our pupils is an important aspect of life at St Cedd's School. To this end, our baccalaureate-style Year 6 curriculum, HOLDFAST, leads to awards in recognition of 'Holistic Opportunities to Learn and Develop, Furthering Achievement, Service and Talent'.

As a member of the Choir Schools Association, our Choristers sing in the Cathedral Choir and the Junior and Senior Chamber Choirs sing at Evensong in Chelmsford Cathedral.

Nurturing the future
For almost 90 years, boys and girls at St Cedd's School have been enjoying a quality of education that is among the very best you will find. We provide the best start in our vibrant Pre-School where the children thrive in a colourful and nurturing environment that widens their horizons and instils in them a love of learning.

Breakfast Club operates from 7:30am-8:00am and a wrap-around care programme is open until 6:00pm. Fees include curriculum-linked extra-curricular activities, 1-1 learning support, lunch and the majority of after-school clubs.

To attend an open day or to arrange an individual tour, please contact Mrs Abbott on 01245 392810 or email admissions@stcedds.org.uk.

England – East

St John's College School

73 Grange Road, Cambridge,
Cambridgeshire CB3 9AB

Tel: 01223 353652
Email: admissions@sjcs.co.uk
Website: www.sjcs.co.uk
Headmaster: Mr N. Chippington MA(Cantab), FRCO
School type: Co-educational Day & Boarding Preparatory
Age range of pupils: 4–13 years

No. of pupils enrolled as at 01/01/2022: 464
Fees per annum as at 01/01/2022:
Boarders: £26,715
Choristers: £8,925
Years 3-8: £16,920
Year 2: £14,160
Year 1 & Reception: £13,605

St John's College School is a leading independent co-educational day and boarding school, set in the heart of Cambridge, which offers an exceptional educational experience to boys and girls aged 4-13. It is described by the Good Schools Guide as "a joyous place that's buzzing".

At St John's, we believe in a childhood filled with affection, in which children know that they are known and valued, in which they learn to trust themselves and each other, in which they find and express their voices, discover the differences they can make for themselves and others, learn to think for themselves, to question, to collaborate, to be independent, and to own and take charge of their learning and their lives.

A St John's education is about the whole child. At its core is our focus on pastoral care and well-being, starting with our

Emotions for Learning programme which is at the very foundation of what we do and how we are as a school. We believe that education at its best is a profound act of care. If we care, then we will notice. If we notice, then we will act on a child's behalf. If we act for each child, then each of our children will achieve their best and become their best selves. To be known, to be noticed, to be valued, to be cared for - fundamental things for all of us, these are the essentials of a good childhood, and they are at the heart of the St John's way.

Our children become independent learners and creative thinkers prepared to question, with their curiosity very much alive. They get the best from themselves and achieve very highly within and beyond the classroom. We aim for our children to develop a real generosity of spirit, to know and care about how to get the best from others and to do well when they are with us and when they are long beyond our walls.

We focus on creativity throughout the school, both in the way we teach and the way children learn. We prefer to enable children to develop the skills they will need to succeed in the future rather concentrate purely on gaining knowledge, gathering facts and passing exams, although these have their place in any educational environment. This different approach creates the right environment for our pupils to find their true voice and realise their potential, secure in the knowledge that they are cared for and supported by the community around them and equipped with the skills to problem-solve, collaborate and adapt.

Our youngest children are full of questions, rich with curiosity. We work to preserve and strengthen their questioning and thinking skills. From the earliest age we give them the essential tools, knowledge and understanding, but we also aim to give them more. Our Flexible Learning programme incorporates child-led independent learning, creative and critical thinking, digitally enhanced learning, philosophy, compassion and loving kindness, as well as outdoor learning, which benefits from the addition of a landscaped forest garden. An Enrichment programme has been implemented with our nine to 13 year olds every Thursday afternoon to explore the development of sustainability projects, as well as cross-curricular work in computing, the arts, design technology, maths and science, and to give space to My Mind (incorporating mindfulness, study skills, tai chi, PSHEE and philosophy, as a foundation for the skills necessary for critical thinking, self-management of learning and management of self). The aim is to foster children's ability to possess their own learning, to engage their innate curiosity and creativity, and to encourage them to connect with their feelings about themselves and the world.

It is from this strong foundation that, despite being non-selective at our main 4+ intake, our pupils go on to achieve at the highest levels. This is confirmed by the results of our recent Inspection Report where the quality of pupils' academic and other achievements and the quality of their personal development were graded 'Excellent'. Our exam results are outstanding and on average, nearly half of our leavers gain scholarships to the strongest schools each year.

FIND OUT MORE

Visit our school and get to know us, as we are, during the normal school day on an Open Morning or an individually arranged tour. It is important to us that you should have an opportunity to see the school in action, tour each of the school's sites (usually with the children) and experience its atmosphere, as well as meet us to discuss the school's educational approach and ask any questions.

To find out more and to arrange your visit or book a place on one of our Open Mornings, please contact the Registrar, Mrs Emma Luck (01223 353652) or admissions@sjcs.co.uk)

England – East

Wymondham College Prep School

Golf Links Road, Wymondham, Norfolk NR18 9SZ
Tel: 01953 609000 (option 3)
Email: admin@wymondhamcollegeprepschool.org
Website: www.wymondhamcollegeprepschool.org
Headteacher: Mr Jon Timmins

School type: State primary with boarding (Years 5&6 only)
Age range of pupils: 4–11 years
No. of pupils enrolled as at 01/01/2022: 150 (will grow annually to a maximum of 452)
Fees per annum as at 01/01/2022:
Full Boarding: £12,165

Introduction

The Prep is located in rural Norfolk on the same site as Wymondham College and provides pupils with the time and space for a full and rounded education. Every effort is taken to provide an environment that is empathic, inspirational and aspirational, where every child can flourish and be successful in their school life.

Academic

The Prep delivers a considered, broad, balanced and knowledge rich curriculum that ensures pupils have the desired knowledge, skills and cultural capital to best access the secondary curriculum when they leave. Pupils experience a range of lessons including Science, History, Geography, Music, French, Dance and Games. Pupils in Reception continue to learn through play but also receive lessons in PSHE, Character, Music, Dance, Games, French alongside phonics, Talk for Writing and Mathematics.

The Prep ensures that high standards are achieved right across the school and we encourage each child to strive to be the very best. From developing our pupils' understanding of early stone-age man, or the inner workings of a piano, to mastering the ability to calculate an unknown in algebra, our teachers continually ignite interest in the classroom.

Our inspirational staff ensure that each pupil receives an education that will support and challenge them as individuals, put smiles on their faces and give them endless things to talk about with enthusiasm when they get home.

The Whole Child

An outstanding education is not purely about academic success; it is about developing socially and emotionally too; and we are committed to the development of the 'whole child'. The personal development of your child enables them to experience an education that goes beyond the curriculum; equipping pupils with important personal, social and emotional skills ready for the challenges and delights of our diverse and changing world.

Your child's tutor is a key component in our pastoral care, monitoring your child's development and will provide you with a vital link to help at every turn. We take great delight in our pupils' achievements, consoling them when it doesn't quite work out, embedding in them 'bouncebackability', and enabling your child to become a successful and positive member of modern society.

Co-curricular

In the co-curriculum, we remain committed to the promotion of the all-round pupil; one who is rewarded for their efforts in the curriculum, the co-curriculum and in their community.

Pupils enjoy a number of opportunities at the Prep, on the sports field, the stage, in a club or on a trip. We operate an engaging clubs list to enable those pupils, of which 95% of pupils choose to participate, to try something new or enjoy something they already love.

We appreciate that there is a need to support families with the demands placed upon them and, as such, our wrap around care is available from 7.45am with our Early Birds Breakfast Club, through to 6pm with our Extended Day provision.

England – East

Boarding

The boarding house, Underwood Hall, has been carefully designed to provide a safe and homely environment for our young boarders to grow. Nestled in the 85-acre Wymondham College site the mixed boarding house benefits from small group same gender dormitories, creating camaraderie and providing individual space. The house itself benefits from a range of community areas enabling boarders to bond together over a favourite film in the lounge or relax in the snug for a board game or book, giving our boarders the time and space to relax.

Choosing to join us in year 5 as a boarder, enables the development of meaningful friendships and characteristics, preparing them for the challenges of secondary education, particularly as a secondary school boarder.

The boarders are able to access the various facilities on offer at the Prep School and the College, with a variety of indoor and outdoor spaces immediately on the house's doorstep, ensuring that our boarders always have the space for meaningful endeavour and relaxation, creating friendships and fond memories.

Our boarders' home from home will be well staffed with a caring and well-meaning team who will be there to

support them as they delight in their achievements, consoling them when it doesn't quite work out and enabling them to flourish.

We provide a wide variety of weekend and evening adventures and activities for the boarders to take part in, with plenty of opportunities to visit the beach, forests, and historic Norwich.

Overall

The Prep fosters an environment that enables both academic achievement and personal development; one which promotes the mastery of skills, whilst allowing pupils varied opportunities. A school which is borne of a strong moral compass, excellent teaching, an engaging curriculum, meaningful rewards and true adaptation will enable your child to be successful. We are proud of our independent, confident, active and, above all, happy pupils.

England – East

York House School

Sarratt Road, Croxley Green,
Rickmansworth, Hertfordshire WD3 4LW
Tel: 01923 772395
Email: yhsoffice@york-house.com
Website: www.york-house.com
Headmaster: Mr Jon Gray BA(Ed)

School type:
Co-educational Day Preparatory
Age range of pupils: 3–13 years
No. of pupils enrolled as at 01/01/2022: 395
Fees per term as at 01/01/2022:
Day: £3,876–£5,164

York House School is a traditional prep school for girls and boys aged between 3 and 13. Founded in 1910, we have been in our stunning location just outside the town of Rickmansworth and village of Croxley Green in Hertfordshire since 1966. The school is proud of its 50 acres, which includes the main school building, purpose built classroom blocks, two halls, a dining room, drama studio, library, music room, amphitheatre and art room alongside playing areas, sport pitches, a smallholding with rescue animals, a mountain biking track, a fruit orchard and obstacle course.

Curriculum time is devoted to developing and nurturing a solid base in their academic subjects, particularly English and Maths. As a guide York House uses the Early Years Foundation Stage, the National Curriculum from Year 1 to Year 6, and the ISEB 13+ Common Entrance Curriculum in Y7 and Y8, to inform their curriculum. However, they have taken advantage of the freedom offered to them as an Independent School to design an engaging curriculum that fits the ethos of the school and meets the needs of the pupils.

York House prides itself on the breadth of subjects offered to all pupils, regardless of age. In the Pre-Prep, pupils have weekly lessons in French, Swimming, PE, Games, Drama, Computing and Music, all taught by specialist teachers. In addition to this, as pupils progress through the school they will also have captivating curriculum lessons in Outdoor Learning, Latin, Trivium, (York House's unique subject which embraces 21st Century Skills like research, critical thinking and public speaking) and STEM. The majority of their pupils are working beyond age related expectations in English and Maths. This allows them the opportunity to enrich their curriculum

England – East

with exciting lessons and engaging experiences; their expert teaching ensures that pupils not only make outstanding progress, but also develop a love of learning. York House strongly believe that learning is not confined to sitting behind a desk and often extends beyond the classroom walls altogether. York House make the most of their wonderful setting and exciting Outdoor Learning facilities, as well as an array of educational visits and trips each year.

Due to the wide variety of lessons on offer, pupil's progression in the academic subjects is always paramount. York House have a firm commitment to ensuring that children fulfil their academic potential, and this guides them at all times. Regular tracking of academic progress and strong communication with home helps to ensure that, by the time they leave York House, they are well prepared for their move to Senior Schools.

The York House Way is very much the basis and foundation of their pastoral care. They aim to create a culture and to share a common language based around the student aims. It is now embedded in what the pupil's say, what they write, hashtag and tweet and of what the school does. It drives the curriculum and pastoral decisions and provides clear outcomes for co-curricular activities. It is a phrase that now embodies the school, its staff and its pupils; it is a phrase that defines York House. The RULER approach has been a welcomed inclusion to everyday life at York House, working in harmony with the York House Way in creating truly empathetic, caring students who understand their emotions and feelings, as well as the emotions of others.

Sport is an integral part of life at York House, with pupils timetabled to make the most of our unique sporting facilities for over five hours a week- this does not include after school and break time clubs, or even morning practices! York House has a 'sport for all' mentality where they look to develop pupils' confidence, ability and understanding in a vast array of sports. York House promotes lifelong participants in sport and physical activity through nurturing their enjoyment and passion by providing links with local club communities throughout the academic year.

The Arts at York House includes Music, Art and Drama; these creative subjects are an anchor point in our rigorous and robust curriculum. Within the Arts, York House believes in creating opportunities to showcase children's work in an encouraging and supportive fashion. York House thrives on celebrating the children's achievements through performances, exhibitions and concerts.

The outdoors is one of the best places to learn and York House pupils have designated lesson time to learning new skills on their extensive school grounds; mountain bike riding, traversing, orienteering, den building, fishing and fire lighting to name a few. York House has a small holding area with a wide range of animals that the children are allowed to take care of during the school day also.

The use of the outdoors and the unique natural environment is one of our greatest assets in the promotion of the health and well-being of their pupils. Understanding the calming and nurturing influence animals and nature can have, especially to those who have specific emotional needs, and making this as accessible to as many pupils, as often as possible, has been life changing for those students.

York House aims to give your child the best possible preparation for his or her future studies and adult life. They encourage pupils to develop a self-disciplined and hard-working approach which will help them achieve good academic results, whilst also encouraging them to follow the York House aims to be their best self:

- I aim to have a positive outlook
- I aim to be self-reliant (for only when you are truly self-reliant are you in a position to help others)
- I aim to leave people and places better than I found them

Every child has talents and York House aims to discover, nurture and develop them to their full potential. York House looks forward to welcoming you to explore #TheYorkHouseWay during a meeting and tour with their Headmaster, Mr Jon Gray.

England – East Midlands

Spratton Hall

(Founded 1951)
Smith Street, Spratton,
Northamptonshire NN6 8HP
Tel: 01604 847292

Fax: 01604 820844
Email: registrar@sprattonhall.com
Website: www.sprattonhall.com
Head Master: Mr Simon Clarke
Appointed: January 2014
School type:
Co-educational Day Preparatory

Religious Denomination:
Church of England
Age range of pupils: 4–13 years
No. of pupils enrolled as at 01/01/2022: 380
Fees per annum as at 01/01/2022:
Day: £10,725–£16,275
Average class size: 15.5

Spratton Hall embodies the values of a traditional prep school and academic achievement is always encouraged and rewarded. However, we are an all-round school, and as such, we help children develop their strengths wherever they lie, be they in Sport, Drama, Art, STEM, or Music.

Recently recognised by The Week as being a "great all-round school", we have 50 acres of first-rate facilities, including: a purpose-built theatre, art studios, science labs, an indoor sports dome, floodlit AstroTurf and multiple sports courts, tracks, pitches and cricket nets. Our 65 extracurricular activities further ensure that we have something to delight and inspire every child.

In our Pre-prep department, determination and kindness are woven into all areas of the curriculum, and children receive daily individual support from highly experienced Early Years teachers. To complement their classroom-based learning, they also enjoy regular PE, Dance, Music, Art, Drama and Forest School sessions. In 2021 the Pre-Prep School was proud to be shortlisted for 'Pre-Prep School of the Year'.

With a 100% pass rate at Common Entrance and multiple annual scholarships to top public schools, the rigorous academic curriculum is balanced with fun inter-house competitions, school trips and our exceptional pastoral care.

Our dedicated Head of Pastoral Care oversees the wellbeing and welfare of all pupils, and a well-resourced learning support team are always on hand to help children overcome any academic obstacles they may meet. Meanwhile parents are supported with extended school days, free wraparound care, and local minibus routes.

To experience a typical school day, personal, tours with the Head Master can be booked at **www.sprattonhall.com**. When you visit the website, you can also order a prospectus, or take a 360° virtual tour of our facilities.

England – Greater London

Holy Cross Preparatory School

(Founded 1931)
George Road, Kingston upon Thames,
Surrey KT2 7NU
Tel: 020 8942 0729
Email: secretary@holycrossprep.com

Website: www.holycrossprepschool.co.uk
Headteacher: Mrs S Hair BEd(Hons)
School type: Girls' Day Preparatory
Age range of girls: 3–11 years

At Holy Cross Prep School for Girls, on George Road in Kingston, you will notice immediately that they identify and nurture your daughter's talents from the very start. Their emphasis on understanding the strengths and personal make-up of each individual girl has, their parents say, become the hallmark of a Holy Cross education.

Why is this so important?
They say it is because, from their long experience of teaching girls and being alongside them as they make the journey through these all- important early years, they know that for every child there is a key - their very own special key that will unlock their future. It is a key that will lead on to a life of broad horizons, confidence in their abilities and in their preparedness to meet life's challenges with a smile. This, they believe, lies at the heart of their school.

The earlier this key is found, the better because as all parents know, the early years are the most formative (the Holy Cross pre-school begins at 3). They tell us that having very good teachers at a very young age make a very big difference, which is why they have so many specialist teachers right from the get go. On top of this, the character formation that happens there, based on a robust and visible Christian value system, provides a solid base for senior school and beyond.

The results of this are obvious for all to see. The girls, as you would hope and expect, leave Holy Cross with an enviably impressive educational springboard - their scholarship board bears this out.

But that is not the only point. The girls will also have formed their own, unique foundations, built to the specifications of their own temperament, their own talents, their own heart.

And, as a direct result of this, the girls leave Holy Cross happy and confidently curious and, the school community tell us, will run at life with joy and with an expectation of success.

No other prep school in the area has a campus like it in terms of size or facilities.

It occasionally happens that a very important step for your family turns out to be ...right on your doorstep.

In this magical corner of Kingston it seems that the girls have their eyes opened to all that is possible for them ...to the limitless things they can achieve.

England – Greater London

Benedict House Preparatory School

1-5 Victoria Road, Sidcup, Kent DA15 7HD
Tel: 020 8300 7206
Email: secretary@benedicthouseprepschool.co.uk
Website: www.benedicthouseprepschool.co.uk

Headteacher: Mr Craig Wardle
School type: Co-educational Day Preparatory
Age range of pupils: 3–11 years

Benedict House Prep school in Sidcup is known for its small class sizes, warm family environment and academic excellence. The school, part of Chatsworth Schools, prides itself on the positive relationships fostered within the school community and the tailored education every child receives. Benedict House children achieve highly in the classroom, on the sports field, on the stage and in the music department.

Benedict House has always been noted for the excellence of its teaching and the consequent high standard of academic achievement among its pupils. The children are well prepared for the challenge of secondary school and the school's success rate is unparalleled among local state and independent schools, with a consistently high percentage of pupils gaining entry into selective Grammar Schools. In 2021, Year 6 pupils achieved the best ever 11+ pass rate in the history of the School, with 100% passing the Kent test and 80% passing the Bexley test.

2021 also saw Benedict House named as 14th best prep school in England by the prestigious Sunday Times 100 Best Primary and Prep Schools list, Parent Power. This reflects the findings from a recent Ofsted visit that *"The teachers are well informed, enthusiastic and committed. Relationships between adults and pupils are good, leading to an extremely positive climate in classrooms, promoting effective learning."* The children at Benedict House benefit from a well rounded education at highly competitive fees.

The relationship between teacher and child is at the centre of the Benedict House learning experience. The school cultivates a caring atmosphere in which all children can feel relaxed and at home; where staff get to know every child in the school, and not just those in their own classes. Teachers promote the joy of learning, develop personal potential, dispel the fear of failure, nurture self-confidence, develop study skills and encourage kindness and consideration for others.

Benedict House believes in nurturing the physical well-being of pupils through sport and promote inclusive, active and enthusiastic participation. All children participate in a broad range of physical activities throughout the year including: football, touch rugby, netball, gymnastics, dance, cricket, rounders, athletics and swimming. Benedict House employs specialist coaches to deliver sports tuition and to ensure pupils get the most from their involvement in terms of their physical development, aptitude and enjoyment. In addition to the school's own recreation area, Benedict House children are fortunate to have the use of extensive, specialist sports facilities. These include large pitches, netball courts and swimming pools, all of which are within a short walk from the school.

It is only when children feel safe and secure in their environment that they can develop all their gifts and talents to the full. The school strongly believes that the closer the affinity between staff and parents, the greater the benefits to children. That is why Benedict House attach such value to growing the partnership between home and school. It strengthens the sense of family.

The school provides a broad range of after-school activities designed to further

England – Greater London

develop and deepen children's interests and skills. The after-school clubs run until 4:30pm each evening and regularly include activities such as arts and crafts, drama, sewing, jewellery making, cookery, dancing, sports. In addition, the school operates a Breakfast Club an After-School Care Session.

Everything that happens at Benedict House has the pupils and their individual needs at heart. The school creates an environment in which children are happy, motivated to achieve and enthusiastic about their learning.

England – Greater London

St Catherine's Prep

ST CATHERINE'S SCHOOL
— TWICKENHAM —

(Founded 1914)

Cross Deep, Twickenham,
Middlesex TW1 4QJ
Tel: 020 8891 2898
Fax: 020 8744 9629
Email: info@stcatherineschool.co.uk
Website: www.stcatherineschool.co.uk
Headmistress:
Mrs Johneen McPherson MA

Appointed: September 2018
School type: Girls' Day Preparatory
Age range of girls: 4–11 years
No. of pupils enrolled as at 01/01/2022: 102
Fees per annum as at 01/01/2022:
Day: £12,480–£13,470
Average class size: 13
Teacher/pupil ratio: 1:9

St Catherine's Prep marks the beginning of an outstanding education for girls, which leads on to St Catherine's Senior School and Sixth Form. Ours is a Catholic school which warmly welcomes girls of all faiths, and we are especially proud of the creative, curious and motivated girls in Prep.

The girls in Early Years enjoy our impressive, purpose-built facilities, including spacious grounds, an indoor swimming pool, large hall and library. An excellent beginning to school years is ensured by our dedicated and experienced staff, whose warm care and focus on each child helps to foster learning and confidence.

In Key Stage One, the emphasis remains on social and personal skills, alongside an increased focus on literacy and numeracy. Each teacher works with her class to encourage a love of learning, and visits and excursions provide enrichment that supports our exciting curriculum. Specialist teaching in French, Music, Swimming, Physical Education and Information Technology continues and many pupils also enjoy individual instrumental lessons.

Our commitment to excellence in teaching and learning continues at Key Stage Two. Pupils thrive on stimulating tasks designed to promote risk taking and resilience. The girls develop excellent thinking and collaborative skills, and they know how to have fun while they learn. Specialist teaching is enhanced by the introduction of Food and Nutrition, Drama, and Design and Technology. As Prep years

England – Greater London

draw to a close, our Year 6 pupils enjoy automatic entry to the Senior School, and almost all girls take up this opportunity.

There is a rich and varied programme of clubs and activities in Prep - ranging from early morning swim squad, to Glee Club and Philosophy for Children - which ensures that pupils make the most of every minute of the day. Many also take advantage of our wrap around care, beginning with Breakfast Club and finishing with After School Care.

St Catherine's offers a values-based education where pupils flourish, and we are proud that our relatively small size helps to ensure we know and care for each girl. The inclusive Catholic life of the School places great emphasis on friendship and community, and is at the centre of all that we do. Through prayer, singing, stories and discussion, the girls reflect upon Gospel values and the world around them, developing a sense of belonging and enjoying warm relationships with peers and staff.

Our all-girls' education also helps us to focus on the needs of our pupils, to give them opportunities to develop and celebrate their gifts and talents, and to grow in self-worth and confidence. We rather like the fact that at St Catherine's 'the girls are the best at everything', and we encourage our pupils to be ambitious as they begin to think about their potential.

St Catherine's girls are encouraged and supported, and we focus on character, helping to create independent and caring young people who are eager to embrace all that life offers.

England – Greater London

Merton Court Preparatory School

(Founded 1899)
38 Knoll Road, Sidcup, Kent DA14 4QU
Tel: 020 8300 2112

Email: office@mertoncourtprep.co.uk
Website: mertoncourtprep.co.uk
Headmaster: Mr Dominic Price BEd, MBA
School type:
Co-educational Day Preparatory

Age range of pupils: 3–11 years
No. of pupils enrolled as at 01/01/2022: 320
Fees per term as at 01/01/2022:
Day: £3,095–£4,675

SPRINGBOARD TO SUCCESS

Merton Court Prep in Sidcup, combines academic excellence with a healthy holistic approach

Founded in 1899, this well-established co-educational, proprietorial school teaches 320 pupils from the age of three to those taking their 11+. It is a place where opportunities make all the difference. Merton Court's aims are very clear - to inspire a passion for learning, through excellent teaching and outstanding personal achievement and to create a unique family ethos, in an atmosphere of warmth, trust and friendliness, with the highest quality of pastoral care.

Merton Court's academic success sees pupils gain places at local well-regarded Grammar and Independent schools. Smooth transition to Senior school is helped by the fact that, like at Secondary school, Merton Court pupils move classroom, from an early age, for different subjects, which are taught by teachers with specialist knowledge, instead of staying put with just one teacher. Indeed, children receive an outstanding introduction to learning from the very start, in our Early Years Foundation stage, which is rated Excellent by the Independent Schools' Inspectorate.

Equally, we promote traditional values in a safe, exciting and stimulating environment, giving each individual child the best possible start to their life story.

Most of all, our aim is to develop children with clear opinions and a 'go for it' attitude, ready to take their place as global citizens, through the excellent provision of extensive enrichment activities and opportunities.

Merton Court boasts grass and Astro pitches, a sports hall, a swimming pool (we were 2018 Primary English Schools' Swimming Association Champions) and dedicated science, music, art, dance and IT areas, but what sets us apart is our beautiful 17-acre grounds including a Forest School - part nature reserve, part outdoor activity area, where children can explore, follow trails, build camps and enjoy mud slides and mud kitchens. All these facilities are for the children's exclusive use, to make sure they enjoy the best days of their lives.

England – Greater London

Woodford Green Preparatory School

Glengall Road, Woodford Green,
Essex IG8 0BZ

Tel: 020 8504 5045
Email: admissions@wgprep.co.uk
Website: www.wgprep.co.uk
Headmaster: Mr J P Wadge
Appointed: September 2015
School type:
Co-educational Day Preparatory

Age range of pupils: 3–11 years
No. of pupils enrolled as at 01/01/2022: 385
Fees per term as at 01/01/2022:
Day: £3,725
Average class size: 24
Teacher/pupil ratio: 1:12

Known locally as the "Red School" because of the scarlet uniforms, Woodford Green Preparatory School was founded in 1932 to provide a non-denominational Christian education for boys and girls aged from 3 to 11 years, a tradition that has been maintained throughout and is now enriched by welcoming children of all faiths and none. The school is highly regarded by parents as successful in terms of ensuring children are safe, happy and well prepared for achieving excellent results in 11+ entrance examinations. We aim to provide a learning community that lights the flame within and empowers all children to reach their educational and personal potential. Our vision is to be known as a school where every pupil is nurtured, encouraged to be curious and achieves their very best.

Our latest independent school inspection report (2014) highlights our outstanding work. Our school ensures that "pupils' personal development is excellent" and that "the quality of pupils' achievements and learning is excellent and reflects the school's aims". It was also noted by the inspectors that our children "are confident, self-aware and have high esteem. Pupils have a keen moral sense, awareness of others and accept responsibility willingly".

The friendly, supportive environment, in which excellent work and behaviour fosters interest and independence, encourages all children to do their very best. We have purpose-built areas for science, sport, art, music, computing and French, complemented by specialist teachers. We have excellent teachers and modern facilities throughout the school, including a fabulous library which is regularly used by the whole school to foster a love of reading. In the Early Years, highly qualified staff ensure that children have an outstanding foundation for the rest of their education both here at WGPS and beyond.

Our links with parents are very active and we strive to give parents excellent opportunities to be involved in school life and their children's progress.

We look forward to welcoming you to our very happy and successful school.

England – London

Blackheath Prep

(Founded 1998)
4 St Germans Place, Blackheath,
London, SE3 0NJ

Tel: 020 8858 0692
Email: info@blackheathprep.co.uk
Website: www.blackheathprep.co.uk
Head: Alex Matthews
School type:
Co-educational Day Preparatory
Age range of pupils: 3–11 years

No. of pupils enrolled as at 01/01/2022: 385
Fees per term as at 01/01/2022:
Nursery: £2,890–£4,910 per term
Pre-Preparatory (Reception to Year 2):
£4,740 per term
Preparatory (Years 3 to 6): £5,130 per term

Blackheath Prep is an outstanding, co-educational prep school for children aged 3 to 11. Located in an idyllic setting on the edge of the heath close to Blackheath Village, our five-acre site offers superb specialist facilities, and plenty of space for our pupils to have the freedom to learn and play in our large playgrounds, forest school areas and 2.5 acre playing field.

Our seven core values of kindness, curiosity, freedom, ambition, courage, community and joy inform all that we do and how we behave as a school community. They guide our approach to teaching and learning, to pastoral care and to wellbeing, and our engagement with those around us.

At Blackheath Prep we are ambitious for your child and who they can become. We're committed to achieving academic excellence within an ethos of strong pastoral care. We deliver this through a balanced and challenging curriculum that captures children's imagination and encourages their creativity. We nurture our pupils both academically and pastorally, enabling them to be happy, confident and inquisitive children.

Through a broad range of subjects, inspiring teaching and plenty of extra-curricular activities, we ensure that our school is a really exciting place to be where curiosity is stimulated, and a love of learning is encouraged.

We provide opportunities for our pupils to engage with every aspect of school life; in the arts, on the sports field and in the classroom as well as excellent wraparound care activities. We encourage our pupils to develop long-held passions, to try new things, to succeed and fail, to lead and serve, to play and explore, to give and give generously.

Above all, we are a kind, friendly and joyful school.

England – London

Devonshire House Preparatory School

(Founded 1989)

2 Arkwright Road, Hampstead, London, NW3 6AE
Tel: 020 7435 1916
Email: enquiries@dhprep.co.uk
Website: www.devonshirehouseschool.co.uk
Headmistress: Mrs S. Piper BA(Hons)
School type: Preparatory, Pre-preparatory & Nursery Day School

Religious Denomination: Non-denominational
Age range of boys: 2.5–13 years
Age range of girls: 2.5–11 years
No. of pupils enrolled as at 01/01/2022: 543
Boys: 317 **Girls:** 226
Fees per annum as at 01/01/2022:
Day: £9,870–£20,475

Devonshire House, the co-educational preparatory and pre-preparatory school with its own nursery, is a place where families come together for their children's most formative years. The School's commitment is to outstanding care and education, to help discover, inspire and develop pupils' talents and to support them throughout their years at the School and in their move to their next schools.

The results for senior school entry are exceptionally good, with some forty scholarships and exhibitions to senior schools in the last three years. However, the School is perhaps proudest that this is achieved in such a creative and happy school with its broad curriculum and with so many extra-curricular activities.

"Pupils leave the school as confident, resilient young people who have a strong self-esteem and a well-developed understanding of how to improve their own learning." ISI Inspection Report.

The School aims to create adaptable and creative minds, for a changing world.

The Head, Senior Leadership Team and Staff are committed to an open, trusting dialogue with parents about their children and to be available to advise and help throughout each child's school career.

Pupils learn how to work hard for their own achievements and to work with others with commitment, understanding and co-operation. They learn many things - traditional and innovative - and above all they learn how to grow their talents and how they may want to apply them in their lives.

Devonshire House has fine buildings, with substantial grounds and games areas, in the heart of Hampstead.

The School seeks to inspire not only a love of learning, but a love of thinking for oneself and the strength and resilience to do so, to make the most of life and to help others along this journey.

"A wonderful experience for my children. I am truly thankful for all the teachers and friends in DHS." Junior School Parent

England – London

Hawkesdown House School Kensington

Hawkesdown House School
Endeavour • Courage • Truth

27 Edge Street, Kensington,
London, W8 7PN

Tel: 020 7727 9090
Email: admin@hawkesdown.co.uk
Website: www.hawkesdown.co.uk
Headmistress: Mrs S Gillam BEd (Cantab)
Appointed: January 2022
School type: Co-educational Independent Preparatory Day

Religious Denomination: Non-denominational
Age range of pupils: 2–8 years
No. of pupils enrolled as at 01/01/2022: 100
Fees per annum as at 01/01/2022:
Day: £4,725–£21,120
Average class size: 14
Teacher/pupil ratio: 1:9

A love of learning and a nurturing environment are at the heart of Hawkesdown House. The School achieves academic excellence and first-class entry results to pupils' next schools, with a broad and exciting curriculum and in days filled with variety, laughter and busy purpose.

Parents are fiercely loyal to this educational philosophy, the success of which is borne out in the excellent results and in the creative, thoughtful, happy pupils. Many of the pupils coming to the School live within walking distance and the School is an important part of the Kensington community.

"Hawkesdown nurtures its pupils, encourages fun but also achieves academic success." Good Schools Guide

Hawkesdown ensures the development of the creative and adaptable thinking that is so vital in a fast-changing world. This is combined with dedicated teaching of the still important traditional subjects and teaching and inspiration towards kindness, initiative, courtesy, cooperative working, and persistence.

The School excels in matching pupils happily and successfully to future schools and spends time with parents ensuring that the transition is smooth and free from stress. In the last few years, leavers have gone to St Paul's Junior's, Westminster Cathedral Choir School, King's College Junior, Westminster Under School, Sussex House, Caldicott, Summer Fields and St Philip's School, amongst others.

England – London

Lyndhurst House Prep School

(Founded 1952)
24 Lyndhurst Gardens, Hampstead, London, NW3 5NW

Tel: 020 7435 4936
Email: jorrett@lyndhursthouse.co.uk
Website: www.lyndhursthouse.co.uk
Head of School:
Mr Andrew Reid MA (Oxon)
Appointed: September 2008
School type: Boys' Day Preparatory

Age range of boys: 4–13 years
No. of pupils enrolled as at 01/01/2022: 125
Fees per annum as at 01/01/2022:
Day: £18,360–£20,790
Average class size: 15
Teacher/pupil ratio: 1:8

"A wonderful, nurturing and supportive environment. My son goes in every morning with a smile on his face." Year One Parent

Lyndhurst House has an outstanding history of achievement and exceptional pastoral care. The boys win places, by scholarship or at Common Entry, particularly to the major London independent day senior schools. The School takes boys from the ages of four to thirteen.

The School's approach helps boys build self-confidence, easy, happy friendships and the key skills to discover, innovate and achieve. The boys have self-respect, respect for others and a very strong sense of commitment.

Individual attention to support academic progress and personal development have always been at the forefront at Lyndhurst.

The School seeks to understand what matters most to each family and encourages parents to visit as early as possible to meet the Head. It is a privilege for any school to have the care and responsibility of a child's early education and at Lyndhurst House this is supported by the close open relationship with parents.

"Pupils are extremely considerate, caring and respectful of each other and all members of their school community. This is strongly encouraged by positive relationships with staff, firmly underpinned by strong values." ISI Inspection Report

The dynamic between exceptional academic education and the nurture and wider development of personality are complementary, and Lyndhurst House has a long record of success delivering this combination.

Lyndhurst is a warm, friendly place where boys discover and grow their talents and initiative. The School develops adaptable and innovative skills, but also helps the boys to understand that some things remain as important as ever: kindness and understanding others' perspectives; being able to be independent, but being kind to oneself; hard work. These all matter as much as ever, as does learning to find ways to relax.

In the coming years, much in society and the workplace generally will change radically, and the education at Lyndhurst emphasises adaptability, independent thought and the building of the skills and character, to be resilient at all stages of life.

"His confidence has grown and he has formed lovely friendships with his peers. We think the staff at Lyndhurst do an amazing job." Year One Parent

England – London

North Bridge House Prep School Regent's Park

(Founded 1939)
1 Gloucester Avenue, London, NW1 7AB
Tel: 020 7428 1520
Email: admissionsenquiries@northbridgehouse.com
Website: www.northbridgehouse.com

Head of School: Mr James Stenning
School type: Co-educational Day
Age range of pupils: 4–13 years
No. of pupils enrolled as at 01/01/2022: 385
Fees per annum as at 01/01/2022:
Day: £18,960–£20,520

Occupying a grand former convent at the edge of Regent's Park, North Bridge House (NBH) Prep School has a longstanding reputation for providing a fully rounded education and achieving first-class results. Year after year, the school sees students gain entry to the top senior schools in the country, often with prestigious academic, art, drama, music and sport scholarships.

From the very start of their educational journey - in Reception - children benefit from specialist teaching in the Arts, languages and sport, while the school delivers a progressively knowledge-rich curriculum at each key stage, designed to stretch pupils further than in a junior school setting. The rich and varied academic programme is tailored to challenge and reward every pupil, ranging from Critical Thinking and Philosophy, Politics and Economics; to Latin and Mandarin.

Pupils are taught entirely by subject specialists from Year 5, while classes remain small to ensure teaching and learning is truly tailored to the individual.

The school is continually recognised not only for its academic excellence, but for its individualised approach to pupils' all-round development and wellbeing. Awarded Outstanding in all areas of inspection, *"A major strength of the school is the manner in which it consistently promotes the children's personal and emotional development."* (School Inspection Service)

The school's focus on nurturing confidence and cultivating character ensures children are fully prepared for the next stage of their school career, benefiting from outstanding tuition and guidance for the various 11+ and 13+ senior school pathways.

NBH works closely with families to choose the right school for their child according to their individual strengths and interests, providing bespoke preparation for every path to success. Boys and girls have the option of the UK's leading destination schools, or a stress-free all-through education which does not compromise on academic excellence. Internal students are prioritised for places at the high-achieving NBH Senior Schools.

NBH Prep School is fully equipped with modern and specialist teaching facilities, including an art studio; soundproof music pods for one-to-one tuition, practice and recording; a stage-lit drama studio; an indoor gym; and science laboratories. In addition, pupils enjoy using the library in and out of class time, extensive use of iPads, and are all provided with their own 1-2-1 devices.

Sport is essential to NBH Prep's focus on pupil wellbeing and personal development. PE and games sessions are held in the school gym and Regent's Park, which is also the school's home ground for its many sporting fixtures. Pupils also benefit from rock-climbing at a local sports club and winter cricket at Lord's. The school's extracurricular offering is broad, diverse and character-building, with activities ranging from music, art, and drama to chess, cookery, design technology, Spanish, ballet and street dance.

The school's inspection report also lauds the "outstanding leadership" and recognises pupils' exemplary behaviour, which "is founded on the high levels of mutual trust and respect between pupils and staff". NBH Prep School promotes happy, self-assured children who "make excellent progress in their learning and development and are extremely well prepared for the next stage of their education."

To find out more about the benefits of an NBH Prep School education, book a visit at northbridgehouse.com

England – London

St Paul's Cathedral School

ST PAUL'S CATHEDRAL SCHOOL

(Founded 12th Century or earlier)
2 New Change, London, EC4M 9AD
Tel: 020 7248 5156
Fax: 020 7329 6568

Email: admissions@spcs.london.sch.uk
Website: www.spcslondon.com
Headmaster: Simon Larter-Evans BA (Hons), PGCE, FRSA
Appointed: September 2016
School type: Co-educational Pre-Prep, Day Prep & Boarding Choir School
Religious Denomination: Church of England, admits pupils of all faiths

Age range of pupils: 4–13 years
No. of pupils enrolled as at 01/01/2022: 258
Boys: 157 **Girls:** 101
Fees per annum as at 01/01/2022:
Day: £15,174–£16,338
Full Boarding: £9,178
Average class size: 15-20
Teacher/pupil ratio: 1:10

Curriculum
A broad curriculum, including the International Primary Curriculum, prepares all pupils for 11+, 13+, scholarship and Common Entrance examinations.

There is a strong musical tradition and choristers' Cathedral choral training is outstanding. A wide variety of games and other activities is offered. At the latest ISI inspection in May 2017, the school was rated 'Excellent'.

Entry requirements
Entry at 4+, 7+ and 11+ years: Pre-prep and day pupils interview and short test; Choristers voice trials and tests held throughout the year for boys between 6½-8½ years. Scholarships available at 11+ years.

St Paul's Cathedral School is a registered charity (No. 312718), which exists to provide education for the choristers of St Paul's Cathedral and for children living in the local area.

England – London

St Benedict's School

(Founded 1902)
54 Eaton Rise, Ealing, London, W5 2ES

Tel: 020 8862 2000
Email: admissions@stbenedicts.org.uk
Website: www.stbenedicts.org.uk
Headmaster: Mr A Johnson BA
Appointed: September 2016
School type: Co-educational Day
Age range of pupils: 3–18 years

No. of pupils enrolled as at 01/01/2022: 1073
Boys: 702 **Girls:** 371 **Sixth Form:** 203
Fees per annum as at 01/01/2022:
Day: £13,995–£18,330
Average class size: Junior School: 17; Senior School: 18; Sixth Form: 7
Teacher/pupil ratio: 1:10

St Benedict's is London's leading independent Catholic coeducational school, in leafy Ealing. Within a caring, happy community, St Benedict's has strong academic standards. The Junior School and Nursery offer a holistic education for children aged 3 to 11, which continues through the Senior School and Sixth Form. St Benedict's, which welcomes children of other Christian denominations and faiths, is committed to supporting all children to develop their full potential.

Inspirational teaching and exceptional pastoral care are at the heart of the education we offer.

The Junior School and Nursery provide a supportive, friendly and vibrant co-educational environment in which to learn. In the Nursery a carefully planned and child-centred programme enables and extends learning and development. The Junior School provides a broad and balanced curriculum based on a rigorous academic core. Sharing excellent facilities with the Senior School, and participating in a programme of cross-curricular activities, helps ease the transition at 11+ to the Senior School, which is on the same site.

There are extensive opportunities in music, art, sport and drama. St Benedict's has a proud sporting tradition, which promotes the highest sporting aspirations while encouraging everyone to enjoy sport, fitness and teamwork. Music is excellent, with several choirs and many instrumental ensembles. A wide range of co-curricular activities is offered, and an after-school club is available at the Junior School.

There has been huge investment in building and facilities at St Benedict's. Having opened our new Sixth Form Centre and Art Department in 2015, a new Nursery and Pre-Prep Department opened in September 2017, providing our youngest pupils with a first-rate learning environment.

St Benedict's School is unique. Come and visit and see what we have to offer. You can be sure of a warm Benedictine welcome.

England – London

England – London

St. Anthony's School for Girls

Ivy House, 94-96 North End Road,
London NW11 7SX
Tel: 020 3869 3070
Email: admissions@stanthonysgirls.co.uk
Website: www.stanthonysgirls.co.uk
Head of School: Mr Donal Brennan

School type: Girls' Day Preparatory
Religious Denomination: Catholic
Age range of girls: 2.5–11 years
No. of pupils enrolled as at 01/01/2022: 85
Fees per annum as at 01/01/2022:
Day: £18,000

St Anthony's School for Girls and Nursery is a confident, nurturing, family school offering a high-quality education within an environment which delivers a happy, healthy academically challenging curriculum.

The school is located at Ivy House, adjacent to Golders Hill Park and is a short bus ride from its sister school St Anthony's Boys in Hampstead.

St Anthony's Girls achieves outstanding 11+ results, regularly receiving offers from a plethora of academic north London schools: Highgate to Channing, South Hampstead High to Haberdasher's School for Girls; Francis Holland Girls to City of London, North London Collegiate to Mill Hill and further afield to Queenswood, Wycombe Abbey, and St Swithun's.

The school owes its success to committed pupils, ambitious teachers and supportive parents who embrace the recipe for success which has been established at the school.

A touch of kindness never goes amiss at St Anthony's, where it is seen as a fundamental tenet to a happy school experience. Adults model and engage in mutually respectful exchanges which the children in turn will role-play as best practice in their relationships. Observing a year 6 girl taking time out from her friends at playtime to sit with a year 1 girl who needed some quiet solace is not an uncommon expression of kindness at St Anthony's.

The girls at St Anthony's are curious: encouraged to ask questions and Big Questions at our Talk Time Assembly leads to robust discussions on the eternal questions. "What does it mean to be thoughtful, why is it difficult to share, why do leaves fall off trees to why are the days shortening during September?" In this environment of curiosity, the girls grow in courage and confidence and can verbalise complex thoughts and feelings.

Respect is witnessed in many ways at St Anthony's. All adults feel valued as equals in the eyes of the girls, the sense of community is strengthened where children develop a confident respect for themselves as unique, valuable individuals. An appreciation for all those who care for them from their parents to their teachers to the bus drivers to the chef who prepares their lunch. Being

respectful of their world and the need to be guardians for future generations ensure that the girls are quick to respond to global and community causes. It is not uncommon for the child-led, charities committee to launch an appeal among their peers to host fundraising events for the koala bears, refugee women and local homeless children.

Being inspired to embrace new challenges is at the heart of the teaching at St Anthony's. From Forest School activities to specialist Music, Drama, Mandarin, French, Rhythmic Gymnastics, Ballet, Science and Sports interwoven into the girls' timetable allow for the girls to have their imagination enriched and developed. From a buffet of creative teaching comes a perfect blend of original and individualised responses. The school clubs schedule further embeds this with girls choosing from Netball, Cross-Country, Yoga, Maths, Environmental Club, Debating, Minnie-Vinnies, Rhythmic Gymnastics, Irish Dancing, Science and Musical Drama.

St Anthony's Girls take responsibility for their actions, accepting praise, being willing to give compliments to others and understanding that at times saying sorry is important. Sincerity and fairness matter hugely to the girls allowing for happy confident relationships to develop at the school.

The establishment of a co-ed nursery at St. Anthony's School for Girls in September 2021 has been a huge success. Families seeking a nurturing and kind learning environment founded upon the values of both the boys' and girls' schools, which is academically enriching at the same time, have been delighted with the experience to date.

The curriculum is informed by the EYFS (Early Years) programme and is designed to encourage curiosity, interaction, independence and most importantly, a love of learning.

The nursery programme aims to help prepare children for reception. Teachers ensure children develop key skills as well as knowledge and an understanding of the world around them, with regular 'learning in nature' lessons at Golders Hill Park.

Children will also be stronger communicators and self-assured as learners owing to the carefully planned timetable they follow. Drama, music, French, Mandarin, sport and dance have been interwoven into the nursery schedule allowing pupils to benefit from the rich specialist curriculum on offer across the school.

The nursery children enjoy talk time, singing and celebration assemblies, feel inspired by 'Whacky Wednesday' science focus, participate in all major school events, such as Harvest Food Appeal,

STEAM week, remembrance service, the Christmas show and the end of term disco.

The nursery children have enjoyed a very colourful and creative autumn term, finding treasure buried in the sandpit at Golders Hill Park, travelling to space in their own bespoke spaceship, welcoming their teddy bears to school on 'Hug a Bear Day' and discovering the fossilised remains of a dinosaur in the nursery sandpit.

We look forward to welcoming families for personalised tours with the headteacher.

England – London

St. Anthony's School for Boys

ST. ANTHONY'S SCHOOL FOR BOYS

(Founded 1952)

90 Fitzjohn's Avenue, Hampstead, London, NW3 6NP
Tel: 020 7431 1066
Email: pahead@stanthonysprep.co.uk
Website: www.stanthonysprep.org.uk
Head of School:
Mr Richard Berlie MA (Cantab)
School type: Boys' Day Prep with Co-educational Nursery

Religious Denomination:
Roman Catholic, all faiths welcome
Age range of boys: 2.5–13 years
Age range of girls: 2.5–4 years
No. of pupils enrolled as at 01/01/2022: 280
Fees per term as at 01/01/2022:
Co-Ed Nursery: £2,800–£4,800 per term
Boys Prep School: £6,750–£6,950 per term

St Anthony's School for Boys is an academic IAPS preparatory school for boys between the ages of 4 and 13 with a Co-Ed Nursery for children between the ages of 2.5-4. It is Roman Catholic but welcomes boys of other faiths. The school has a family atmosphere, relaxed and unstuffy, but with a rigorous approach to learning. It is not a 'hot house' and great care is taken to ensure that pupils feel happy and at ease in the school environment. The majority of boys transfer to leading independent school.

The school operates a two-form entry with approximately 20 boys in each class from Reception up to and including Year 6. About half the year group leave St Anthony's to join Year 7 senior schools including UCS, City of London and Highgate. The remaining pupils stay on to prepare for Common Entrance at the end of Year 8 before proceeding to leading boarding and day schools such as Harrow, Eton, St Paul's and Westminster.

The school is not super-selective and promotes a caring, nurturing environment promoting the holistic education of each child. The school views itself as a greenhouse rather than a hothouse, where Pastoral and academic expectations are high amongst parents and staff. The school adds significant value to pupils' learning and there is great emphasis on regular communication between boys, staff and pupils.

St Anthony's achieved 'Excellent' in all categories of the ISI full-school inspection in November 2019 - the school is now pursuing an ambitious development plan incorporating digital literacy with outstanding academic, pastoral and co-curricular provision.

School Life
The school follows the EYFS programme for boys in Reception who will also start learning French (or another modern language) and Mandarin. The curriculum from Year 1 through to Year 6 is shaped by the National Curriculum Key Stages with greater academic content and rigour. In Years 7 and 8 boys are prepared to sit Common Entrance papers (in June of Year 8) before joining 13+ schools.

Lessons are planned around maximising pupil outcomes especially deepening knowledge and understanding of topics. The added dimension is encouraging the boys to enquire and think, to problem-solve and to respond individually as well as part of a group.

Sport, music and drama are all incorporated into the timetable. There is plenty of scope for boys to perform or play from elementary to the highest standard. In addition, there is a host of clubs and hobbies offered before and after school.

England – London

England – London

The Village Prep School

(Founded 1985)
2 Parkhill Road, Belsize Park,
London, NW3 2YN
Tel: 020 7485 4673
Email: admin@thevillageprepschool.com

Website: www.thevillageprepschool.com
Head of School: Ms Morven MacDonald
School type: Girls' Day Preparatory
Age range of girls: 2.5–11 years

The Village Prep School in Belsize Park, wholeheartedly believes that every child should achieve their full potential through exceptional teaching tailored to individual needs. The school offers their 2.5 - 11 year old girls, meaningful and exciting learning experiences that go well beyond the curriculum and take advantage of the school's huge outdoor space right in the heart of Belsize Park. Village Prep girls achieve fantastic results and 2021 saw the school's best ever Year 6 results with 16 scholarships to an impressive range of leading London Day Schools including City of London School for Girls, South Hampstead and St Paul's.

The school's commitment to nurturing a love of learning is evident in the breadth of opportunities afforded to the girls. The new Head Morven MacDonald, who joined the school in September 2021 after 7 years at Garden House in Chelsea has a passion for nurturing a love a learning and this is evident in every area of school life. Teachers are courageous and exciting in their approach to teaching and the facilities at the Village, including half an acre of outdoor space, permit these opportunities to happen with ease. The school's outdoor space includes a full-sized floodlit netball court, a large grassed area, an adventure playground, an outdoor classroom and fruit trees and herb gardens. Beyond this space there is a well-equipped theatre which is used for gymnastics, dance, ballet, yoga, indoor games and fencing as well as the girls wonderful theatrical productions.

Sport is an important part of life at The Village Prep, and as a partner school of Saracens Rugby Club and associate school of Saracens Mavericks Netball Club, the girls have the opportunity to see top class sport and to gain coaching tips from experienced professionals. As part of Chatsworth Schools, the school also benefits from invaluable expertise by being part of a family of schools.

The Village Prep is not afraid to do things differently and as a result, girls are both nurtured and thriving academically. At the heart of the school's approach is their 'no homework' policy, which means from aged 7, girls are given homework slots during the school day. The Village believe this helps girls develop excellent independent study skills as well as providing immediate feedback for teachers. Moreover, girls leave school at 4.30pm having completed their homework, attended an extra-curricular club and therefore, home time is for family discussions, reading and play! This

England – London

approach promotes a love of learning and ensures girls are refreshed and focused for the next day.

Throughout the school, teachers nurture a commitment to protect the planet. This is reflected across the school from the hessian backing on display boards, to the school's work with a local social enterprise group and the way in which the girls are given awareness of the impact of their food choices by highlighting the carbon footprint of the different food options served at lunchtime. The Village Prep's eco approach is an important part of their school ethos.

The school aims to equip the girls with the right skills to be the best they can be in the world. This includes an education that goes beyond the normal curriculum, such as the Village Business Award which provides girls with an initial investment which they can use to create and subsequently sell their own products to raise money for local charities.

As the girls reach their last year at The Village Prep the school seeks to make every moment count through enrichment and responsibility as well as exam preparation. There is a bespoke approach to the 11+ and in their final year, girls complete weekly practise examinations tailored to their individual needs and also enjoy art appreciation lessons which teach them how to form ideas and learn how to share them. Every Village Prep girl receives the support and input they need to demonstrate their full potential.

To find out more about The Village Prep, you can listen to Morven MacDonald's podcast 'It Takes a Village' via the school website and Spotify.

England –North-West

Bridgewater School

(Founded 1950)
Drywood Hall, Worsley Road, Worsley, Manchester, Greater Manchester M28 2WQ

Tel: 0161 794 1463
Email: admin@bwslive.co.uk
Website: www.bridgewater-school.co.uk
Head Teacher: Mrs JAT Nairn CertEd(Distinction)
School type: Co-educational Day
Age range of pupils: 3–18 years

No. of pupils enrolled as at 01/01/2022: 452
Fees per annum as at 01/01/2022:
Prep school (Kindergarten to Year 6): £8,905 (£3,060 per term)
Senior school (Years 7 to 13): £11,876 (£4,081 per term)

At Bridgewater School, we celebrate, support and nurture individuality.

We provide independent education for girls and boys aged 3-18 years in an inspirational setting that is inclusive, stimulating, supportive and totally focused on helping your child to be everything they can be.

We are proud of our family ethos, our consistently outstanding results and our forward-thinking academic environment. But most of all, we are proud to be part of each child's individual journey.

Ever since the school's inception in 1950, our family ethos has ensured that every child is known and recognised throughout their own unique learning journey. Although the scale and stature of the school have grown alongside our new buildings and facilities, we are still small enough to know each young person by name and develop a true understanding of their specific needs and abilities.

Whether your child joins us at the very start of their learning journey, as a Prep School pupil or at Senior School or Sixth Form level, our consistently high teaching standards and varied extra-curricular activities start in our Early Years Foundation Stage and continue throughout the school, enriching students' experiences and underpinning the excellent personal development of all our pupils.

The result is a vibrant community where children can flourish, learning together and achieving together, as they each follow their own path towards fulfilling their individual potential.

To experience our approach for yourself visit bridgewater-school.co.uk and take a virtual tour of our impressive grounds and facilities, or call 0161 794 1463 / email admin@bwslive.co.uk to arrange a personal visit, when we would be delighted to show you all the highly individual features which set our school apart and make it the perfect location for your child's future.

England – North-West

The Queen's School

(Founded 1878)
City Walls Road, Chester,
Cheshire CH1 2NN

Tel: 01244 312078
Email: admissions@thequeensschool.co.uk
Website: www.thequeensschool.co.uk
Headmistress:
Mrs Sue Wallace-Woodroffe
Head of Lower School: Ms Iona Carmody
School type: Girls' Independent Day School

Age range of girls: 4–18 years
No. of pupils enrolled as at 01/01/2022: 450
Fees per term as at 01/01/2022:
Lower School: £3,280 (Rec-Y2)–£3,475 (Y3-6) per term
Senior School: £4,805 per term
Average class size: 15
Teacher/pupil ratio: 1:8

The Queen's School is an outstanding independent day school for girls aged 4-18 located in the historic city of Chester. From day one, girls are taught that they will succeed, helping them to develop a growth mind set, the advantages of which include increased perseverance, positive wellbeing and self-regulation and reduced stress. Pupils are given self belief and the opportunities to explore and try new things. In particular Queen's girls are encouraged to:
- Think independently
- Collaborate confidently
- Aspire globally

Providing outdoor learning opportunities is part of the fabric that makes up The Queen's School's curriculum, giving pupils the opportunity to reconnect with the outdoor world beyond the classroom, boosting environmental stewardship, academic learning and personal development. Forest activities and the Beach School programme at The Lower School help children develop many skills that are hard to teach in the classroom. They encourage children to be active, assess situations, take risks and make decisions, with lots of activities to develop both fine and gross motor skills.

The school fosters a global perspective by immersing the girls in experiences that develop a deep understanding and appreciation of other cultures. They want pupils to contribute successfully in the global community by developing the attitudes, knowledge, and skills needed to live and work in today's interconnected world, matched with global competence to participate as empathetic, engaged, and effective citizens of the world.

All of this takes place in a caring environment where no one gets lost or slips through the net. Being a smaller school dedicated to the education of girls, pupils are offered a level of pastoral and academic support that is second to none. Learning is enhanced through a wide range of extra-curricular opportunities and individually tailoring the approach to each child enables them to achieve outstanding academic results, whilst developing the skills and mind-set to thrive in a changing world.

England – South-East

Aberdour School

Aberdour floret qui laborat
(Founded 1928)
Brighton Road, Burgh Heath, Tadworth, Surrey KT20 6AJ

Tel: +44 (0)1737 354119
Email: enquiries@aberdourschool.co.uk
Website: www.aberdourschool.co.uk
Headmaster: Mr S. D. Collins
School type: Independent Co-educational Day

Age range of pupils: 2–11 years
No. of pupils enrolled as at 01/01/2022: 343
Fees per annum as at 01/01/2022:
Day: £4,710–£16,272

Finding the brilliance in every child
Enquire now for September 2022
Independent day school for girls and boys aged 2-11 years

Every child has the potential to shine. At Aberdour, we aim to find the brilliance in every child, by providing an individual tailored education that identifies their potential and maximises their opportunities to learn, grow and succeed.

Founded in 1928 Aberdour is a thriving and extremely successful preparatory school for girls and boys aged 2-11 years. Set in 12 acres of beautiful Surrey parkland, Aberdour is truly a hidden gem, providing a safe and happy haven for your child. With our many purpose-built facilities for learning, sport and play, your child can develop his or her talents and skills whilst experiencing an exceptional breadth of opportunity both inside and outside the classroom.

Aberdour developed Personalised Achievement Learning® in 2007, providing a truly personalised education with breadth and flexibility. We have supported P.A.L® with major investments in our staff, our systems, our buildings, our IT and our resources, and the combination of a child-focused education. Through P.A.L®, we believe that every child will fulfil their individual potential if we nurture the talent that is within them, whatever that talent may be. Genuinely innovative teaching has made a real difference to the children's skills, achievements and enjoyment of life. We invite you to come see for yourself.

Please visit our website for information on our Admissions process and to contact our Registrar.

England – South-East

Barrow Hills School

(Founded 1950)

Roke Lane, Witley, Godalming, Surrey GU8 5NY
Tel: +44 (0)1428 683639
Email: info@barrowhills.org
Website: www.barrowhills.org
Headmaster: Mr Philip Oldroyd
Appointed: September 2019
Chairman of Governors: Mrs Justine Voisin

School type: Co-educational Day Preparatory
Age range of pupils: 2–13 years
No. of pupils enrolled as at 01/01/2022: 216
Fees per annum as at 01/01/2022:
Day: £16,785
Average class size: 15-19
Teacher/pupil ratio: 1:12

Barrow Hills School is committed to delivering an exceptional, all-round independent education with a strong family ethos, focusing on the whole child. All that the School does is inspired by the qualities in its pupil profile and the importance of developing strong core values. Barrow Hills encourages its children to be Curious; Scholarly; Compassionate; Generous; Brave; Responsible; Joyful and Truthful.

Set in 33 acres of Surrey Hills countryside in Witley near Godalming, Surrey, the coeducational preparatory school for children aged 2 to 13 prides itself on offering a nurturing, progressive environment for children to thrive.

School life centres on a broad curriculum. Alongside academics, music, art and drama also play a major role. An outstanding range of sports aims to encourage every level and ability.

Through its partner school, King Edward's Witley, Barrow Hills children have access to facilities beyond the reach of most stand-alone preparatory schools, and parents can see their children benefit from the seamless transition from prep school to senior school.

Boys and girls leave Barrow Hills, usually at 13, to join the finest independent schools, including King Edward's Witley.

Over the last two years, all children have progressed successfully onto their chosen senior school at the end of Year 8, with over a third of the children gaining a scholarship. The School includes a caring Nursery and Pre-Preparatory School providing children with the same special, caring and nurturing environment that is unique to Barrow Hills. This ensures a consistent, stable and secure learning environment as the child progresses through the School.

For more information please visit: www.barrowhills.org.

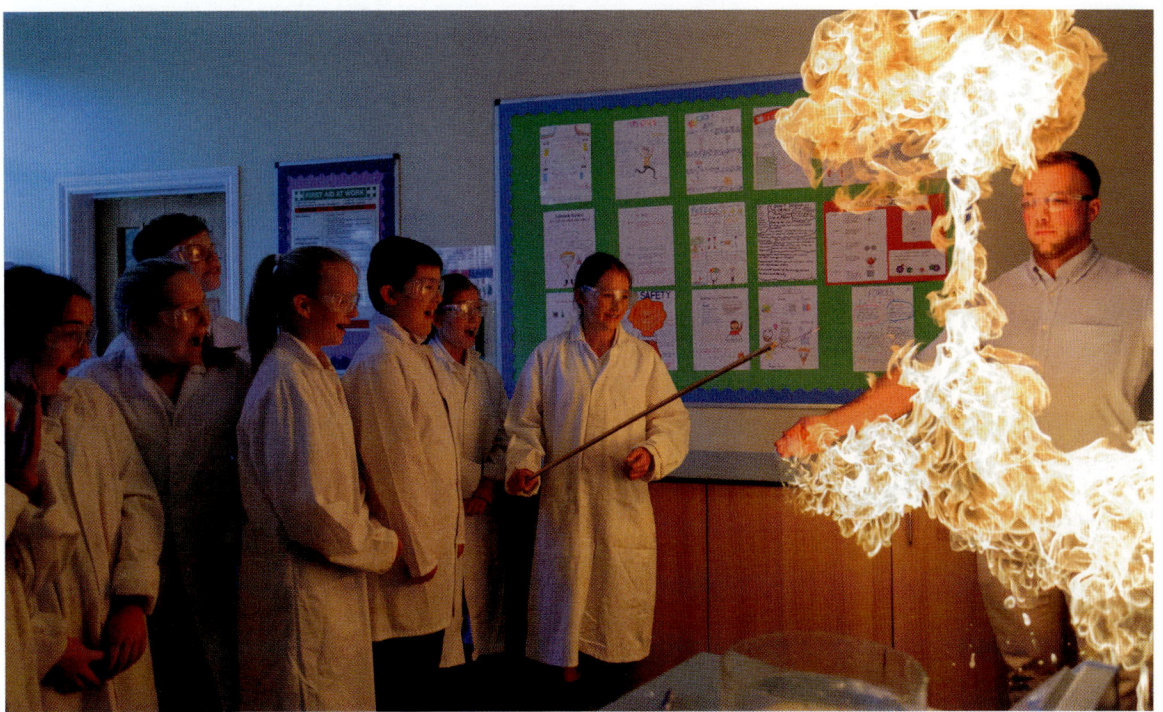

England – South-East

Ballard School

BESPOKE EDUCATION

(Founded 1895)

Fernhill Lane, New Milton,
Hampshire BH25 5SU
Tel: 01425 626900
Email: registrar@ballardschool.co.uk
Website: www.ballardschool.co.uk
Headmaster: Mr Andrew McCleave
School type: Co-educational Day

Age range of pupils: 2–16 years
No. of pupils enrolled as at 01/01/2022: 451
Fees per term as at 01/01/2022:
Day: £3,015–£5,550
Average class size: 10-18
Teacher/pupil ratio: 1:9

"Quite simply a remarkable school." (Parent)

"Ballard has been a massive influence on him, and he is unrecognisable to the youngster who started there only a short time ago, it is, without doubt, one of the best moves we made for him." (Parent)

Ballard is an award-winning, co-educational, independent day school for children from Nursery to GCSE, set in 34 acres on the edge of the New Forest and South Coast. New leadership has turned 'excellent & outstanding' (ISI) into exceptional, with pupil numbers at a five-year high. By listening to and working alongside their pupils, providing outstanding opportunities and encouraging them to be the best they can be, Ballard nurtures well-rounded, happy individuals with a healthy outlook on life.

Helping others is part of their DNA. Our Lower Prep curriculum includes Life Skills lessons, which includes charity work and emotional intelligence, alongside household skills. Recently, three pupils chose to set up a fundraising page for their local hospice, asking for donations rather than birthday presents, raising over £1,000! Ballard couldn't be more proud - they call it, 'The Ballard Way.'

All pupils use the School's fantastic facilities, which include an Olympic sized astro-turf, swimming pool, and 200-seater Performing Arts Centre. Pre-Prep pupils receive specialist Sports, Music, Forest School, Beach School, French and Dance tuition.

Furthermore, they offer additional peripatetic lessons from a very early age. Children look after chickens, bees and allotments, as well as having plenty of space to roam and explore. By Year 6, the majority of lessons are taught by GCSE specialists.

A diverse and inspiring range of activities and trips nurture self-confidence, aspiration and help develop each child's personality. With over 120 weekly activities on offer, from solving fiendish puzzles or saving the planet to Celtic harps or mixed rugby training, every day at Ballard inspires.

Ballard invests in and embraces innovative educational initiatives and programmes. With 75" top of the range digital display boards in every classroom, pupils embrace new technology. Their teachers know the educational foundations that need to be laid and which skills are essential for future academic success. With three libraries and two librarians, one a published author, Ballard also understands the benefits of books. Weekly 'Drop Everything & Read' sessions, combined with Reading Cloud and Accelerated Reader software, are the backbone of their literacy drive, building skills for future success.

"With your help and encouragement, he is now keen to read, he even read the whole book last night and is excited to read more! This is a huge turning point for him, so thank you!" (Parent)

Ballard excels in so many areas, offering pupils plenty of opportunities to develop skills and gain experience. With GCSE results consistently higher than the national average, here are some of their highlights:

STEM - Regional winners at TeenTech Solent and Soroptomist.
Arts - Artsmark Gold, 100% success in LAMDA, New Era and Arts Award;

England – South-East

performing with Gareth Malone at the Royal Albert Hall; biennial dance production plus an annual production for each section of School including Matilda Jr. and Jungle Book Jr. this year.

Sport - National success; Schools Sport Gold, athletics, cross-country, hockey, netball and swimming.

Life - Silver Eco-School; International School Award; Erasmus+; GL Centre of Assessment Excellence.

Amy's Story

"There's so many things I love about Ballard, especially their family ethos. There's no hierarchy and friendships are made across year groups. Everyone's included and opportunities to mentor younger pupils create bonds, trust and support for the mentee.

At Ballard, teachers tailor their lessons to the pupils - it's not one-size-fits-all. They encourage us to fulfil our potential, but don't place us under unnecessary pressure. These relationships with teachers are vital to our achievements. Staff always make time to listen, often sacrificing their lunch.

Opportunities at Ballard are countless. The amount of activities is awe-inspiring. There's an extensive range of trips to cater for all interests, both locally and abroad; creating lasting memories. I particularly loved the Tuscany music trip. We sang in a sacred Florentine church and on-top of the Leaning Tower, as well as dancing with locals to Wonderland in the piazza. These trips shape you; enhancing knowledge and encouraging independence.

I love Ballard's inclusivity; nobody is left out. You don't have to be the best - as long as you have a passion or interest, you are welcome. Activities aren't gender-oriented either, so at Ballard, girls play football and boys play netball. Our amazing productions are 'West-End worthy' because we all get involved. Young and old, boys and girls - it takes all sorts to achieve great things. Sport for all, music for all, learning for all.

As I read this back, I wonder how we do it all. My years here have been exceptional and I will miss Ballard immensely." Amy, a former Head Girl.

Contact Us

There is a wealth of information at www.ballardschool.co.uk, including a Virtual Open Day. For all enquiries, please email: registrar@ballardschool.co.uk or call 01425 626900.

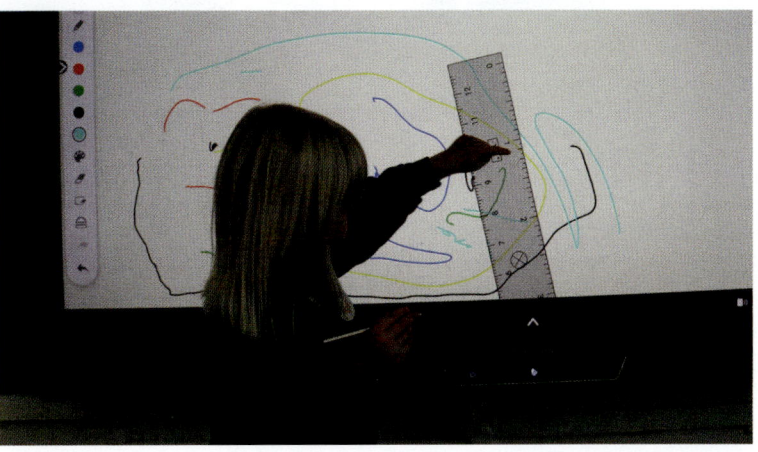

99

England – South-East

Coworth Flexlands School

Inspiring Minds, Nurturing Spirit

(Founded 1963)

Valley End, Chobham, Surrey GU24 8TE
Tel: 01276 855707
Email: secretary@coworthflexlands.co.uk
Website: www.coworthflexlands.co.uk
Head of School: Miss Nicola Cowell
Appointed: September 2018
School type: Independent Day School
Age range of boys: 2.5–7 years
Age range of girls: 2.5–11 years
No. of pupils enrolled as at 01/01/2022: 120
Boys: 17 **Girls:** 103
Fees per term as at 01/01/2022:
Nursery: £1,040 (3 mornings)–£3,056 (5 days) per term
Pre-prep: £3,525 –£3,575 per term
Prep: £4,500 –£4,800 per term

Coworth Flexlands Prep School is an Independent School for girls, with a co-ed Nursery and Pre-Prep. Nursery starts at the age of 2 1/2, where children are fully immersed in school life. Nestled between the villages of Sunningdale, Windlesham and Chobham, you will find a happy, high-achieving school where children are inspired and nurtured.

The school is ideally located in acres of beautiful grounds on the Surrey/Berkshire borders with a forest school for outdoor learning and a wide range of facilities and opportunities.

The importance of inspiring minds and nurturing individual spirits is at the heart of the school.

Inspiring minds is developing the child's curiosity through a challenging, investigative curriculum where they are encouraged to question the world around them and foster a lifelong love of learning. This approach sees every pupil reaching and growing their potential at a pace which is right for them. Our pupils have specialist teaching across a broad spectrum right from nursery upwards.

Nurturing spirit is the aspect in the childs' life that makes them smile! Pupil development, pastoral care and the Christian ethos of the school builds self-esteem, self-confidence and allows them to feel connected to others and themselves.

As pupils end their time at Coworth Flexlands, they are guided to choose the right school for them. The girls move on to top senior schools with many gaining academic, sport and musical scholarships each year. The boys head off to local prep schools well prepared for their future education.

Open Mornings
Friday 22 April 2022 at 10am
Friday 10 June 2022 at 10am

England – South-East

Eton End School

(Founded 1936)
35 Eton Road, Datchet, Slough, Berkshire SL3 9AX
Tel: 01753 541075
Email: admin@etonend.org
Website: www.etonend.org

Head of School: Mrs Sophie Banks MEd
School type: Coeducational Day
Age range of pupils: 3–11 years
No. of pupils enrolled as at 01/01/2022: 244
Fees per annum as at 01/01/2022:
Day: £10,266–£13,119

Eton End is a coeducational day school and nursery for children aged three to 11 years, situated on the fringes of Datchet and Eton and positioned in six acres of semi-wooded land. Having been established in 1936 to educate the children of Eton Masters, it is a school which successfully merges tradition with a forward thinking approach to teaching and learning. The links with Eton College continue to this day, enabling our pupils to experience numerous opportunities which extend and enrich their learning.

The children at Eton End achieve excellent academic standards, developing a life-long love of learning in small classes. The highly qualified specialist staff bring the broad curriculum alive with their enthusiasm and expertise and use of the outdoor space is maximised to enhance this.

The Independent Schools Inspectorate (ISI) inspection report (May 2019) found Eton End to be 'Excellent' in all areas and with teaching and learning at the heart of all we do, excellent academic results are achieved. ISI stated that Eton End develops children's 'skills, knowledge and understanding to a high level and teaches them how to apply these skills across the curriculum'.

Eton End children are confident and articulate with strong communication skills, displaying excellent attitudes to learning from an early age. Encouraging the children to be resilient and to persevere, showing self-awareness and an ability to reflect on their progress is key. The children at Eton End display a strong sense of self-confidence, resilience and commitment to improve their learning and performance in readiness for the next stage of their lives. Empathising with peers, encouraging others and, most importantly, learning to respect one another are essential skills for life which are developed and nurtured at Eton End.

The opportunities available to the pupils at Eton End enable every child to find their strengths, both inside and outside of the classroom. With the wonderful space available and our bespoke 'Outdoor Learning Centre', the opportunities for outdoor learning are endless. An Eton End Education is not only about teaching the children a body of knowledge but also about preparing them for life in the 21st Century. This year we have revamped the Dining Room and built a bespoke Food Technology area, which will enhance the children's life skills further.

A full after school programme of clubs and activities is available for pupils to enjoy, enabling them to develop alternative skills in the comfort of the school environment. Happiness and wellbeing are pivotal to an Eton End education and we work hard to ensure that our happy children thrive.

Eton End offers pupils an excellent all-rounded education, whilst ensuring they experience a childhood they will cherish.

Please contact us to chat to our Registrar or make an appointment to meet the Headmistress and tour the school on 01753 541075

England – South-East

Eagle House School

(Founded 1820)
Sandhurst, Berkshire GU47 8PH
Tel: 01344 772134

Email: info@eaglehouseschool.com
Website: www.eaglehouseschool.com
Headmaster:
Mr A P N Barnard BA(Hons), PGCE
Appointed: September 2006
School type: Co-educational Day & Boarding Preparatory
Age range of pupils: 3–13 years

No. of pupils enrolled as at 01/01/2022: 394
Boys: 224 **Girls:** 170
No. of boarders: 45
Fees per annum as at 01/01/2022:
Day: £18,615
Full Boarding: £25,905
Average class size: 18
Teacher/pupil ratio: 1:8

Eagle House is a coeducational, boarding and day Prep, Pre-Prep and Nursery located in Berkshire, but close to the borders of Surrey and Hampshire. The school was founded in 1820 and is proud of its 200 years heritage. Superb grounds and excellent facilities are the background to an experience where success, confidence and happiness are paramount. The Good Schools Guide describes Eagle House as a 'progressive, kind and buzzy' school. Tradition is important but putting children's learning at the heart of what we do and embracing change enables them to thrive in the 21st century.

The school is proud of its academic record, preparing children for a host of top independent schools and boasting a diverse and robust curriculum. Eagle House received an 'excellent' rating in all areas from the ISI inspection team.

Younger pupils follow the International Primary Curriculum and our older children no longer sit the Common Entrance examinations, allowing pupils to embark on Curriculum 200, a new, rich, robust, assessment-led curriculum that will furnish senior schools with a valuable portfolio of academic data, removing the shackles of the traditional exam-based system. Great teaching, new technology and a focus on the basics mean that children make good progress and love to be in the classroom. Independent learning is a focus for all children and our Extended Project programme helps drive inquisitive minds.

At Eagle House we unashamedly offer lots as part of our Golden Eagle activities experience. Children benefit from a huge range of opportunities in sport, music, drama, art, outward bound and community programmes. Our focus on service means that the school regularly gets involved with local people, particularly the elderly. The Arts play a big part at Eagle House. Music fills every corner of the school with regular concerts both small and large consisting of choirs, ensembles and orchestras. Choir tours to Holland and Belgium have taken place and children regularly perform in various concerts out of school. Drama is popular and aside from a big annual production there are smaller performances and actors perform each year at the Edinburgh Fringe Festival. Art and design are part of the curriculum and children are encouraged to be creative in all sorts of ways. Technology-led projects teach pupils to experiment with software and applications.

Busy children are happy and fulfilled children and we like to think that all pupils are Learning for Life. Learning for Life means that children benefit from the best all-round education. They can feel confident in the classroom, on the games field, on stage, in the concert hall and in the community. Everyone is given the chance to stretch themselves in every area. Challenge is an important part of growing up and at Eagle House we learn that success and failure are both positive experiences. Bright learning environments including a new Pre-Prep and Music complex, new Science laboratories, a modern well-equipped library, design and textile workshops, outdoor learning areas and wonderful sporting facilities are important but it is the community that shapes a young person.

Through the excellent pastoral care

England – South-East

and tutor system, coupled with a buddy structure, ensuring children have an older pupil to support them, Eagle House seeks to develop wellbeing from the youngest to the oldest. Recognising how to be a positive influence within a community is also part of the Eagle House journey. Through our wonderful Learning for Life programme that teaches children about themselves and the wider community, we aim to make all our pupils responsible and independent as well as able to show empathy and understanding towards others. Time for reflection in chapel and assemblies also improves the way we look at the world and mindfulness sessions help us all take stock. Boarding is a popular option and allows children to experience a varied evening programme of activities as well as being part of a vibrant and caring community. Boarding encourages independence but it is also great fun and whether weekly or flexi, boarders have the most wonderful time. Our new common room area allows boarders time to relax amongst friends on big sofas or gather around the large kitchen table for a chat whilst munching on a bowl of cereal!

We often say that Eagle House children have the time of their lives and we firmly believe this. Learning for Life at Eagle House opens the doors to all sorts of opportunities and this results in children who are highly motivated and enthusiastic in all they do. Eagle House buzzes with achievement and laughter - not a bad way to grow up!

Eagle House is a registered charity (No 309093) for the furtherance of education.

England – South-East

Greenfield School

(Founded 1935)

Old Woking Road, Woking, Surrey GU22 8HY
Tel: 01483 772525
Email: schooloffice@greenfield.surrey.sch.uk
Website: www.greenfield.surrey.sch.uk
Headmistress: Mrs. Tania Botting MEd

School type: Co-educational Day Preparatory & Nursery
Age range of pupils: 6 months–11 years
No. of pupils enrolled as at 01/01/2022: 335
Fees per annum as at 01/01/2022:
Nursery: £6,096–£21,675
Preparatory: £12,228 –£14,361

Greenfield School is found on the outskirts of Woking Town Centre, a popular commuter town known for its excellent transport links. The School has a long history within the town and has occupied numerous different urban sites, but is now proudly situated on a 10+ acre plot where the children benefit from many excellent facilities.

The ethos at Greenfield is incredibly strong and influences every decision made by the leadership team in order to maintain a culture of kindness and inclusion. Greenfield is academically non-selective but thanks to its excellent teaching, high staff numbers, flexible teaching groups and broad curriculum, results are consistently impressive.

Academic children earn places at some of the most prestigious academic schools in the country, many with accompanying scholarships, whilst those who are creative frequently receive offers to study Art, Drama or Music as a scholar, or at a specialist Performing Arts School. In addition, scholarships for sport, all-round achievement and even design & technology feature regularly on the honours boards.

Two forms in each year group offers the perfect balance between a small school and one which has the capacity to offer the children outstanding facilities and opportunities, whilst maintaining the much-loved family-feeling. A large extension, due to open in Summer 2022, houses a new sports hall, dining room, music recital space, music practice rooms, drama studio, multi-media suite, teaching rooms and a courtyard garden. Outside, the grounds include two forest schools and multiple sports pitches as well as tennis/netball courts and a MUGA due to be installed later this year. The site is large, but not so big that the children cannot be trusted to move about independently, and the design of the extension keeps all the indoor facilities under one roof.

Greenfield offers boys and girls a relevant, varied, exciting education up to age 11 (Year 6) and has its own 50 week nursery onsite for babies 6 months+. A superb wrap-around provision offers families flexibility ranging from 07:30 through to 18:00 Monday to Friday, with holiday clubs throughout most of the school term breaks too.

Visitors are encouraged and appointments can be made for mutually convenient times during the working week.

England – South-East

Highfield and Brookham Schools

(Founded 1907)
Highfield Lane, Liphook,
Hampshire GU30 7LQ
Tel: 01428 728000

Email: admissions@highfieldandbrookham.co.uk
Website: www.highfieldandbrookham.co.uk
Headteachers:
Mr Phillip Evitt MA (Hons), PGCE &
Mrs Sophie Baber BA (Hons), PGCE, PG Cert
School type: Co-educational Day & Boarding

Age range of pupils: 2–13 years
No. of pupils enrolled as at 01/01/2022: 448
Boys: 236 **Girls:** 212
Fees per term as at 01/01/2022:
£3,925–£9,475 per term
Average class size: 16
Teacher/pupil ratio: 1:8

"We were immediately struck by the warmth of Highfield and Brookham Schools. It's hard to put my finger on exactly what it is, but it's like being wrapped up in a big hug! The children who showed us around were charismatic and confident without being arrogant, polite without being insincere and rosy cheeked with muddy knees as they spent so much time outside! We were looking for a school that could accommodate all three of our children, even though they have different strengths and weaknesses. Highfield and Brookham offered our family the whole package and it was an easy decision to make."

Discover the very best education possible for boys and girls aged 2-13 at Highfield and Brookham Schools. We are Nursery, Pre-prep and Prep schools with day and boarding options set in 175 acres in the South Downs National Park on the borders of Hampshire, Surrey and West Sussex, yet only an hour from London.

At Highfield and Brookham, we have a strong reputation for academic excellence, feeding some of the top senior schools in the country including Down House, Eton, Marlborough, Radley, Winchester and Wellington.

Children at Highfield and Brookham grow up with a love of learning. Our enviable facilities and stunning setting enable us to offer a broad curriculum where teaching and learning takes place in and out of the classroom. Our children develop skills to help them thrive in Sport, Music, Drama and Art and our wide range of extra-curricular activities encourages children to discover their strengths, uncover their passions and develop life skills. Our track record in securing every child a place at their first-choice senior school is flawless and our academic ambition means we achieve excellent scholarship success at 11+ and 13+.

Choosing Highfield and Brookham is your opportunity to make a positive impact on your child's learning journey, ensuring they grow up as happy, well-rounded individuals, full of life, keen and ready to tackle the next stage of their education.

England – South-East

Highfield Preparatory School

(Founded 1918)
2 West Road, Maidenhead,
Berkshire SL6 1PD
Tel: 01628 624918
Email: office@highfieldprep.org

Website: www.highfieldprep.org
Headteacher: Mrs Joanna Leach
School type: Girls' Day Preparatory
Age range of boys: 2–7 years
Age range of girls: 2–11 years

Highfield Prep School in Maidenhead, part of the Chatsworth Schools family of schools, is known for its small classes, specialist teachers, nurturing environment and access to outstanding local sporting facilities. We all want the best for our children and a Highfield education is a rich, yet affordable experience with a bespoke, personalised approach to teaching children in a kind and supportive environment.

Highfield recently extended its co-educational provision and are now welcoming boys from Nursery up to the end of Year 2, so that more families can benefit from all that the school has to offer. From Year 3 onwards Highfield is a girls' only school as from experience the school believes that this setting allows girls to thrive and fulfil their full potential. From Year 3 - Year 6 at Highfield, all the scientists are girls; all the mathematicians are girls - there are no glass ceilings and no assumptions about what girls like or prefer because no one is saying 'that subject is for boys'. Highfield girls leave with confidence in STEAM-related skills along with great self confidence in their all-round academic performance.

At Highfield great value is placed on giving pupils the opportunity to flourish in all areas of school life. The school creates a sense of happiness and warmth in which pupils are motivated to work and play to the best of their abilities. Both inside and outside the classroom, Highfield generates a sense of vitality based on the principle that learning is fun. The school has an outstanding team of experienced teachers and support staff, committed to making every family's time as rewarding and fulfilling as possible.

Sport sits firmly at the heart of the curriculum with the busy, vibrant school providing pupils with the opportunity to learn new skills, challenge themselves and work as a team. At Highfield, sport is for all and there is a comprehensive physical education curriculum, which begins in Pre-Prep. Highfield have always had fantastic success in sports which the school believes is down to their access to outstanding local sporting facilities, the on-site netball court and sports hall and the dedicated sports teaching team.

At Highfield pupils and staff are excited by Science, Technology, Engineering, Computing and the Arts and the power and potential they have to enrich learning across the curriculum. Highfield believes that inspiring pupils to be creative and confident is hugely important if they are to excel and achieve in the 21st Century and pupils are encouraged to embrace their creativity and gain a better understanding of themselves.

One of Highfield's many strengths is the extra-curricular programme that helps pupils develop their passions and talents, as well as building valuable life skills. The range of opportunities at Highfield is unparalleled and there is something for everyone to enjoy; this is all part of the school's mission to meet the interests and needs of every pupil.

England – South-East

Highfield girls move on to a range of leading schools age 11 and all girls are well prepared for 11+ and independent senior school entrance examinations. The school offers independent senior school exam prep classes and mock interviews and have an impressive track record of girls reaching their senior school of choice, frequently with scholarships. When the time comes to leave Highfield, girls do so as confident, resilient, curious independent learners who are ready to take on any challenge they choose.

Nothing holds back Highfield children and the school community works together to enable outstanding futures for all.

England – South-East

Kent College Junior School

KENT COLLEGE
CANTERBURY
(Founded 1885)
Harbledown, Canterbury, Kent CT2 9AQ

Tel: 01227 762436
Email: admissions@kentcollege.co.uk
Website: kentcollege.com/junior-index.php
Head: Mr Simon James
Appointed: September 2020
Deputy Head: Mrs Anouska Blaza
School type: Co-educational Day & Boarding Preparatory

Age range of pupils: 0–11 years
No. of pupils enrolled as at 01/01/2022: 200
No. of boarders: 15
Fees per annum as at 01/01/2022:
Day: £10,587–£16,473
Full Boarding: £26,901
Teacher/pupil ratio: 1:7

Kent College is a very happy and successful school for boys and girls aged 0-18, which is situated in the south east of England on the outskirts of the beautiful and historic city of Canterbury. Canterbury is less than one hour from the centre of London by train and very close to all of the London airports.

The Garden Cottage Nursery (0-3yrs) and Prep School (3-11yrs) are based in an idyllic 14 acre site, just one mile from the centre of Canterbury. This day and boarding school offers a British education with an innovative approach to learning, full of opportunities for children to grow and develop their skills and talents.

The school has a thriving Music Department and our Choristers regularly perform at national level. There are a wide range of sports on offer from hockey to football and the school hosts regular athletic and cross country with events as well as taking students on sports tours during the year. Art and Drama are also well catered for with the installation of a new Art department in the main school house and the development of an outdoor theatre.

We believe in making the timetable appropriate for each individual child. All children in the Junior school take part in our Gifted, Really Enthusiastic, Able and Talented Programme which enables the children to increase their performance even further in their chosen area. These lessons are given curriculum time and are delivered by specialist teachers who develop individual programmes for each pupil based on their needs and interests.

The areas of choice are geared towards maximising each child's chances of winning a scholarship to the Senior School or gaining entry to the school of their choice.

Kent College has a long history of welcoming boarding pupils from abroad, as well as from British families resident in the UK or working overseas. The Junior school Boarding House takes children from the age of 7 upwards and is a cosy family environment.

Our full range of 50 after school clubs offer a variety of interesting, challenging and fun activities for the children to enjoy whilst expanding their skills and knowledge.

We are also lucky to have a working farm where students can join the Farm Club and learn to care for and show animals at the Kent Show. Horse Riding lessons are available in the school's riding arena and our NESA team successfully competes in events all over the country.

England – South-East

Milbourne Lodge School

Arbrook Lane, Esher, Surrey KT10 9EG
Tel: 01372 462737

Email: registrar@milbournelodge.co.uk
Website: www.milbournelodge.co.uk
Head: Mrs Judy Waite
School type: Co-educational Day Preparatory

Age range of pupils: 4–13 years
No. of pupils enrolled as at 01/01/2022: 276
Boys: 224 **Girls:** 52
Fees per annum as at 01/01/2022:
Day: £13,695–£17,205

Milbourne Lodge is a selective Prep School for boys and girls aged 4 to 13. Founded in 1912, the school has a long-standing tradition of preparing children for Senior School Entrance and Scholarship exams to the most prestigious and well known public schools in the country including: St Paul's, Westminster, Eton, Charterhouse, Epsom College, Wellington, Winchester and Benenden. In the past 5 years alone over 50 academic, art, music and sports scholarships have been won by our pupils.

We strive to set the academic bar high, to value sport and extra-curricular activities, to instil a sense of responsibility and good manners and to develop children that are resilient and confident.

Our academic curriculum, taught by a highly experienced and dedicated team of staff, is supported by excellent music, art, IT & sports programmes, with games played every day. A strong emphasis is also placed on pastoral care and the school provides a warm and supportive environment in which each child feels valued and can flourish.

The latest SIS Inspection awarded Milbourne Lodge 'Outstanding in all Areas' status. The Inspectors stated that: *'Milbourne Lodge provides an outstanding education for its pupils. The pupils' academic attainment is very high and their achievements are exceptional.'*

Milbourne Lodge is a very energetic school which provides endless opportunities and variety. Every child is encouraged to build on their own particular talents and to discover new ones. Here at Milbourne we work hard and play hard!

'Our overriding objective is to prepare your child for his or her senior school. We will prepare each child to be ready to relish the experience of their new school, to be confident in their own skin and to be eager to take the next steps', Judy Waite, Head.

Located in Esher, Surrey, the School is situated in over 8 acres of beautiful grounds within easy access of the A3 and M25. A daily bus runs from SW London.

England – South-East

Priory School of Our Lady of Walsingham

(Founded 1993)

Beatrice Avenue, Whippingham,
Isle of Wight PO32 6LP
Tel: 01983 861222
Email: mail@prioryschool.org.uk
Website: www.prioryschool.org.uk
Headmaster: Mr Edmund Matyjaszek
Appointed: 2009

School type: Co-educational Day
Age range of pupils: 4–18 years
No. of pupils enrolled as at 01/01/2022: 170
Boys: 85 **Girls:** 85
Fees per annum as at 01/01/2022:
Day: £6,900–£9,990
Average class size: 16 max

Priory School of our Lady of Walsingham was founded in 1993 out of the Girls Boarding School Upper Chine in Shanklin on the Isle of Wight.

In 2012 it moved to the historic Whippingham site on the Osborne Estate where Queen Victoria built to Prince Albert's design a school to cater for the children of the village and the estate.

HRH Princess Beatrice of York unveiled a plaque in 2014 to celebrate 150 years of continuous education on the site. The school has close links with St Mildred's Church and Osborne House, where more than once our school choirs have sung.

The school has two core principles that inform its ethos: academic rigour and pastoral care. We maintain a maximum class size in all academic subjects of 16, splitting the class into smaller tutor groups or allocating "Second Teachers" to ensure this ratio. We believe this underpins our academic success with 100% GCSE pass rates in recent years and an enviable track record of admissions to Russell Group universities; and our pupils' behaviour and conduct, favourably commented on by Ofsted reports. The most recent report in 2018 rated the school Outstanding in both its Early Years provision and its Pupil Personal Development & Welfare. Many comment on its family atmosphere which is informed by its strong Christian foundation and ethos that underpins the religiously and ethnically diverse nature of its student and staff body.

We compete vigorously in both island and mainland sports fixtures with professional sports coaches on staff, and are especially strong in expressive arts, with school productions in the modern Anthony Minghella Theatre in Newport, the county town, and dedicated LAMDA lessons. Pupils have won several Island Design Competitions and the school's Science Department has had Good Schools Guide awards twice in the last few years.

Specialist teachers in IT, French & Spanish, PE, Music & Drama teach from Reception Year upwards to provide a rich, varied and stimulating learning environment.

Fast becoming the school of choice for many families moving out of metropolitan environments, Priory School offers a proven quality of education set in the history and beauty of the Isle of Wight.

England – South-East

Spring Grove School

(Founded 1963)

Harville Road, Wye, Kent TN25 5EZ
Tel: 01233 812337
Email: office@springgroveschool.co.uk
Website: www.springgroveschool.co.uk
Head of School: Mrs Therésa Jaggard
School type: Co-educational Day Preparatory

Age range of pupils: 2–11 years
No. of pupils enrolled as at 01/01/2022: 226
Boys: 111 **Girls:** 115
Fees per annum as at 01/01/2022:
Day: £9,459–£13,290
Teacher/pupil ratio: 1:8

Spring Grove is a happy, family school for boys and girls aged 2-11 set in 14 acres of beautiful Kent countryside. The school is located in Wye, between Ashford and Canterbury, and close to the high-speed train link into London St Pancras. As an independent Prep school it offers a first-class education, preparing children for both grammar and senior independent school entry and scholarships.

Spring Grove offers a wide range of subjects and extra-curricular activities. Our children are happy and confident, and the school is renowned for its friendly, family atmosphere. Spring Grove Nursery, which caters for children from the age of 2 to 4, is on the same site as the Prep school, and while it is a safe and separate space, the preschool children benefit from sharing staff and facilities with the older children in the school. The Nursery also has its own beautiful walled garden where the children play all year round.

Spring Grove's Home Learning website allows a full timetable to be delivered online through a child-friendly and interactive platform if the need arises. Every child from Reception class upwards has a school Chromebook and some lessons in school are taught via Google Classroom, allowing a seamless transition from in-school to Home Learning when necessary.

Outdoor learning is integral to the Spring Grove curriculum, and all children from Reception upwards regularly visit the school's award-winning Forest School, situated on a permanent site near Wye. The school also has an active pupil-led Eco Committee, and in 2020 Spring Grove became an Eco Council Green Flag school. The creative and performing arts are also an important part of everyday life for all Spring Grove children with specialist music, dance and art teachers and ensembles including an orchestra, choir and folk band. This year Spring Grove hopes to achieve its Artsmark status - a quality standard awarded by Arts Council England.

England – South-East

St Andrew's Prep

St Andrew's Prep
EASTBOURNE

(Founded 1877)
Meads Street, Eastbourne,
East Sussex BN20 7RP

Tel: 01323 733203
Email: admissions@standrewsprep.co.uk
Website: www.standrewsprep.co.uk
Headmaster: Tom Gregory BA(Hons), PGCE
School type: Co-educational Day & Boarding Preparatory

Age range of pupils: 9 months–13 years
No. of pupils enrolled as at 01/01/2022: 374
Fees per term as at 01/01/2022:
£3,565 (Reception)–£8,915 (full boarding) per term
Average class size: Av 16 Max 20
Teacher/pupil ratio: 1:10

St Andrew's Prep is an 'Excellent' rated Prep School offering wrap-around care and located on the beautiful sunshine coast of Eastbourne. With 21st century technology, environmental issues and society continuing to change at a fast pace, we recognise our responsibility to equip our pupils with minds to tackle this modern, high-tech world. Our talented staff is dedicated to preparing the children for the future; teaching them life-long learning, problem-solving and thinking skills alongside leadership and teamwork opportunities and, perhaps most important of all, the tools to become good citizens. The school was quick to react to the Coronavirus crisis and is proud of its outstanding remote and blended learning offering.

Our staff work hard to develop the right attitude towards academic study and encourage our pupils to think for themselves so that they can tackle challenges confidently. Over the last four years, the school's Year 8 pupils have won 114 scholarships to their senior schools including Eastbourne College, Brighton College, Hurst, Gordonstoun King's Canterbury, Millfield and St Edward's Oxford across academics, art, dance, design, drama, performing arts and sport.

"A forward-thinking seaside prep school in an enviable location with a focus on bringing out the best in all children and developing creativity, thinking skills and self-expression." - Muddy Stilettos

Brimming with opportunities
However, success for our pupils appears in many forms. Opportunities for artistic expression abound in our Creative and Performing Arts programme including Art, DTI (Design, Technology & Innovation), Dance, Drama and Music. The Cultural Curriculum encourages our pupils to be inventive, resourceful and imaginative and it plays a central role in providing our pupils with rewarding opportunities.

In sport, our aim is to promote enjoyment and an understanding of the values and ideals of good sportsmanship that are the essence of team sports. There are teams for every ability and this ensures that each child represents the school. However, our sporting pedigree is excellent with school representatives frequently reaching national finals and occasionally winning medals.

- 2021, 2020, 2019 Included in top 50 cricket schools by the Cricketer magazine
- 2021 U13 Girls Hockey National Finalists
- 2021 U13 Boys Table Tennis Sussex Champions
- 2020 U13 Boys Hockey National Finalists
- 2019-20 U13 Girls Hockey National Finalists
- 2020 U11 and U13 Table Tennis Regional Finalists
- 2019 U11 boys football team reached the ISFA finals
- 2019 U13 boys cricket team were placed third in the country
- 2019 U13 boys hockey finished 14th in the country

England – South-East

- 2019 U13 boys team finished 12th at National Hockey finals
- 2019 Girls 1st hockey team finished 12th in the country at the IAPS National Hockey finals
- 2019 1st XI finished 4th in the Rugby Sussex Cup
- 2019 U10A rugby team had an unbeaten season
- 2019 Nine pupils reached the National swimming finals

In addition to the titles above, our pupils have also scored much individual success at national, regional, county and IAPS level in wind-surfing, riding, cross-country and chess over the last few years.

Our after-school and optional Saturday morning activities are plentiful. Martial arts, skiing, pottery, mountain biking and golf are a small selection of the vast array of options available to inspire our enthusiastic youngsters.

Beautiful, healthy, seaside location and great facilities
St Andrew's Prep is just a five minute walk to the sea and is nestled at the foot of the South Downs, yet London is near enough for educational and boarding trips. With nature on our front door, we offer unique Forest and Beach Schools - both providing opportunities to complement classroom study with outdoor learning. The children may try woodcarving, pond dipping and shelter building or build a fire around which they drink hot chocolate and toast marshmallows or they may simply play games using the natural resources available to them. The school facilities are excellent and include a 4 lane 20m indoor pool, a Music school, an Art, Design and Innovation block, teaching blocks, pavilion, a rifle range, two libraries and three ICT suites. In 2016, a game-changing Sports Hall and Dance Studio was unveiled and the school pavilion and boarding house have just been refurbished at a cost of more than £200,000.

"This is a strong supportive community; very different, parents say, to London type schools, where the parents are vying for position." The Good Schools Guide

A growing boarding house
The school's boarding house, Colstocks, is in the heart of the school. The House is lively and full of fun but also offers its boarders a place to relax and enjoy the company of friends from around the world. On weekends, our experienced Housemaster and his team offer activities and weekend trips to venues including the British Museum, Thorpe Park, rock climbing, go-karting and trampolining. The school is happy to provide supervised transport to and from London and the airports.

Visit St Andrew's Prep
We would be delighted to welcome you to St Andrew's Prep where we are sure you will gain a real sense of the energy and the happiness and engagement in learning of our children.

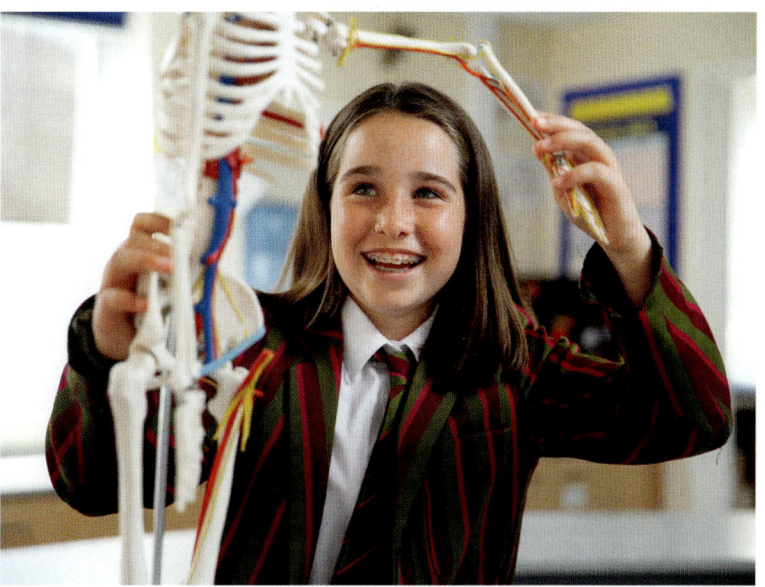

England – South-East

St Swithun's Prep

St Swithun's
WINCHESTER

(Founded 1884)
Alresford Road, Winchester,
Hampshire SO21 1HA

Tel: 01962 835750
Fax: 01962 835779
Email: prepoffice@stswithuns.com
Website: www.stswithuns.com
Head of School: Mr Jonathan Brough
Appointed: 2020
School type: Girls' Day School with Co-educational Preschool

Age range of boys: 3–4 years
Age range of girls: 3–11 years
No. of pupils enrolled as at 01/01/2022: 186
Fees per annum as at 01/01/2022:
Preschool: £11,670 (all day)
Reception, Years 1 and 2: £11,670
Years 3, 4, 5 and 6: £15,180

St Swithun's Prep School is a magical place with children's happiness at its core. You can fe el the positive energy as you walk through the door. Confidence is fundamental to success so all activities are characterised by a palpable sense of fun and enjoyable challenge to ensure that pupils flourish, whilst simultaneously encouraging them to be courageous in everything that they do. The children learn that not all days are perfect and are taught to persevere and develop resilience, allowing them to be ready to take all opportunities that life presents.

Children are encouraged to be compassionate - to be kind and caring - and to be respectful to everyone else. Welcoming those of all faiths and those of none and, developing the children's appreciation of diversity is of the utmost importance at St Swithun's.

The weekly timetable is rich and varied; emphasising the core subjects but balancing them with a huge amount of sports, humanities, arts, languages and extra-curricular opportunities, such as sailing, gardening, ballet, music and baking. The children at St Swithun's have the chance to sample a wide range of experiences and to shine wherever their interests lie.

The teaching and learning environment is spectacular both inside and outside. Set in 45 acres of grounds overlooking the South Downs, the prep school was purpose built in 2015 and has its own specialist facilities, including a gym, theatre, and teaching kitchen. It also benefits from sharing the senior school facilities, such as the swimming pool and athletics track.

To find out more about all that St Swithun's has to offer, please explore the website www.stswithuns.com or make an appointment to speak with Prep School Head Jonathan Brough. Please contact 01962 835750 or email prepoffice@stswithuns.com. Keep up to date with the latest news by following @StSwithunsPrep on Twitter.

England – South-West

Exeter Cathedral School

(Founded 12th century)
The Chantry, Palace Gate, Exeter, Devon EX1 1HX

Tel: 01392 255298
Email: admissions@exetercs.org
Website: www.exetercathedralschool.co.uk
Headmaster: James Featherstone
Appointed: 2016
School type: Co-educational, Day & Boarding, Preparatory
Age range of pupils: 3–13 years

No. of pupils enrolled as at 01/01/2022: 266
Boys: 165 **Girls:** 101
No. of boarders: 9
Fees per term as at 01/01/2022:
Day: £2,823–£4,623
Full Boarding: £2,722
Teacher/pupil ratio:
1:10 (Pre-Prep) & 1:13 (Prep)

Exeter Cathedral School is a flourishing day and boarding Prep School for girls and boys.

Founded in the 12th century as a choir school, today we are a vibrant independent Prep School which offers an outstanding educational experience to our 275 pupils, and which is proud to educate the Choristers of Exeter Cathedral.

Our ancient foundations and our wonderful location (in the heart of the city yet nestled safely in the lee of the Cathedral) sit harmoniously alongside our traditional values and our modern, forward-thinking approach, to deliver an education which focuses on developing the whole child.

Our small class sizes, our commitment to nurturing our pupils, our focus on individualised pastoral care and academic rigour, our exciting range of extra-curricular activities, our unparalleled heritage and history, our outstanding provision in sport, and the world-class musical education we offer all of our pupils means that Exeter Cathedral School is a place where children can flourish, aim high, discover, grow, and be happy.

Above all, we are a school where people matter, and where we work with families to help our pupils acquire the right habits for life.

A warm welcome

We host a number of open days and taster events which take place throughout the year. We warmly invite families to discover the joy of an education at Exeter Cathedral School and why its pupils flourish.

For further information, please contact our Admissions Manager, Katharine Pearce, on 01392 255298 or admissions@exetercs.org

England – South-West

Hazlegrove Prep School

Hazlegrove House, Sparkford, Somerset BA22 7JA

Tel: +44 (0)1963 442606
Email: admissions@hazlegrove.co.uk
Website: www.hazlegrove.co.uk
Headmaster: Mr Mark White MA (Hons)
Appointed: September 2017
School type: Co-educational Day & Boarding Preparatory

Age range of pupils: 2–13 years
No. of pupils enrolled as at 01/01/2022: 364
Fees per term as at 01/01/2022:
Day: £3,076–£6,237
Full Boarding: £7,235–£9,232
Average class size: 14
Teacher/pupil ratio: 1:9

Hazlegrove is an Independent Day and Boarding Preparatory School for 360 boys and girls. Established in 1947, the school enjoys an inspiring setting within 200 acres of parkland in Somerset and benefits from outstanding facilities. Hazlegrove believes it is important that children, from an early age, should have the breadth of opportunity to develop their abilities and potential whilst enjoying the benefit of a caring, nurturing and secure environment.

Hazlegrove is committed to celebrating childhood. A Hazlegrovian in the 21st century is a child that is empathetic, kind and connected to the world; one who is independent but knows that developing relationships and a sense of duty to the community are integral to a successful life. A vibrant and creative curriculum, exceptional pastoral care and stunning rural Somerset location combine to make children feel nurtured, motivated, inspired and encouraged to love learning for life.

The curriculum has a real, hands-on feel where children participate and are not just spectators. Staff are passionate about developing in the children, genuine awe, wonder and curiosity at the complexities of life and the world - past, present and future. The breadth and balance in the curriculum give pupils an opportunity to get excited about the lessons they have each day.

Sport is a clear strength and significant success is achieved by pupils in team and individual sports. Drama and music are part of the school's DNA with a vast array of choirs, ensemble groups and theatre productions. Every pupil performs in a drama production every year.

The children at Hazlegrove are surrounded with care. That care includes at its core, staff for whom going many extra miles is an everyday thing, and who unashamedly make time to talk about the children. It includes a dedicated Pastoral Leadership Team which meets twice a week, a tutor system, a pastoral care curriculum embedded in everything, and an ever-developing framework for social and emotional literacy and support.

Hazlegrove pupils move on to a wide variety of senior schools aged 13, having taken Common Entrance or Scholarship examinations. Hazlegrove pupils move on to a wide variety of senior schools aged 13, having taken Common Entrance or Scholarship examinations. Over the last four years, a total of 121 scholarships and Awards have been gained to 28 different schools.

Outstanding facilities with a continual programme of investment in its buildings and facilities ensure that Hazlegrove pupils have the best start possible both now and in the future.

For further information, please contact admissions@hazlegrove.co.uk, 01963 442 606

England – South-West

King's Hall School

(Founded 1957)

Kingston Road, Taunton,
Somerset TA2 8AA
Tel: 01823 285920
Email: admissions@kings-taunton.co.uk
Website: www.kingshalltaunton.co.uk
Head: Mr Justin Chippendale

School type:
Co-educational Day & Boarding
Age range of pupils: 2–13 years
No. of pupils enrolled as at 01/01/2022: 320
Fees per annum as at 01/01/2022:
Day: £8,265–£17,670
Average class size: 20 max
Teacher/pupil ratio: 1:9

King's Hall School is a coeducational Pre-Prep and Prep school with around 320 pupils, offering both day and boarding. Set in a beautiful countryside location surrounded by farmland, the school is only a couple of minutes' drive from the centre of Taunton in Somerset.

The school respects traditional values and boarding is a strong feature, which contributes to the tangible family atmosphere that exists in the school. Children enjoy a challenging all-round education in a progressive and stimulating environment.

We have a very popular Pre-Prep located in its own dedicated area of the school, having full access to our extensive facilities and grounds. Our Nursery is a friendly, happy and welcoming setting for children aged 2 to 4 years, and every child has their very own key worker who focuses on individual needs and supports each child through their time with us. When the time comes for moving up to Reception, we take the children and their parents on a tour of the facilities so they can see more of what we have to offer for the next stage of their child's development. This gentle and smooth transition helps children to become familiar with their new surroundings and to feel like part of one big school family.

When children first join us in Prep, they will open the door to an exciting new world of opportunities and challenges, both inside and outside the classroom. Our teachers are welcoming, engaging and passionate. All children study the core subjects of English, maths, science, geography, history, modern foreign languages (MFL), and religious studies, and our broad curriculum also embraces Latin, the visual and creative arts (including music, art and drama), design technology, and an imaginative programme of PE and games.

Across the school site, pupils benefit from traditional and modern facilities: a bright modern science faculty, new cookery school, adventure playground, outdoor swimming pool, astros and extensive grass pitches, a huge indoor sports centre and gym equipment, as well as an arts centre that acts as the hub for music and performing arts events. The school's 2.5km 'King's Loop' is popular for cross-country running at lunch times!

Opportunities are extensive, as is the school's co-curricular offering: Forest School, riding lessons at the school's off-site equestrian centre, archery, ballet, fencing, cookery, multi-sports and outdoor adventure are but some of the activities available.

King's Hall has a senior school, King's College, Taunton, and the two schools benefit from having their own independent sites, furnished with excellent age-appropriate facilities and attitudes to maximise the opportunities for the children in their care.

There is a close working relationship between the schools and transitioning from King's Hall to King's College is seamless. A great many pupils start at 2 and finish their education with us at 18. The two-site model enables those joining at 11 to find their feet before moving to King's College at 13. Scholarships are available for pupils with exceptional ability. These are awarded at 11+ and continue at King's College up to age 18.

Justin Chippendale, Headmaster at King's Hall added: *"At King's Hall we provide a fabulous educational experience. We aim to maximise potential and to help develop children to be the best they can be. The school is open and friendly, with solid structures in place to support children with all aspects of their lives. They leave us ready and prepared for the next part of their educational journey."*

England – South-West

Millfield Preparatory School

(Founded 1945)

Edgarley Hall, Glastonbury,
Somerset BA6 8LD
Tel: 01458 832446
Email: admissions@millfieldprep.com
Website: www.millfieldschool.com/prep
Headmaster: Dan Thornburn
Appointed: January 2022

School type:
Co-educational Day & Boarding
Age range of pupils: 2–13 years
No. of pupils enrolled as at 01/01/2022: 434
Fees per annum as at 01/01/2022:
£11,475–£30,255

Founded in 1945, Millfield Prep offers an exceptional, all-round educational experience that puts the individual at the centre, in order to develop and discover their brilliance. Nestled in 200 acres of beautiful Somerset countryside, Millfield Prep is an independent, co-educational day and boarding school for pupils aged 2-13, and provides the ideal environment in which to grow up, foster a love of learning and create lifelong childhood memories.

We pride ourselves on providing an exceptional, all-round education where every child can discover their brilliance. Our fundamental belief is that every child is unique and that they all have their own special talents which they enjoy and excel at, and the school's outstanding facilities and teaching provision help immerse pupils in limitless opportunities.

Our focus is teaching pupils a broad, balanced and individually tailored programme, and promoting confidence, health and wellbeing through involvement in sport and physical activity. All our pupils gain a real sense of achievement from the variety of co-curricular activities on offer. Pupils can choose from a wide range of clubs, from Pottery and Sailing to Rock Climbing and Lego Modelling - there is something for everyone.

Millfield Prep's outstanding facilities allow pupils to excel. Whether it's swimming in our 25-metre indoor heated swimming pool, playing golf on our 9- or 18-hole golf courses, or horse riding in our fantastic equestrian centre which features over 120 acres of hacking trails and a British Eventing (BE) cross-country course, we provide opportunities in a wide variety of fields.

95% of Millfield Prep pupils move up to Millfield in Year 9 to continue their education.

We award a number of Academic, Art, Music and Sports Scholarships each year for entry into Years 6, 7 and 8. We also welcome applications for scholarships from good all-rounders; boys and girls who have reached a good standard academically and show promise in specific areas such as Art, Music or Sport.

England – South-West

Monkton Prep School

(Founded 1886)
Church Road, Combe Down, Bath, Bath & North-East Somerset BA2 7ET
Tel: 01225 831200

Email: mpsadmissions@monkton.org.uk
Website: www.monktoncombeschool.com
Head: Mrs Catherine Winchcombe
Appointed: 2020
School type: Co-educational Day & Boarding Preparatory
Age range of pupils: 2–13 years (boarding from 8)

No. of pupils enrolled as at 01/01/2022: 305
Fees per term as at 01/01/2022:
Kindergarten - Year 2:
£3,407–£3,504 per term
Years 3-8 (Day): £4,115 –£5,995 per term
Years 3-8 (Boarding):
£8,000 –£8,640 per term
Average class size: 16
Teacher/pupil ratio: 1:9

Monkton Prep School is a small school with a big heart. It's built on strong relationships, a Christian foundation and a culture of care designed to give each child a sense of belonging and firm roots from which to grow.

We are a school where children learn about themselves by exploring their own world and a place where they grow in confidence through a sense of belonging. They begin to recognise their own value by valuing others and develop a love of learning through imagination, innovation and creativity.

Being a small school allows us to develop excellent relationships and really get to know our pupils, gaining the insight and understanding to provide outstanding learning and pastoral care. We have a strong sense of family and commitment to a vibrant boarding ethos which help our students to feel unconditionally valued.

We recognise the potential of each individual, helping children to develop their talents by developing a better understanding of themselves and giving them the self-confidence to thrive, experiment and explore.

We are a small school, but our children enjoy an expansive outdoor setting, with space for exploration and adventure, as well as first-rate facilities for games and early years' sports.

England – South-West

Taunton School

(Founded 1847)
Staplegrove Road, Taunton,
Somerset TA2 6AD

Tel: +44 (0)1823 703703
Email: enquiries@tauntonschool.co.uk
Website: www.tauntonschool.co.uk
Headmaster, Taunton School:
Mr. Lee Glaser
Appointed: January 2015
Headmaster, Taunton Prep School:
Mr. Andrew Edwards
School type:
Co-educational Boarding & Day

Religious Denomination:
Non-denominational
Age range of pupils: 0–18 years
No. of pupils enrolled as at 01/01/2022: 1000
Fees per annum as at 01/01/2022:
Prep: £3,020–£9,190
Senior: £6,960–£12,960
International: £7,275–£14,260
Average class size: 10
Teacher/pupil ratio: 1:7

Introduction
Founded in 1847, Taunton School is one of the South West's leading co-educational independent day and boarding schools for children aged 0–18 years. Set in a beautiful 52-acre site, Taunton School nurtures the individual in a friendly and broad-minded atmosphere, equipping our young people with the life skills to enable them to shape the world in the 21st century.

Information
Taunton School is a lively, international community where we aim to challenge, nurture and inspire young people to succeed in a global community.

Pupils leaving Taunton School go on to top universities including Oxbridge and Russell Group universities. We are one of the only schools in the UK to offer four unique Sixth Form pathways: the popular IB Diploma, A-levels, Level 3 BTEC Diploma in Business and in Sport & Exercise Science and our newly launched Pre-foundation and Foundation course in Business, which are specifically for international students.

Taunton School consists of a caring and experienced Nursery and Pre-Preparatory School, inspiring Preparatory School and an innovative Senior School and International School, which all share the same spacious 56-acre campus, as well as Taunton School International Middle School which is located in The Grange, a beautiful, traditional manor house close to Taunton School. Our outstanding campus includes a brand new £4 million Dining Hall, extensive sports fields, specific Music, Art and D&T departments and a 19th century Grade II listed Chapel built in 1907.

Excellent Boarding
The School offers a supportive boarding environment for children from 7 to 18 years. At the Preparatory School level (aged 7–13 years), boarding life is very much an extension of family life. Taunton Prep School boarders live in Thone boarding house, which is for boys and girls and has recently received a significant £350,000 refurbishment. It has excellent facilities and recreational areas, including a computer room and movie room. We support the children to learn to do things for themselves to be more confident and

England – South-West

to provide them with a tremendous breath of exciting opportunities in all areas of school life.

In the Senior School boarding environment, our young adults have access to abundant cultural and sporting activities. With close friends at hand, they have the opportunity to develop life skills within a relaxed but well-controlled atmosphere.

Exceptional academic results

As a completely non-selective school, Taunton School has achieved consistently excellent GCSE results and some of the most exceptional A-level and International Baccalaureate results in South West England. Approximately 96% of all Sixth Form leavers usually take up university or college places. The school usually sends three or four students per year to Oxford or Cambridge although the number has been as high as seven.

International Baccalaureate at Taunton School

We have been offering the IB Diploma since becoming an IB World School in 2007. During that time over 300 students have obtained the diploma and its popularity continues to grow not just with students, but also with universities and employers.

In 2021, of all the 26 students who passed their Diploma, seven scored 40 or more points including one student achieving the maximum 45 points. The average points score per candidate of 36.4 was well in excess of the world average of 33 and was the highest achieved in the 14 years of running the IB Diploma at Taunton School.

Military Families

Military families have been part of Taunton School for many years and contribute greatly to our broad and diverse community. As well rounded, independent individuals, they enjoy the stability, consistency and undisrupted education that Taunton School can offer, whether it's through full, weekly or flexible boarding. We believe that every child should benefit from an exceptional education, which is why we offer significant financial support for military families in receipt of CEA. View military families fees information on our website.

England – West Midlands

Birchfield School

(Founded 1935)
Albrighton, Wolverhampton,
Shropshire WV7 3AF
Tel: 01902 372534
Email: admissions@birchfieldschool.co.uk
Website: www.birchfieldschool.co.uk

Headmistress: Sarah Morris
School type: Co-educational Day
Age range of pupils: 4–16 years
No. of pupils enrolled as at 01/01/2022: 142
Fees per annum as at 01/01/2022:
Day: £7,500–£11,000

Birchfield School is a preparatory and senior school for boys and girls aged 4 to 16. In a new and exciting development, the senior school recently extended its provision with the first ever Year 9 class due to join in September 2023 and sit a comprehensive 3 year GCSE programme.

The school's mission is to inspire and nurture every pupil in its care, exploring and expanding their individual potential, and to encourage them within a caring community to hold in the highest esteem mutual respect, kindness, aspiration and diligence. Birchfield pupils receive a truly rounded education and pupils move on with exemplary manners, social skills and a love of learning.

In November 2021, ISI inspectors, in judging the school 'Excellent' in all categories, noted that pupils 'make excellent progress' and 'achieve highly in all areas'. Referring to Birchfield as an 'extremely harmonious and happy community', the report concluded that 'from the earliest age, pupils are enthusiastic and ambitious learners, with a genuine desire to succeed.'

Birchfield School offers first class specialist teaching with small class sizes and offers a range of facilities including two IT suites, an outdoor Early Years classroom, a 6,000 title library, a Food Technology room and a much-loved Forest School.

With 20 acres of extensive playing fields, including three cricket squares and practice nets and a multi-purpose astro-turf sports arena, pupils are well served with superb facilities. Sport forms an important part of the curriculum with all pupils offered the opportunity to play in sports teams.

Art, Music and Drama also play a key role in the school with pupils taking part in art competitions, drama productions, as well as learning a musical instrument and performing regularly.

Birchfield is supported by Prepcare Nursery which operates on the school site and accepts children from 6 weeks old.

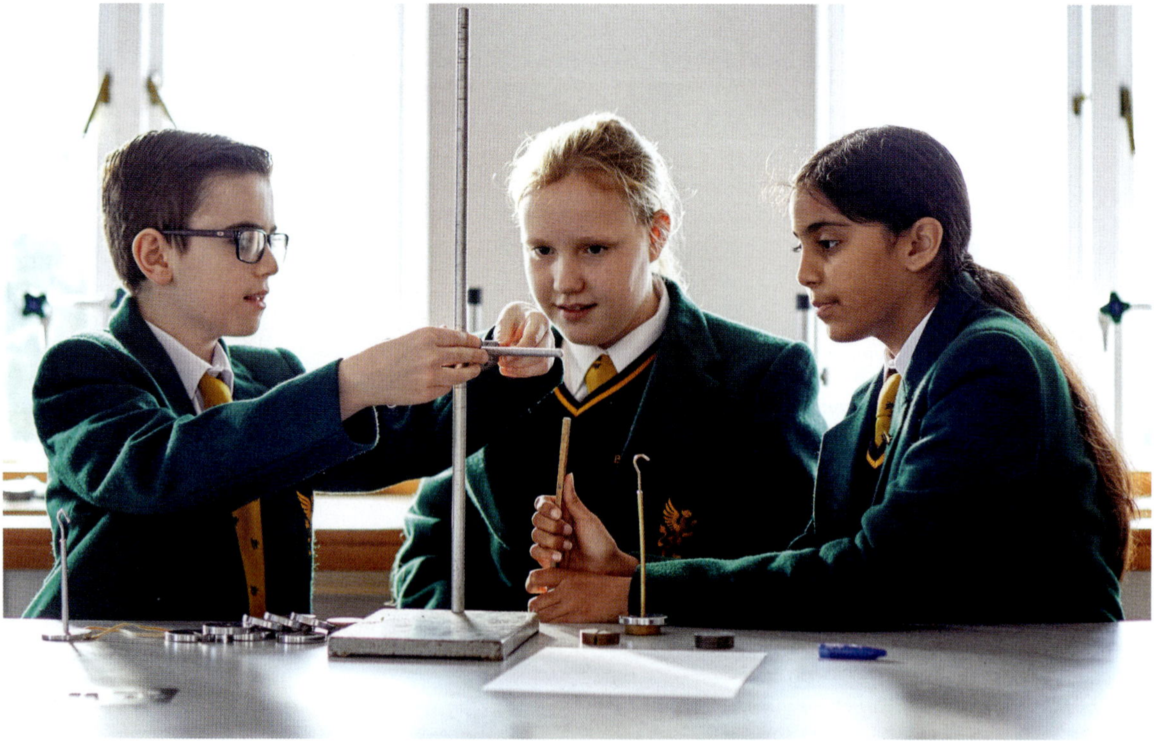

England – West Midlands

Moor Park

(Founded 1964)
Richards Castle, Ludlow, Shropshire SY8 4DZ

Tel: 01584 876 061
Email: head@moorpark.org.uk
Website: www.moorpark.org.uk
Headmaster: Mr Charles G O'B Minogue
Appointed: September 2015
School type: Co-educational Day, Full & Flexi Boarding
Age range of pupils: 0–13 years

No. of pupils enrolled as at 01/01/2022: 214
Boys: 108 **Girls:** 106
Fees per term as at 01/01/2022:
Day: £2,225–£6,215
Full Boarding: £7,700–£9,225
Average class size: 14
Teacher/pupil ratio: 1:8

Moor Park is a co-educational, boarding and day school accepting children from 3 months to 13 years of age.

Children often start in the Tick Tock Nursery, which provides a secure, nurturing and fun environment for our very youngest children. They transfer to the Pre-Prep Nursery and Kindergarten in the term that they turn 3. Children are then carefully prepared to start more formal schooling by a team of well-qualified and caring staff.

Our children are prepared mentally, emotionally and physically to move on with confidence to the full range of schools nationally. Eton, Harrow, Cheltenham Ladies' College and Radley, as well as the more local schools, are regular destinations and children also develop the independence they will need to succeed in a rapidly changing world whilst making full use of the 85 acres of beautiful grounds. An impressive proportion of our leavers win scholarships in a variety of disciplines. These include academic and extra-curricular awards to some of the top senior schools in the country.

It is also worth saying that Moor Park is a school where children of all abilities thrive and where children are treated as unique individuals. All of this is underpinned by a culture of kindness founded on Catholic principles, which ensures that all children are valued for who they are. Passionate teachers and an average class size of around 14 also make a difference.

Not every child can be good at everything but every child can be good at something and finding something for every child is something that we take seriously. Moor Park's facilities and, more importantly, enthusiastic and dedicated staff ensure that the school is well placed to get the best out of every child.

England – West Midlands

Moreton Hall

Moreton Hall Prep
Scholarship | Gaiety | Humanity

(Founded 1913)
Weston Rhyn, Oswestry,
Shropshire SY11 3EW
Tel: 01691 776028

Email: moretonhallprep@moretonhall.com
Website: www.moretonhall.org/moreton-prep
Head: Mr John Bond
School type: Co-educational Day & Boarding Preparatory

Age range of pupils: 6 months–11 years
No. of pupils enrolled as at 01/01/2022: 150
Fees per annum as at 01/01/2022:
Day: £10,650–£15,135
Full Boarding: £24,570
Average class size: 14

Our Prep School is an aspirational, joyous and nurturing independent preparatory school for children aged 6 months to 11 years old.

As an integral part of Moreton Hall, which was named TES Boarding School of the Year 2021, the Prep School is located in the centre of the school grounds, taking full advantage of the 100 acres of parkland and the extensive facilities of one of England's premier independent boarding schools, including our own farm.

Built on a solid foundation of teaching excellence, the Prep School shares the Senior School's high academic aspirations and uniquely joyous and nurturing family environment. Children are not only happy here, they flourish - academically, socially and personally. Our Prep School received the highest ranking of excellent in its most recent ISI inspection, with inspectors commenting: *"The quality of pupils' personal development is excellent."* Our teaching staff are exceptional and lie at the heart of the school's success. They are passionate about positive learning and skilled in teaching, bringing out the best in each individual pupil.

Our core teaching staff is augmented by specialists from our Senior School, including in sport, music, drama and spoken English, which is a hallmark of a Moreton education.

Moreton's liberal approach gives children the freedom to be themselves: playful, curious and confident. Instead of petty and punitive rules, we have a mutually beneficial loop of respect and trust between teachers and pupils. With small class sizes, every child is valued and understood. Our pastoral care is of the highest quality, ensuring pupils feel safe and are supported and encouraged to take on challenges, to persevere and find success and joy in all that they do.

Outdoor education, child-centred exploration and sensitive guidance are the keys to our success in the Early Years, Year 1 and Year 2. As children move along to the junior stage, they are encouraged to aspire to individual academic, creative and sporting goals. Our rich extra-curricular programme develops interests and resilience. Recognising the demands of modern, busy family life, we provide a variety of wrap around support, including after-school and holiday clubs, prep sessions and evening meals, as well as flexi and full-time boarding.

Located in beautiful north Shropshire, our Prep School's central location means we are only one hour from three of England's largest cities: Manchester, Liverpool and Birmingham, and 30 minutes from the market towns of Chester and Shrewsbury. We also welcome students from nearby North Wales, Wrexham and Herefordshire, as well as London. We warmly invite you to visit us and discover the Moreton Magic for yourself.

England – West Midlands

Priory School

(Founded 1936)
39 Sir Harry's Road, Edgbaston,
Birmingham, West Midlands B15 2UR
Tel: 0121 440 4103
Email: enquiries@prioryschool.net

Website: www.prioryschool.net
Headmaster: Mr J Cramb
School type: Co-educational Day
Age range of pupils: 6 months–18 years

Priory School is a centre of excellence where children and young people flourish, nurtured by a faith-based framework, permeating everything that we do.

Our resolute success and culture of aspiration begins with excellent standards of teaching and learning delivered within small classes and developed to meet the needs of the individual. It is enhanced by the quality of relationships between all members of the school community, built on honesty and respect and supported by a diverse and tailored curriculum to challenge and inspire.

Our trailblazing 'through school approach' offers a seamless educational transition from six months to eighteen years providing our pupils with a strong sense of belonging and stability, and an opportunity to grow into responsible and successful young people fully equipped for life after school.

Beyond the classroom, an incredibly diverse range of opportunities ensures each young person can excel spiritually, artistically, culturally and physically. We are a centre of sporting excellence, ensuring that students who compete at regional and national level in their chosen disciplines are also supported academically.

You are cordially invited to come along and see how your son or daughter will benefit from a Priory education.

Come and confirm for yourself that Priory gives you the 'edge' in Edgbaston and beyond!

England – West Midlands

Pattison School

86-90 Binley Road, Coventry,
West Midlands CV3 1FQ
Tel: 024 7645 5031
Email: office@pattisons.co.uk

Website: www.pattisons.co.uk
Head of School: Mr Graeme Delaney
School type: Co-educational Day
Age range of pupils: 2–18 years

Coventry based Pattison is a non-selective school for pupils aged 2 to 18 that offers excellent tuition and personal care where each student can shine. Founded in 1949 and now part of Chatsworth Schools, Pattison is a very special school because of its highly acclaimed performing arts pedigree combined with a strong academic focus. Students can take advantage of confidence-building performance opportunities in dance, drama and music, as well as a first-class education. This is all within a family environment with all the advantages of an uninterrupted all-through education and a strong focus on pastoral care.

All children from the age of four to Year 9 have a Speech and Drama lesson as part of their timetable. This lesson enables pupils to develop into confident, articulate members of society. From a young age, pupils are also encouraged to express themselves through dance and to develop the physical control and discipline required to dance, through weekly lessons. In music, specialist staff teach all pupils from the Early Years to Year 10 and pupils are encouraged to join the Junior and Senior choirs, which take part in performances throughout the year, as well as competing successfully in local festivals.

At all levels, the Performing Arts are taught by specialist teachers and most pupils coming to Pattison take advantage of the vast range of dance activities. Individual timetables are designed for all pupils, based on their interest, experience and ability. A Sports Club also takes place three times a week at lunchtimes for those who are not dance enthusiasts.

Being a small school, Pattison's celebrates and values each child's individuality, and staff take the time to get to know every pupil, supporting them, helping them and encouraging them to learn at their own pace. This pastoral care continues right through their time at Pattison. Children are supported, challenged or extended depending on their individual needs, so that they are always working to their full potential. All children are given the opportunity to develop their learning and interests as individuals and within small groups.

In the Early Years, learning through play develops into phonics and numeracy through games and group activities. It is in these early years that Pattison children develop a life-long passion for learning and a deep thirst for knowledge about the world around them.

At Pattison, there is one class comprising both Years 1 and 2 children. This means children between the ages of 5 to 7 have two years to learn the Key Stage 1 objectives. This gives the younger children a better chance of meeting those learning objectives and allows the older children

England – West Midlands

time to grow in confidence. Pattison has two classes at Key Stage 2: the Lower Juniors (Years 3 and 4) and the Upper Juniors (Years 5 and 6). Good literacy and numeracy skills are essential at this stage and Pattison believes that mixed age and ability is an ideal environment in which to encourage this.

Age 11, Pattison pupils progress to the Senior School as happy, accomplished, self-confident, well-mannered young people, respectful of each other. The Pattison Senior School courses are based on the National Curriculum which lead to G.C.S.E. examinations as well as a BTEC in IT. Non-examination subjects include Art, RE, PSHEE, Citizenship and Music.

Pattison is proud of its pupils fantastic achievements. Some children leave the school at age 16 and the majority of these children continue on to further education and university. Other children chose to stay on at Pattison until age 18 to participate in the schools excellent Musical Theatre Course which prepares students for careers both as performers and teachers. Students who leave Pattison at the end of the Musical Theatre Course are extremely well prepared for this with qualifications and skills in dance, drama and singing.

Every Pattison student has the opportunity to shine and fulfil their full potential, in preparation for a bright future.

England – West Midlands

The Old Hall School

(Founded 1845)

Stanley Road, Wellington, Shropshire TF1 3LB
Tel: 01952 223117
Email: admissions@oldhall.co.uk
Website: www.oldhall.co.uk
Headmaster: Mr Martin Stott
School type: Co-educational Day

Age range of pupils: 4–11
No. of pupils enrolled as at 01/01/2022: 232
Fees per annum as at 01/01/2022:
Day: £8,850–£13,920
Average class size: Circa 20
Teacher/pupil ratio: 1:10

Founded in 1845, The Old Hall School is a co-educational day school (4-11 years), housed in spectacular premises, located alongside Wrekin College, in beautiful Shropshire. Old Hall prides itself on being a progressive school, which also represents the traditions of all that is best in education; a community committed to the belief that every child has talents which need to be identified and developed.

Pupils are encouraged to develop a desire to learn, to think for themselves and to aim high in setting their own personal goals. Achievement and individuality are recognised and celebrated in many ways both inside and outside the classrooms; the children are encouraged to recognise and appreciate each other's achievements, celebrate success modestly and accept disappointment with grace.

The school offers first-class facilities; a double sports hall, 25-metre indoor swimming pool, an artificial playing surface and grass pitches offer an excellent sports and games environment, whilst specialist music and drama areas help to promote high standards in the performing arts.

A suite of specialist learning support rooms reflects the School's commitment to the needs of the individual.

A dedicated team of professionals who encourage pupils to fulfil their potential in a happy and secure environment enrich the broad curriculum.

Through the academic curriculum and caring pastoral system, the school aims to lay solid foundations in the development of well-motivated, confident and happy individuals who are always willing to give of their best on the road to high achievement.

Please do come and visit us to see for yourself all we can offer your child.

England – West Midlands

West House School

(Founded 1895)

24 St James's Road, Edgbaston, Birmingham, West Midlands B15 2NX
Tel: 0121 440 4097
Fax: 0121 440 5839
Email: secretary@westhouseprep.com
Website: www.westhouseprep.com
Headmaster:
Mr Alistair M J Lyttle BA(Hons), PGCE, NPQH

School type: Boys' Day Prep with Co-educational Nursery
Age range of boys: 1–11 years
Age range of girls: 1–4 years
No. of pupils enrolled as at 01/01/2022: 350
Fees per term as at 01/01/2022:
Day: £2,200–£4,226
Average class size: 17 (two form entry)
Teacher/pupil ratio: 1:12

Situated in the leafy oasis of the Calthorpe Estate, West House School has occupied the same site since its foundation in 1895. Since that time, the school has evolved significantly to become an independent preparatory school for boys aged 4-11 years, with a co-educational Early Years setting offering care for children aged from 12 months. West House is a member of The Independent Association of Preparatory Schools and, as such, upholds the requirement to provide a 'world class education'.

West House is a non-denominational school, guided by Christian principles. It is divided into three departments - Prep (Years 3-6), Pre-Prep (Years 1 & 2) and the Early Years Foundation Stage (Nursery - Reception).

With five acres of beautiful grounds, less than two miles from Birmingham city centre, the school lies at the heart of a thriving community. It is surrounded by many outstanding cultural and recreational facilities. These enrich the lives of all pupils and complement a broad and balanced curriculum through which boys explore and extend their talents in sport, music and performing arts.

The school continues to boast a unique family atmosphere of which founding Headmaster, Arthur Perrott Cary Field, would have been proud. However, in the spirit of combining the best of its traditions with an education that prepares pupils for life in the middle part of the 21st century, it remains determined to be at the forefront of innovation.

Employing 45 full-time and part-time academic staff, West House has grown considerably during the last five years to accommodate approximately 310 pupils - 130 of whom attend the EYFS Department.

Pupils are prepared for a wide range of senior schools and standards at 11+ are consistently high, with most Year 6 boys transferring to local grammar schools, King Edward's School, Birmingham and Solihull School.

Further details about the school can be found at www.westhouseprep.com

England – Yorkshire & Humberside

Ackworth School

(Founded 1779)
Pontefract Road, Ackworth, Pontefract, West Yorkshire WF7 7LT

Tel: 01977 233 600
Email: admissions@ackworthschool.com
Website: www.ackworthschool.com
Headteacher:
Mr. Anton Maree BA Rhodes (HDE)
Appointed: September 2014
School type:
Coeducational Day & Boarding

Religious Denomination: Quaker
Age range of pupils: 2.5–18 years
No. of pupils enrolled as at 01/01/2022: 510
Fees per term as at 01/01/2022:
Day: £3,000–£4,935
Full Boarding: £8,436–£10,692
Average class size: 16
Teacher/pupil ratio: 1:12

Ackworth has always been a co-educational, boarding and day school. For 240 years, we have maintained a passion for teaching and learning. We are proud of our traditions and family values, but equally proud of our innovative approach to co-education.

Ackworth is a dynamic and forward-thinking school. We strive to develop resilient individuals who not only think creatively, but also act ethically and with responsibility. We encourage our students to express themselves with confidence, to embody the Quaker value of speaking respectfully to others, but also in a way that is true to themselves and their beliefs.

First-class teaching is at the heart of any good school and Ackworth benefits greatly from the quality and experience of its teaching staff. Our aim is to provide a broad and balanced curriculum based on the National Curriculum but taking advantage of the flexibility we enjoy as an independent school. We encourage students to make curriculum choices which suit them best and much advice and guidance is on offer to help them to do this.

Located in a beautiful rural setting in Yorkshire, we offer broad educational opportunities from nursery age to sixth form, for day pupils and boarders.

Some of these opportunities are:
- proven academic performance
- a safe and supportive atmosphere
- the strength of quiet reflection
- excellent sport, music, drama, visual arts and recreational facilities

The School embraces the Quaker ethos of looking for the good in people, encouraging the individual and providing a friendly, supportive environment. First class teaching, a broad curriculum and superb facilities provide the foundations for a stimulating learning environment.

England – Yorkshire & Humberside

Bootham Junior School

AGES 3-18

(Founded 1823)

Rawcliffe Lane, York,
North Yorkshire YO30 6NP
Tel: 01904 655021
Email: junior@boothamschool.com
Website: www.boothamschool.com
Head: Mrs Helen Todd

School type:
Co-educational Day Preparatory
Age range of pupils: 3–11 years
Fees per term as at 01/01/2022:
Day: £2,430–£3,630

Bootham Junior School is situated on the outskirts of the beautiful and historic city of York. With purpose built classrooms, outdoor play areas and plenty of green space, the school provides pupils from ages 3-11 the space and environment to thrive. Classes are small to ensure each child benefits from individual attention and support and standards are high, both academically and pastorally.

As a Quaker school, Bootham emphasises responsibility for self and for others - with a premium on integrity, honesty and trustworthiness from an early age.

Through a lively curriculum and a varied range of activities, dedicated staff strive to embed the necessary skills for the educational challenges that pupils will face in the years ahead.

Bootham has an excellent reputation for its pastoral care and maintaining the health and well-being of pupils is extremely important. Staff work with parents and guardians and welcome active support and involvement. Good work habits, co-operation and tolerance create the happy, family atmosphere for which the School is known.

Comments below are from the latest Independent Schools Inspectorate report.

"Throughout the school, the pupils' spiritual development is outstanding. Pupils of all ages absorb the school's Quaker ethos which embodies the key spiritual principles of unity, peace and tolerance. In doing so, pupils, including the youngest, develop into kind, compassionate human beings with a keen sense of service and duty to others and a firm moral compass. From the central Quaker tenet of looking for the best in each individual, they gain self-awareness and from the school's emphasis on celebrating and cherishing individuality, they gain high levels of self-confidence and self-esteem, whilst remaining strongly empathetic to others."

England – Yorkshire & Humberside

Brontë House School

(Founded 1934)

Apperley Bridge, Bradford, West Yorkshire BD10 0PQ
Tel: 0113 250 2811
Email: admissions@woodhousegrove.co.uk
Website: www.woodhousegrove.co.uk
Head: Mrs Sarah Chatterton

School type: Co-educational Day
Age range of pupils: 2–11 years
No. of pupils enrolled as at 01/01/2022: 312
Boys: 176 **Girls:** 136
Fees per annum as at 01/01/2022:
£9,765 - £12,978 (fees include all wraparound care, meals and clubs)

Brontë House School – a bright beginning for a bright future

Brontë House is an independent, co-educational school in Yorkshire welcoming pupils from 2 to 11 years. Set in large, beautiful grounds with sports fields, a separate woodland and play area for our Nursery pupils and ample parking for stress free drop off and collection.

Our latest ISI inspection rated our school as "Excellent".

At Brontë House, all of our wrap-around care, co-curricular activities and meals – plus swimming lessons from Reception upwards – are included in our fees.

For busier families we also offer a 51 week contract for Pre-Nursery and Nursery pupils as well as a term-time only option.

Learning at primary school is not just academic. It is the softer, social skills that develop during this time that are the key to future happiness. Brontë House is the perfect size for your child to flourish. Classes are small enough to allow teachers to get to know each individual child's academic strengths and challenges, as well as the way in which they are best motivated to learn; yet large enough to provide children with a wide social circle in which to foster friendships.

"The best thing about Brontë House is how happy it makes my child. To see my daughter so positive about school, making friends and feeling safe and supported in the school is invaluable." Brontë Parent

Sport plays an important role in life at Brontë House, giving our pupils so much more than just physical fitness. It is a delight to watch personalities flourish within a team, leadership skills develop and resilience grow. Our specialist sports staff know every child is different and create a sports offering that is inclusive yet challenging – and most importantly, a lot of fun.

"Since coming to Brontë, my child has blossomed. They now look forward to school each day and have rediscovered their love of learning." Brontë Parent

Performing Arts is considered an integral part of every pupil's experience at the school; developing confidence, creativity and teamwork. We encourage all our pupils to learn a musical instrument and whatever a child's musical tastes or ability, they have ample opportunity to get involved.

The Grovian values we encourage in Nursery, are supported throughout our school. We cultivate confidence, commitment, resilience and respect knowing that these qualities will allow future generations to flourish and prepare them for life; school life, teenage life, family life and work life.

By moving through to our senior school, Woodhouse Grove, we can offer your child a seamless education from 2 to 18 years.

England – Yorkshire & Humberside

The Froebelian School

(Founded 1913)

Clarence Road, Horsforth, Leeds, West Yorkshire LS18 4LB
Tel: 0113 2583047
Fax: 0113 2580173
Email: office@froebelian.co.uk
Website: www.froebelian.com
Head Teacher:
Mrs Catherine Dodds BEd (Hons), PGCE
Appointed: 2015

School type:
Co-educational Day Preparatory
Age range of pupils: 3–11 years
No. of pupils enrolled as at 01/01/2022: 181
Boys: 93 **Girls:** 88
Fees per annum as at 01/01/2022:
Day: £5,535–£8,250
Teacher/pupil ratio: 1:10

We lay solid foundations for a future relevant lifelong love of learning.

A truly nurturing environment for your child to grow.

Situated in Horsforth and acknowledged as one of the North's leading independent prep schools, we welcome over 180 pupils between the ages of 3 and 11.

Children are at the heart of everything we do and we are passionate that they enjoy a positive experience, in a caring, structured and secure environment. To ensure we are laying solid foundations for a lifelong love of learning, to gain knowledge and skills, and develop personal attributes, relevant to their futures, we have made significant investment in our early years provision creating bespoke-designed classrooms and continuous access to an exceptional outdoor space.

"We knew from our first visit to the school that it was perfect. Every day our instincts are justified, as we watch our little girl blossom into a confident, delightful and happy little person." A Parent

With 51 weeks a year provision for all children, our plans for further investment and development in STEAM and Sport, balance both academic and co-curricular spheres of school life and honour our school motto – 'Giving a flying start to the citizens of tomorrow.'

Our aim is to provide a first class, future focused all-round education with committed and supportive pastoral care enabling us to develop the whole child. Therefore, our children regularly secure a place at their first choice of senior school and we enjoy an excellent scholarship success rate.

The most recent Independent Schools Inspectorate report judged the School as 'excellent' (the highest level) for the quality of the pupils' achievements and personal development.

"The children and staff work harmoniously together creating a special place, with a uniquely happy atmosphere." ISI Inspectorate

Our children adore their school, love learning and there is a true sense of fun - please do come and meet them.

"The pupils' attitudes to learning are exceptional." ISI Inspectorate

The school is easily accessible from most areas of Leeds, Bradford and Harrogate. Visit www.froebelian.com to find out more.

England – Yorkshire & Humberside

Scarborough College

(Founded 1896)

Filey Road, Scarborough,
North Yorkshire YO11 3BA
Tel: +44 (0)1723 360620
Fax: +44 (0)1723 377265
Email: admin@scarboroughcollege.co.uk
Website: www.scarboroughcollege.co.uk
Headmaster: Mr Guy Emmett

School type:
Co-educational Day & Boarding
Age range of pupils: 3–18 years
No. of pupils enrolled as at 01/01/2022: 484
Fees per annum as at 01/01/2022:
Day: £8,022–£15,741
Full Boarding: £24,528–£32,277
Teacher/pupil ratio: 1:8

The Scarborough College Prep School is a small, safe and friendly haven for children aged five to eleven, with the Little Owls nursery adjacent and the Scarborough College Senior School right across. A thriving Prep School, numbers have doubled in the last seven years, despite the financial crisis and global Covid pandemic.

The Scarborough College Prep School merged with its prestigious neighbour Bramcote Prep School in 2012. The Prep School remains true to the traditions of a prep school and takes full advantage of being co-located with an active and successful senior school as well as its excellent and extensive facilities. In addition to small class sizes and specialist teachers from Year 3, pupils enjoy access to a wide range of sporting facilities, science and arts classrooms, LAMDA provision and private music tuition to name but a few. Pupils in Year 3 and up take full advantage of first class education by subject specialists who either come from across the Senior School or teach the children in specialist classrooms in the Senior School. This enables a much smoother transition to the Senior School and its offering of different subjects.

A well-balanced and healthy lunch is taken in the senior school. Provided by renowned independent school caterers Holroyd and Howe, all lunches offer three varieties of hot meal, daily homemade soup, an extensive salad bar and delicious deserts.

Sport is an important and daily focus in the Prep School and teams have been successful in sports such as cricket, hockey, netball and rugby; including being crowned North of England Champions in hockey a few years ago. Representative sports are practiced daily in the junior school and from Reception onwards, children have daily games lessons. Using the Scarborough College fleet of minibuses, the players in the junior school often go out on fixtures to take on local rivals. Though the school does not have its own swimming pool, a nearby holiday park is used for weekly swimming lessons.

Under the enthusiastic guidance of a Prep School performing arts coordinator, the Prep School enjoys a busy calendar of musical and dramatic events. With

England – Yorkshire & Humberside

an infants', junior school and chamber choir; the Prep School is a place where music takes centre stage. Midweek music concerts, participation at the Eskdale Festival and the Prep School Production are but a small number of performances on the agenda each year.

The unique location is a key feature of the Prep School. Not only do all children live less than 30 minutes' drive from the school, the close proximity to the beach and the moors means outdoor education is thriving. As early as the Little Owls nursery, children enjoy Beach, Forest and Adventure School. Science, Geography and History lessons take place along the stunning coastline, at nearby Dalby Forest or in the school's own allotment. Trips away to nearby farms, meandering rivers and interesting rock formations are as frequent as trips on foot to sunny South Beach for a game of beach cricket.

Pupils in Year 6 start focusing on their transition to the Senior School and the vast majority will earn a place at Scarborough College. In recent years, more than 95% of all Year 6 pupils continued to Scarborough College. The Prep School does not offer SATs and Year 6 is more than just a year of learning and transitioning. Pupils' highlights of Year 6 are the camping trips and the annual Yorkshire Three Peaks Challenge.

To find out more about the Scarborough College Prep School, please visit scarboroughcollege.co.uk/educational-journey/scarborough-college-prep-school/ or contact Mr Chris Barker, Head of the Prep School, on 01723 360620. We would be delighted to show you around the school or arrange for a taster day. Alternatively, you can look out for our Open Mornings and our special open days that take place at the end of each month, Friday's For You.

England – Yorkshire & Humberside

Woodhouse Grove School

WOODHOUSE GROVE SCHOOL
(Founded 1812)
Apperley Bridge, Bradford,
West Yorkshire BD10 0NR

Tel: 0113 250 2477
Email: admissions@woodhousegrove.co.uk
Website: www.woodhousegrove.co.uk
Headmaster: Mr James Lockwood
School type: Co-educational Day & Boarding
Age range of pupils: 11–18 years

No. of pupils enrolled as at 01/01/2022: 751
Boys: 410 **Girls:** 341 **Boarders:** 80
Sixth form: 200
Fees per annum as at 01/01/2022:
Day: £14,490 - £14,694
Boarding: £30,555 - £30,720

Woodhouse Grove School is a co-educational day and boarding school located in Yorkshire. With our Prep School, Brontë House, we can provide a seamless education from 2 to 18 years. Boarding is from Year 7.

Our campus is set in idyllic countryside with outstanding facilities, yet only four miles from Leeds Bradford Airport and with direct train links to Leeds City Centre. With artificial pitches, competition pool, climbing wall, recording studio and 230 seater theatre, the opportunities for our students are endless.

Offering an "all-round" education and academic excellence - Woodhouse Grove is proof that both can flourish under one roof, as confirmed by our 'Excellent' rating in the latest ISI inspection (2017).

The Grove is well known for its ability to produce well-rounded, go-getting, entrepreneurial young people. The school's sporting heritage and success is firmly established – and it's performing arts offering is second to none. Combine this co-curricular pedigree with a strong academic ethos, as explained by our Deputy Head, Ed Wright, and it's a win-win for parents and pupils.

"We see learning and academic success as a collaborative effort between the teacher and student. Every member of staff works incredibly hard to get to know their individual students – to understand their drives and motivations, how they learn and what they want to achieve."

Grovian values are instilled in pupils from the start of their Grovian journey and include being kind and generous, committed and resilient, enterprising and resourceful.

To be a "Grovian" is something that benefits pupils long after they leave the school gates for the last time. The school's alumni – or "Old Grovians" – form a close, altruistic network across a huge variety of fields – from Red Arrows Team Leader to Engineer; Chief Executive to the West End.

Our school ethos, outlined by Headmaster, James Lockwood,

"At Woodhouse Grove we appreciate that every child has their own unique personality, talents and skills. We nurture and celebrate this individuality at all stages of their education.

Prospective parents are impressed by the confidence, commitment and respect shown by our students and choose Woodhouse Grove to deliver their child's education and unlock their potential.

We recognise this potential could lie anywhere – so we offer every pupil a huge array of opportunities and experiences. We take pride in identifying and honing their strengths as well as giving them the confidence to tackle any challenges.

I am proud of our holistic approach which prepares each and every Grovian for life beyond the classroom."

Invest in your child's future, find out more at www.woodhousegrove.co.uk

Prep schools in Scotland

Scotland

Merchiston Castle School

A BOARDING AND DAY SCHOOL FOR BOYS AGED 7-18

(Founded 1833)
294 Colinton Road, Edinburgh, EH13 0PU

Tel: 0131 312 2200
Email: admissions@merchiston.co.uk
Website: www.merchiston.co.uk
Headmaster: Mr Jonathan Anderson
Appointed: August 2018
Deputy Head: Mr Danny Rowlands (Wellbeing), Dr Dale Cartwright (Learning and Teaching)

School type: Boys' Boarding & Day
Age range of boys: 7–18 years
No. of pupils enrolled as at 01/01/2022: 400
No. of boarders: 260
Fees per annum as at 01/01/2022:
Day: £15,330–£26,040
Full Boarding: £22,080–£35,880
Teacher/pupil ratio: 1:9

Building Strong Foundations from Age 7

Many schools can boast about their exceptional academic results, university success rates, extensive sporting and co-curricular programmes, welcoming atmospheres and stunning grounds and facilities. Indeed, we can do that as well.

What makes us different, however, is a combination of things: our size, a genuine focus on the needs of the individual, and the fact that we really understand boys and how to get the very best out of them.

It is a potent trio. It is what enables us to know our boys really well and to understand what makes them tick. It is why we can support them in a way that is material and motivating to them. It is the reason your son will strive for personal excellence and want to be the best version of himself. It is the secret of their, and our, success.

Our mission is to provide a caring community for every boy, which treats him as an individual, unearths and nurtures his talents, encourages him to pursue excellence in all he does, and enables him to flourish.

Our community's wellbeing is central; without it, no one will ever achieve their best. That is why wellbeing underpins everything we do. Our boys thrive because they are known, understood, valued, and supported in everything they do.

Merchiston is a remarkable school where boys make lifelong friends and community connections whilst gaining a world-class, global, outward-looking education.

We would love to talk to you about your son and, more importantly, talk with him to work out what makes him tick, discuss where he wants to go next and make sure he has the toolkit to get there.

Merchiston's young men leave us as rounded individuals, not only having achieved the highest level of personal academic success but with a sense of who they are and with respect for others, having learnt what it means to have true integrity and character. **Our success proves that what we do works.**

Curriculum - Merchiston Juniors

The curriculum at Merchiston Juniors is designed with the following principles in mind: challenge and enjoyment, breadth, progression, depth, personalisation and choice, coherence and relevance.

Our curriculum provides the opportunity for individual study, creativity, leadership, co-operative learning, self- and peer assessment and target setting. Co-curricular activities in the arts and sport provide numerous additional opportunities to be challenged, to flourish and to succeed. We look to develop successful learners, confident individuals, responsible citizens and effective contributors. We believe that the wide range of opportunities on offer allows each learner to thrive and develop in a rounded manner.

Outdoor Learning

We are incredibly fortunate to be able to use the outdoors every day to help develop and extend our pupils' skills and enhance our curriculum. Our pupils forage and collect eggs for baking, incorporate nature walks into descriptive writing, collect autumnal leaves for Art lessons, perform drama under the spectacular tree canopy and much more.

Home from Home

The School provides a stimulating, challenging, yet supportive and encouraging environment where your son can grow up surrounded by his friends within our unique house structure.

A housemother ensures the smooth-running of the domestic side of the House and provides valuable pastoral wellbeing support. An enthusiastic and committed

Scotland

team of tutors and prefects allows us to provide exciting recreational and social activities, designed to meet the needs of every boy. Boys leave Merchiston Juniors eager and ready to make the most of the opportunities available to them in the Senior School, and detailed discussions take place to ensure their smooth transition to life in the Senior School.

Links with Girls' Schools
Merchiston also benefits from its strong links with girls' schools for drama performances, cultural events and social gatherings.

Scholarships and Financial Assistance
A range of scholarships are available at ages 10+. A financial concession is not automatically applied to a Scholarship but, where parents wish, they may apply for means-tested financial assistance.

Admissions
The Junior School at Merchiston is very special, which is perhaps something of a hidden gem. To arrange a visit, please contact Mrs Kay Wilson, Director of Admissions, on +44 (0)131 312 2201.

Scotland

St Leonards School

(Founded 1877)
The Pends, St Andrews, Fife KY16 9QJ
Tel: 01334 472126

Email: registrar@stleonards-fife.org
Website: stleonards-fife.org
Head: Mr Simon Brian
School type:
Co-educational Day & Boarding
Religious Denomination:
Non-denominational

Age range of pupils: 5–18 years
No. of pupils enrolled as at 01/01/2022: 577
Fees per annum as at 01/01/2022:
Day: £9,840–£15,939
Full Boarding: £24,342–£37,920
Average class size: 12-20
Teacher/pupil ratio: 1:7

St Leonards is an independent, co-educational boarding and day school situated in an historic campus at the heart of the seaside, university town of St Andrews. It offers a world of opportunities for pupils from age five to 18 to excel academically and develop interests outside the classroom, ultimately ensuring that they leave as rounded, courteous, and confident individuals, fully equipped to tackle the challenges of today's rapidly changing world.

St Leonards was named Scotland's Independent School of the Year 2019 by The Sunday Times Good Schools Guide, and is proud to be an all-through International Baccalaureate (IB) World School, delivering the inspiring Primary Years Programme (PYP), followed by the Middle Years Programme (MYP), and two Sixth Form pathways in the form of the Career-related Programme (CP) or the Diploma Programme (DP). GCSEs are offered in Years 10 and 11. This approach to learning ensures a seamless and coherent journey for pupils as they move up through the school, from Year 1 to Year 13.

St Leonards is both international and progressive in outlook, yet rooted in Scottish tradition. Junior pupils have a dedicated teaching and learning area within the school campus, whilst also accessing and enjoying facilities in Senior areas of the school. From Year 1 upwards, pupils are taught by subject specialists for PE, Games, Music, Drama, and French, and from Year 3 the pupils also enjoy specialist teaching for Art.

In line with the IB Learner Profile, pupils

Scotland

are encouraged to be principled, caring, open-minded, knowledgeable, reflective, internationally-minded and balanced inquirers, thinkers, communicators, and risk-takers. All of these values align with the school's ethos of embedding outdoor learning as part of a rounded education, delivered both within the green and historic grounds, and beyond, on the beach, in the woods and on the water.

Beach School is a highlight of the weekly timetable, with PYP pupils enjoying lessons on the East Sands, just a two-minute walk from the school campus. These lessons are vibrant and varied, and include everything from honing subtraction skills by creating and solving problems in the sand, to investigating forces using ropes, barrels and found objects. Class reading books are taken down to the pier on bright days, to the fire pit in twilight hours, and into one of the school's two cosy yurts, complete with wood-burning stoves, in wet weather.

In addition, pupils enjoy developing their beekeeping, gardening, and bushcraft skills, both in curriculum lessons and as after-school activities, and prove themselves as 'risk-takers' with fun termly 'dooks' in the North Sea - those who choose to complete three dooks become fully fledged members of the Polar Bear Club!

A diverse programme of after-school activities opens doors to music, drama, dance, languages, film, arts and crafts, and a whole host of team and individual sports including hockey, rugby, football, lacrosse, swimming, running, and golf. St Leonards' leading five-tier Golf Programme, in partnership with the St Andrews Links Trust, caters for pupils from age eight upwards, with a dedicated tier for Junior pupils. Pupils enrolled on the programme have unrivalled access to the outstanding Links courses in the 'Home of Golf', as well as expert coaching and state-of-the-art sporting technology.

Boarding at St Leonards is available from age 10 and, thanks to an ambitious £5 million refurbishment programme over the past five years, all three houses are equipped with state-of-the-art kitchens and spacious communal areas, which are regularly used for fun evening and weekend activities. Study bedrooms have been fitted with new built-in beds and desk spaces with modern storage, lighting and USB charging points - some of the rooms even offer views over the school playing fields to the sea beyond.

Each house has a distinct décor and unique personality. For example, St Rule, the Junior boarding house at St Leonards, is a real 'home from home' with a playful and informal aesthetic, and family at its heart. There are comfy bean bags for movie nights, as well as table tennis and pool for evening games. The design of all three houses is underpinned by the same ethos: to provide a truly special boarding experience that is rooted in tradition, but continually adapting and evolving to meet the needs of today's young people.

At St Leonards, the healthy balance of outstanding sporting and co-curricular programmes alongside academic studies and outdoor learning opportunities ensures that pupils leave equipped with the skills to succeed in today's ever-changing world. Truly an education 'Ad Vitam'.

Scotland

Craigclowan Preparatory School

(Founded 1952)

Edinburgh Road, Perth,
Perth & Kinross PH2 8PS
Tel: 01738 626310
Fax: 01738 440349
Email: headspa@craigclowan-school.co.uk
Website: www.craigclowan-school.co.uk
Head of School: John Gilmour

Appointed: October 2014
School type: Co-educational Day
Age range of pupils: 3–13 years
No. of pupils enrolled as at 01/01/2022: 212
Fees per term as at 01/01/2022:
Day: £4,950
Average class size: 14
Teacher/pupil ratio: 1:9

Craigclowan Prep School, set on a hillside to the South of the Fair City of Perth, provides a warm and nurturing environment for boys and girls aged 3-13. Surrounded by stunning grounds with magnificent views over Perthshire, the school has a distinguished history, a reputation for the highest standards and expectations and a passion for childhood.

The learning environment delivers a modern education within a framework of proven traditional values, effectively balancing the best of old and new in education. Beginning with the youngest pupils, who join the nursery after their third birthday, children's input in planning activities is valued, engendering curiosity within each child and promoting opportunities to explore, progress and flourish at their own pace.

With a friendly, caring and supportive ethos, the staff are able to get to know the children closely and treat them as individuals in all they do. Each child at Craigclowan will have a talent or gift for something; the school's mission is to discover and nurture this to allow them to thrive. Every pupil is encouraged to achieve their all-round potential, academically, on the sports field and in more than 50 extra-curricular activities on offer, ranging from skiing, on the school's own dry ski slope, to art clubs, judo, kayaking, bushcraft skills and fencing.

The school is a hive of activity and the outdoor classroom, all-weather training ground, sports fields, Forest School and trim trail are in daily use. The children make the most of the world outside the classroom through a wide range of outdoor activities that build confidence and resilience, encourage creativity and problem solving and ensure rosy cheeks and muddy boots. Wellie boots are a must!

When it comes to moving on to senior school, pupils attend a wide variety of top UK schools, both north and south of the border, many with scholarships. The values that are instilled in pupils during their journey through Craigclowan, are the qualities that allow them to thrive after they leave.

Prep schools in Wales

Wales

St Gerard's School

(Founded 1915)

Ffriddoedd Road, Bangor,
Gwynedd LL57 2EL
Tel: 01248 351656
Email: sgadmin@st-gerards.org
Website: www.st-gerards.org
Head Teacher: Mr Campbell Harrison
Appointed: September 2016

School type: Co-educational Day
Age range of pupils: 4–18 years
No. of pupils enrolled as at 01/01/2022: 143
Fees per annum as at 01/01/2022:
Day: £7,695–£11,655
Teacher/pupil ratio: 1:10

Welcome to St Gerard's School Trust
St Gerard's is a small independent day school that has a happy, secure, family atmosphere in which the pupils thrive. Since its foundation over a hundred years ago the school has maintained a kind and caring ethos which also sets high standards of behaviour for the students.

St Gerard's School Trust has consistently high academic results and has the experience to provide the individual attention each child needs to fulfil their potential. Despite the COVID-19 pandemic our teachers continued to deliver a full curriculum with outstanding A level and GCSE results. We pride ourselves on providing a nurturing environment, allowing children to develop into well rounded students ready to move on to adulthood confident in their own abilities.

Children from the earliest years learn to share with and care for others and the older children work and interact in an atmosphere that encourages them to be resilient, compassionate and trustworthy. There are lots of different activities that the children can take part in to enrich their learning experience.

Through the hard work of staff and pupils and the support of parents we hope to develop analytical, critical and compassionate thinkers who are capable of achieving happiness and success in their life.

We are very proud of our school and all that is achieved here. The best advertisement for our school is our students and we invite you to come and meet them and see the school in action.

Arrangements can be made to visit throughout the whole of the year.

Senior School
Our senior school offers a small educational community that is focused on the potential of each pupil. Our pupils, staff and parents work in partnership toward our aim of achieving optimum progress together. The senior school at St Gerard's is located in the original convent building with two more recent extensions to house purpose-built classrooms. The senior school is in close proximity to the junior school. This allows the interchange of staff expertise and the opportunity for interaction between junior and senior pupils' with the aim of benefiting the pupils' education.

At the senior school our teachers are subject specialists and individual year groups move from classroom to classroom

Wales

to curricular need. Subject teachers are responsible for the design and delivery of their schemes of work as they align to the national curriculum and exam board specifications. Work is planned with close liaison, communication and support from the headteacher. Each member of staff in the senior school is linked to a form group to help monitor pupils' personal welfare as well as their academic progress.

Our small class sizes in the senior school allow for individual attention for each pupil. Teachers are aware of individual pupils' strengths and target individual areas for improvement.

Junior School

Our junior school offers every child the opportunity to achieve his or her potential. Our children, staff and parents work in partnership toward our aim of achieving together. The junior school at St Gerard's is housed in a purpose-built block adjacent to the senior school. The close proximity with the senior school allows the interchange of staff expertise, further benefiting pupils' education.

Class teachers are responsible for the children's welfare and delivery of the curriculum. Work is planned with close liaison, communication and support from the headteacher.

During planning, staff share the preparation of work, drawing on different experiences, knowledge and expertise to ensure work is relevant and well-matched to meet the needs of the children. In this way, we are able to utilise the strengths of our staff team and enhance the quality of learning and teaching here at St Gerard's.

The pupils are mainly taught by form teachers with some subject lessons taught by senior school.

We aim for us all to:

- feel safe and valued as part of a caring community that celebrates success
- be independent thinkers / learners who are able to seek solutions creatively and co-operatively
- inspire an 'enquiring' mind and ask questions
- experience and actively participate in a relevant, enjoyable curriculum that evolves to meet the needs of all
- listen and articulate responses showing consideration to others
- be polite and courteous
- be proactive in our responsibilities towards the community, society, the environment and economy, linking 'real life' with our learning
- understand and respect diversity
- be aware of and recognise our own learning needs and be involved in planning future steps and targets
- develop a sense of self-esteem and be well-balanced, healthy individuals
- contribute to our wider community by being considerate of others.

Directory

Channels Islands D149
Central & West D151
East D157
East Midlands D165
Greater London D169
London D175
North-East D185
North-West D187
South-East D193
South-West D205
West Midlands D211
Yorkshire & Humberside D217
Northern Ireland D221
Scotland D223
Wales D227

Please note the following: The user will find Essex and Hertfordshire in Greater London and East of England; Kent and Surrey in Greater London and South-East. When seeking schools in any of these counties, therefore, the user is advised to check both regional sections.

UK region map – Directories

Channel Islands

KEY TO SYMBOLS
- Boys' school
- Girls' school
- International school
- Tutorial or sixth form college
- A levels
- Boarding accommodation
- Bursaries
- International Baccalaureate
- Learning support
- Entrance at 16+
- Vocational qualifications
- Independent Association of Prep Schools
- The Headmasters' & Headmistresses' Conference
- Independent Schools Association
- Girls' School Association
- Boarding Schools' Association
- Society of Heads

Unless otherwise indicated, all schools are coeducational day schools. Single-sex and boarding schools will be indicated by the relevant icon.

Channel Islands

Guernsey

Elizabeth College Junior School
Beechwood, Queen's Road, St Peter Port, Guernsey GY1 1PU
Tel: 01481 722123
Headteacher: Mr Richard Fyfe
Age range: 2.5–11 years

The Ladies' College
Les Gravées, St Peter Port, Guernsey GY1 1RW
Tel: 01481 721602
Principal: Ms Ashley Clancy
Age range: G2.5–18 years

Jersey

Beaulieu Convent School
Wellington Road, St Helier, Jersey JE2 4RJ
Tel: 01534 731280
Headmaster: Mr C Beirne
Age range: B16–19 years G3–19 years

De La Salle College
Wellington Road, St Saviour, Jersey JE2 7TH
Tel: 01534 754100
Head of College: Mr Jason Turner
Age range: 3–18 years

FCJ Primary School
Deloraine Road, St Saviour, Jersey JE2 7XB
Tel: 01534 723063
Headteacher: Ms Donna Lenzi
Age range: 4–11 years

Helvetia House School
14 Elizabeth Place, St Helier, Jersey JE2 3PN
Tel: 01534 724928
Headmistress: Mrs Lindsey Woodward BA, DipEd
Age range: G4–11 years

St George's Preparatory School
La Hague Manor, Rue de la Hague, St Peter, Jersey JE3 7DB
Tel: 01534 481593
Headmaster: Mr Cormac Timothy
Age range: 2–11 years

St Michael's Preparatory School
La Rue de la Houguette, Five Oaks, St Saviour, Jersey JE2 7UG
Tel: 01534 856904
Head of School: Mr Mike Rees
Age range: 3–14 years
No. of pupils: 317
Fees: Day £11,175–£17,565

Victoria College Preparatory School
Pleasant Street, St Helier, Jersey JE2 4RR
Tel: 01534 723468
Head Teacher: Mr Dan Pateman
Age range: B7–11 years

Central & West

Buckinghamshire D152
Gloucestershire D152
Oxfordshire D153
West Berkshire D154
Wiltshire D155

KEY TO SYMBOLS
- Boys' school
- Girls' school
- International school
- Tutorial or sixth form college
- A levels
- Boarding accommodation
- Bursaries
- International Baccalaureate
- Learning support
- Entrance at 16+
- Vocational qualifications
- (IAPS) Independent Association of Prep Schools
- (HMC) The Headmasters' & Headmistresses' Conference
- (ISA) Independent Schools Association
- (GSA) Girls' School Association
- (BSA) Boarding Schools' Association
- (S) Society of Heads

Unless otherwise indicated, all schools are coeducational day schools. Single-sex and boarding schools will be indicated by the relevant icon.

England – Central & West

Buckinghamshire

Akeley Wood School
Akeley Wood, Buckingham,
Buckinghamshire MK18 5AE
Tel: 01280 814110
Headmaster: Mr Simon Antwis
Age range: 12 months–18 years
No. of pupils: 700 VIth100
Fees: Day £10,665–£15,900

Ashfold School
Dorton House, Dorton, Aylesbury,
Buckinghamshire HP18 9NG
Tel: 01844 238237
Headmaster: Mr Colin MacIntosh
Age range: 3–13 years

Broughton Manor Preparatory School
Newport Road, Broughton, Milton Keynes, Buckinghamshire MK10 9AA
Tel: 01908 665234
Heads: Mr J Smith & Mrs R Smith
Age range: 2 months–11 years

Caldicott
Crown Lane, Farnham Royal,
Buckinghamshire SL2 3SL
Tel: 01753 649300
Headmaster: Mr Jeremy Banks BA (Hons) QTS, MEd
Age range: B7–13 years

Chesham Preparatory School
Two Dells Lane, Chesham,
Buckinghamshire HP5 3QF
Tel: 01494 782619
Headmaster: Mr Jonathan Beale
Age range: 3–13 years

Child First Aylesbury Pre-School
35 Rickfords Hill, Aylesbury,
Buckinghamshire HP20 2RT
Tel: 01296 433224
Age range: 3–5 years

CROWN HOUSE PREPARATORY SCHOOL
For further details see p. 48
Bassetsbury Manor, Bassetsbury Lane, High Wycombe,
Buckinghamshire HP11 1QX
Tel: 01494 529927
Email: office@crownhouseschool.co.uk
Website: www.crownhouseschool.co.uk
Headteacher: Mrs Sarah Hobby
Age range: 3–11 years

Dair House School
Bishops Blake, Beaconsfield Road, Farnham Royal,
Buckinghamshire SL2 3BY
Tel: 01753 643964
Headmaster: Mr Terry Wintle BEd(Hons)
Age range: 3–11 years

Davenies School
Station Road, Beaconsfield,
Buckinghamshire HP9 1AA
Tel: 01494 685400
Headmaster: Mr Carl Rycroft BEd (Hons)
Age range: B4–13 years
No. of pupils: 343
Fees: Day £11,985–£17,985

Gateway School
1 High Street, Great Missenden,
Buckinghamshire HP16 9AA
Tel: 01494 862407
Head of School: Mrs Cath Bufton-Green
Age range: 2–11 years

GODSTOWE PREPARATORY SCHOOL
For further details see p. 52
Shrubbery Road, High Wycombe, Buckinghamshire
HP13 6PR
Tel: 01494 529273
Email: schooloffice@godstowe.org
Website: www.godstowe.org
Headmistress: Ms Sophie Green
Age range: B3–7 years G3–13 years

GRIFFIN HOUSE PREPARATORY SCHOOL
For further details see p. 50
Little Kimble, Aylesbury,
Buckinghamshire HP17 0XP
Tel: 01844 346154
Email: secretary@griffinhouseschool.co.uk
Website: www.griffinhouseschool.co.uk
Headmaster: Mr Tim Walford
Age range: 3–11 years

Heatherton School
10 Copperkins Lane, Amersham,
Buckinghamshire HP6 5QB
Tel: 01494 726433
Headmaster: Mrs Nicola Nicoll
Age range: B3–4 years G3–11 years
No. of pupils: 148
Fees: Day £1,140–£13,335

HIGH MARCH
For further details see p. 53
23 Ledborough Lane, Beaconsfield,
Buckinghamshire HP9 2PZ
Tel: 01494 675186
Email: office@highmarch.co.uk
Website: www.highmarch.co.uk
Head of School: Mrs Kate Gater
Age range: B3–4 years G3–11 years
No. of pupils: 280
Fees: Day £5,850–£16,185

Milton Keynes Preparatory School
Tattenhoe Lane, Milton Keynes,
Buckinghamshire MK3 7EG
Tel: 01908 642111
Head of School: Mr Simon Driver
Age range: 2 months–11 years

Pipers Corner School
Pipers Lane, Great Kingshill, High Wycombe,
Buckinghamshire HP15 6LP
Tel: 01494 718 255
Headmistress: Mrs H J Ness-Gifford BA(Hons), PGCE
Age range: G4–18 years

Swanbourne House School
Swanbourne, Milton Keynes,
Buckinghamshire MK17 0HZ
Tel: 01296 720264
Head of School: Mrs Jane Thorpe
Age range: 4–13 years

The Beacon School
15 Amersham Road,
Chesham Bois, Amersham,
Buckinghamshire HP6 5PF
Tel: 01494 433654
Headmaster: Mr William Phelps
Age range: B3–13 years

The Grove Independent School
Redland Drive, Loughton, Milton Keynes, Buckinghamshire MK5 8HD
Tel: 01908 690590
Principal: Mrs Deborah Berkin
Age range: 3 months–13 years

The Webber Independent School
Soskin Drive, Stantonbury Fields, Milton Keynes,
Buckinghamshire MK14 6DP
Tel: 01908 574740
Principal: Mrs Hilary Marsden
Age range: 6 months–16 years

Thornton College
College Lane, Thornton, Milton Keynes, Buckinghamshire MK17 0HJ
Tel: 01280 812610
Headteacher: Mrs Val Holmes
Age range: G3–18 years (Boarding from age 7)
No. of pupils: 402
Fees: Day £10,545–£16,815 WB £18,525–£23,445 FB £23,040–£28,575

Walton Pre-Preparatory School & Nursery
The Old Rectory, Walton Drive, Milton Keynes,
Buckinghamshire MK7 6BB
Tel: 01908 678403
Head of School: Mrs Chantelle McLaughlan
Age range: 2 months–5 years

Gloucestershire

Airthrie School
29 Christchurch Road, Cheltenham, Gloucestershire GL50 2NY
Tel: 01242 512837
Headteacher: Mrs Sara Jackson
Age range: 3–11
No. of pupils: 168
Fees: Day £6,770–£9,930

Beaudesert Park School
Minchinhampton, Stroud,
Gloucestershire GL6 9AF
Tel: 01453 832072
Headmaster: Mr J P R Womersley BA, PGCE
Age range: 3–13
No. of pupils: 450
Fees: Day £5,745–£17,661 FB £22,677

England – Central & West

BERKHAMPSTEAD SCHOOL
For further details see p. 46
Pittville Circus Road, Cheltenham, Gloucestershire GL52 2QA
Tel: 01242 523263
Email: office@berkhampsteadschool.co.uk
Website: www.berkhampsteadschool.co.uk
Headmaster: Richard Cross
Age range: 3 months–11 years
No. of pupils: 254
Fees: Day £2,820–£4,045

Bredon School
Pull Court, Bushley, Tewkesbury, Gloucestershire GL20 6AH
Tel: 01684 293156
Headmaster: Mr Nick Oldham
Age range: 7–18 years

Cheltenham College Preparatory School
Thirlestaine Road, Cheltenham, Gloucestershire GL53 7AB
Tel: 01242 522697
Headmaster: Mr Tom O'Sullivan
Age range: 7–13 years

Dean Close Pre-Preparatory & Preparatory School
Lansdown Road, Cheltenham, Gloucestershire GL51 6QS
Tel: +44 (0)1242 512217
Headmaster Preparatory School: Mr Paddy Moss
Age range: 2+–13

Dean Close St John's
Castleford Hill, Tutshill, Gloucestershire NP16 7LE
Tel: 01291 622045
Head: Mr Nick Thrower
Age range: 3 months–13 years

Hatherop Castle School
Hatherop, Cirencester, Gloucestershire GL7 3NB
Tel: 01285 750206
Headmaster: Mr Nigel Reed M.Ed, B.Sc (Hons), PGCE
Age range: 2–13
No. of pupils: 210
Fees: Day £6,285–£10,455 FB £15,270–£16,110

Hopelands Preparatory School
38 Regent Street, Stonehouse, Gloucestershire GL10 2AD
Tel: 01453 822164
Headmistress: Mrs S Bradburn
Age range: 3–11
No. of pupils: 76
Fees: Day £6,996–£10,155

Kitebrook Preparatory School
Kitebrook House, Moreton-in-Marsh, Gloucestershire GL56 0RP
Tel: 01608 674350
Headmistress: Mrs Susan McLean
Age range: 3–13
No. of pupils: 304

OneSchool Global UK Bristol Campus
Station Road, Wanswell, Berkeley, Gloucestershire GL13 9RS
Tel: 01453 511282
Age range: 7–18 years

OneSchool Global UK Gloucester Campus
Eastbrook Road, Gloucester, Gloucestershire GL4 3DB
Tel: 01452 417722
Age range: 7–18 years

Rendcomb College
Rendcomb, Cirencester, Gloucestershire GL7 7HA
Tel: 01285 831213
Headmaster: Mr R Jones BA(Hons), MEd
Age range: 3–18
No. of pupils: 350 VIth72
Fees: Day £2,070–£7,775 WB £8,140–£9,785 FB £8,925–£11,995

St Edward's Preparatory School
London Road, Charlton Kings, Cheltenham, Gloucestershire GL52 6NR
Tel: 01242 538900
Headmaster: Mr Stephen McKernan BA(Hons) MEd NPQH
Age range: 1–11
No. of pupils: 295
Fees: Day £7,770–£12,975

The Acorn School
Church Street, Nailsworth, Gloucestershire GL6 0BP
Tel: 01453 836508
Headmaster: Mr Graeme E B Whiting
Age range: 7–18
No. of pupils: VIth30
Fees: Day £6,675–£12,045

The King's School
Gloucester, Gloucestershire GL1 2BG
Tel: 01452 337337
Headmaster: David Morton
Age range: 3–18
No. of pupils: VIth80
Fees: Day £7,350–£19,185

The Richard Pate School
Southern Road, Cheltenham, Gloucestershire GL53 9RP
Tel: 01242 522086
Headmaster: Mr Robert MacDonald
Age range: 3–11 years
No. of pupils: 300
Fees: Day £3,330–£10,410

Westonbirt Prep School
Westonbirt, Tetbury, Gloucestershire GL8 8QG
Tel: 01666 881400
Headmaster: Mr Sean Price
Age range: 3–11
Fees: Day £2,680–£3,865

Wycliffe College
Bristol Road, Stonehouse, Gloucestershire GL10 2AF
Tel: 01453 822432
Senior School Head: Mr Nick Gregory BA, MEd
Age range: 3–19
No. of pupils: 696
Fees: Day £9,675–£20,985 FB £20,625–£38,115

Wynstones School
Whaddon Green, Gloucester, Gloucestershire GL4 0UF
Tel: 01452 429220
Chair of the College of Teachers: Marianna Law-Lindberg
Age range: 3–18
No. of pupils: VIth9
Fees: Day £2,820–£9,540 FB £8,160

Oxfordshire

Abingdon Preparatory School
Josca's House, Kingston Road, Frilford, Oxfordshire OX13 5NX
Tel: 01865 391570
Headmaster: Mr Craig Williams MA(Oxon), PGCE
Age range: B4–13 years

Carrdus School
Overthorpe Hall, Banbury, Oxfordshire OX17 2BS
Tel: 01295 263733
Head: Mr Edward Way
Age range: B3–8 G3–11
No. of pupils: 122
Fees: Day £735–£11,625

Chandlings
Bagley Wood, Kennington, Oxford, Oxfordshire OX1 5ND
Tel: 01865 730771
Head: Christine Cook
Age range: 2–11
Fees: Day £10,110–£15,870

Christ Church Cathedral School
3 Brewer Street, Oxford, Oxfordshire OX1 1QW
Tel: 01865 242561
Headmaster: Richard Murray
Age range: B3–13 years G3–4 years

Cokethorpe School
Witney, Oxfordshire OX29 7PU
Tel: 01993 703921
Headmaster: Mr D Ettinger BA, MA, PGCE
Age range: 4–18
No. of pupils: 666 VIth133
Fees: Day £12,600–£19,200

Cothill House
Abingdon, Oxfordshire OX13 6JL
Tel: 01865 390800
Headmaster: Mr D M Bailey
Age range: B8–13 years

CRANFORD HOUSE SCHOOL
For further details see p. 47
Moulsford, Wallingford, Oxfordshire OX10 9HT
Tel: 01491 651218
Email: admissions@cranfordhouse.net
Website: www.cranfordhouse.net
Headmaster: Dr James Raymond
Age range: 3–18 years
No. of pupils: 525
Fees: Day £3,650–£6,175

England – Central & West

Dragon School
Bardwell Road, Oxford,
Oxfordshire OX2 6SS
Tel: 01865 315405
Head: Emma Goldsmith
Age range: 4–13 years
No. of pupils: 798
Fees: Day £7,473 FB £10,931

Emmanuel Christian School
Sandford Road, Littlemore,
Oxford, Oxfordshire OX4 4PU
Tel: 01865 395236
Principal: Mrs Elizabeth Nesbitt
Age range: 3–11
No. of pupils: 43
Fees: Day £5,550

Headington Preparatory School
26 London Road, Oxford,
Oxfordshire OX3 7PB
Tel: +44 (0)1865 759116
Head: Mrs Jane Crouch BA (Hons), MA
Age range: G3–11
No. of pupils: 280

Magdalen College School
Cowley Place, Oxford,
Oxfordshire OX4 1DZ
Tel: 01865 242191
Master: Helen Pike
Age range: B7–18
No. of pupils: 669 VIth161
Fees: Day £17,799–£18,477

MOULSFORD PREPARATORY SCHOOL
For further details see p. 54
Moulsford-on-Thames,
Oxfordshire OX10 9HR
Tel: 01491 651438
Email: admissions@moulsford.com
Website: www.moulsford.com
Headmaster: Mr B Beardmore-Gray
Age range: B4–13 years
No. of pupils: 372
Fees: FB £7,850

New College School
2 Savile Road, Oxford,
Oxfordshire OX1 3UA
Tel: 01865 285 560
Head of School: Dr Matthew Jenkinson
Age range: B4–13 years
No. of pupils: 156
Fees: Day £11,100–£17,700

Our Lady's Abingdon School
Radley Road, Abingdon-on-Thames, Oxfordshire OX14 3PS
Tel: 01235 524658
Principal: Mr Stephen Oliver
Age range: 7–18 years
No. of pupils: 374 VIth61
Fees: Day £11,280–£16,815

Oxford High School GDST
Belbroughton Road, Oxford,
Oxfordshire OX2 6XA
Tel: 01865 559888
Head: Dr Helen Stringer
Age range: G4–18
No. of pupils: 900
Fees: Day £9,000–£15,546

Oxford Montessori School
Forest Farm, Elsfield, Oxford,
Oxfordshire OX3 9UW
Tel: 01865 352062
Age range: 5–10
No. of pupils: 169

Rupert House School
90 Bell Street, Henley-on-Thames, Oxfordshire RG9 2BN
Tel: 01491 574263
Headmistress: Mrs C Lynas
Age range: B4–7 G4–11
No. of pupils: 214
Fees: Day £5,640–£13,785

Rye St Antony
Pullens Lane, Oxford,
Oxfordshire OX3 0BY
Tel: 01865 762802
Headmistress: Miss A M Jones BA, PGCE
Age range: B3–11 G3–18
No. of pupils: 400 VIth70
Fees: Day £9,870–£15,330 WB £21,000–£24,690 FB £22,230–£25,935

Sibford School
Sibford Ferris, Banbury,
Oxfordshire OX15 5QL
Tel: 01295 781200
Head of School: Toby Spence
No. of pupils: VIth840
Fees: Day £9,180–£14,739 WB £26,154–£26,670 FB £28,077–£28,644

St Helen and St Katharine
Faringdon Road, Abingdon,
Oxfordshire OX14 1BE
Tel: 01235 520173
Headmistress: Mrs Rebecca Dougall BA MA
Age range: G9–18
No. of pupils: 730
Fees: Day £5,665

St Hugh's School
Carswell Manor, Faringdon,
Oxfordshire SN7 8PT
Tel: 01367 870700
Head of School: Mr James Thompson
Age range: 3–13
Fees: Day £12,285–£21,195 WB £23,655–£25,350

St John's Priory School
St John's Road, Banbury,
Oxfordshire OX16 5HX
Tel: 01295 259607
Headmistress: Tracey Wilson
Age range: 3–11
Fees: Day £6,715–£9,450

St Mary's Preparatory School
13 St Andrew's Road, Henley-on-Thames, Oxfordshire RG9 1HS
Tel: 01491 573118
Headmaster: Mr Rob Harmer (BA)Hons
Age range: 2–11 years
No. of pupils: 129
Fees: Day £4,010

Summer Fields
Mayfield Road, Oxford,
Oxfordshire OX2 7EN
Tel: 01865 454433
Headmaster: Mr David Faber MA(Oxon)
Age range: B4–13 years

The King's School, Witney
New Yatt Road, Witney,
Oxfordshire OX29 6TA
Tel: 01993 778463
Principal: Mr Matthew Cripps
Age range: 3–16 years
No. of pupils: 200
Fees: Day £6,073

The Manor Preparatory School
Faringdon Road, Abingdon,
Oxfordshire OX13 6LN
Tel: 01235 858458
Headmaster: Mr Alastair Thomas
Age range: 2–11 years
No. of pupils: 372

Windrush Valley School
The Green, London Lane,
Ascott-under-Wychwood,
Oxfordshire OX7 6AN
Tel: 01993 831793
Headteacher: Mrs Amanda Douglas
Age range: 3–11 years
No. of pupils: 120
Fees: Day £7,005–£7,341

West Berkshire

Brockhurst & Marlston House Schools
Hermitage, Newbury, West Berkshire RG18 9UL
Tel: 01635 200293
Headmaster: Mr David Fleming MA (Oxon), MSc
Age range: 2 1/2–13 years

Cheam School
Headley, Newbury, West Berkshire RG19 8LD
Tel: +44 (0)1635 268242
Headmaster: Mr Martin Harris
Age range: 3–13 years

Horris Hill
Newtown, Newbury, West Berkshire RG20 9DJ
Tel: 01635 40594
Headmaster: Dr S Bailey
Age range: B4–13 years

St Gabriel's
Sandleford Priory, Newbury, West Berkshire RG20 9BD
Tel: 01635 555680
Principal: Mr Richard Smith MA (Hons), MEd, PGCE
Age range: B6 months–11 G6 months–18
No. of pupils: 469 VIth40
Fees: Day £10,668–£17,418

St Michael's School
Harts Lane, Burghclere, Newbury, West Berkshire RG20 9JW
Tel: 01635 278137
Headmaster: Rev. Fr. John Brucciani
Age range: B5–18 G5–11

Wiltshire

Avondale School
High Street, Bulford, Salisbury,
Wiltshire SP4 9DR
Tel: 01980 632387
Head of School: Mr Ben Coombes
Age range: 2–11
Fees: Day £8,097

Chafyn Grove School
33 Bourne Avenue, Salisbury,
Wiltshire SP1 1LR
Tel: 01722 333423
Headmaster: Mr Simon Head
Age range: 3–13
No. of pupils: 265

Emmaus School
School Lane, Staverton,
Trowbridge, Wiltshire BA14 6NZ
Tel: 01225 782684
Head: Mrs M Wiltshire
Age range: 5–16
No. of pupils: 75
Fees: Day £3,500–£4,400

Godolphin Preparatory School
Laverstock Road, Salisbury,
Wiltshire SP1 2RB
Tel: 01722 430 652
Headmistress: Emma Hattersley
Age range: G3–11
No. of pupils: 100
Fees: Day £7,125–£13,935
WB £21,540 FB £25,230

Heywood Prep
The Priory, Corsham,
Wiltshire SN13 0AP
Tel: 01249 713379
Headmistress: Rebecca Mitchell
Age range: 2–11
No. of pupils: 140
Fees: Day £5,760–£8,985

Leehurst Swan School
Campbell Road, Salisbury,
Wiltshire SP1 3BQ
Tel: 01722 333094
Headmaster: Mr Terence Ayres
Age range: Reception–16 years
Fees: Day £8,985–£15,300

Maranatha Christian School
Queenlaines Farm, Sevenhampton,
Swindon, Wiltshire SN6 7SQ
Tel: 01793 762075

Meadowpark School & Nursery
The Old School House, High
Street, Cricklade, Swindon,
Wiltshire SN6 6DD
Tel: 01793 752600
Age range: 0–11 years

OneSchool Global UK Salisbury Campus
The Hollows, Wilton, Salisbury,
Wiltshire SP2 0JE
Tel: 01722 741910
Age range: 7–18 years

Pinewood School
Bourton, Swindon, Wiltshire SN6 8HZ
Tel: 01793 782205
Headmaster: Mr P J Hoyland
Age range: 3–13
No. of pupils: 313
Fees: Day £8,790–£17,895
WB £22,260

Prior Park Preparatory School
Calcutt Street, Cricklade,
Wiltshire SN6 6BB
Tel: 01793 750275
Headteacher: Guy Barrett
Age range: 2–13
No. of pupils: 240
Fees: Day £6,900–£14,460

Salisbury Cathedral School
The Old Palace, 1 The Close,
Salisbury, Wiltshire SP1 2EQ
Tel: 01722 555300
Head Master: Mr Clive Marriott BEd MA
Age range: 3–13

Sandroyd School
Rushmore, Tollard Royal,
Salisbury, Wiltshire SP5 5QD
Tel: 01725 516264
Headmaster: Mr Alastair Speers
Age range: 2–13 years

St Francis School
Marlborough Road, Pewsey,
Wiltshire SN9 5NT
Tel: 01672 563228
Headmaster: Mr David Sibson
Age range: 0–13
Fees: Day £4,821–£12,571

St Margaret's Preparatory School
Curzon Street, Calne,
Wiltshire SN11 0DF
Tel: 01249 857220
Head of School: Mr Luke Bromwich
Age range: 2–11 years
No. of pupils: 180

Stonar School
Cottles Park, Atworth,
Melksham, Wiltshire SN12 8NT
Tel: 01225 701740
Head of School: Mr Matthew Way
Age range: 2–18 years
No. of pupils: 370
Fees: Day £9,120–£17,715
FB £24,450–£36,960

Warminster School
Church Street, Warminster,
Wiltshire BA12 8PJ
Tel: +44 (0)1985 210100
Headmaster: Mr Matt Williams BA MA
Age range: 2–18 years
No. of pupils: 550
Fees: Day £5,740 FB £11,770

East

Bedfordshire D158
Cambridgeshire D158
Essex D159
Hertfordshire D160
Norfolk D161
Suffolk D162

*See also Greater London (D169) for schools in Essex and Hertfordshire

KEY TO SYMBOLS
- Boys' school
- Girls' school
- International school
- Tutorial or sixth form college
- (A) A levels
- Boarding accommodation
- (£) Bursaries
- (IB) International Baccalaureate
- Learning support
- Entrance at 16+
- Vocational qualifications
- (IAPS) Independent Association of Prep Schools
- (HMC) The Headmasters' & Headmistresses' Conference
- (ISA) Independent Schools Association
- (GSA) Girls' School Association
- (BSA) Boarding Schools' Association
- (S) Society of Heads

Unless otherwise indicated, all schools are coeducational day schools. Single-sex and boarding schools will be indicated by the relevant icon.

England – East

Bedfordshire

Bedford Girls' School
Cardington Road, Bedford,
Bedfordshire MK42 0BX
Tel: 01234 361900
Headmistress: Ms Gemma Gibson
Age range: G7–18 years

Bedford Greenacre Independent School
58-60 Shakespeare Road,
Bedford, Bedfordshire MK40 2DL
Tel: 01234 352031
Head of School: Mr Ian Daniel
Age range: 3–18 years

Bedford Modern School
Manton Lane, Bedford,
Bedfordshire MK41 7NT
Tel: 01234 332500
Headmaster: Mr Alex Tate
Age range: 7–18 years
No. of pupils: 1289
Fees: Day £10,528–£14,443

Bedford Preparatory School
De Parys Avenue, Bedford,
Bedfordshire MK40 2TU
Tel: 01234 362274
Headmaster: Mr Ian Silk
Age range: B7–13 years

King's House School
33-43 High Street, Leagrave,
Luton, Bedfordshire LU4 9JY
Tel: 01582 491430
Head of School: Mr Jade Pawaar
Age range: 4–13 years

OneSchool Global UK Biggleswade Campus
The Oaks, Potton
Road, Biggleswade,
Bedfordshire SG18 0EP
Tel: 01767 602800
Age range: 7–18 years

OneSchool Global UK Dunstable Campus
Ridgeway Avenue, Dunstable,
Bedfordshire LU5 4QL
Tel: 01582 665676
Age range: 7–18 years

Orchard School & Nursery
Higham Gobion Road,
Barton le Clay, Bedford,
Bedfordshire MK45 4RB
Tel: 01582 882054
Headmistress: Mrs Anne Burton
Age range: 0–9 years

Pilgrims Pre-Preparatory School
Brickhill Drive, Bedford,
Bedfordshire MK41 7QZ
Tel: 01234 369555
Head: Mrs J Webster
BEd(Hons), EYPS
Age range: 3 months–7 years

Polam School
45 Lansdowne Road, Bedford,
Bedfordshire MK40 2BU
Tel: 01234 261864
Head: Darren O'Neil
Age range: 1–7 years
No. of pupils: 110
Fees: Day £10,080

St George's School
28 Priory Road, Dunstable,
Bedfordshire LU5 4HR
Tel: 01582 661471
Head of School: Mr Stuart Compton
Age range: 3–11 years

Cambridgeshire

Cambridge Steiner School
Hinton Road, Fulbourn, Cambridge,
Cambridgeshire CB21 5DZ
Tel: 01223 882727
Head of School: Ms Sarah Fox
Age range: 2.5–16 years

Kimbolton School
Kimbolton, Huntingdon,
Cambridgeshire PE28 0EA
Tel: 01480 860505
Headmaster: Mr Jonathan Belbin
Age range: 4–18 years

King's College School
West Road, Cambridge,
Cambridgeshire CB3 9DN
Tel: 01223 365814
Head: Mrs Yvette Day
BMus, MMus, GDL
Age range: 4–13 years

King's Ely Acremont & Nursery
30 Egremont Street, Ely,
Cambridgeshire CB6 1AE
Tel: 01353 660700
Head of School: Ms
Faye Fenton-Stone
Age range: 2–7 years

KING'S ELY JUNIOR
For further details see p. 61
Ely, Cambridgeshire CB7 4DB
Tel: 01353 660707
Email: admissions@kingsely.org
Website: www.kingsely.org
Head: Mr Richard Whymark
Age range: 7–13 years
No. of pupils: 374
Fees: Day £15,690–£17,121
FB £25,017–£26,415

Magdalene House Preparatory School
Chapel Road, Wisbech,
Cambridgeshire PE13 1RH
Tel: 01945 583631
Senior Deputy Head, Prep School: Mrs Keryn Neaves
Age range: 3–11 years

Oaks International School
Cherry Hinton Road, Cambridge,
Cambridgeshire CB1 8DW
Tel: +44 (0) 1223 416938
Headteacher: Ms
Amanda Gibbard
Age range: 2–11 years

Sancton Wood School
2 St Paul's Road, Cambridge,
Cambridgeshire CB1 2EZ
Tel: +44 (0)1223 471703
Head of School: Mr Richard Settle
Age range: 1–16 years

St Faith's
Trumpington Road, Cambridge,
Cambridgeshire CB2 8AG
Tel: 01223 352073
Headmaster: Dr Crispin Hyde-Dunn
Age range: 4–13 years

ST JOHN'S COLLEGE SCHOOL
For further details see p. 66
73 Grange Road, Cambridge,
Cambridgeshire CB3 9AB
Tel: 01223 353652
Email: admissions@sjcs.co.uk
Website: www.sjcs.co.uk
Headmaster: Mr N. Chippington
MA(Cantab), FRCO
Age range: 4–13 years
No. of pupils: 464

St Mary's School
Bateman Street, Cambridge,
Cambridgeshire CB2 1LY
Tel: 01223 353253
Headmistress: Ms Charlotte Avery
Age range: G4–18 years

Stephen Perse Junior School, Fitzwilliam Building
Shaftesbury Road, Cambridge,
Cambridgeshire CB2 8AA
Tel: 01223 454700 (Ext:2000)
Age range: 5–11 years

Stephen Perse Nurseries & Early Years
Cambridge Road,
Madingley, Cambridge,
Cambridgeshire CB23 8AH
Tel: 01223 454700 (Ext:5000)
Age range: 1–5 years

The Perse Pelican Pre-Prep & Nursery
92 Glebe Road, Cambridge,
Cambridgeshire CB1 7TD
Tel: 01223 403940
Head: Ms Francesca Heftman
Age range: 3–7 years

The Perse Prep School
Trumpington Road, Cambridge,
Cambridgeshire CB2 8EX
Tel: 01223 403920
Head: Mr James Piper
Age range: 7–11 years

The Peterborough School
Thorpe Road, Peterborough,
Cambridgeshire PE3 6AP
Tel: 01733 343357
Headmaster: Mr A D
Meadows BSc(Hons)
Age range: 6 weeks–18 years
No. of pupils: 440
Fees: Day £11,028–£17,061

Whitehall School
117 High Street, Somersham,
Cambridgeshire PE28 3EH
Tel: 01487 840966
Head of School: Chris Holmes
Age range: 6 months–11 years

England – East

Essex

Alleyn Court School
Wakering Road, Southend-on-Sea, Essex SS3 0PW
Tel: 01702 582553
Headmaster: Mr Rupert W.J. Snow B.Ed, NPQH
Age range: 2.5–11 years

BRENTWOOD PREPARATORY SCHOOL
For further details see p. 56
Shenfield Road, Brentwood, Essex CM15 8BD
Tel: +44 (0)1277 243300
Email: prepadmissions@brentwood.essex.sch.uk
Website: www.brentwoodschool.co.uk
Headmaster: Mr Jason Whiskerd
Age range: 3–11 years
No. of pupils: 591

Colchester High School
Wellesley Road, Colchester, Essex CO3 3HD
Tel: 01206 573389
Headteacher: Ms Karen Gracie-Langrick
Age range: 2–16 years
No. of pupils: 320
Fees: Day £9,465–£13,620

Coopersale Hall School
Flux's Lane, off Stewards Green Road, Epping, Essex CM16 7PE
Tel: 01992 577133
Headmistress: Miss Kaye Lovejoy
Age range: 2–11
No. of pupils: 275
Fees: Day £10,350–£10,575

Elm Green Preparatory School
Parsonage Lane, Little Baddow, Chelmsford, Essex CM3 4SU
Tel: 01245 225230
Principal: Ms Ann Milner
Age range: 4–11
No. of pupils: 220
Fees: Day £8,844

Felsted Preparatory School
Felsted, Great Dunmow, Essex CM6 3JL
Tel: 01371 822610
Headmaster: Mr Simon James
Age range: 4–13 years

Gosfield School
Cut Hedge Park, Halstead Road, Gosfield, Halstead, Essex CO9 1PF
Tel: 01787 474040
Headteacher: Mr Guy Martyn
Age range: 4–18
No. of pupils: VIth21
Fees: Day £6,690–£15,525

HEATHCOTE SCHOOL
For further details see p. 58
Eves Corner, Danbury, Chelmsford, Essex CM3 4QB
Tel: 01245 223131
Email: enquiries@heathcoteschool.co.uk
Website: www.heathcoteschool.co.uk
Head of School: Mrs Samantha Scott
Age range: 2–11 years
No. of pupils: 105
Fees: Day £9,450

Herington House School
1 Mount Avenue, Hutton, Brentwood, Essex CM13 2NS
Tel: 01277 211595
Principal: Mr R. Dudley-Cooke
Age range: 3–11
No. of pupils: 130
Fees: Day £1,955–£3,865

Holmwood House Preparatory School
Chitts Hill, Lexden, Colchester, Essex CO3 9ST
Tel: 01206 574305
Headmaster: Alexander Mitchell
Age range: 4–13
No. of pupils: 302
Fees: Day £10,140–£17,895 FB £35

Littlegarth School
Horkesley Park, Nayland, Colchester, Essex CO6 4JR
Tel: 01206 262332
Headmaster: Mr Peter H Jones
Age range: 2–11 years
No. of pupils: 318
Fees: Day £3,205–£3,723

Maldon Court Preparatory School
Silver Street, Maldon, Essex CM9 4QE
Tel: 01621 853529
Headteacher: Elaine Mason
Age range: 3–11
Fees: Day £8,236

New Hall School
The Avenue, Boreham, Chelmsford, Essex CM3 3HS
Tel: 01245 467588
Principal: Mrs Katherine Jeffrey MA, BA, PGCE, MA(Ed Mg), NPQH
Age range: 1–18 years
No. of pupils: 1400
Fees: Day £9,621–£20,502 WB £18,234–£28,026 FB £21,177–£32,472

OneSchool Global UK Colchester Campus
Sudbury Road, Stoke By Nayland, Colchester, Essex CO6 4RW
Tel: 01206 264210
Age range: 7–18 years

Oxford House School
2-4 Lexden Road, Colchester, Essex CO3 3NE
Tel: 01206 576686
Head Teacher: Mrs Sarah Leyshon
Age range: 2–11
No. of pupils: 158

Saint Nicholas School
Hillingdon House, Hobbs Cross Road, Harlow, Essex CM17 0NJ
Tel: 01279 429910
Headmaster: Mr D Bown
Age range: 4–16
No. of pupils: 400
Fees: Day £9,960–£12,660

Saint Pierre School
16 Leigh Road, Leigh-on-Sea, Southend-on-Sea, Essex SS9 1LE
Tel: 01702 474164
Headmaster: Mr Peter Spencer-Lane
Age range: 2 1/2–11 years

ST CEDD'S SCHOOL
For further details see p. 65
178a New London Road, Chelmsford, Essex CM2 0AR
Tel: 01245 392810
Email: info@stcedds.org.uk
Website: www.stcedds.org.uk
Head: Mr Matthew Clarke
Age range: 3–11 years
No. of pupils: 400
Fees: Day £9,240–£11,820

St John's School
Stock Road, Billericay, Essex CM12 0AR
Tel: 01277 623070
Head Teacher: Mrs F Armour BEd(Hons)
Age range: 2–16 years
No. of pupils: 392
Fees: Day £5,328–£13,500

St Margaret's Preparatory School
Hall Drive, Gosfield, Halstead, Essex CO9 1SE
Tel: 01787 472134
Headteacher: Mrs Carolyn Moss
Age range: 2–11 years
Fees: Day £3,240–£4,055

St Mary's School
Lexden Road, Colchester, Essex CO3 3RB
Tel: 01206 572544 Admissions: 01206 216420
Principal: Mrs H K Vipond MEd, BSc(Hons), NPQH
Age range: B3–4 G3–16
No. of pupils: 430
Fees: Day £6,855–£14,985

St Michael's Church Of England Preparatory School
198 Hadleigh Road, Leigh-on-Sea, Southend-on-Sea, Essex SS9 2LP
Tel: 01702 478719
Head: Steve Tompkins BSc(Hons), PGCE, MA, NPQH
Age range: 3–11
No. of pupils: 271
Fees: Day £4,104–£9,600

St Philomena's Catholic School
Hadleigh Road, Frinton-on-Sea, Essex CO13 9HQ
Tel: 01255 674492
Head of School: Mrs P Mathews ACIS, BA Hons, PGCE, MA, NPQH
Age range: 4–11
Fees: Day £6,240–£7,500

St. Anne's Preparatory School
154 New London Road, Chelmsford, Essex CM2 0AW
Tel: 01245 353488
Head of School: Valerie Eveleigh
Age range: 3–11 years

Stephen Perse Junior School, Dame Bradbury's School
Ashdon Road, Saffron Walden, Essex CB10 2AL
Tel: 01223 454700 (Ext: 4000)
Age range: 1–11 years

The Christian School (Takeley)
Dunmow Road, Brewers End, Takeley, Bishop's Stortford, Essex CM22 6QH
Tel: 01279 871182
Headmaster: M E Humphries
Age range: 3–16
Fees: Day £6,012–£8,436

Thorpe Hall School
Wakering Road, Southend-on-Sea, Essex SS1 3RD
Tel: 01702 582340
Headmaster: Mr Andrew Hampton
Age range: 2–16 years
No. of pupils: 359
Fees: Day £9,000–£12,600

Ursuline Preparatory School
Old Great Ropers, Great Ropers Lane, Warley, Brentwood, Essex CM13 3HR
Tel: 01277 227152
Headmistress: Mrs Pauline Wilson MSc
Age range: 3–11
Fees: Day £6,450–£12,015

England – East

Widford Lodge Preparatory School
Widford Road, Chelmsford, Essex CM2 9AN
Tel: 01245 352581
Headteacher: Miss Michelle Cole A.C.I.B. – P.G.C.E.
Age range: 2 1/2–11 years

Woodlands School, Great Warley
Warley Street, Great Warley, Brentwood, Essex CM13 3LA
Tel: 01277 233288
Head: Mr David Bell
Age range: 3 months–11 years

Woodlands School, Hutton Manor
428 Rayleigh Road, Hutton, Brentwood, Essex CM13 1SD
Tel: 01277 245585
Head: Paula Hobbs
Age range: 3 months–11 years

Hertfordshire

ABBOT'S HILL SCHOOL
For further details see p. 55
Bunkers Lane, Hemel Hempstead, Hertfordshire HP3 8RP
Tel: 01442 240333
Email: registrar@abbotshill.herts.sch.uk
Website: www.abbotshill.herts.sch.uk
Headmistress: Mrs K Gorman BA, MEd (Cantab)
Age range: G4–16 years
No. of pupils: 482

Aldenham School
Elstree, Hertfordshire WD6 3AJ
Tel: 01923 858122
Head of School: Mr Andrew Williams
Age range: 3–18

Aldwickbury School
Wheathampstead Road, Harpenden, Hertfordshire AL5 1AD
Tel: 01582 713022
Headmaster: Mr V W Hales
Age range: B4–13 years

Beechwood Park School
Markyate, St Albans, Hertfordshire AL3 8AW
Tel: 01582 840333
Headmaster: Mr E Balfour BA (Hons), PGCE
Age range: 3–13 years

Berkhamsted School
Overton House, 131 High Street, Berkhamsted, Hertfordshire HP4 2DJ
Tel: 01442 358001
Principal: Mr Richard Backhouse MA(Cantab)
Age range: 3–18 years
No. of pupils: 2001 VIth408
Fees: Day £10,830–£22,170 WB £29,850 FB £35,610

Bishop's Stortford College Prep School
Maze Green Road, Bishop's Stortford, Hertfordshire CM23 2PQ
Tel: 01279 838583
Head of the Prep School: Mr Bill Toleman
Age range: 4–13 years

Charlotte House Preparatory School
88 The Drive, Rickmansworth, Hertfordshire WD3 4DU
Tel: 01923 772101
Head: Miss P Woodcock
Age range: G3–11
No. of pupils: 140
Fees: Day £3,432–£12,102

Duncombe School
4 Warren Park Road, Bengeo, Hertford, Hertfordshire SG14 3JA
Tel: 01992 414100
Headmaster: Mr Jeremy Phelan M.A. (Ed)
Age range: 2–11 years
No. of pupils: 301
Fees: Day £10,380–£14,565

Edge Grove School
Aldenham Village, Hertfordshire WD25 8NL
Tel: 01923 855724
Head of School: Miss Lisa McDonald
Age range: 3–13 years
No. of pupils: 501

Egerton Rothesay School
Durrants Lane, Berkhamsted, Hertfordshire HP4 3UJ
Tel: 01442 865275
Headteacher: Mr Colin Parker BSc(Hons), Dip.Ed (Oxon), PGCE, C.Math MIMA
Age range: 6–19

Gurukula - The Hare Krishna Primary School
Hartspring Cottage, Elton Way, Watford, Hertfordshire WD25 8HB
Tel: 01923 851 005
Head of School: Ms Gunacuda Dasi (Gwyneth Milan)
Age range: 4–12 years

Haberdashers' Aske's School for Girls
Aldenham Road, Elstree, Borehamwood, Hertfordshire WD6 3BT
Tel: 020 8266 2300
Head of School: Ms Rose Hardy
Age range: G4–18
No. of pupils: 1190
Fees: Day £17,826–£19,311

Heath Mount School
Woodhall Park, Watton-at-Stone, Hertford, Hertfordshire SG14 3NG
Tel: 01920 830230
Headmaster: Mr Chris Gillam BEd(Hons)
Age range: 3–13 years
No. of pupils: 492 B270 G222
Fees: Day £12,435–£19,185

High Elms Manor School
High Elms Lane, Watford, Hertfordshire WD25 0JX
Tel: 01923 681 103
Headmistress: Ms Liadain O'Neill BA (Hons), AMI 0-3, AMI 3-6, Early Years FdA Dist.+
Age range: 2–12
No. of pupils: 100
Fees: Day £10,500–£12,675

HOWE GREEN HOUSE SCHOOL
For further details see p. 59
Great Hallingbury, Bishop's Stortford, Hertfordshire CM22 7UF
Tel: 01279 657706
Email: schooloffice@howegreenhouse.essex.sch.uk
Website: www.howegreenhouseschool.co.uk
Headmistress: Ms Deborah Mills BA (Hons) Q.T.S
Age range: 2–11 years
No. of pupils: 177
Fees: Day £433–£4,313

KINGSHOTT
For further details see p. 62
Stevenage Road, St Ippolyts, Hitchin, Hertfordshire SG4 7JX
Tel: 01462 432009
Email: admissions@kingshottschool.com
Website: www.kingshottschool.com
Headmaster: Mr David Weston
Age range: 3–13 years
No. of pupils: 400
Fees: Day £6,555–£14,115

Little Acorns Montessori School
Lincolnsfield Centre, Bushey Hall Drive, Bushey, Hertfordshire WD23 2ER
Tel: 01923 230705
Head of School: Lola Davies BPA, AMIDip
Age range: 12 months–6
No. of pupils: 28
Fees: Day £2,120

Lochinver House School
Heath Road, Little Heath, Potters Bar, Hertfordshire EN6 1LW
Tel: 01707 653064
Headmaster: Mr Ben Walker BA(Hons)
Age range: B4–13 years
No. of pupils: 345
Fees: Day £12,060–£15,840

Lockers Park
Lockers Park Lane, Hemel Hempstead, Hertfordshire HP1 1TL
Tel: 01442 251712
Headmaster: Mr Gavin Taylor
Age range: B4–13 years
No. of pupils: 171
Fees: Day £11,505–£18,225 WB £26,325

Longwood School
Bushey Hall Drive, Bushey, Hertfordshire WD23 2QG
Tel: 01923 253715
Head Teacher: Claire May
Age range: 3 months–11
Fees: Day £3,705–£7,800

Manor Lodge School
Rectory Lane, Ridge Hill, Shenley, Hertfordshire WD7 9BG
Tel: 01707 642424
Head of School: Mrs A Lobo BEd(Hons)
Age range: 3–11
No. of pupils: 427
Fees: Day £11,100–£12,300

Merchant Taylors' Prep
Moor Farm, Sandy Lodge Road, Rickmansworth, Hertfordshire WD3 1LW
Tel: 01923 825648
Headmaster: Dr Karen McNerney BSc (Hons), PGCE, MSc, EdD
Age range: B3–13 years

England – East

Radlett Preparatory School
Kendal Hall, Watling Street,
Radlett, Hertfordshire WD7 7LY
Tel: 01923 856812
Principal: Mr M Pipe BA Hons, QTS
Age range: 4–11

Sherrardswood School
Lockleys, Welwyn,
Hertfordshire AL6 0BJ
Tel: 01438 714282
Headmistress: Mrs Anna Wright
Age range: 2–18
No. of pupils: 357
Fees: Day £10,383–£16,113

St Albans High School for Girls
Townsend Avenue, St Albans,
Hertfordshire AL1 3SJ
Tel: 01727 853800
Headmistress: Amber Waite
Age range: G4–18
No. of pupils: 940 VIth170

St Christopher School
Barrington Road, Letchworth,
Hertfordshire SG6 3JZ
Tel: 01462 650 850
Head: Richard Palmer
Age range: 3–18
No. of pupils: 511 VIth78
Fees: Day £4,590–£18,075 WB £19,950–£24,675 FB £31,650

St Edmund's College & Prep School
Old Hall Green, Nr Ware,
Hertfordshire SG11 1DS
Tel: 01920 824247
Headmaster: Mr Matthew Mostyn BA (Hons) MA (Ed)
Age range: 3–18
No. of pupils: 852
Fees: Day £9,882–£18,345 WB £24,165–£27,630 FB £28,302–£32,460

St Edmund's Prep
Old Hall Green, Ware,
Hertfordshire SG11 1DS
Tel: 01920 824239
Head: Mr Steven Cartwright BSc (Surrey)
Age range: 3–11
No. of pupils: 185
Fees: Day £10,650–£13,365

St Francis' College
Broadway, Letchworth Garden City, Hertfordshire SG6 3PJ
Tel: 01462 670511
Headmistress: Mrs B Goulding
Age range: G3–18
No. of pupils: 460 VIth75
Fees: Day £9,990–£16,980 WB £22,350–£26,475 FB £27,990–£31,995

St Hilda's
High Street, Bushey,
Hertfordshire WD23 3DA
Tel: 020 8950 1751
Headmistress: Miss Sarah-Jane Styles MA
Age range: B2–4 G2–11
Fees: Day £12,012–£12,843

St Hilda's School
28 Douglas Road, Harpenden,
Hertfordshire AL5 2ES
Tel: 01582 712307
Headmaster: Mr Dan Sayers
Age range: G2.5–11 years
No. of pupils: 150
Fees: Day £3,154–£4,115

St Joseph's In The Park
St Mary's Lane, Hertingfordbury,
Hertford, Hertfordshire SG14 2LX
Tel: 01992 513810
Head of School: Mr Douglas Brown
Age range: 3–11
No. of pupils: 150
Fees: Day £5,718–£16,899

St Margaret's School, Bushey
Merry Hill Road, Bushey,
Hertfordshire WD23 1DT
Tel: +44 (0)20 8416 4400
Headteacher: Lara Péchard
Age range: 2–18 years
No. of pupils: 530

St. John's Prep. School
The Ridgeway, Potters Bar,
Hertfordshire EN6 5QT
Tel: +44 (0)1707 657294
Head Teacher: Mrs C Tardios
Age range: 4–11

Stanborough School
Stanborough Park, Garston,
Watford, Hertfordshire WD25 9JT
Tel: 01923 673268
Acting Head Teacher: Ms Eileen Hussey
Age range: 3–17
No. of pupils: 300
Fees: Day £6,630–£10,224 WB £10,350–£13,995

Stormont
The Causeway, Potters Bar,
Hertfordshire EN6 5HA
Tel: 01707 654037
Head Teacher: Miss Louise Martin
Age range: G4–11
Fees: Day £12,300–£13,050

The Haberdashers' Aske's Boys' School
Butterfly Lane, Elstree,
Borehamwood,
Hertfordshire WD6 3AF
Tel: 020 8266 1700
Headmaster: Gus Lock MA (Oxon)
Age range: B5–18 years
No. of pupils: 1428
Fees: Day £15,339–£20,346

The King's School
Elmfield, Ambrose Lane,
Harpenden, Hertfordshire AL5 4DU
Tel: 01582 767566
Principal: Mr Clive John Case BA, HDE
Age range: 4–16
Fees: Day £7,680

The Purcell School, London
Aldenham Road, Bushey,
Hertfordshire WD23 2TS
Tel: 01923 331100
Headteacher: Dr Bernard Trafford
Age range: 10–18
No. of pupils: 180
Fees: Day £25,707 FB £32,826

Tring Park School for the Performing Arts
Mansion Drive, Tring,
Hertfordshire HP23 5LX
Tel: 01442 824255
Principal: Mr Stefan Anderson MA, ARCM, ARCT
Age range: 8–19 years
No. of pupils: 370 VIth171
Fees: Day £15,405–£24,885 FB £26,190–£37,605

Westbrook Hay Prep School
London Road, Hemel Hempstead,
Hertfordshire HP1 2RF
Tel: 01442 256143
Headmaster: Mark Brain
Age range: 3–13 years
No. of pupils: 340
Fees: Day £10,905–£15,690

YORK HOUSE SCHOOL
For further details see p. 70
Sarratt Road, Croxley Green, Rickmansworth,
Hertfordshire WD3 4LW
Tel: 01923 772395
Email: yhsoffice@york-house.com
Website: www.york-house.com
Headmaster: Mr Jon Gray BA(Ed)
Age range: 3–13 years
No. of pupils: 395
Fees: Day £3,876–£5,164

Norfolk

All Saints School
School Road, Lessingham,
Norwich, Norfolk NR12 0DJ
Tel: 01692 582083
Head of School: Samantha Dangerfield
Age range: 7–16
Fees: Day £3,600–£5,400

Beeston Hall School
Beeston Regis, West Runton,
Cromer, Norfolk NR27 9NQ
Tel: 01263 837324
Headmaster: Mr Fred de Falbe BA(Hons) PGCE
Age range: 4–13
Fees: Day £8,550–£17,730 FB £18,360–£23,820

Downham Preparatory School & Montessori Nursery
The Old Rectory, Stow Bardolph,
Kings Lynn, Norfolk PE34 3HT
Tel: 01366 388066
Principal: Mrs E J Laffeaty-Sharpe
Age range: 3 months–13 years

Glebe House School
2 Cromer Road, Hunstanton,
Norfolk PE36 6HW
Tel: 01485 532809
Headmaster: Mr Crofts
Age range: 0–13
No. of pupils: 110
Fees: Day £8,316–£13,290

England – East

Gresham's Nursery and Pre-Prep School
Market Place, Holt,
Norfolk NR25 6BB
Tel: 01263 714575
Head: Ms Sarah Hollingsworth
Age range: 2–7 years

Gresham's Prep School
Cromer Road, Holt,
Norfolk NR25 6EY
Tel: 01263 714600
Head: Mrs Cathy Braithwaite
Age range: 7–13
No. of pupils: 240
Fees: Day £15,120–£18,630 FB £26,100

Langley Preparatory School at Taverham Hall
Taverham, Norwich,
Norfolk NR8 6HU
Tel: 01603 868206
Headmaster: Mr Mike A Crossley NPQH, BEd(Hons)
Age range: 2–13
Fees: Day £10,275–£14,175 WB £18,315

Norwich High School for Girls GDST
95 Newmarket Road,
Norwich, Norfolk NR2 2HU
Tel: 01603 453265
Headmistress: Mrs Kirsty von Malaise
Age range: G3–18
No. of pupils: VIth120
Fees: Day £9,198–£14,562

Norwich School
70 The Close, Norwich,
Norfolk NR1 4DD
Tel: 01603 728430
Head Master: Steffan D A Griffiths
Age range: 4–18
No. of pupils: 1065
Fees: Day £10,998–£16,212

Norwich Steiner School
Hospital Lane, Norwich,
Norfolk NR1 2HW
Tel: 01603 611175
Headteacher: Mr Andrew Vestrini
Age range: 3–18
No. of pupils: 91
Fees: Day £3,830–£7,010

NOTRE DAME PREPARATORY SCHOOL
For further details see p. 63
147 Dereham Road,
Norwich, Norfolk NR2 3TA
Tel: 01603 625593
Email: admissions@notredameprepschool.co.uk
Website: www.notredameprepschool.co.uk
Headmaster: Mr Rob Thornton MA
Age range: 2–11 years

OneSchool Global UK Swaffham Campus
Turbine Way, Swaffham,
Norfolk PE37 7XD
Tel: 01760 336939
Age range: 7–18 years

Riddlesworth Hall Preparatory School
Hall Lane, Diss, Norfolk IP22 2TA
Tel: 01953 681 246
Acting Headmaster: Mr A Bentley
Age range: 2–13
Fees: Day £6,435–£8,970 FB £18,000–£20,100

Thetford Grammar School
Bridge Street, Thetford,
Norfolk IP24 3AF
Tel: 01842 752840
Headmaster: Mr Michael Brewer
Age range: 3–18
No. of pupils: 200
Fees: Day £8,250–£13,665

Town Close School
14 Ipswich Road, Norwich,
Norfolk NR2 2LR
Tel: 01603 620180
Headteacher: Mr Chris Wilson
Age range: 3–13 years
No. of pupils: 450
Fees: Day £3,081–£4,673

WYMONDHAM COLLEGE PREP SCHOOL
For further details see p. 68
Golf Links Road, Wymondham,
Norfolk NR18 9SZ
Tel: 01953 609000 (option 3)
Email: admin@wymondhamcollegeprepschool.org
Website: www.wymondhamcollegeprepschool.org
Headteacher: Mr Jon Timmins
Age range: 4–11 years
No. of pupils: 150
Fees: FB £12,165

Suffolk

Barnardiston Hall Preparatory School
Barnardiston, Nr Haverhill,
Suffolk CB9 7TG
Tel: 01440 786316
Headmaster: Lt Col K A Boulter MA(Cantab)
Age range: 6 months–13 years
No. of pupils: 220
Fees: Day £8,235–£13,725 WB £18,975 FB £20,580

Brookes UK
Flempton Road, Risby, Bury St Edmunds, Suffolk IP28 6QJ
Tel: 01284 760531
Director: Mr D Rose
Age range: 2–16 years

Culford Preparatory School
Culford, Bury St Edmunds,
Suffolk IP28 6TX
Tel: 01284 385383
Head of School: Mrs Claire Bentley
Age range: 7–13
No. of pupils: 240
Fees: Day £12,375–£16,215 FB £23,970–£25,755

Culford Pre-Preparatory School
Fieldgate House, Bury St Edmunds, Suffolk IP28 6TX
Tel: 01284 385412
Head of School: Mrs Claire Bentley
Age range: 1–7
Fees: Day £9,475–£10,200

FAIRSTEAD HOUSE SCHOOL
For further details see p. 57
Fairstead House, Fordham Road,
Newmarket, Suffolk CB8 7AA
Tel: 01638 662318
Email: secretary@fairsteadhouse.co.uk
Website: www.fairsteadhouseschool.co.uk
Head of School: Mr Michael Radford
Age range: 3 months–11 years
No. of pupils: 95
Fees: Day £10,704–£11,934

Finborough School
The Hall, Great Finborough,
Stowmarket, Suffolk IP14 3EF
Tel: 01449 773600
Principal: Mr Steven Clark
Age range: 2–18 years
Fees: Day £9,630–£14,880 WB £18,030–£24,150 FB £22,440–£30,090

Framlingham College
College Road, Framlingham,
Suffolk IP13 9EY
Tel: 01728 723789
Headmaster: Mrs Louise North
Age range: 2–18
No. of pupils: 700
Fees: Day £8,409–£19,176 FB £29,823

Framlingham College Prep School
Brandeston, Suffolk IP13 7AH
Tel: +44 (0)1728 685331
Head of Prep School: Matthew King
Age range: 3–13
No. of pupils: 265
Fees: Day £9,129–£15,888 FB £23,906

Ipswich High School
Woolverstone, Ipswich,
Suffolk IP9 1AZ
Tel: 01473 780201
Head of School: Mr Mark Howe
Age range: 3–18 years
No. of pupils: 450
Fees: Day £10,300–£16,285 FB £34,650

IPSWICH PREP SCHOOL
For further details see p. 60
3 Ivry Street, Ipswich,
Suffolk IP1 3QW
Tel: 01473 282800
Email: prepenquiries@ipswich.school
Website: www.ipswich.school
Headmistress: Amanda Childs
Age range: 0–11 years
No. of pupils: 353
Fees: Day £10,914–£13,410

England – East

OLD BUCKENHAM HALL SCHOOL
For further details see p. 64
Old Buckenham Hall, Brettenham Park, Ipswich, Suffolk IP7 7PH
Tel: 01449 740252
Email: admissions@obh.co.uk
Website: www.obh.co.uk
Headmaster: Mr David Griffiths
Age range: 3–13 years
No. of pupils: 242
Fees: Day £6,947 FB £9,052

Orwell Park School
Nacton, Ipswich, Suffolk IP10 0ER
Tel: 01473 659225
Headmaster: Mr Adrian Brown MA(Cantab)
Age range: 2 1/2–13 years
No. of pupils: 270

Saint Felix School
Halesworth Road, Southwold, Suffolk IP18 6SD
Tel: 01502 722175
Headmaster: Mr. James Harrison
Age range: 2–18
No. of pupils: 312 VIth65
Fees: Day £7,485–£16,185 WB £17,670–£22,470 FB £23,370–£28,170

South Lee Preparatory School
Nowton Road, Bury St Edmunds, Suffolk IP33 2BT
Tel: 01284 754654
Headmaster: Mr Mervyn Watch BEd (Hons)
Age range: 2–13
Fees: Day £9,645–£11,820

St Joseph's College
Belstead Road, Ipswich, Suffolk IP2 9DR
Tel: 01473 690281
Principal: Mrs Danielle Clarke
Age range: 3–18

Stoke College
Stoke-by-Clare, Sudbury, Suffolk CO10 8JE
Tel: 01787 278141
Head: Dr Gareth P Lloyd
Age range: 3–18
Fees: Day £6,132–£14,979 WB £20,829–£24,231 FB £27,096–£31,518

Summerhill School
Leiston, Suffolk IP16 4HY
Tel: 01728 830540
Principal: Mrs Zoe Readhead
Age range: 5–17
No. of pupils: 69
Fees: Day £5,475–£11,205 FB £12,069–£19,041

The Old School Henstead
Toad Row, Beccles, Suffolk NR34 7LG
Tel: 01502 741150
Head: Mr W J McKinney
Age range: 2–11
No. of pupils: 123
Fees: Day £6,990–£10,077

Woodbridge School
Burkitt Road, Woodbridge, Suffolk IP12 4JH
Tel: +44 (0)1394 615000
Acting Head: Miss Shona Norman
Age range: 4–18
No. of pupils: 901
Fees: Day £9,741–£16,505 FB £30,885

Woodbridge School Prep
Church Street, Woodbridge, Suffolk IP12 1DS
Tel: +44 (0)1394 382673
Head of School: Mrs N Mitchell
Age range: 4–11

East Midlands

Derbyshire D166
Leicestershire D166
Lincolnshire D167
Northamptonshire D167
Nottinghamshire D168
Rutland D168

KEY TO SYMBOLS
- Boys' school
- Girls' school
- International school
- Tutorial or sixth form college
- A levels
- Boarding accommodation
- Bursaries
- International Baccalaureate
- Learning support
- Entrance at 16+
- Vocational qualifications
- (IAPS) Independent Association of Prep Schools
- (HMC) The Headmasters' & Headmistresses' Conference
- (ISA) Independent Schools Association
- (GSA) Girls' School Association
- (BSA) Boarding Schools' Association
- (S) Society of Heads

Unless otherwise indicated, all schools are coeducational day schools. Single-sex and boarding schools will be indicated by the relevant icon.

England – East Midlands

Derbyshire

Barlborough Hall School
Park Street, Barlborough,
Chesterfield, Derbyshire S43 4ES
Tel: 01246 810511
Headteacher: Mrs Karen Keeton
Age range: 3–11 years

Dame Catherine Harpur's School
Rose Lane, Ticknall, Derby,
Derbyshire DE73 7JW
Tel: 01332 862792
Head: Ms Whyte
Age range: 3–11
No. of pupils: 28
Fees: Day £4,794

Derby Grammar School
Rykneld Hall, Rykneld Road, Littleover, Derby,
Derbyshire DE23 4BX
Tel: 01332 523027
Head: Dr Ruth Norris
Age range: B7–18 G16–18
No. of pupils: 255
Fees: Day £8,823–£13,449

Derby High School
Hillsway, Littleover, Derby,
Derbyshire DE23 3DT
Tel: 01332 514267
Headteacher: Mrs Amy Chapman
Age range: 3–18

Emmanuel School
Juniper Lodge, 43 Kedleston Road,
Derby, Derbyshire DE22 1FP
Tel: 01332 340505
Headteacher: Mr Ben Snowdon
Age range: 3–16

Normanton House School
Normanton House, Village Street,
Derby, Derbyshire DE23 8DF
Tel: 01332 769333
Head of School: Mrs Nazia Iqbal
Age range: 5–16

Ockbrook School
The Settlement, Ockbrook,
Derby, Derbyshire DE72 3RJ
Tel: 01332 673532
Head: Mr Tom Brooksby
Age range: 2–18
No. of pupils: 409 VIth55
Fees: Day £8,955–£13,170

Old Vicarage School
11 Church Lane, Darley Abbey,
Derby, Derbyshire DE22 1EW
Tel: 01332 557130
Headmaster: Mr M J Adshead
Age range: 3–13
No. of pupils: 95
Fees: Day £7,650–£8,124

Repton Prep
Milton, Derby, Derbyshire DE65 6EJ
Tel: 01283 707100
Headmaster: Mr R Relton
Age range: 3–13 years

S. Anselm's School
Stanedge Road, Bakewell,
Derbyshire DE45 1DP
Tel: 01629 812734
Headmaster: Peter Phillips BA (Hons), MA, PGCE (SPLD), NPQH
Age range: 3–13
No. of pupils: 215
Fees: Day £10,950–£20,700 FB £26,100

St Peter & St Paul School
Brambling House, Hady Hill,
Chesterfield, Derbyshire S41 0EF
Tel: 01246 278522
Headteacher: Mrs Jill Phinn
Age range: 3 months–11 years
No. of pupils: 120
Fees: Day £8,658–£9,159

St Wystan's School
High Street, Repton,
Derbyshire DE65 6GE
Tel: 01283 703258
Head Teacher: Ms Kara Lebihan
Age range: 3–11
Fees: Day £4,500–£8,655

Watchorn Christian School
Watchorn Church, Derby Road,
Alfreton, Derbyshire DE55 7AQ
Tel: 07387 721877

Leicestershire

Al-Aqsa Schools Trust
The Wayne Way, Leicester,
Leicestershire LE5 4PP
Tel: 0116 2760953
Headteacher: Mrs Amina Patel
Age range: 5–16
No. of pupils: 231

Brooke House Day School
Croft Road, Cosby, Leicester,
Leicestershire LE9 1SE
Tel: 0116 286 7372
Head: Mrs Joy Parker
Age range: 3–16 years

Fairfield Prep School
Leicester Road, Loughborough,
Leicestershire LE11 2AE
Tel: 01509 215172
Headmaster: Mr Andrew Earnshaw
Age range: 3–11 years
No. of pupils: 530

Jameah Girls Academy
49 Rolleston Street, Leicester,
Leicestershire LE5 3SD
Tel: 0116 262 7745
Headteacher: Ms Erfana Bora
Age range: G6–16
No. of pupils: 142

Leicester Grammar Junior School
London Road, Great Glen,
Leicester, Leicestershire LE8 9FL
Tel: 0116 259 1950
Head of School: Mrs S Ashworth Jones
Age range: 3–11 years
No. of pupils: 391
Fees: Day £11,493–£12,212

Leicester High School for Girls
454 London Road, Leicester,
Leicestershire LE2 2PP
Tel: 0116 2705338
Headmaster: Mr Alan Whelpdale
Age range: G3–18
No. of pupils: 435 VIth60
Fees: Day £2,995–£4,065

Leicester Islamic Academy
320 London Road, Leicester,
Leicestershire LE2 2PJ
Tel: 01162 705343
Headteacher: Mrs S Khan
Age range: 3–11

Leicester Prep School
2 Albert Road, Leicester,
Leicestershire LE2 2AA
Tel: 0116 2707414
Headmaster: Paul Hitchcock
Age range: 3–11
No. of pupils: 130
Fees: Day £7,800

Loughborough Amherst School
Gray Street, Loughborough,
Leicestershire LE11 2DZ
Tel: 01509 263901
Headmaster: Dr Julian Murphy
Age range: 4–18 years
No. of pupils: 305

Ratcliffe College
Fosse Way, Ratcliffe on the Wreake,
Leicester, Leicestershire LE7 4SG
Tel: +44 (0)1509 817000
Headmaster: Mr J Reddin BSc, MSc, NPQH
Age range: 3–18

St Crispin's School
4-6 St Mary's Road, Stoneygate,
Leicester, Leicestershire LE2 1XA
Tel: 0116 2707648
Head Master: Andrew Atkin
Age range: 2–16 years

Stoneygate School
6 London Road, Great Glen,
Leicester, Leicestershire LE8 9DJ
Tel: 0116 259 2282
Headmaster: Mr J F Dobson
Age range: 4–16 years
No. of pupils: 180
Fees: Day £11,469–£14,379

The Dixie Grammar School
Station Road, Market Bosworth,
Leicestershire CV13 0LE
Tel: 01455 292244
Headmaster: Richard Lynn MA
Age range: 3–18
No. of pupils: 474 VIth71
Fees: Day £8,835–£12,015

England – East Midlands

Lincolnshire

Ayscoughfee Hall School
Welland Hall, London Road,
Spalding, Lincolnshire PE11 2TE
Tel: 01775 724733
Headmistress: Mrs Clare Ogden BA(Hons), PGCE
Age range: 3–11
No. of pupils: 146
Fees: Day £4,560–£6,720

Bicker Preparatory School & Early Years
School Lane, Bicker, Boston, Lincolnshire PE20 3DW
Tel: 01775 821786
Head of School: Ms Anne Daynes BEd Hons
Age range: 3–11 years

Copthill Independent Day School
Barnack Road, Uffington, Stamford, Lincolnshire PE9 3AD
Tel: 01780 757506
Headmaster: Mr J A Teesdale BA(Hons), PGCE
Age range: 2–11
No. of pupils: 300
Fees: Day £9,255–£10,350

Dudley House School
1 Dudley Road, Grantham, Lincolnshire NG31 9AA
Tel: 01476 400184
Headmistress: Mrs Jenny Johnson
Age range: 3–11
No. of pupils: 50
Fees: Day £5,220

Grantham Preparatory International School
Gorse Lane, Grantham, Lincolnshire NG31 7UF
Tel: +44 (0)1476 593293
Headmistress: Mrs K A Korcz
Age range: 3–11
No. of pupils: 140
Fees: Day £9,786

Greenwich House School
106 High Holme Road, Louth, Lincolnshire LN11 0HE
Tel: 01507 609252
Headmistress: Mrs J Brindle
Age range: 9 months–11 years

Handel House Preparatory School
The Northolme, Gainsborough, Lincolnshire DN21 2JB
Tel: 01427 612426
Headmistress: Mrs Victoria Haigh
Age range: 2–11

Kirkstone House School
Main Street, Baston, Peterborough, Lincolnshire PE6 9PA
Tel: 01778 560350
Head: Mrs C Jones BSocSc
Age range: 3–18
No. of pupils: 234
Fees: Day £9,498–£11,640

Lincoln Minster School
Upper Lindum Street, Lincoln, Lincolnshire LN2 5RW
Tel: 01522 551300
Head of School: Mrs Maria Young
Age range: 4–18 years
No. of pupils: 500

St George's Preparatory School & Little Dragons Nursery
126 London Road, Boston, Lincolnshire PE21 7HB
Tel: 01205 317600
Headteacher: Mrs Sarah Whelan B.Ed (Hons) EYPS

St Hugh's School
Cromwell Avenue, Woodhall Spa, Lincolnshire LN10 6TQ
Tel: 01526 352169
Head: C Ward BEd(Hons)
Age range: 2–13
No. of pupils: 195
Fees: Day £8,880–£14,928 FB £18,750

Stamford Junior School
Kettering Road, Stamford, Lincolnshire PE9 2LR
Tel: 01780 484400
Headteacher: Mr Matthew O'Reilly
Age range: 2–11 years

Viking School
140 Church Road North, Skegness, Lincolnshire PE25 2QJ
Tel: 01754 765749
Principal: Mrs S J Barker
Age range: 3–11
No. of pupils: 100
Fees: Day £4,050–£4,350

Witham Hall Preparatory School
Witham-on-the-Hill, Bourne, Lincolnshire PE10 0JJ
Tel: +44(0)1778 590222
Headmaster: Mr Charles Welch B.Ed (Hons)
Age range: 4–13
No. of pupils: 250
Fees: Day £9,555–£16,080 FB £21,690

Northamptonshire

Beachborough School
Westbury, Nr. Brackley, Northamptonshire NN13 5LB
Tel: 01280 700071
Headmaster: Mr Christian Pritchard
Age range: 2–13 years
No. of pupils: 400
Fees: Day £3,190–£5,970

Laxton Junior School
East Road, Oundle, Northamptonshire PE8 4BX
Tel: 01832 277159
Head of School: Mr Sam Robertson
Age range: 4–11
No. of pupils: 260
Fees: Day £9,720–£14,115

Maidwell Hall
Maidwell, Northampton, Northamptonshire NN6 9JG
Tel: 01604 686234
Headmaster: Mr R A Lankester MA, PGCE
Age range: 4–13
Fees: FB £27,966

Northampton High School GDST
Newport Pagnell Road, Hardingstone, Northampton, Northamptonshire NN4 6UU
Tel: 01604 765765
Headmistress: Adele O'Doherty
Age range: G2–18 years
No. of pupils: 600
Fees: Day £3,346–£4,918

OneSchool Global UK Northampton Campus
Billing Road East, Northampton, Northamptonshire NN3 3LF
Tel: 01604 633819
Age range: 7–18 years

Overstone Park School
Overstone Park, Overstone, Northampton, Northamptonshire NN6 0DT
Tel: 01604 643787
Principal: Mrs M F Brown BA(Hons), PGCE
Age range: 0–18
No. of pupils: 85

Pitsford School
Pitsford Hall, Pitsford, Northampton, Northamptonshire NN6 9AX
Tel: 01604 880306
Headteacher: Dr Craig Walker
Age range: 3–18 years
Fees: Day £8,751–£15,183

Quinton House School
Upton Hall, Upton, Northampton, Northamptonshire NN5 4UX
Tel: 01604 752050
Headteacher: Mr Tim Hoyle
Age range: 2–18 years
No. of pupils: 390
Fees: Day £8,040–£11,985

SPRATTON HALL
For further details see p. 72
Smith Street, Spratton, Northamptonshire NN6 8HP
Tel: 01604 847292
Email: registrar@sprattonhall.com
Website: www.sprattonhall.com
Head Master: Mr Simon Clarke
Age range: 4–13 years
No. of pupils: 380
Fees: Day £10,725–£16,275

St Peter's School
52 Headlands, Kettering, Northamptonshire NN15 6DJ
Tel: 01536 512066
Head of School: Mark Thomas
Age range: 2–11
No. of pupils: 161

Wellingborough School
Wellingborough, Northamptonshire NN8 2BX
Tel: 01933 222427
Headmaster: Mr A N Holman
Age range: 3–18
No. of pupils: VIth145
Fees: Day £9,420–£15,990

Winchester House School
High Street, Brackley, Northamptonshire NN13 7AZ
Tel: 01280 702483
Head: Ms Antonia Lee
Age range: 3–13 years

England – East Midlands

Nottinghamshire

Colston Bassett Preparatory School
School Lane, Colston bassett, Nottingham, Nottinghamshire NG12 3FD
Tel: 01949 81118
Headteacher: Mrs C Newcombe
Age range: 4–11
Fees: Day £7,098

Coteswood House Pre-school & Day Nursery
19 Thackeray's Lane, Woodthorpe, Nottingham, Nottinghamshire NG5 4HT
Tel: 0115 9676551
Age range: 2–5 years

Fig Tree Primary School
30 Bentinck Road, Nottingham, Nottinghamshire NG7 4AF
Tel: 0115 978 8152
Head of School: Mrs Nabeela Hussain
Age range: 5–11

Highfields School
London Road, Newark, Nottinghamshire NG24 3AL
Tel: 01636 704103
Head of School: Mrs S H Lyons
Age range: 2–11
No. of pupils: 140
Fees: Day £10,080

Hollygirt School
Elm Avenue, Nottingham, Nottinghamshire NG3 4GF
Tel: 0115 958 0596
Headmistress: Mrs Pam Hutley BA(Hons), PGCE, MSc
Age range: 3–16
No. of pupils: 200
Fees: Day £9,300–£12,234

Iona School
310 Sneinton Dale, Nottingham, Nottinghamshire NG3 7DN
Tel: 01159 415295
Chair of College: Richard Moore
Age range: 3–11
Fees: Day £6,724

Jamia Al-Hudaa Residential College
Forest House, Berkeley Avenue, Mapperley Park, Nottingham, Nottinghamshire NG3 5TT
Tel: 0115 9690800
Principal: Raza ul-Haq Siakhvy
Age range: 11–19
No. of pupils: 224

Nottingham Girls' High School GDST
9 Arboretum Street, Nottingham, Nottinghamshire NG1 4JB
Tel: 0115 9417663
Head: Miss Julie Keller
Age range: G3–18
No. of pupils: 691
Fees: Day £9,873–£14,016

Nottingham High Infant and Junior School
Waverley Mount, Nottingham, Nottinghamshire NG7 4ED
Tel: 0115 978 6056
Age range: 4–11 years
No. of pupils: 1158
Fees: Day 10,986–16,047

OneSchool Global UK Nottingham Campus
Wellington Street, Long Eaton, Nottingham, Nottinghamshire NG10 4HR
Tel: 0115 973 3568
Age range: 7–18 years

Plumtree School
Church Hill, Plumtree, Nottingham, Nottinghamshire NG12 5ND
Tel: 0115 937 5859
Head Teacher: Phil Simpson
Age range: 3–11
Fees: Day £6,540

Salterford House School
Salterford Lane, Calverton, Nottingham, Nottinghamshire NG14 6NZ
Tel: 0115 9652127
Head: Ms Kimberley Venables
Age range: 3–11
No. of pupils: 124
Fees: Day £7,800–£7,890

Saville House School
11 Church Street, Mansfield Woodhouse, Mansfield, Nottinghamshire NG19 8AH
Tel: 01623 625068
Joint Head: Mrs See & Mrs Hill
Age range: 3–11
No. of pupils: 89
Fees: Day £5,475

St Joseph's School
33 Derby Road, Nottingham, Nottinghamshire NG1 5AW
Tel: 0115 9418356
Head Teacher: Mr Ashley Crawshaw
Age range: 1–11
Fees: Day £7,728

The Orchard School
South Leverton, Retford, Nottinghamshire DN22 0DJ
Tel: 01427 880395
Principal: Mrs S M Fox BA, PGCE
Age range: 5–16
No. of pupils: 150
Fees: Day £4,770–£7,575

Wellow House School
Wellow, Newark, Nottinghamshire NG22 0EA
Tel: 01623 861054
Principal: Kirsty Lamb
Age range: 3–13
No. of pupils: 152
Fees: Day £7,485–£11,985

Worksop College Preparatory School, Ranby House
Retford, Nottinghamshire DN22 8HX
Tel: 01777 714387 (Admissions)
Headmaster: C S J Pritchard MA, BA(Hons), QTS
Age range: 3–11 years
No. of pupils: 190
Fees: Day £8,385–£13,485 FB £19,485–£20,085

Rutland

Brooke Priory School
Station Approach, Oakham, Rutland LE15 6QW
Tel: 01572 724778
Headmaster: Mr R Outwin-Flinders BEd (Hons)
Age range: 2–11
No. of pupils: 193
Fees: Day £7,395–£9,195

Greater London

Essex D170
Hertfordshire D170
Kent D171
Middlesex D171
Surrey D172

*See also East (D157) for schools in Essex and Hertfordshire; South-East (D193) for schools in Kent and Surrey

KEY TO SYMBOLS

- ♂ Boys' school
- ♀ Girls' school
- 🌐 International school
- 16· Tutorial or sixth form college
- Ⓐ A levels
- Boarding accommodation
- £ Bursaries
- IB International Baccalaureate
- Learning support
- 16· Entrance at 16+
- Vocational qualifications
- (IAPS) Independent Association of Prep Schools
- (HMC) The Headmasters' & Headmistresses' Conference
- (ISA) Independent Schools Association
- (GSA) Girls' School Association
- (BSA) Boarding Schools' Association
- (S) Society of Heads

Unless otherwise indicated, all schools are coeducational day schools. Single-sex and boarding schools will be indicated by the relevant icon.

England – Greater London

Essex

Al-Noor Primary School
619-629 Green Lane, Goodmayes, Ilford, Essex IG3 9RP
Tel: 020 8597 7576
Headteacher: Mrs Someera Butt
Age range: 4-10

Avon House Preparatory School
490 High Road, Woodford Green, Essex IG8 0PN
Tel: 020 8504 1749
Headteacher: Mrs Amanda Campbell
Age range: 3-11
No. of pupils: 268
Fees: Day £3,530-£3,950

Bancroft's School
High Road, Woodford Green, Essex IG8 0RF
Tel: 020 8505 4821
Head: Mr Simon Marshall MA, PGCE (Cantab), MA, MPhil (Oxon)
Age range: 7-18
No. of pupils: 1120 VIth247

Beehive Preparatory School
233 Beehive Lane, Redbridge, Ilford, Essex IG4 5ED
Tel: 020 8550 3224
Head Teacher: Mr Jamie Gurr
Age range: 4-11

Braeside School
130 High Road, Buckhurst Hill, Essex IG9 5SD
Tel: 020 8504 1133
Headmistress: Ms Chloe Moon
Age range: G3-16
Fees: Day £3,200-£4,400

Chigwell School
High Road, Chigwell, Essex IG7 6QF
Tel: 020 8501 5700
Headmaster: Mr M E Punt M.A. M.Sc. P.G.C.E.
Age range: 4-18
Fees: Day £4,250-£6,295 FB £10,995

Daiglen School
68 Palmerston Road, Buckhurst Hill, Essex IG9 5LG
Tel: 020 8504 7108
Headteacher: Mrs P Dear
Age range: 3-11 years
Fees: Day £3,375-£3,425

Eastcourt Independent School
1-5 Eastwood Road, Goodmayes, Ilford, Essex IG3 8UW
Tel: 020 8590 5472
Headmistress: Mrs Christine Redgrave BSc(Hons), DipEd, MEd
Age range: 4-11 years
No. of pupils: 220
Fees: Day £2,600

Gidea Park Preparatory School & Nursery
2 Balgores Lane, Gidea Park, Romford, Essex RM2 5JR
Tel: 01708 740381
Head of School: Mr Callum Douglas
Age range: 2-11 years
No. of pupils: 100
Fees: Day £10,775

Guru Gobind Singh Khalsa College
Roding Lane, Chigwell, Essex IG7 6BQ
Tel: 020 8559 9160
Principal: Mr Amarjit Singh Toor BSc(Hons), BSc, BT
Age range: 3-19
Fees: Day £5,892-£6,720

Immanuel School
Havering Grange, Havering Road, Romford, Essex RM1 4HR
Tel: 01708 764449
Head of School: Mr Simon Reeves
Age range: 3-16

Loyola Preparatory School
103 Palmerston Road, Buckhurst Hill, Essex IG9 5NH
Tel: 020 8504 7372
Headmistress: Mrs K R Anthony
Age range: B3-11 years
No. of pupils: 200
Fees: Day £11,085

Maytime Montessori Nursery - Cranbrook Road
341 Cranbrook Road, Ilford, Essex IG1 4UF
Tel: 020 8554 3079

Maytime Montessori Nursery - Eastwood Road
2 Eastwood Road, Goodmayes, Essex IG3 8XB
Tel: 020 8599 3744

Maytime Montessori Nursery - Wanstead Road
293 Wanstead Park Rd, Ilford, Essex IG1 3TR
Tel: 020 8554 6344
Age range: 0-6

Oakfields Preparatory School
Harwood Hall, Harwood Hall Lane, Upminster, Essex RM14 2YG
Tel: 01708 220117
Headmistress: Katrina Carroll
Age range: 2-11 years
No. of pupils: 202
Fees: Day £10,296-£11,121

Oaklands School
8 Albion Hill, Loughton, Essex IG10 4RA
Tel: 020 8508 3517
Group Managing Principal: Mr M Hagger
Age range: 2-16
No. of pupils: 243
Fees: Day £10,350-£10,575

Park School for Girls
20-22 Park Avenue, Ilford, Essex IG1 4RS
Tel: 020 8554 2466
Head Teacher: Mrs Androulla Nicholas BSc Hons (Econ) PGCE
Age range: G4-16
No. of pupils: 160
Fees: Day £2,375-£3,580

St Aubyn's School
Bunces Lane, Woodford Green, Essex IG8 9DU
Tel: 020 8504 1577
Headmaster: Mr Leonard Blom BEd(Hons) BA NPQH
Age range: 3-13 years

St Mary's Hare Park School & Nursery
South Drive, Gidea Park, Romford, Essex RM2 6HH
Tel: 01708 761220
Headteacher: Mr Ludovic Bernard
Age range: 2-11
No. of pupils: 180
Fees: Day £8,775

The Ursuline Preparatory School Ilford
2-8 Coventry Road, Ilford, Essex IG1 4QR
Tel: 020 8518 4050
Headteacher: Mrs Victoria McNaughton
Age range: G3-11
No. of pupils: 159
Fees: Day £7,320-£9,828

WOODFORD GREEN PREPARATORY SCHOOL
For further details see p. 79
Glengall Road, Woodford Green, Essex IG8 0BZ
Tel: 020 8504 5045
Email: admissions@wgprep.co.uk
Website: www.wgprep.co.uk
Headmaster: Mr J P Wadge
Age range: 3-11 years
No. of pupils: 385
Fees: Day £3,725

Hertfordshire

Lyonsdown School
3 Richmond Road, New Barnet, Barnet, Hertfordshire EN5 1SA
Tel: 020 8449 0225
Acting Co-Heads: Rittu Hall & Julia Windsor
Age range: G3-11 years
No. of pupils: 180
Fees: Day £3,681-£11,766

The Royal Masonic School for Girls
Rickmansworth Park, Rickmansworth, Hertfordshire WD3 4HF
Tel: 01923 773168
Headmaster: Mr Kevin Carson M.Phil (Cambridge)
Age range: G4-18
No. of pupils: 930 VIth165
Fees: Day £11,475-£17,475 WB £20,115-£27,495 FB £21,225-£29,835

England – Greater London

Kent

Ashgrove School
116 Widmore Road,
Bromley, Kent BR1 3BE
Tel: 020 8460 4143
Principal: Dr Patricia Ash CertEd,
BSc(Hons), PhD, CMath, FIMA
Age range: 3–11 years

Babington House School
Grange Drive, Chislehurst,
Kent BR7 5ES
Tel: 020 8467 5537
Headmaster: Mr Tim Lello
MA, FRSA, NPQH
Age range: 3–18
No. of pupils: 432

**BENEDICT HOUSE
PREPARATORY SCHOOL**
For further details see p. 74
1-5 Victoria Road, Sidcup,
Kent DA15 7HD
Tel: 020 8300 7206
Email: secretary@
benedicthouseprepschool.
co.uk
Website: www.benedict
houseprepschool.co.uk
Headteacher: Mr Craig Wardle
Age range: 3–11 years

Bickley Park School
24 Page Heath Lane, Bickley,
Bromley, Kent BR1 2DS
Tel: 020 8467 2195
Headmaster: Mr Patrick Wenham
Age range: B2 1/2–13
years G2 1/2–4 years

Bishop Challoner School
228 Bromley Road, Shortlands,
Bromley, Kent BR2 0BS
Tel: 020 8460 3546
Headteacher: Mrs Paula Anderson
Age range: 3–18
No. of pupils: 340
Fees: Day £3,150–£4,500

**Breaside Preparatory
School**
41-43 Orchard Road,
Bromley, Kent BR1 2PR
Tel: 020 8460 0916
Executive Principal: Mrs Karen A
Nicholson B.Ed, NPQH, Dip EYs
Age range: 2 1/2–11 years
No. of pupils: 376
Fees: Day £11,580–£13,494

Bromley High School GDST
Blackbrook Lane, Bickley,
Bromley, Kent BR1 2TW
Tel: 020 8781 7000/1
Head: Mrs A M Drew
BA(Hons), MBA (Dunelm)
Age range: G4–18

Farringtons Junior School
Perry Street, Chislehurst,
Kent BR7 6LR
Tel: 020 8467 0395
Head of Junior School:
Jack Charlton
Age range: 3–11 years

**MERTON COURT
PREPARATORY SCHOOL**
For further details see p. 78
38 Knoll Road, Sidcup,
Kent DA14 4QU
Tel: 020 8300 2112
Email: office@
mertoncourtprep.co.uk
Website: mertoncourtprep.co.uk
Headmaster: Mr Dominic
Price BEd, MBA
Age range: 3–11 years
No. of pupils: 320
Fees: Day £3,095–£4,675

**St Christopher's
The Hall School**
49 Bromley Road,
Beckenham, Kent BR3 5PA
Tel: 020 8650 2200
Headmaster: Mr A Velasco
MEd, BH(Hons), PGCE
Age range: 3–11
No. of pupils: 305
Fees: Day £3,750–£9,165

St. David's Prep
Justin Hall,, Beckenham Road,
West Wickham, Kent BR4 0QS
Tel: 020 8777 5852
Principal: Mrs J Foulger
Age range: 4–11
No. of pupils: 155
Fees: Day £5,850–£8,550

West Lodge School
36 Station Road, Sidcup,
Kent DA15 7DU
Tel: 020 8300 2489
Head Teacher: Mr Robert Francis
Age range: 3–11
No. of pupils: 163
Fees: Day £5,475–£9,150

Wickham Court School
Schiller International,
Layhams Road, West
Wickham, Kent BR4 9HW
Tel: 020 8777 2942
Principal: Mrs Samantha Da Costa
Age range: 2–16
No. of pupils: 121
Fees: Day £6,983.40–£12,344.55

Middlesex

**ACS Hillingdon
International School**
Hillingdon Court, 108 Vine
Lane, Hillingdon, Uxbridge,
Middlesex UB10 0BE
Tel: +44 (0) 1895 259 771
Head of School: Mr Martin Hall
Age range: 4–18

Alpha Preparatory School
21 Hindes Road, Harrow,
Middlesex HA1 1SH
Tel: 020 8427 1471
Head: Mr P Fahy
Age range: 3–11 years

Ashton House School
50-52 Eversley Crescent,
Isleworth, Middlesex TW7 4LW
Tel: 020 8560 3902
Headteacher: Mrs Angela Stewart
Age range: 3–11 years

**Buckingham
Preparatory School**
458 Rayners Lane, Pinner,
Harrow, Middlesex HA5 5DT
Tel: 020 8866 2737
Head of School: Mrs Sarah Hollis
Age range: B3–11 years G3–4 years

Buxlow Preparatory School
5/6 Castleton Gardens,
Wembley, Middlesex HA9 7QJ
Tel: 020 8904 3615
Headteacher: Mr Ralf Furse
Age range: 2–11
Fees: Day £8,970–£9,330

**Hampton Prep and
Pre-Prep School**
Gloucester Road, Hampton,
Middlesex TW12 2UQ
Tel: 020 8979 1844
Headmaster: Mr Tim Smith
Age range: 3–11 years

Holland House School
1 Broadhurst Avenue, Edgware,
Middlesex HA8 8TP
Tel: 020 8958 6979
Headteacher: Mrs Emily Brown
Age range: 4–11
No. of pupils: 147

Jack and Jill School
30 Nightingale Road, Hampton,
Middlesex TW12 3HX
Tel: 020 8979 3195
Principal: Miss K Papirnik BEd(Hons)
Age range: B2–5 G2–7
No. of pupils: 155
Fees: Day £4,608–£13,143

**Lady Eleanor Holles
(Junior Department)**
177 Uxbridge Road, Hampton
Hill, Middlesex TW12 1BD
Tel: 020 8979 2173
Head of School: Mrs Paula Mortimer
Age range: G7–11
Fees: Day £17,229

Newland House School
Waldegrave Park, Twickenham,
Middlesex TW1 4TQ
Tel: 020 8865 1234
Headmaster: Mr D A Alexander
Age range: B3–13 G3–11
No. of pupils: 425
Fees: Day £3,848–£4,306

**North London
Collegiate School**
Canons, Canons Drive,
Edgware, Middlesex HA8 7RJ
Tel: +44 (0)20 8952 0912
Headmistress: Mrs Sarah Clark
Age range: G4–18 years
No. of pupils: 1080
Fees: Day £5,956–£7,049

**Northwood College
for Girls GDST**
Maxwell Road, Northwood,
Middlesex HA6 2YE
Tel: 01923 825446
Head of School: Mrs
Rebecca Brown
Age range: G3–18 years
No. of pupils: 844

Orley Farm School
South Hill Avenue, Harrow,
Middlesex HA1 3NU
Tel: 020 8869 7600
Headmaster: Mr Tim Calvey
Age range: 4–13 years

**Quainton Hall
School & Nursery**
91 Hindes Road, Harrow,
Middlesex HA1 1RX
Tel: 020 8861 8861
Headmaster: S Ford BEd
(Hons), UWE Bristol
Age range: B2–13 G2–11
Fees: Day £11,850–£13,050

England – Greater London

Radnor House
Pope's Villa, Cross Deep,
Twickenham, Middlesex TW1 4QG
Tel: 020 8891 6264
Head: Mr Darryl Wideman
MA Oxon, PGCE
Age range: 9–18

Reddiford School
36-38 Cecil Park, Pinner,
Middlesex HA5 5HH
Tel: 020 8866 0660
Headteacher: Mrs J
Batt CertEd, NPQH
Age range: 3–11
No. of pupils: 320
Fees: Day £4,860–£11,565

Roxeth Mead School
Buckholt House, 25 Middle Road,
Harrow, Middlesex HA2 0HW
Tel: 020 8422 2092
Headmistress: Mrs A Isaacs
Age range: 3–7
No. of pupils: 54
Fees: Day £4,800–£10,665

ST CATHERINE'S PREP
For further details see p. 76
Cross Deep, Twickenham,
Middlesex TW1 4QJ
Tel: 020 8891 2898
Email: info@stcatherineschool.co.uk
Website: www.stcatherineschool.co.uk
Headmistress: Mrs Johneen McPherson MA
Age range: G4–11 years
No. of pupils: 102
Fees: Day £12,480–£13,470

St Christopher's School
71 Wembley Park Drive,
Wembley, Middlesex HA9 8HE
Tel: 020 8902 5069
Headteacher: Mr G. P. Musetti
Age range: 4–11
Fees: Day £9,006–£9,906

St Helen's College
Parkway, Hillingdon, Uxbridge,
Middlesex UB10 9JX
Tel: 01895 234371
Head: Mrs. Shirley Drummond
BA, PGCert, MLDP, FCCT
Age range: 2–11 years
No. of pupils: 380
Fees: Day £10,200–£12,600

St Helen's School
Eastbury Road, Northwood,
Middlesex HA6 3AS
Tel: +44 (0)1923 843210
Headmistress: Dr Mary Short BA, PhD
Age range: G3–18
No. of pupils: VIth165

St John's School
Potter Street Hill, Northwood,
Middlesex HA6 3QY
Tel: 020 8866 0067
Headmaster: Mr Sean Robinson
Age range: B3–13 years

St Martin's School
40 Moor Park Road, Northwood,
Middlesex HA6 2DJ
Tel: 01923 825740
Headmaster: Mr S Dunn BEd (Hons)
Age range: B3–13 years

St. Catherine's School
Cross Deep, Twickenham,
Middlesex TW1 4QJ
Tel: 020 8891 2898
Headmistress: Mrs Johneen McPherson MA
Age range: G4–18 years
No. of pupils: 449
Fees: Day £12,480–£16,125

Tashbar of Edgware
Mowbray Road, Edgware,
Middlesex HA8 8JL
Age range: B3–11

The Hall Pre-Preparatory School & Nursery
The Grange Country House,
Rickmansworth Road,
Northwood, Middlesex HA6 2RB
Tel: 01923 822807
Headmistress: Mrs S M Goodwin
Age range: 1–7
Fees: Day £4,650–£9,900

The Mall School
185 Hampton Road, Twickenham,
Middlesex TW2 5NQ
Tel: 0208 977 2523
Headmaster: Mr D C Price BSc, MA
Age range: B4–11 years

The St Michael Steiner School
Park Road, Hanworth Park,
London, Middlesex TW13 6PN
Tel: 0208 893 1299
Age range: 3–16 (17 from Jul 2014)
No. of pupils: 101
Fees: Day £3,850–£9,500

Twickenham Preparatory School
Beveree, 43 High Street,
Hampton, Middlesex TW12 2SA
Tel: 020 8979 6216
Headmaster: Mr Oliver Barrett
Age range: B4–13 years G4–11 years

Surrey

Al-Khair School
109-117 Cherry Orchard Road,
Croydon, Surrey CR0 6BE
Tel: 020 8662 8664
Headteacher: Mrs Aisha Chaudhry
Age range: 5–16 years

Broomfield House School
Broomfield Road, Kew Gardens,
Richmond, Surrey TW9 3HS
Tel: 020 8940 3884
Head Teacher: Mr N O York
BA(Hons), MA, MPhil, FRSA
Age range: 3–11
No. of pupils: 160
Fees: Day £4,389–£15,054

Collingwood School
3 Springfield Road, Wallington,
Surrey SM6 0BD
Tel: 020 8647 4607
Headmaster: Mr Leigh Hardie
Age range: 3–11 years

Croydon High School GDST
Old Farleigh Road, Selsdon,
South Croydon, Surrey CR2 8YB
Tel: 020 8260 7500
Headmistress: Mrs Emma Pattison
Age range: G3–18
No. of pupils: 580 VIth75

Cumnor House Kindergarten & PreSchool, South Croydon
91 Pampisford Road, South
Croydon, Surrey CR2 6DH
Tel: 020 8660 4480
Head of School: Miss Emma Edwards
Age range: 2–4 years

Cumnor House School for Boys
168 Pampisford Road, South
Croydon, Surrey CR2 6DA
Tel: 020 8645 2614
Headmaster: Mr Daniel Cummings
Age range: B2–13 years
No. of pupils: 423
Fees: Day £3,880–£4,655

Cumnor House School for Girls
1 Woodcote Lane, Purley,
Surrey CR8 3HB
Tel: 020 8668 0050
Headmistress: Mrs Amanda McShane
Age range: G4–11 years

Date Valley School Trust
Mitcham Court, Cricket Green,
Mitcham, Surrey CR4 4LB
Tel: +44 (0)20 8648 4647
Headteacher: Neena Lone
Age range: 3–11

Educare Small School
12 Cowleaze Road, Kingston
upon Thames, Surrey KT2 6DZ
Tel: 020 8547 0144
Head Teacher: Mrs E Steinthal
Age range: 3–11
No. of pupils: 46
Fees: Day £6,240

Elmhurst School
44-48 South Park Hill Rd, South
Croydon, Surrey CR2 7DW
Tel: 020 8688 0661
Head Teacher: Mr Tony Padfield
Age range: B3–11 years

Falcons Prep Richmond
41 Kew Foot Road, Richmond,
Surrey TW9 2SS
Tel: 020 8948 9490
Headmistress: Ms Olivia Buchanan
Age range: B7–13
Fees: Day £14,250–£17,835

HOLY CROSS PREPARATORY SCHOOL
For further details see p. 73
George Road, Kingston upon
Thames, Surrey KT2 7NU
Tel: 020 8942 0729
Email: secretary@holycrossprep.com
Website: www.holycrossprepschool.co.uk
Headteacher: Mrs S Hair BEd(Hons)
Age range: G3–11 years

Homefield Preparatory School
Western Road, Sutton,
Surrey SM1 2TE
Tel: 0208 642 0965
Headmaster: Mr John Towers
Age range: B4–13 years
No. of pupils: 350
Fees: Day £6,345–£13,650

England – Greater London

Kew College
24-26 Cumberland Road,
Kew, Surrey TW9 3HQ
Tel: 020 8940 2039
Head: Mrs Jane Bond
BSc, MA(Ed), PGCE
Age range: 3–11 years
No. of pupils: 296
£ ✎

Kew Green Preparatory School
Layton House, Ferry Lane, Kew Green, Richmond, Surrey TW9 3AF
Tel: 020 8948 5999
Headmaster: Mr J Peck
Age range: 4–11
No. of pupils: 280
Fees: Day £6,120
✎

King's House School
68 King's Road, Richmond,
Surrey TW10 6ES
Tel: 020 8940 1878
Head: Mr Mark Turner
BA, PGCE, NPQH
Age range: B3–13 years G3–4 years
No. of pupils: 460
Fees: Day £1,860–£6,190
♂ Ⓐ ✎

Laleham Lea School
29 Peaks Hill, Purley, Surrey CR8 3JJ
Tel: 020 8660 3351
Headteacher: Ms K Barry
Age range: 3–11 years
No. of pupils: 131
Fees: Day £9,207
£ ✎

Oakwood Independent School
Godstone Road, Purley,
Surrey CR8 2AN
Tel: 020 8668 8080
Headmaster: Mr Ciro Candia BA(Hons), PGCE
Age range: 3–11
No. of pupils: 176
Fees: Day £9,030–£9,840
£

Old Palace of John Whitgift School
Old Palace Road, Croydon,
Surrey CR0 1AX
Tel: 020 8688 2027
Head: Mrs. C Jewell
Age range: G3–18 years
No. of pupils: 650
Fees: Day £3,300–£5,536
♂ Ⓐ £

Old Vicarage School
46-48 Richmond Hill,
Richmond, Surrey TW10 6QX
Tel: 020 8940 0922
Headmistress: Mrs G D Linthwaite
Age range: G3–11 years
No. of pupils: 200
Fees: Day £5,200
♂

Park Hill School
8 Queens Road, Kingston upon Thames, Surrey KT2 7SH
Tel: 020 8546 5496
Headmaster: Mr Alistair Bond
Age range: 2–11
No. of pupils: 100
Fees: Day £10,440
✎

Rokeby School
George Road, Kingston upon Thames, Surrey KT2 7PB
Tel: 020 8942 2247
Head: Mr J R Peck
Age range: B4–13 years
♂ ✎

Royal Russell Junior School
Coombe Lane, Croydon,
Surrey CR9 5BX
Tel: 020 8651 5884
Junior School Headmaster:
Mr James C Thompson
Age range: 3–11
No. of pupils: 300
Fees: Day £11,160–£14,220

Seaton House School
67 Banstead Road South,
Sutton, Surrey SM2 5LH
Tel: 020 8642 2332
Headmistress: Mrs Debbie Morrison Higher Diploma in Education (RSA)
Age range: B3–5 G3–11
No. of pupils: 164
Fees: Day £10,188
♂

Shrewsbury House School
107 Ditton Road, Surbiton,
Surrey KT6 6RL
Tel: 020 8399 3066
Executive Head: Ms Joanna Hubbard MA BA(Hons) PGCE PGDipSEN
Age range: B7–13 years
♂ ✎

St David's School
23/25 Woodcote Valley Road,
Purley, Surrey CR8 3AL
Tel: 020 8660 0723
Headmistress: Cressida Mardell
Age range: 3–11
No. of pupils: 167
Fees: Day £6,375–£10,650
£ ✎

Staines Preparatory School
3 Gresham Road, Staines-upon-Thames, Surrey TW18 2BT
Tel: 01784 450909
Head of School: Ms Samantha Sawyer B.Ed (Hons), M.Ed, NPQH
Age range: 3–11 years
No. of pupils: 307
Fees: Day £10,560–£12,660
£ ✎

Surbiton High School
13-15 Surbiton Crescent, Kingston upon Thames, Surrey KT1 2JT
Tel: 020 8546 5245
Principal: Mrs Rebecca Glover
Age range: B4–11 G4–18
No. of pupils: 1210 VIth186
Fees: Day £10,857–£17,142
♂ Ⓐ £ ✎

Sutton High School GDST
55 Cheam Road, Sutton,
Surrey SM1 2AX
Tel: 020 8642 0594
Headmistress: Mrs Katharine Crouch
Age range: G3–18
No. of pupils: 600 VIth60
Fees: Day £10,095–£17,043
♂ Ⓐ £ ✎

The Study School
57 Thetford Road, New Malden, Surrey KT3 5DP
Tel: 020 8942 0754
Head of School: Mrs Donna Brackstone-Drake
Age range: 3–11
No. of pupils: 134
Fees: Day £4,860–£11,388

Unicorn School
238 Kew Road, Richmond,
Surrey TW9 3JX
Tel: 020 8948 3926
Headmaster: Mr Kit Thompson
Age range: 3–11
Fees: Day £7,170–£13,170
£ ✎

Westbury House
80 Westbury Road, New Malden, Surrey KT3 5AS
Tel: 020 8942 5885
Head of School: Matthew Burke
Age range: 3–11
Fees: Day £4,860–£11,115

London

Central London D176
East London D176
North London D176
North-West London D177
South-East London D179
South-West London D180
West London D182

KEY TO SYMBOLS
- Boys' school
- Girls' school
- International school
- Tutorial or sixth form college
- A levels
- Boarding accommodation
- Bursaries
- International Baccalaureate
- Learning support
- Entrance at 16+
- Vocational qualifications
- (IAPS) Independent Association of Prep Schools
- (HMC) The Headmasters' & Headmistresses' Conference
- (ISA) Independent Schools Association
- (GSA) Girls' School Association
- (BSA) Boarding Schools' Association
- (S) Society of Heads

Unless otherwise indicated, all schools are coeducational day schools. Single-sex and boarding schools will be indicated by the relevant icon.

England – London

Central London

Charterhouse Square School
40 Charterhouse Square,
London EC1M 6EA
Tel: 020 7600 3805
Head of School: Mrs Caroline Lloyd BEd (Hons)
Age range: 3–11 years

City of London School for Girls
St Giles' Terrace, Barbican,
London EC2Y 8BB
Tel: 020 7847 5500
Headmistress: Mrs E Harrop
Age range: G7–18
No. of pupils: 725

Dallington School
8 Dallington Street, Islington,
London EC1V 0BW
Tel: 020 7251 2284
Headteacher: Maria Blake
Age range: 3–11
No. of pupils: 103
Fees: Day £11,490–£14,490

ST PAUL'S CATHEDRAL SCHOOL
For further details see p. 85
2 New Change,
London EC4M 9AD
Tel: 020 7248 5156
Email: admissions@spcs.london.sch.uk
Website: www.spcslondon.com
Headmaster: Simon Larter-Evans BA (Hons), PGCE, FRSA
Age range: 4–13 years
No. of pupils: 258
Fees: Day £15,174–£16,338 FB £9,178

The Lyceum School
65 Worship Street,
London EC2A 2DU
Tel: +44 (0)20 7247 1588
Head of School: Ms Hilary Wyatt NPQH, MA, PGCE
Age range: 3–11
Fees: Day £16,185

East London

Al-Falah Primary School
48 Kenninghall Road,
Hackney, London E5 8BY
Tel: 020 8985 1059
Headteacher: Mr M A Hussain
Age range: 5–11

Al-Mizan School
46 Whitechapel Road,
London E1 1JX
Tel: 020 7650 3070
Head: Mr Askor Ali
Age range: B7–11

Beis Trana Girls' School
186 Upper Clapton Road,
London E5 9DH
Tel: 020 8815 8000
Head of School: Mrs M Shmaya
Age range: G3–16

Faraday Prep School
Old Gate House, 7 Trinity Buoy Wharf, London E14 0JW
Tel: 020 8965 7374
Head Teacher: Lucas Motion
Age range: 4–11
No. of pupils: 100
Fees: Day £3,686

Forest School
College Place, Snaresbrook,
London E17 3PY
Tel: 020 8520 1744
Warden: Mr Cliff Hodges
Age range: 4–18
No. of pupils: 1355 VIth260
Fees: Day £13,095–£18,681

Gatehouse School
Sewardstone Road, Victoria Park, London E2 9JG
Tel: 020 8980 2978
Head of School: Mrs Sevda Corby
Age range: 3–11 years
No. of pupils: 489
Fees: Day £4,130–£4,353

Grangewood Independent School
Chester Road, Forest Gate, London E7 8QT
Tel: 020 8472 3552
Headteacher: Mrs B A Roberts B.Ed (Hons); PG Cert (SEN)
Age range: 2–11
No. of pupils: 71
Fees: Day £5,157–£6,751

Hyland House School
Holcombe Road, Tottenham,
, London N17 9AD
Tel: 0208 520 4186
Head Teacher: Mrs Gina Abbequaye
Age range: 3–11
Fees: Day £2,520

Lubavitch House School (Junior Boys)
135 Clapton Common,
London E5 9AE
Tel: 020 8800 1044
Head: Mr R Leach
Age range: B5–11
No. of pupils: 101

Normanhurst School
68-74 Station Road,
Chingford, London E4 7BA
Tel: 020 8529 4307
Headmistress: Mrs Claire Osborn
Age range: 2–16
No. of pupils: 250
Fees: Day £10,350–£13,050

Pillar Box Montessori Nursery & Pre-Prep School
107 Bow Road, London E3 2AN
Tel: 020 8980 0700
Director: Lorraine Redknapp
Age range: 0–5
Fees: Day £12,000

Quwwat-ul Islam Girls School
16 Chaucer Road, Forest Gate, London E7 9NB
Tel: 020 8548 4736
Headteacher: Ms Shazia Member
Age range: G4–11

River House Montessori School
3-4 Shadwell Pierhead, Glamis Road, London E1W 3TD
Tel: 020 7538 9886
Headmistress: Miss S Greenwood
Age range: 3–16
Fees: Day £3,410–£3,625

Snaresbrook Preparatory School
75 Woodford Road, South Woodford, London E18 2EA
Tel: 020 8989 2394
Head of School: Mr Ralph Dalton
Age range: 3–11
Fees: Day £8,922–£11,934

Talmud Torah Machzikei Hadass School
1 Belz Terrace, Clapton,
London E5 9SN
Tel: 020 8800 6599
Headteacher: Rabbi C Silbiger
Age range: B3–16

Winston House Preparatory School
140 High Road, London E18 2QS
Tel: 020 8505 6565
Head Teacher: Mrs Marian Kemp
Age range: 3–11

North London

Annemount School
18 Holne Chase, Hampstead Garden Suburb, London N2 0QN
Tel: 020 8455 2132
Principal: Mrs G Maidment BA(Hons), MontDip
Age range: 2–7 years

Avenue Pre-Prep & Nursery School
2 Highgate Avenue,
Highgate, London N6 5RX
Tel: 020 8348 6815
Principal: Mrs. Mary Fysh
Age range: 2–8

Beis Chinuch Lebonos Girls School
Woodberry Down Centre,
Woodberry Down, London N4 2SH
Tel: 020 88097 737
Age range: G2–16

Beis Malka Girls School
93 Alkham Road, London N16 6XD
Tel: 020 8806 2070
Age range: G2–16

Beis Rochel D'Satmar Girls School
51-57 Amhurst Park, London N16 5DL
Tel: 020 8800 9060
Headmistress: Mrs E Katz
Age range: G2–18

Bnois Jerusalem School
79-81 Amhurst Park,
London N16 5DL
Tel: 020 8211 7136
Age range: G3–16

Bobov Primary School
87-90 Egerton Road,
London N16 6UE
Tel: 020 8809 1025
Headmaster: Mr Chaim Weissman
Age range: B3–13

Channing School
The Bank, Highgate, London N6 5HF
Tel: 020 8340 2328
Head: Mrs B M Elliott
Age range: G4–18
No. of pupils: 746 VIth108
Fees: Day £17,610–£19,410

Dwight School London
6 Friern Barnet Lane,
London N11 3LX
Tel: 020 8920 0600
Head: Chris Beddows
Age range: 2–18 years

Finchley & Acton Yochien School
6 Hendon Avenue, Finchley,
London N3 1UE
Tel: 020 8343 2191
Headteacher: J Tanabe
Age range: 2–6
No. of pupils: 145

Grange Park Preparatory School
13 The Chine, Grange Park, Winchmore Hill, London N21 2EA
Tel: 020 8360 1469
Headteacher: Miss F Rizzo
Age range: G4–11
No. of pupils: 90
Fees: Day £10,300–£10,378

Highgate
North Road, Highgate,
London N6 4AY
Tel: 020 8340 1524
Head Master: Mr A S Pettitt MA
Age range: 3–18
No. of pupils: 1541 VIth312
Fees: Day £18,165–£20,970

England – London

Highgate Junior School
Cholmeley House, 3 Bishopswood Road, London N6 4PL
Tel: 020 8340 9193
Principal: Mr S M James BA
Age range: 7–11
Fees: Day £19,230

Highgate Pre-Preparatory School
7 Bishopswood Road, London N6 4PH
Tel: 020 8340 9196
Principal: Mrs Diane Hecht
Age range: 3–7
No. of pupils: 150
Fees: Day £18,165

Keble Prep
Wades Hill, Winchmore Hill, London N21 1BG
Tel: 020 8360 3359
Headmaster: Mr P Gill BA (Hons)
Age range: B4–13 years

Kerem School
Norrice Lea, London N2 0RE
Tel: 020 8455 0909
Head Teacher: Miss Alyson Burns
Age range: 3–11
Fees: Day £9,435

Norfolk House School
10 Muswell Avenue, Muswell Hill, London N10 2EG
Tel: 020 8883 4584
Headteacher: Mr Paul Jowett
Age range: 2–11
No. of pupils: 220
Fees: Day £4,143

North London Rudolf Steiner School
1-3 The Campsbourne, London N8 7PN
Tel: 020 8341 3770
Age range: 0–7
No. of pupils: 40

Palmers Green High School
Hoppers Road, Winchmore Hill, London N21 3LJ
Tel: 020 8886 1135
Headmistress: Mrs Wendy Kempster
Age range: G3–16
No. of pupils: 300
Fees: Day £5,880–£15,930

Pardes House Primary School
Hendon Lane, Finchley, London N3 1SA
Tel: 020 8343 3568
Headteacher: Rabbi J Sager MA, B.Ed, NPQH, FCCT
Age range: B4–11 years

Rosemary Works Independent School
1 Branch Place, London N1 5PH
Tel: 020 7739 3950
Head: Rob Dell
Age range: 3–11
No. of pupils: 104
Fees: Day £14,097

Salcombe Preparatory School
224-226 Chase Side, Southgate, London N14 4PL
Tel: 020 8441 5356
Headmistress: Mrs Sarah-Jane Davies BA(Hons) QTS MEd
Age range: 3–11
No. of pupils: 250
Fees: Day £11,673

St Paul's Steiner School
1 St Paul's Road, Islington, London N1 2QH
Tel: 020 7226 4454
College of Teachers: College of Teachers
Age range: 2–14
No. of pupils: 136

Sunrise Nursery, Stoke Newington
1 Cazenove Road, Stoke Newington, Hackney, London N16 6PA
Tel: 020 8806 6279
Principal: Didi Ananda Manika

Sunrise Primary School
55 Coniston Road, Tottenham, London N17 0EX
Tel: 020 8806 6279 (Office); 020 8885 3354 (School)
Head: Mrs Mary-Anne Lovage MontDipEd, BA
Age range: 2–11
No. of pupils: 30
Fees: Day £5,550

Talmud Torah Chaim Meirim School
26 Lampard Grove, London N16 6XB
Tel: 020 8806 0898
Principal: Rabbi S Hoffman
Age range: B4–13

Talmud Torah Yetev Lev School
111-115 Cazenove Road, London N16 6AX
Tel: 020 8806 3834
Age range: B2–11 years

Tayyibah Girls School
88 Filey Avenue, Hackney, London N16 6JJ
Tel: 020 8880 0085
Headmistress: Mrs N B Qureishi MSc
Age range: G5–18

The Children's House Upper School
King Henry's Walk, London N1 4PB
Tel: 020 7249 6273
Head of School: Kate Orange
Age range: 4–7 years
Fees: Day £5,310

The Gower School Montessori Nursery
18 North Road, Islington, London N7 9EY
Tel: 020 7700 2445
Principal: Miss Emma Gowers
Age range: 3 months–5 years
No. of pupils: 237

The Gower School Montessori Primary
10 Cynthia Street, Barnsbury, London N1 9JF
Tel: 020 7278 2020
Principal: Miss Emma Gowers
Age range: 4–11
No. of pupils: 237
Fees: Day £15,576

TTTYY School
14 Heathland Road, London N16 5NH
Tel: 020 8802 1348
Head of School: Rabbi A Friesel
Age range: B2–13

Vita et Pax School
Priory Close, Southgate, London N14 4AT
Tel: 020 8449 8336
Headteacher: Miss Gillian Chumbley
Age range: 3–11
Fees: Day £9,360

Yesodey Hatorah Senior Girls' School
Egerton Road, London N16 6UB
Tel: 020 8826 5500
Acting Head Teacher: Mrs C Neuberger
Age range: 3–16
No. of pupils: 920

North-West London

Al-Sadiq & Al-Zahra Schools
134 Salusbury Road, London NW6 6PF
Tel: 020 7372 7706
Headteacher: Dr M Movahedi
Age range: 4–16

Arnold House School
1 Loudoun Road, St John's Wood, London NW8 0LH
Tel: 020 7266 4840
Headmaster: Mr Giles F Tollit
Age range: B3–13 years

Beis Soroh Schneirer
Arbiter House, Wilberforce Road, London NW9 6AX
Tel: 020 8201 7771
Head of School: Mrs Sonia Mossberg
Age range: G2–11

Belmont, Mill Hill Preparatory School
The Ridgeway, London NW7 4ED
Tel: 020 8906 7270
Headmaster: Mr Leon Roberts MA
Age range: 7–13 years
No. of pupils: 550
Fees: Day £19,560

DEVONSHIRE HOUSE PREPARATORY SCHOOL
For further details see p. 81
2 Arkwright Road, Hampstead, London NW3 6AE
Tel: 020 7435 1916
Email: enquiries@dhprep.co.uk
Website: www.devonshirehouseschool.co.uk
Headmistress: Mrs S. Piper BA (Hons)
Age range: B2.5–13 years G2.5–11 years
No. of pupils: 543
Fees: Day £9,870–£20,475

Golders Hill School
666 Finchley Road, London NW11 7NT
Tel: 020 8455 2589
Headmistress: Mrs A T Eglash BA(Hons)
Age range: 2–7
No. of pupils: 180
Fees: Day £1,575–£13,827

Goodwyn School
Hammers Lane, Mill Hill, London NW7 4DB
Tel: 020 8959 3756
Principal: Struan Robertson
Age range: 3–11
No. of pupils: 193
Fees: Day £5,436–£11,943

Grimsdell, Mill Hill Pre-Preparatory School
Winterstoke House, Wills Grove, Mill Hill, London NW7 1QR
Tel: 020 8959 6884
Head: Mrs Kate Simon BA, PGCE
Age range: 3–7 years
No. of pupils: 188
Fees: Day £15,095

Hampstead Hill Pre-Prep & Nursery School
St Stephen's Hall, Pond Street, Hampstead, London NW3 2PP
Tel: 020 7435 6262
Principal: Mrs Andrea Taylor
Age range: B2–7+ G2–7+
Fees: Day £10,175–£16,830

Heathside School Hampstead
84a Heath Street, Hampstead, London NW3 1DN
Tel: +44 (0)20 3058 4011
Headteacher: Katherine Vintiner
Age range: 2–13 years
No. of pupils: 230
Fees: Day £16,800–£19,400

England – London

Hendon Prep School
20 Tenterden Grove, Hendon, London NW4 1TD
Tel: 020 8203 7727
Head of School: Mrs Tushi Gorasia
Age range: 2–11 years
No. of pupils: 165
Fees: Day £6,975–£15,600

Hereward House School
14 Strathray Gardens, Hampstead, London NW3 4NY
Tel: 020 7794 4820
Headmaster: Mr P Evans
Age range: B4–13 years
Fees: Day £15,615–£16,065

ICS London
7B Wyndham Place, London W1H 1PN
Tel: +44 (0)20 729 88800
Head of School: David Laird
Age range: 3–19 years
No. of pupils: 175
Fees: Day £19,650–£28,770

IRIS School
100 Carlton Vale, London NW6 5HE
Tel: 020 7372 8051
Headteacher: Mr Seyed Abbas Hosseini
Age range: 6–16 years

LYNDHURST HOUSE PREP SCHOOL
For further details see p. 83
24 Lyndhurst Gardens, Hampstead, London NW3 5NW
Tel: 020 7435 4936
Email: jorrett@lyndhursthouse.co.uk
Website: www.lyndhursthouse.co.uk
Head of School: Mr Andrew Reid MA (Oxon)
Age range: B4–13 years
No. of pupils: 125
Fees: Day £18,360–£20,790

Maple Walk Prep School
62A Crownhill Road, London NW10 4EB
Tel: 020 8963 3890
Head Teacher: Claire Murdoch
Age range: 4–11
No. of pupils: 190
Fees: Day £3,580

Maria Montessori School - Hampstead
26 Lyndhurst Gardens, Hampstead, London NW3 5NW
Tel: +44 (0)20 7435 3646
Director of School: Miss L Kingston
Age range: 2–12
No. of pupils: 100
Fees: Day £6,270–£13,560

Naima Jewish Preparatory School
21 Andover Place, London NW6 5ED
Tel: 020 7328 2802
Headmaster: Mr Bill Pratt
Age range: 3–11

Nancy Reuben Primary School
Finchley Lane, Hendon, London NW4 1DJ
Tel: 020 82025646
Head: Anthony Wolfson
Age range: 3–11
No. of pupils: 207

North Bridge House Nursery and Pre-Prep Hampstead
8 Netherhall Gardens, London NW3 5RR
Tel: 020 7428 1520
Head of School: Mrs Christine McLelland
Age range: 2–7 years
No. of pupils: 190

North Bridge House Nursery and Pre-Prep West Hampstead
85-87 Fordwych Rd, London NW2 3TL
Tel: 020 7428 1520
Head of School: Mrs Christine McLelland
Age range: 2–7 years

NORTH BRIDGE HOUSE PREP SCHOOL REGENT'S PARK
For further details see p. 84
1 Gloucester Avenue, London NW1 7AB
Tel: 020 7428 1520
Email: admissionsenquiries@northbridgehouse.com
Website: www.northbridgehouse.com
Head of School: Mr James Stenning
Age range: 7–13 years
No. of pupils: 385
Fees: Day £18,960–£20,520

Rainbow Montessori School
13 Woodchurch Road, Hampstead, London NW6 3PL
Tel: 020 7328 8986
Head Mistress: Maggy Miller MontDip
Age range: 2–5
Fees: Day £12,240–£12,417

Saint Christina's School
25 St Edmunds Terrace, Regent's Park, London NW8 7PY
Tel: 020 7722 8784
Headteacher: Miss J Finlayson
Age range: 3–11
No. of pupils: 224
Fees: Day £13,500

Sarum Hall School
15 Eton Avenue, London NW3 3EL
Tel: 020 7794 2261
Headteacher: Victoria Savage
Age range: G3–11
No. of pupils: 184

South Hampstead High School GDST
3 Maresfield Gardens, London NW3 5SS
Tel: 020 7435 2899
Head of School: Mrs V Bingham
Age range: G4–18
No. of pupils: 900
Fees: Day £15,327–£18,654

Southbank International School - Hampstead
16 Netherhall Gardens, London NW3 5TH
Tel: 020 7243 3803
Principal: Shirley Harwood
Age range: 3–11 years
No. of pupils: 210

St Christopher's School
32 Belsize Lane, Hampstead, London NW3 5AE
Tel: 020 7435 1521
Head: Emma Crawford-Nash
Age range: G4–11
No. of pupils: 235
Fees: Day £14,700

St John's Wood Pre-Preparatory School
St Johns Hall, Lords Roundabout, London NW8 7NE
Tel: 020 7722 7149
Principal: Adrian Ellis
Age range: 3–7

St Margaret's School
18 Kidderpore Gardens, Hampstead, London NW3 7SR
Tel: 020 7435 2439
Principal: Mr M Webster BSc, PGCE
Age range: G4–16
No. of pupils: 156
Fees: Day £12,591–£14,589

St Martin's School
22 Goodwyn Avenue, Mill Hill, London NW7 3RG
Tel: 020 8959 1965
Head Teacher: Mrs Samantha Mbah
Age range: 3–11
No. of pupils: 90
Fees: Day £7,800

St Mary's School Hampstead
47 Fitzjohn's Avenue, Hampstead, London NW3 6PG
Tel: 020 7435 1868
Head Teacher: Mrs Harriet Connor-Earl
Age range: G2 years 9 months–11 years
No. of pupils: 300
Fees: Day £8,625–£15,945

St Nicholas School
22 Salmon Street, London NW9 8PN
Tel: 020 8205 7153
Headmaster: Mr Matt Donaldson BA (Hons), PGCE, PGDip (Surv)
Age range: 3 months–11
No. of pupils: 80
Fees: Day £8,550–£8,850

ST. ANTHONY'S SCHOOL FOR GIRLS
For further details see p. 88
Ivy House, 94-96 North End Road, , London NW11 7SX
Tel: 020 3869 3070
Email: admissions@stanthonysgirls.co.uk
Website: www.stanthonysgirls.co.uk
Head of School: Mr Donal Brennan
Age range: G2.5–11 years
No. of pupils: 85
Fees: Day £18,000

ST. ANTHONY'S SCHOOL FOR BOYS
For further details see p. 90
90 Fitzjohn's Avenue, Hampstead, London NW3 6NP
Tel: 020 7431 1066
Email: pahead@stanthonysprep.co.uk
Website: www.stanthonysprep.org.uk
Head of School: Mr Richard Berlie MA (Cantab)
Age range: B2.5–13 years G2.5–4 years
No. of pupils: 280

The Academy School
3 Pilgrims Place, Rosslyn Hill, Hampstead, London NW3 1NG
Tel: 020 7435 6621
Headteacher: Mr Garth Evans BA (Lond)

The American School in London
One Waverley Place, London NW8 0NP
Tel: 020 7449 1221
Head: Robin Appleby
Age range: 4–18
No. of pupils: 1350
Fees: Day £27,050–£31,200

The Cavendish School
31 Inverness Street, Camden Town, London NW1 7HB
Tel: 020 7485 1958
Headmistress: Miss Jane Rogers
Age range: G3–11
No. of pupils: 260
Fees: Day £15,300

England – London

The Hall School
23 Crossfield Road, Hampstead, London NW3 4NU
Tel: 020 7722 1700
Headmaster: Mr Chris Godwin
Age range: B4–13 years

The King Alfred School
Manor Wood, North End Road, London NW11 7HY
Tel: 020 8457 5200
Head: Robert Lobatto MA (Oxon)
Age range: 4–18
No. of pupils: 650 VIth100
Fees: Day £15,531–£18,723

The Mulberry House School
7 Minster Road, West Hampstead, London NW2 3SD
Tel: 020 8452 7340
Headteacher: Ms Victoria Playford BA Hons, QTS
Age range: 2–7 years
No. of pupils: 223

THE VILLAGE PREP SCHOOL
For further details see p. 92
2 Parkhill Road, Belsize Park, London NW3 2YN
Tel: 020 7485 4673
Email: admin@thevillageschool.org.uk
Website: www.thevillageschool.org.uk
Head of School: Ms Morven MacDonald
Age range: G2.5–11 years

Torah Vodaas
Brent Park Road, West Hendon Broadway, London NW9 7AJ
Tel: 020 3670 4670
Head of School: Rabbi Y Feldman
Age range: B2–11

Trevor-Roberts School
55-57 Eton Avenue, London NW3 3ET
Tel: 020 7586 1444
Headmaster: Simon Trevor-Roberts BA
Age range: 5–13
Fees: Day £14,700–£16,200

University College School Hampstead (UCS) Junior
11 Holly Hill, Hampstead, London NW3 6QN
Tel: 020 7435 3068
Headmaster: Mr Lewis Hayward
Age range: B7–11 years

University College School Hampstead (UCS) Pre-Prep
36 College Crescent, Hampstead, London NW3 5LF
Tel: 020 7722 4433
Headmistress: Ms Zoe Dunn
Age range: B4–7 years

South-East London

Alleyn's School
Townley Road, Dulwich, London SE22 8SU
Tel: 020 8557 1500
Head of School: Jane Lunnon
Age range: 4–18 years

Blackheath High School GDST
Vanbrugh Park, Blackheath, London SE3 7AG
Tel: 020 8853 2929
Head: Mrs Carol Chandler-Thompson BA (Hons) Exeter, PGCE Exeter
Age range: G3–18
No. of pupils: 780

BLACKHEATH PREP
For further details see p. 80
4 St Germans Place, Blackheath, London SE3 0NJ
Tel: 020 8858 0692
Email: info@blackheathprep.co.uk
Website: www.blackheathprep.co.uk
Head: Alex Matthews
Age range: 3–11 years
No. of pupils: 385

Colfe's Junior School
Horn Park Lane, Lee, London SE12 8AW
Tel: 020 8463 8240
Head: Ms C Macleod
Age range: 3–11
No. of pupils: 355
Fees: Day £13,230–£13,995

Dulwich College
Dulwich Common, , London SE21 7LD
Tel: 020 8693 3601
Master: Dr J A F Spence
Age range: B0–18 years
Fees: Day £21,672 WB £42,408 FB £45,234

Dulwich College Kindergarten & Infants School
Eller Bank, 87 College Road, London SE21 7HH
Tel: 020 8693 1538
Head: Mrs Miranda Norris
Age range: 3 months–7 years
No. of pupils: 180

Dulwich Prep London
42 Alleyn Park, Dulwich, London SE21 7AA
Tel: 020 8766 5500
Head Master: Miss Louise Davidson
Age range: B3–13 years G3–5 years

Eltham College
Grove Park Road, Mottingham, London SE9 4QF
Tel: 0208 857 1455
Headmaster: Guy Sanderson
Age range: 7–18
No. of pupils: 911 VIth199

Eltham College Junior School
Grove Park Road, London SE9 4QF
Tel: 020 8857 1455
Headmaster: Keith John BSc, PGCE
Age range: B7–11
No. of pupils: 213
Fees: Day £10,320

Greenwich Steiner School
Woodlands, 90 Mycenae Road, Blackheath, London SE3 7SE
Tel: 020 8858 4404
Head of School: Mr Adrian Dow
Age range: 3–14
No. of pupils: 180
Fees: Day £7,310–£8,100

Heath House Preparatory School
37 Wemyss Road, Blackheath, London SE3 0TG
Tel: 020 8297 1900
Head Teacher: Mrs Sophia Laslett CertEd PGDE
Age range: 3–11
No. of pupils: 125
Fees: Day £13,485–£14,985

Herne Hill School
The Old Vicarage, 127 Herne Hill, London SE24 9LY
Tel: 020 7274 6336
Headteacher: Mrs Ngaire Telford
Age range: 2–7
No. of pupils: 296
Fees: Day £6,225–£14,955

James Allen's Girls' School
144 East Dulwich Grove, Dulwich, London SE22 8TE
Tel: 020 8693 1181
Head of School: Mrs Sally-Anne Huang MA, MSc
Age range: G4–18
No. of pupils: 1075

Kings Kids Christian School
100 Woodpecker Road, Newcross, London SE14 6EU
Tel: 020 8691 5813
Headteacher: Mrs M Okenwa
Age range: 5–11

London Christian School
40 Tabard Street, London SE1 4JU
Tel: 020 3130 6430
Headmistress: Miss N Collett-White
Age range: 3–11
No. of pupils: 105
Fees: Day £9,390

Oakfield Preparatory School
125-128 Thurlow Park Road, West Dulwich, London SE21 8HP
Tel: 020 8670 4206
Head of School: Mrs Moyra Thompson
Age range: 2–11 years
No. of pupils: 310
Fees: Day £12,324

Octavia House School, Vauxhall
Vauxhall Primary School, Vauxhall Street, London SE11 5LG
Tel: 020 3651 4396 (option 1)
Executive Headteacher: Mr P Foster
Age range: 5–14

Octavia House School, Walworth
Larcom House, Larcom Street, , London SE17 1RT
Tel: 020 3651 4396 (option 2)
Executive Headteacher: Mr P Foster

Riverston School
63-69 Eltham Road, Lee Green, London SE12 8UF
Tel: 020 8318 4327
Principal: Michael Lewis
Age range: 9 months–19 years

Rosemead Preparatory School & Nursery, Dulwich
70 Thurlow Park Road, London SE21 8HZ
Tel: 020 8670 5865
Headmaster: Mr Phil Soutar
Age range: 2–11
No. of pupils: 366
Fees: Day £10,272–£11,286

St Dunstan's College
Stanstead Road, London SE6 4TY
Tel: 020 8516 7200
Headmaster: Mr Nicholas Hewlett
Age range: 3–18
No. of pupils: 870

St Olave's Preparatory School
106 Southwood Road, New Eltham, London SE9 3QS
Tel: 020 8294 8930
Headteacher: Miss Claire Holloway BEd, QTS
Age range: 3–11
No. of pupils: 220
Fees: Day £10,848–£12,300

Sydenham High School GDST
15 & 19 Westwood Hill, London SE26 6BL
Tel: 020 8557 7004
Headmistress: Mrs Katharine Woodcock
Age range: G4–18
No. of pupils: 665

England – London

The Pointer School
19 Stratheden Road,
Blackheath, London SE3 7TH
Tel: 020 8293 1331
Headmaster: Mr Adam M
Greenwood BSc (Hons),
PGCE, GCGI, MBA
Age range: 3–11 years

The Villa School & Nursery
54 Lyndhurst Grove, Peckham,
London SE15 5AH
Tel: 020 7703 6216
Head Teacher: Louise Maughan
Age range: 2–7

South-West London

Al-Risalah Secondary School
145 Upper Tooting Road,
London SW17 7TJ
Tel: 020 8767 6057
Executive Principal: Suhayl Lee
Age range: 11–16 years

Beechwood Nursery School
55 Leigham Court Road,
Streatham, London SW16 2NJ
Tel: 020 8677 8778
Age range: 0–5

Bertrum House Nursery
290 Balham High Road,
London SW17 7AL
Tel: 020 8767 4051
Age range: 2–5

Broomwood Hall Lower School
50 Nightingale Lane,
London SW12 8TE
Tel: 020 8682 8840
Head: Miss Jo Townsend
Age range: 4–8
No. of pupils: 320
Fees: Day £5,610

Cameron Vale School
4 The Vale, Chelsea,
London SW3 6AH
Tel: 020 7352 4040
Headmistress: Mrs Bridget Saul
Age range: 4–11
Fees: Day £19,305

Dolphin School
106 Northcote Road,
London SW11 6QW
Tel: 020 7924 3472
Principal: Mr Sam Gosden
Age range: 2–11 years
No. of pupils: 162
Fees: Day £6,285–£14,085

Donhead Preparatory School
33 Edge Hill, Wimbledon,
London SW19 4NP
Tel: 020 8946 7000
Headmaster: Mr P J J Barr
Age range: B4–11 years

Eaton House Belgravia
3-5 Eaton Gate, London SW1W 9BA
Tel: 020 7924 6000
Head of School: Mr Huw May
Age range: B3–11 years

Eaton House The Manor
58 Clapham Common
Northside, London SW4 9RU
Tel: 020 7924 6000
Head: Mr Oliver Snowball
Age range: G4–11
Fees: Day £16,143

Eaton House The Manor Pre Prep and Nursery
58 Clapham Common
Northside, London SW4 9RU
Tel: 020 7924 6000
Nursery Head of School: Miss Roosha
Age range: B3.5–8
Fees: Day £16,143

Eaton House The Manor Prep School
58 Clapham Common
Northside, London SW4 9RU
Tel: 020 7924 6000
Head: Mrs Sarah Segrave
Age range: B8–13
Fees: Day £19,743

Eaton Square School Belgravia
79 Eccleston Square,
London SW1V 1PP
Tel: +44 (0)20 7931 9469
Principal: Mr Sebastian Hepher
Age range: 4–11

Eaton Square School Kensington
24 Elvaston Place, London SW7 5NL
Tel: +44 (0)20 7225 3131
Headmistress: Mrs Trish Watt
Age range: 4–11

Eveline Day & Nursery Schools
14 Trinity Crescent, Upper
Tooting, London SW17 7AE
Tel: 020 8672 4673
Headmistress: Ms Eveline Drut
Age range: 3 months–11 years
No. of pupils: 80
Fees: Day £13,859

Falcons School for Girls
11 Woodborough Road,
Putney, London SW15 6PY
Tel: 020 8992 5189
Headmistress: Ms Sara Williams-Ryan
Age range: G4–11
Fees: Day £7,800–£15,705

Falkner House
19 Brechin Place, South
Kensington, London SW7 4QB
Tel: 020 7373 4501
Headteacher: Mrs Anita Griggs BA(Hons), PGCE
Age range: B3–11 G3–11

Finton House School
171 Trinity Road, London SW17 7HL
Tel: 020 8682 0921
Head of School: Mr Ben Freeman
Age range: 4–11
No. of pupils: 300
Fees: Day £15,378–£15,588

Francis Holland School, Sloane Square, SW1
39 Graham Terrace,
London SW1W 8JF
Tel: 020 7730 2971
Head: Mrs Lucy Elphinstone MA(Cantab)
Age range: G4–18
No. of pupils: 520 VIth70
Fees: Day £17,760–£20,085

Garden House School
Boys' School & Girls' School,
Turk's Row, London SW3 4TW
Tel: 020 7730 1652
Boys' Head: Mr Christian Warland BA(Hons), LLB.
Age range: 3–11
No. of pupils: 490
Fees: Day £17,700–£22,800

Glendower School
86/87 Queen's Gate,
London SW7 5JX
Tel: 020 7370 1927
Headmistress: Mrs Sarah Knollys BA, PGCE
Age range: G4–11+
No. of pupils: 206
Fees: Day £19,200

Hall School Wimbledon Junior School
17, The Downs, Wimbledon,
London SW20 8HF
Tel: 020 8879 9200
Headmaster: Mr. A Hammond
Age range: 5–11 years

Harrodian
Lonsdale Road, London SW13 9QN
Tel: 020 8748 6117
Headmaster: Mr James R Hooke
Age range: 4–18 years
No. of pupils: 1023
Fees: Day £5,000–£8,000

Hill House
17 Hans Place, Chelsea,
London SW1X 0EP
Tel: 020 7584 1331
Headmaster: Mr Richard Townend
Age range: 4–13
No. of pupils: 600
Fees: Day £15,000–£18,600

Hornsby House School
Hearnville Road, Balham,
London SW12 8RS
Tel: 020 8673 7573
Headmaster: Mr Edward Rees
Age range: 4–11
Fees: Day £14,280–£15,345

Hurlingham Nursery School
The Old Methodist Hall, Gwendolen
Avenue, London SW15 6EH
Tel: 020 8103 0807
Headmaster: Mr Simon Gould
Age range: 2–4 years

Hurlingham School
122 Putney Bridge Road,
Putney, London SW15 2NQ
Tel: 020 8103 1083
Headmaster: Mr Simon Gould
Age range: 4–11

Ibstock Place School
Clarence Lane, London SW15 5PY
Tel: 020 8876 9991
Head of School: Mr Christopher Wolsey
Age range: 4–18 years
No. of pupils: 990
Fees: Day £5,870–£7,450

Kensington Prep School
596 Fulham Road, London SW6 5PA
Tel: 0207 731 9300
Head of School: Mrs Caroline Hulme-McKibbin
Age range: G4–11
No. of pupils: 289
Fees: Day £17,193

Knightsbridge School
67 Pont Street, Knightsbridge,
London SW1X 0BD
Tel: +44 (0)20 7590 9000
Head of School: Shona Colaço
Age range: 3–13
Fees: Day £18,756–£19,965

L'Ecole de Battersea
Trott Street, Battersea,
London SW11 3DS
Tel: 020 7371 8350
Principal: Mrs F Brisset
Age range: 3–11
No. of pupils: 260
Fees: Day £13,740

L'Ecole des Petits
2 Hazlebury Road, Fulham,
London SW6 2NB
Tel: 020 7371 8350
Principal: Mrs F Brisset
Age range: 3–6
No. of pupils: 125
Fees: Day £13,365

London Steiner School
9 Weir Road, Balham,
London SW12 0LT
Tel: 0208 772 3504
Age range: 3–14

England – London

Lycée Français Charles de Gaulle de Londres
35 Cromwell Road,
London SW7 2DG
Tel: 020 7584 6322
Head of School: Didier Devilard
Age range: 3–18 years
No. of pupils: 3450
Fees: Day £8,617–£14,782

Newton Prep
149 Battersea Park Road,
London SW8 4BX
Tel: 020 7720 4091
Headmistress: Mrs Alison Fleming BA, MA Ed, PGCE
Age range: 3–13 years
No. of pupils: 628
Fees: Day £9,975–£21,135

Northcote Lodge
26 Bolingbroke Grove,
London SW11 6EL
Tel: 020 8682 8888
Head: Mr Clive Smith-Langridge
Age range: B8–13
No. of pupils: 260
Fees: Day £6,880

Oliver House Preparatory School
7 Nightingale Lane,
London SW4 9AH
Tel: 020 8772 1911
Headteacher: Mr Rob Farrell
Age range: 3–11
No. of pupils: 144
Fees: Day £6,600–£15,090

Parkgate House School
80 Clapham Common North Side, London SW4 9SD
Tel: +44 (0)20 7350 2461
Principal: Miss Catherine Shanley
Age range: 2.5–11 years
No. of pupils:
Fees: Day £5,940–£15,600

Parsons Green Prep School
1 Fulham Park Road,
Fulham, London SW6 4LJ
Tel: 020 7371 9009
Headmaster: Tim Cannell
Age range: 4–11
No. of pupils: 200
Fees: Day £16,857–£18,201

Prince's Gardens Preparatory School
10–13 Prince's Gardens,
London SW7 1ND
Tel: 0207 591 4622
Headmistress: Mrs Alison Melrose
Age range: 3–11 years

Prospect House School
75 Putney Hill, London SW15 3NT
Tel: 020 8246 4897
Head: Mr Michael Hodge BPED(Rhodes) QTS
Age range: 3–11 years
No. of pupils: 316
Fees: Day £9,480–£19,755

Putney High School GDST
35 Putney Hill, London SW15 6BH
Tel: 020 8788 4886
Headmistress: Mrs Suzie Longstaff BA, MA, PGCE
Age range: G4–18
No. of pupils: 976 VIth150

Queen's Gate School
133 Queen's Gate, London SW7 5LE
Tel: 020 7589 3587
Principal: Mrs R M Kamaryc BA, MSc, PGCE
Age range: G4–18 years
No. of pupils: 500 VIth81

Redcliffe School Trust Ltd
47 Redcliffe Gardens,
Chelsea, London SW10 9JH
Tel: 020 7352 9247
Head: Sarah Lemmon
Age range: 3–11
Fees: Day £6,660–£17,730

Sinclair House Montessori Nursery
159 & 196 Munster Road,
Fulham, London SW6 6AU
Tel: 0207 736 9182
Principal: Mrs Carlotta T M O'Sullivan

Sinclair House Preparatory School
59 Fulham High Street,
Fulham, London SW6 3JJ
Tel: 0207 736 9182
Principal: Mrs Carlotta T M O'Sullivan
Age range: 2–11
No. of pupils: 120
Fees: Day £5,280–£17,025

St Paul's Juniors
St Paul's School, Lonsdale Road, London SW13 9JT
Tel: 020 8748 3461
Head of School: Maxine Shaw
Age range: B7–13 years

St Philip's School
6 Wetherby Place, London SW7 4NE
Tel: 020 7373 3944
Headmaster: Mr Wulffen-Thomas
Age range: B7–13 years

Streatham & Clapham High School GDST
42 Abbotswood Road,
London SW16 1AW
Tel: 020 8677 8400
Headmaster: Dr Millan Sachania
Age range: G3–18
No. of pupils: 603 VIth70
Fees: Day £10,431–£19,743

Sussex House School
68 Cadogan Square,
London SW1X 0EA
Tel: 020 7584 1741
Headmaster: Mr N P Kaye MA(Cantab), ACP, FRSA, FRGS
Age range: B8–13 years

Swedish School
82 Lonsdale Road, London SW13 9JS
Tel: 020 8741 1751
Head of School: Ms. Jenny Abrahamsson
Age range: 3–18
No. of pupils: 300 VIth145
Fees: Day £8,600–£9,100

The Hampshire School, Chelsea
15 Manresa Road, Chelsea,
London SW3 6NB
Tel: 020 7352 7077
Head of School: Dr P Edmonds BEd (Hons) MEd EdD
Age range: 3–13
No. of pupils: 300
Fees: Day £16,965–£17,955

The Merlin School
4 Carlton Drive, London SW15 2BZ
Tel: 020 8788 2769
Principal: Mrs Kate Prest
Age range: 4–8
No. of pupils: 130
Fees: Day £5,241

The Montessori Pavilion - The Kindergarten School
Vine Road, Barnes,
London SW13 0NE
Tel: 07554 277 746
Headmistress: Ms Georgina Dashwood
Age range: 3–8
No. of pupils: 50

The Norwegian School
28 Arterberry Road, Wimbledon, London SW20 8AH
Tel: 020 8947 6617
Head: Mr Ivar Chavannes
Age range: 3–16

The Roche School
11 Frogmore, London SW18 1HW
Tel: 020 8877 0823
Headmistress: Mrs Vania Adams BA(Hons), PGCE, MA
Age range: 2–11 years
No. of pupils: 302
Fees: Day £14,970–£15,690

The Rowans School
19 Drax Avenue, Wimbledon, London SW20 0EG
Tel: 020 8946 8220
Head Teacher: Mrs. Joanna Hubbard MA BA (Hons) PGCE QTS PGDipSEN
Age range: 3–8
Fees: Day £7,905–£13,170

The Study Preparatory School
Wilberforce House, Camp Road, Wimbledon Common, London SW19 4UN
Tel: 020 8947 6969
Head of School: Miss Vicky Ellis BSc (Hons), QTS, MA
Age range: G4–11
No. of pupils: 320
Fees: Day £4,925

The White House Preparatory School & Woodentops Kindergarten
24 Thornton Road, London SW12 0LF
Tel: 020 8674 9514
Principal: Mrs. Mary McCahery
Age range: 2–11
Fees: Day £4,436–£4,740

Thomas's Preparatory School - Battersea
28-40 Battersea High Street,
London SW11 3JB
Tel: 020 7978 0900
Head: Simon O'Malley
Age range: 4–13
No. of pupils: 547
Fees: Day £18,747–£20,868

Thomas's Preparatory School - Clapham
Broomwood Road,
London SW11 6JZ
Tel: 020 7326 9300
Headmaster: Mr Philip Ward BEd(Hons)
Age range: 4–13
No. of pupils: 647
Fees: Day £17,262–£19,518

Thomas's Preparatory School - Fulham
Hugon Road, London SW6 3ES
Tel: 020 7751 8200
Head: Miss Annette Dobson BEd(Hons), PGCertDys
Age range: 4–11
Fees: Day £17,880–£20,016

Tower House School
188 Sheen Lane, London SW14 8LF
Tel: 020 8876 3323
Head: Mr Gregory Evans
Age range: B4–13 years

Ursuline Preparatory School
18 The Downs, Wimbledon,
London SW20 8HR
Tel: 020 8947 0859
Head Teacher: Mrs Caroline Molina BA (Hons)
Age range: B3–4 years G3–11 years
No. of pupils: 169

Wandsworth Preparatory School
The Old Library, 2 Allfarthing Lane, London SW18 2PQ
Tel: 0208 870 4133
Headteacher: Ms Jo Fife
Age range: 4–11
No. of pupils: 100
Fees: Day £4,710

Westminster Abbey Choir School
Dean's Yard, London SW1P 3NY
Tel: 0207 654 4918
Headmaster: Mr Peter Roberts
Age range: B7–10 years

England – London

Westminster Cathedral Choir School
Ambrosden Avenue,
London SW1P 1QH
Tel: 020 7798 9081
Headmaster: Mr Neil McLaughlan
Age range: B4–13
No. of pupils: 150
Fees: Day £16,350–£19,233 FB £10,086

Westminster Under School
27 Vincent Square,
London SW1P 2NN
Tel: 020 7821 5788
Master: Mrs C J Jefferson
Age range: B7–13 years

Willington Prep
Worcester Road, Wimbledon,
London SW19 7QQ
Tel: 020 8944 7020
Head of School: Mr Keith Brown
Age range: 3–11
No. of pupils: 220

Wimbledon Common Preparatory
113 Ridgway, Wimbledon,
London SW19 4TA
Tel: 020 8946 1001
Head Teacher: Mrs Tracey Buck
Age range: B4–8
No. of pupils: 160
Fees: Day £13,185

Wimbledon High School GDST
Mansel Road, Wimbledon,
London SW19 4AB
Tel: 020 8971 0900
Headmistress: Mrs Jane Lunnon
Age range: G4–18
No. of pupils: 900 VIth155
Fees: Day £14,622–£18,810

West London

Abercorn School
38 Portland Place, London W1B 1LS
Tel: 020 7100 4335
Headmaster: Mr Christopher Hammond
Age range: 2–13 years

Avenue House School
70 The Avenue, Ealing,
London W13 8LS
Tel: 020 8998 9981
Headteacher: Mr J Sheppard
Age range: 3–11
No. of pupils: 135
Fees: Day £11,250

Bassett House School
60 Bassett Road, Notting Hill, London W10 6JP
Tel: 020 8969 0313
Headmistress: Mrs Kelly Gray
Age range: 3–11 years
No. of pupils: 120
Fees: Day £5,499–£19,200

Bute House Preparatory School for Girls
Bute House, Luxemburg Gardens, London W6 7EA
Tel: 020 7603 7381
Head of School: Ms Sian Bradshaw
Age range: G4–11 years

Chepstow House School
108a Lancaster Road,
London W11 1QS
Tel: 0207 243 0243
Headteacher: Angela Barr
Age range: 2.5–12 years

Chiswick & Bedford Park Prep School
Priory House, Priory Avenue,
London W4 1TX
Tel: 020 8994 1804
Head of School: Ms Henrietta Adams
Age range: B4–7+ G4–11
No. of pupils: 180
Fees: Day £13,275

Clifton Lodge School
8 Mattock Lane, Ealing,
London W5 5BG
Tel: 020 8579 3662
Head of School: Mrs Beth Friel
Age range: 3–13 years
No. of pupils: 130
Fees: Day £13,065–£15,600

Connaught House School
47 Connaught Square,
London W2 2HL
Tel: 020 7262 8830
Principal: Mrs V Hampton
Age range: 4–11
No. of pupils: 75
Fees: Day £16,650–£18,300

Durston House
12-14 Castlebar Road,
Ealing, London W5 2DR
Tel: 020 8991 6530
Headmaster: Mr Giles Entwisle
Age range: B4–13 years
No. of pupils: 380
Fees: Day £4,490–£5,420

Ecole Francaise Jacques Prevert
59 Brook Green, London W6 7BE
Tel: 020 7602 6871
Headteacher: Delphine Gentil
Age range: 4–11

Fulham Prep School
200 Greyhound Road,
London W14 9SD
Tel: 020 7386 2444
Head of Pre Prep: Di Steven
Age range: 4–18 years
No. of pupils: 675
Fees: Day £18,420–£21,567

Great Beginnings Montessori Nursery
39 Brendon Street, London W1H 5JE
Tel: 020 7258 1066
Head: Mrs Wendy Innes
Age range: 2–6

Greek Primary School of London
3 Pierrepoint Road, Acton,
London W3 9JR
Tel: 020 899 26156
Primary School Head Teacher: Mrs Despoina Kyriakidou BA, MA, QTS
Age range: 1–11

Harvington School
20 Castlebar Road, Ealing,
London W5 2DS
Tel: 020 8997 1583
Headmistress: Mrs Anna Evans
Age range: B3–4 G3–11
No. of pupils: 140
Fees: Day £6,525–£12,615

HAWKESDOWN HOUSE SCHOOL KENSINGTON
For further details see p. 82
27 Edge Street, Kensington,
London W8 7PN
Tel: 020 7727 9090
Email: admin@hawkesdown.co.uk
Website: www.hawkesdown.co.uk
Headmistress: Mrs S Gillam BEd (Cantab)
Age range: 2–8 years
No. of pupils: 100
Fees: Day £4,725–£21,120

Heathfield House School
Heathfield Gardens,
Chiswick, London W4 4JU
Tel: 020 8994 3385
Headteacher: Mrs Goodsman
Age range: 4–11
No. of pupils: 197
Fees: Day £2,471–£3,676

Holland Park Pre Prep School and Day Nursery
5, Holland Road, Kensington,
London W14 8HJ
Tel: 020 7602 9066/020 7602 9266
Head Mistress: Mrs Kitty Mason
Age range: 3 months–8 years
No. of pupils: 39
Fees: Day £9,180–£18,120

Instituto Español Vicente Cañada Blanch
317 Portobello Road,
London W10 5SZ
Tel: +44 (0) 20 8969 2664
Principal: Carmen Pinilla Padilla
Age range: 4–19
No. of pupils: 405

International School of London (ISL)
139 Gunnersbury Avenue,
London W3 8LG
Tel: +44 (0)20 8992 5823
Principal: Mr Richard Parker
Age range: 3–18 years
No. of pupils: 500
Fees: Day £19,000–£26,300

King Fahad Academy
Bromyard Avenue, Acton,
London W3 7HD
Tel: 020 8743 0131
Director General: Dr Tahani Aljafari
Age range: 3–19

La Petite Ecole Francaise
73 Saint Charles Square,
London W10 6EJ
Tel: +44 208 960 1278
Principal: Mme Marjorie Lacassagne
Age range: 3–11

Latymer Prep School
36 Upper Mall, Hammersmith,
London W6 9TA
Tel: 020 7993 0061
Principal: Ms Andrea Rutterford B.Ed (Hons)
Age range: 7–11
No. of pupils: 165
Fees: Day £18,330

Le Herisson
River Court Methodist Church, Rover Court Road, Hammersmith, London W6 9JT
Tel: 020 8563 7664
Director: Maria Frost
Age range: 2–6
Fees: Day £8,730–£8,970

L'Ecole Bilingue
St David's Welsh Church, St Mary's Terrace, London W2 1SJ
Tel: 020 7224 8427
Headteacher: Ms Veronique Ferreira
Age range: 3–11
No. of pupils: 68
Fees: Day £9,960–£10,770

Lloyd Williamson School Foundation
12 Telford Road, London W10 5SH
Tel: 020 8962 0345
Co-Principals: Ms Lucy Meyer & Mr Aaron Williams
Age range: 4 months–16 years
Fees: Day £17,550

London Welsh School Ysgol Gymraeg Llundain
Hanwell Community Centre, Westcott Crescent, London W7 1PD
Tel: 020 8575 0237
Lead Teacher: Mrs Rachel King
Age range: 3–11

England – London

Norland Place School
162-166 Holland Park Avenue,
London W11 4UH
Tel: 020 7603 9103
Headmaster: Mr Patrick Mattar MA
Age range: B4–8 years G4–11 years
Fees: Day £16,107–£18,072

Notting Hill & Ealing High School GDST
2 Cleveland Road, West
Ealing, London W13 8AX
Tel: (020) 8799 8400
Headmaster: Mr Matthew Shoults
Age range: G4–18
No. of pupils: 903 VIth150
Fees: Day £14,313–£18,561

Notting Hill Preparatory School
95 Lancaster Road,
London W11 1QQ
Tel: 020 7221 0727
Head of School: Mrs Sarah Knollys
Age range: 4–13
No. of pupils: 370
Fees: Day £7,130

Orchard House School
16 Newton Grove, Bedford
Park, London W4 1LB
Tel: 020 8742 8544
Headmaster: Mr Kit Thompson
Age range: 3–11 years
No. of pupils: 262
Fees: Day £9,480–£19,755

Pembridge Hall School
18 Pembridge Square,
London W2 4EH
Tel: 020 7229 0121
Headmaster: Mr Henry Keighley-Elstub
Age range: G4–11 years

Queen's College Preparatory School
61 Portland Place, ,
London W1B 1QP
Tel: 020 7291 0660
Headmistress: Mrs Emma Webb
Age range: G4–11

Ravenscourt Park Preparatory School
16 Ravenscourt Avenue,
London W6 0SL
Tel: 020 8846 9153
Headmaster: Mr Carl Howes MA (Cantab), PGCE (Exeter)
Age range: 4–11
No. of pupils: 419
Fees: Day £6,120

Southbank International School - Kensington
36-38 Kensington Park
Road, London W11 3BU
Tel: +44 (0)20 7243 3803
Principal: Siobhan McGrath
Age range: 3–18 years

St Augustine's Priory
Hillcrest Road, Ealing,
London W5 2JL
Tel: 020 8997 2022
Headteacher: Mrs Sarah Raffray M.A., N.P.Q.H
Age range: B3–4 G3–18
No. of pupils: 485
Fees: Day £11,529–£16,398

St Benedict's Junior School and Nursery
5 Montpelier Avenue,
Ealing, , London W5 2XP
Tel: 020 8862 2254
Headmaster: Mr R G Simmons
Age range: 3–11
No. of pupils: 286
Fees: Day £10,560–£11,760

ST BENEDICT'S SCHOOL
For further details see p. 86
54 Eaton Rise, Ealing,
London W5 2ES
Tel: 020 8862 2000
Email: admissions@stbenedicts.org.uk
Website: www.stbenedicts.org.uk
Headmaster: Mr A Johnson BA
Age range: 3–18 years
No. of pupils: 1073 VIth203
Fees: Day £13,995–£18,330

St James Preparatory School
Earsby Street, London W14 8SH
Tel: 020 7348 1777
Headmistress: Mrs Catherine Thomlinson BA(Hons)
Age range: 3–11
Fees: Day £16,425–£17,910

Tabernacle School
32 St Anns Villas, Holland
Park, London W11 4RS
Tel: 020 7602 6232
Headteacher: Mrs P Wilson
Age range: 3–16
Fees: Day £6,500–£9,500

The Falcons Pre-Preparatory School for Boys
2 Burnaby Gardens,
Chiswick, London W4 3DT
Tel: 020 8747 8393
Head of School: Ms Liz McLaughlin
Age range: B2–7 years G2–4 years
Fees: Day £7,500–£15,705

The Japanese School
87 Creffield Road, Acton,
London W3 9PU
Tel: 020 8993 7145
Age range: 6–16

Thomas's Preparatory School - Kensington
17-19 Cottesmore Gardens,
London W8 5PR
Tel: 020 7361 6500
Headmistress: Miss Joanna Ebner MA, BEd(Hons)(Cantab), NPQH
Age range: 4–11
Fees: Day £20,526–£21,789

Wetherby Preparatory School
Bryanston Square, London W1H 2EA
Tel: 020 7535 3520
Headmaster: Mr Nick Baker
Age range: B8–13 years

Wetherby Pre-Preparatory School
11 Pembridge Square,
London W2 4ED
Tel: 020 7727 9581
Headmaster: Mr Mark Snell
Age range: B2 1/2–8 years

North-East

Durham D186
Northumberland D186
Stockton-on-Tees D186
Tyne & Wear D186

KEY TO SYMBOLS
- Boys' school
- Girls' school
- International school
- Tutorial or sixth form college
- A levels
- Boarding accommodation
- Bursaries
- International Baccalaureate
- Learning support
- Entrance at 16+
- Vocational qualifications
- Independent Association of Prep Schools
- The Headmasters' & Headmistresses' Conference
- Independent Schools Association
- Girls' School Association
- Boarding Schools' Association
- Society of Heads

Unless otherwise indicated, all schools are coeducational day schools. Single-sex and boarding schools will be indicated by the relevant icon.

England – North-East

Durham

Barnard Castle Preparatory School
Westwick Road, Barnard Castle, Durham DL12 8UW
Tel: 01833 696032
Headmistress: Mrs Laura Turner
Age range: 4–11 years
No. of pupils: 180
Fees: Day £6,240–£9,450 FB £18,300

Bow, Durham School
South Road, Durham DH1 3LS
Tel: 0191 731 9270
Headmistress: Mrs Sally Harrod
Age range: 3–11 years

Durham High School for Girls
Farewell Hall, Durham DH1 3TB
Tel: 0191 384 3226
Head of School: Mrs Simone Niblock
Age range: G3–18 years
No. of pupils: 347

The Chorister School
The College, Durham DH1 3EL
Tel: 0191 384 2935
Headmaster: Mr Ian Wicks
Age range: 3–13 years

Northumberland

Longridge Towers School
Longridge Towers, Berwick-upon-Tweed, Northumberland TD15 2XQ
Tel: 01289 307584
Headmaster: Mr Jonathan Lee
Age range: 3–19 years
No. of pupils: 313

Mowden Hall School
Newton, Stocksfield, Northumberland NE43 7TP
Tel: 01661 842147
Head: Ms Kate Martin
Age range: 3–13 years

Stockton-on-Tees

Red House School
36 The Green, Norton, Stockton-on-Tees TS20 1DX
Tel: 01642 553370
Headmaster: Mr Ken James LLB
Age range: 3–16
No. of pupils: 363
Fees: Day £4,710–£10,620

Teesside High School
The Avenue, Eaglescliffe, Stockton-on-Tees TS16 9AT
Tel: 01642 782095
Head of School: Mrs K Mackenzie
Age range: 3–18
No. of pupils: 350 VIth70

Yarm Preparatory School
Grammar School Lane, Yarm, Stockton-on-Tees TS15 9ES
Tel: 01642 781447
Headteacher: Mr William Sawyer
Age range: 3–11
No. of pupils: 360
Fees: Day £5,232–£10,755

Tyne & Wear

Argyle House School
19-20 Thornhill Park, Sunderland, Tyne & Wear SR2 7LA
Tel: 0191 5100726
Headteacher: Mr. Chris Johnson
Age range: 3–16
No. of pupils: 233

Dame Allan Junior School
Hunters Road, Spital Tongues, Newcastle upon Tyne, Tyne & Wear NE2 4NG
Tel: 0191 275 0608
Head: Mr A J Edge
Age range: 3–11
No. of pupils: 140
Fees: Day £7,266–£10,419

Gateshead Jewish Primary School
18-22 Gladstone Terrace, Gateshead, Tyne & Wear NE8 4EA
Tel: 0191 477 2154
Age range: 5–11

Newcastle High School for Girls GDST
Tankerville Terrace, Jesmond, Newcastle upon Tyne, Tyne & Wear NE2 3BA
Tel: 0191 201 6511
Acting Head: Mr Michael Tippett
Age range: G3–18 years
No. of pupils: G700
Fees: Day £2,886–£4,470

Newcastle Preparatory School
6 Eslington Road, Jesmond, Newcastle upon Tyne, Tyne & Wear NE2 4RH
Tel: 0191 281 1769
Head of School: Ms Fiona Coleman
Age range: 3–11 years

Newcastle School for Boys
30 West Avenue, Gosforth, Newcastle upon Tyne, Tyne & Wear NE3 4ES
Tel: 0191 255 9300
Headmaster: Mr David Tickner
Age range: B3–18

OneSchool Global UK York (Springwell) Campus
60 Peareth Hall Road, Springwell, Gateshead, Tyne & Wear NE9 7NT
Tel: 01904 663300
Age range: 7–18 years

Royal Grammar School
Eskdale Terrace, Newcastle upon Tyne, Tyne & Wear NE2 4DX
Tel: 0191 281 5711
Headmaster: Mr John Fern
Age range: 7–18
No. of pupils: 1325 VIth341
Fees: Day £10,662–£12,657

Westfield School
Oakfield Road, Gosforth, Newcastle upon Tyne, Tyne & Wear NE3 4HS
Tel: 0191 255 3980
Headmaster: Mr Neil Walker
Age range: G3–18
No. of pupils: 315 VIth50
Fees: Day £7,755–£13,590

North-West

Cheshire D188
Cumbria D188
Greater Manchester D189
Isle of Man D190
Lancashire D190
Merseyshire D191

KEY TO SYMBOLS
- (♂) Boys' school
- (♀) Girls' school
- (🌐) International school
- (16) Tutorial or sixth form college
- (A) A levels
- (⚓) Boarding accommodation
- (£) Bursaries
- (IB) International Baccalaureate
- (✎) Learning support
- (16) Entrance at 16+
- (✿) Vocational qualifications
- (IAPS) Independent Association of Prep Schools
- (HMC) The Headmasters' & Headmistresses' Conference
- (ISA) Independent Schools Association
- (GSA) Girls' School Association
- (BSA) Boarding Schools' Association
- (S) Society of Heads

Unless otherwise indicated, all schools are coeducational day schools. Single-sex and boarding schools will be indicated by the relevant icon.

England – North-West

Cheshire

Abbey Gate College
Saighton Grange, Saighton,
Chester, Cheshire CH3 6EN
Tel: 01244 332077
Head: Mrs Tracy Pollard
Age range: 4–18
No. of pupils: 468 VIth71
Fees: Day £8,955–£12,840
(A)(£)(🙂)

Alderley Edge School for Girls
Wilmslow Road, Alderley
Edge, Cheshire SK9 7QE
Tel: 01625 583028
Head of School: Mrs Helen Jeys
Age range: G2–18
(🎓)(A)(£)(B)(🙂)

Beech Hall School
Beech Hall Drive, Tytherington,
Macclesfield, Cheshire SK10 2EG
Tel: 01625 422192
Headmaster: Mr James Allen
Age range: 6 months–16 years
No. of pupils: 230
Fees: Day £9,720–£13,020
(£)(🙂)

Bowdon Preparatory School for Girls
Ashley Road, Altrincham,
Cheshire WA14 2LT
Tel: 0161 928 0678
Headmistress: Mrs Helen Gee
Age range: G3–11
No. of pupils: 200
(🎓)

Brabyns Preparatory School
34-36 Arkwright Road, Marple,
Stockport, Cheshire SK6 7DB
Tel: 0161 427 2395
Headteacher: Mrs
Lindsay McKenna
Age range: 2–11 years
Fees: Day £1,974–£2,719
(£)(🙂)

Cransley School
Belmont Hall, Great Budworth,
Northwich, Cheshire CW9 6HN
Tel: 01606 891747
Head of School: Mr Richard Pollock
LL.B, PGCE, PG Dip (RNCM)
Age range: 4–16
(£)(🙂)

Greater Grace Christian School
Church Lane, Backford,
Chester, Cheshire CH2 4BE
Tel: 01244 851797
Head Teacher: Mrs A Mulligan
Age range: 5–18

Green Meadow Independent Primary School
Robson Way, Lowton, Warrington,
Cheshire WA3 2RD
Tel: 01942 671138
Head: Mrs S Green
Age range: 4–11

Greenbank Preparatory School
64 Heathbank Road, Cheadle
Hulme, Stockport, Cheshire SK8 6HU
Tel: 0161 485 3724
Head of School: Mr
Malcolm Johnson
Age range: 6 months–11 years
No. of pupils: 283
Fees: Day £9,480
(£)(🙂)

Hale Preparatory School
Broomfield Lane, Hale,
Cheshire WA15 9AS
Tel: 0161 928 2386
Headmaster: Mr J F Connor
Age range: 4–11
No. of pupils: 202
Fees: Day £7,650

Lady Barn House School
Schools Hill, Cheadle,
Cheshire SK7 1JE
Tel: 0161 428 2912
Head of School: Mr M Turner
Age range: 3–11
No. of pupils: 483
Fees: Day £8,640
(£)(🙂)

OneSchool Global UK Northwich Campus
Hartford Manor, Greenbank Lane,
Northwich, Cheshire CW8 1HW
Tel: 01606 210320
Age range: 7–18 years

Pownall Hall School
Carrwood Road, Pownall Park,
Wilmslow, Cheshire SK9 5DW
Tel: 01625 523141
Headmaster: Mr David Goulbourn
Age range: 2–11 years
(🙂)

Terra Nova School
Jodrell Bank, Holmes Chapel,
Crewe, Cheshire CW4 8BT
Tel: 01477 571251
Headmaster: Mr Philip Stewart
Age range: 3–13
No. of pupils: 295
Fees: Day £5,940–£14,697
(🎓)(£)(🙂)

The Firs School
Newton Lane, Upton, Chester,
Cheshire CH2 2HJ
Tel: 01244 322443
Head Teacher: Mrs L Davies
BA (Hons) Durham, PGCE
(Exeter), PGCDL (York), NP+
Age range: 3–11
No. of pupils: 172
Fees: Day £9,147
(£)(🙂)

The Grange School
Bradburns Lane, Hartford,
Northwich, Cheshire CW8 1LU
Tel: 01606 74007 or 77447
Headmistress: Mrs
Deborah Leonard
Age range: 4–18
No. of pupils: 1185 VIth193
Fees: Day £8,340–£11,160
(A)(£)(🙂)

The Hammond School
Mannings Lane, Chester,
Cheshire CH2 4ES
Tel: 01244 305350
Principal: Ms Maggie Evans BA
(Hons) MA, PGCE, NPQH, FRSA
Age range: 6–19
No. of pupils: 280
Fees: Day £8,370–£18,750
FB £20,400–£27,600
(🎓)(A)(🎓)(£)(🙂)

The King's School Chester
Wrexham Road, Chester,
Cheshire CH4 7QL
Tel: 01244 689500
Headmaster: G J Hartley MA, MSc
Age range: 4–18
No. of pupils: 1080 VIth218
Fees: Day £9,150–£13,515
(A)(£)(🙂)

The King's School in Macclesfield
Alderley Road, Prestbury,
Cheshire SK10 4SP
Tel: 01625 260000
Headmaster: Dr Simon Hyde
Age range: 3–18
No. of pupils: 1200 VIth250
Fees: Day £8,235–£12,990
(A)(£)(🙂)

THE QUEEN'S SCHOOL
For further details see p. 95
City Walls Road, Chester,
Cheshire CH1 2NN
Tel: 01244 312078
Email: admissions@
thequeensschool.co.uk
Website:
www.thequeensschool.co.uk
Headmistress: Mrs Sue
Wallace-Woodroffe
Age range: G4–18 years
No. of pupils: 450
(🎓)(A)(£)

The Ryleys School
Ryleys Lane, Alderley Edge,
Cheshire SK9 7UY
Tel: 01625 583241
Headteacher: Mrs Julia Langford
Age range: 1–11 years

Wilmslow Preparatory School
Grove Avenue, Wilmslow,
Cheshire SK9 5EG
Tel: 01625 524246
Headteacher: Mrs Helen Rigby
Age range: 3–11
No. of pupils: 117
Fees: Day £4,635–£10,365
(£)(🙂)

Yorston Lodge School
18 St John's Road, Knutsford,
Cheshire WA16 0DP
Tel: 01565 633177
Headmistress: Mrs J
Dallimore BEd(Hons)
Age range: 3–11
Fees: Day £8,250–£8,310

Cumbria

Austin Friars School
Etterby Scaur, Carlisle,
Cumbria CA3 9PB
Tel: 01228 528042
Headmaster: Mr Matt Harris
Age range: 3–18
No. of pupils: 507 VIth70
Fees: Day £7,653–£14,952
(A)(£)(🙂)

Casterton, Sedbergh Preparatory School
Casterton, Carnforth,
Cumbria LA6 2SG
Tel: 01524 279200
Headmaster: Mr Will Newman
BA(Ed) Hons MA
Age range: 3–13
No. of pupils: 210
(🎓)(£)(🙂)

Hunter Hall School
Frenchfield, Penrith,
Cumbria CA11 8UA
Tel: 01768 891291
Head Teacher: Mrs Donna Vinsome
Age range: 3–11
No. of pupils: 101
Fees: Day £7,749–£8,979
(£)(🙂)

Lime House School
Holm Hill, Dalston, Carlisle,
Cumbria CA5 7BX
Tel: 01228 710225
Headteacher: Mrs Mary Robertson-Barnett MA(Oxon), PGCE
Age range: 7–18 years
No. of pupils: 182
(🎓)(A)(🎓)(£)(🙂)

England – North-West

Windermere School, Elleray Campus
Ambleside Road, Windermere, Cumbria LA23 1AP
Tel: +44 (0) 15394 43308
Head: Mrs Julie King
Age range: 3–11
No. of pupils: 75

Greater Manchester

Abbotsford Preparatory School
211 Flixton Road, Urmston, Manchester, Greater Manchester M41 5PR
Tel: 0161 748 3261
Head of School: Mrs Catherine Howard B.Ed(Hons)
Age range: 3–11 years

Altrincham Preparatory School
Marlborough Road, Bowdon, Altrincham, Greater Manchester WA14 2RR
Tel: 0161 928 3366
Headmaster: Mr N J Vernon
Age range: B2–11 years
No. of pupils: 310
Fees: Day £7,338–£9,579

Beech House School
184 Manchester Road, Rochdale, Greater Manchester OL11 4JQ
Tel: 01706 646309
Principal: Mr A Sartain BSc(Hons), PGCE, DipSp, CBiol, FIBiol
Age range: 2–16
Fees: Day £5,376–£6,546

Beis Ruchel Girls School
1-7 Seymour Road, Crumpsall, Manchester, Greater Manchester M8 5BQ
Tel: 01617 951830
Headmistress: Mrs E Krausz
Age range: G3–11

Bnos Yisroel School
Foigel Esther Shine House, Leicester Road, Manchester, Greater Manchester M7 4DA
Tel: 0161 792 3896
Headmaster: Rabbi R Spitzer
Age range: G2–16

Bolton School
Chorley New Road, Bolton, Greater Manchester BL1 4PA
Tel: 01204 840201
Heads of School: Mr Philip Britton & Miss Sue Hincks
Age range: 0–18 years
Fees: Day £9,966–£12,462

Branwood Preparatory School
Stafford Road, Monton, Eccles, Manchester, Greater Manchester M30 9HN
Tel: 0161 789 1054
Head of School: Mr Andrew Whittell
Age range: 3–11
No. of pupils: 156
Fees: Day £6,597

BRIDGEWATER SCHOOL
For further details see p. 94
Drywood Hall, Worsley Road, Worsley, Manchester, Greater Manchester M28 2WQ
Tel: 0161 794 1463
Email: admin@bwslive.co.uk
Website: www.bridgewater-school.co.uk
Head Teacher: Mrs JAT Nairn CertEd(Distinction)
Age range: 3–18 years
No. of pupils: 452

Bury Catholic Preparatory School
Arden House, 172 Manchester Road, Bury, Greater Manchester BL9 9BH
Tel: 0161 797 5804
Age range: 3–11
No. of pupils: 94
Fees: Day £3,992–£6,638

Bury Grammar Schools
Bridge Road, Bury, Greater Manchester BL9 0HH
Tel: 0161 696 8600
Headmistress: Mrs J Anderson
Age range: B4–7 G4–18
No. of pupils: VIth120
Fees: Day £7,836–£10,755

Cheadle Hulme School
Claremont Road, Cheadle Hulme, Cheadle, Greater Manchester SK8 6EF
Tel: 0161 488 3345
Head: Mr Neil Smith
Age range: 4–18
No. of pupils: 1396 VIth254
Fees: Day £8,950–£11,880

Chetham's School of Music
Long Millgate, Manchester, Greater Manchester M3 1SB
Tel: 0161 834 9644
Joint Principals: Nicola Smith & Tom Redmond
Age range: 8–18 years
No. of pupils: 300

Clarendon Cottage School
Ivy Bank House, Half Edge Lane, Eccles, Manchester, Greater Manchester M30 9BJ
Tel: 0161 950 7868
Headteacher: Mrs A Hartley
Age range: 3–11
No. of pupils: 81
Fees: Day £4,590–£4,740

Clevelands Preparatory School
425 Chorley New Road, Bolton, Greater Manchester BL1 5DH
Tel: 01204 843898
Head of School: Mr Keith Cahillane
Age range: 2–11
No. of pupils: 141
Fees: Day £7,485

Covenant Christian School
The Hawthorns, 48 Heaton Moor Road, Stockport, Greater Manchester SK4 4NX
Tel: 0161 432 3782
Head: Dr Roger Slack
Age range: 5–16
No. of pupils: 32

Farrowdale House Preparatory School
Farrow Street, Shaw, Oldham, Greater Manchester OL2 7AD
Tel: 01706 844533
Headteacher: Miss Z. N. Campbell BA (Hons) PGCE
Age range: 3–11
No. of pupils: 90
Fees: Day £5,790–£6,270

Forest Park Preparatory School
Lauriston House, 27 Oakfield, Sale, Greater Manchester M33 6NB
Tel: 0161 973 4835
Headteacher: Mr Nick Tucker
Age range: 3–11
Fees: Day £1,425–£2,496

Forest Preparatory School
Moss Lane, Timperley, Altrincham, Greater Manchester WA15 6LJ
Tel: 0161 980 4075
Headmaster: Mr Graeme Booth
Age range: 2–11 years
Fees: Day £1,437–£2,538

Hulme Hall Grammar School
Beech Avenue, Stockport, Greater Manchester SK3 8HA
Tel: 0161 485 3524
Headmaster: Mr Dean Grierson
Age range: 2–16 years
No. of pupils: 200
Fees: Day £2,840–£3,300

King of Kings School
142 Dantzic Street, Manchester, Greater Manchester M4 4DN
Tel: 0161 834 4214
Head Teacher: Mrs B Lewis
Age range: 3–18
No. of pupils: 29

Loreto Preparatory School
Dunham Road, Altrincham, Greater Manchester WA14 4GZ
Tel: 0161 928 8310
Headteacher: Mrs Anne Roberts
Age range: G3–11

Manchester High School for Girls
Grangethorpe Road, Manchester, Greater Manchester M14 6HS
Tel: 0161 224 0447
Head Mistress: Mrs Helen F Jeys
Age range: G4–18 years
No. of pupils: 1000

Manchester Junior Girls School
64 Upper Park Road, Salford, Greater Manchester M7 4JA
Tel: 0161 740 0566
Age range: G3–11

Manchester Muslim Preparatory School
551 Wilmslow Road, Withington, Manchester, Greater Manchester M20 4BA
Tel: 0161 445 5452
Head Teacher: Mrs Doris Ghafori-Kanno
Age range: 3–11
No. of pupils: 186
Fees: Day £5,225–£5,500

England – North-West

Monton Village Nursery & Forest School
The School House, Francis Street, Monton, Manchester, Greater Manchester M30 9PR
Tel: 0161 789 0472
Age range: 1–7

Moor Allerton Preparatory School
131 Barlow Moor Road, West Didsbury, Manchester, Greater Manchester M20 2PW
Tel: 0161 445 4521
Headmistress: Mrs Adriana Ewart-Jones
Age range: 3–11
Fees: Day £8,310–£8,550

Oldham Hulme Grammar School
Chamber Road, Oldham, Greater Manchester OL8 4BX
Tel: 0161 624 4497
Principal: Mr CJD Mairs
Age range: 2–18
No. of pupils: 766
Fees: Day £8,220–£11,235

OYY Lubavitch Girls School
Beis Menachem, Park Lane, Salford, Greater Manchester M7 4JD
Tel: 0161 795 0002
Headmistress: Mrs J Hanson
Age range: 2–16
No. of pupils: 82

Prestwich Preparatory School
St Margaret's Building, 400 Bury Old Road, Prestwich, Manchester, Greater Manchester M25 1PZ
Tel: 0161 773 1223
Headmistress: Miss P Shiels
Age range: 2–11
No. of pupils: 122
Fees: Day £6,300

St Ambrose Preparatory School
Hale Barns, Altrincham, Greater Manchester WA15 0HF
Tel: 0161 903 9193
Headmaster: F J Driscoll
Age range: 3–11 years

St Bede's College
Alexandra Park Road, Manchester, Greater Manchester M16 8HX
Tel: 0161 226 3323
Headmaster: Dr Richard Robson
Age range: 3–18
Fees: Day £8,076–£11,325

Stella Maris Junior School
St Johns Road, Heaton Mersey, Stockport, Greater Manchester SK4 3BR
Tel: 0161 432 0532
Headteacher: Mrs N Johnson
Age range: 3–11
No. of pupils: 68
Fees: Day £7,713

Stockport Grammar School
Buxton Road, Stockport, Greater Manchester SK2 7AF
Tel: 0161 456 9000
Headmaster: Dr Paul Owen
Age range: 3–18
No. of pupils: 1439 VIth193
Fees: Day £8,766–£11,700

Tashbar of Manchester
20 Upper Park Road, Salford, Greater Manchester M7 4HL
Tel: 01617 208254
Head of School: Rabbi David Hammond
Age range: B3–12

The Chadderton Preparatory Grammar School
Broadway, Chadderton, Oldham, Greater Manchester OL9 0AD
Tel: 0161 6206570
Headteacher: Mrs Caroline Greenwood
Age range: 2–11
Fees: Day £6,270

The Manchester Grammar School
Old Hall Lane, Fallowfield, Manchester, Greater Manchester M13 0XT
Tel: 0161 224 7201
High Master: Dr Martin Boulton
Age range: B7–18
Fees: Day £12,570

Trinity Christian School
Birbeck Street, Stalybridge, Greater Manchester SK15 1SH
Tel: 0161 303 0674
Head: Mr Michael Stewart
Age range: 3–16
Fees: Day £4,038–£5,874

Withington Girls' School
Wellington Road, Fallowfield, Manchester, Greater Manchester M14 6BL
Tel: 0161 224 1077
Headmistress: Mrs S J Haslam BA
Age range: G7–18
No. of pupils: 660 VIth150
Fees: Day £9,195–£12,252

Isle of Man

The Buchan School
Westhill, Arbory Road, Castletown, Isle of Man IM9 1RD
Tel: +44 (0)1624 820481
Head of School: G R Shaw-Twilley

Lancashire

AKS Lytham
Clifton Drive South, Lytham St Annes, Lancashire FY8 1DT
Tel: 01253 784100
Headmaster: Mr. Mike Walton BA, MA (Ed), PGCE, NPQH
Age range: 2–18
No. of pupils: 800 VIth165
Fees: Day £8,895–£11,787

Ashbridge Independent School
Lindle Lane, Hutton, Preston, Lancashire PR4 4AQ
Tel: 01772 619900
Headteacher: Karen Mehta
Age range: 0–11
No. of pupils: 315
Fees: Day £7,800

Heathland School
Broad Oak, Sandy Lane, Accrington, Lancashire BB5 2AN
Tel: 01254 234284
Principal: Mrs J Harrison BA(Hons), CertEd, FRSA
Age range: 4–16

Highfield Priory School
58 Fulwood Row, Fulwood, Preston, Lancashire PR2 5RW
Tel: 01772 709624
Headteacher: Jeremy M Duke
Age range: 2–11 years
No. of pupils: 210
Fees: Day £8,370

Kirkham Grammar School
Ribby Road, Kirkham, Preston, Lancashire PR4 2BH
Tel: 01772 684264
Headmaster: Mr Daniel Berry
Age range: 3–18 years
No. of pupils: 870 VIth180

Lancaster Steiner School
Lune Road, Lancaster, Lancashire LA1 5QU
Tel: 01524 381876
Age range: 0–11

Moorland School
Ribblesdale Avenue, Clitheroe, Lancashire BB7 2JA
Tel: 01200 423833
Principal: Mr Jonathan Harrison
Age range: 3 months–16 years
Fees: Day £6,996–£9,996 WB £18,000–£22,800 FB £19,800–£24,900

Oakhill School & Nursery
Wiswell Lane, Whalley, Clitheroe, Lancashire BB7 9AF
Tel: 01254 823546
Principal: Ms Jane Buttery BA (Hons) NPQH
Age range: 2–16

OneSchool Global UK Lancaster Campus
Melling Road, Hornby, Lancashire LA2 8LH
Tel: 01524 222159
Age range: 7–18 years

Rossall School
Broadway, Fleetwood, Lancashire FY7 8JW
Tel: +44 (0)1253 774201
Head: Mr Jeremy Quartermain
Age range: 0–18 years
No. of pupils: 821 VIth232
Fees: Day £8,865–£14,430 WB £15,285–£24,840 FB £22,575–£41,175

Scarisbrick Hall School
Southport Road, Scarisbrisk, Ormskirk, Lancashire L40 9RQ
Tel: 01704 841151
Headmaster: Mr J Shaw
Age range: 0–18
Fees: Day £7,185–£11,160

England – North-West

St Anne's College Grammar School
293 Clifton Drive South, Lytham St Annes, Lancashire FY8 1HN
Tel: +44 (0)1253 725815
Principal: Mr S R Welsby
Age range: 2–18
No. of pupils: VIth16
Fees: Day £5,370–£7,320

St Joseph's School, Park Hill
Park Hill, Padiham Road, Burnley, Lancashire BB12 6TG
Tel: 01282 455622
Headmistress: Mrs Annette Robinson
Age range: 3–11
Fees: Day £6,195

St Pius X Preparatory School
Oak House, 200 Garstang Road, Fulwood, Preston, Lancashire PR2 8RD
Tel: 01772 719937
Head of School: Patrick Gush
Age range: 2–11
No. of pupils: 260
Fees: Day £7,800

Stonyhurst St Mary's Hall
Clitheroe, Lancashire BB7 9PU
Tel: 01254 826242
Headmaster: Mr Ian Murphy BA (Hons), PGCE Durham
Age range: 3–13 years

Westholme School
Meins Road, Blackburn, Lancashire BB2 6QU
Tel: 01254 506070
Principal: Mrs Lynne Horner
Age range: 2–18
No. of pupils: 792 VIth72
Fees: Day £7,890–£10,875

Merseyside

Avalon Preparatory School
Caldy Road, West Kirby, Wirral, Merseyside CH48 2HE
Tel: 0151 625 6993
Head of School: Ms Joanna Callaway
Age range: 2–11
No. of pupils: 178
Fees: Day £4,539–£8,469

Birkenhead School
The Lodge, 58 Beresford Road, Birkenhead, Merseyside CH43 2JD
Tel: 0151 652 4014
Headmaster: Mr Paul Vicars
Age range: 3 months–18 years
No. of pupils: VIth103
Fees: Day £8,010–£11,994

Carleton House Preparatory School
145 Menlove Avenue, Liverpool, Merseyside L18 3EE
Tel: 0151 722 0756
Head of School: Mrs Sandy Coleman
Age range: 3–11
No. of pupils: 179
Fees: Day £7,771

Christian Fellowship School
Overbury Street, Edge Hill, Liverpool, Merseyside L7 3HL
Tel: 0151 709 1642
Headteacher: Mrs R Boulton (BA Tons, PGCE)
Age range: 4–16
No. of pupils: 136
Fees: Day £2,628–£5,220

Prenton Preparatory School
Mount Pleasant, Oxton, Wirral, Merseyside CH43 5SY
Tel: 0151 652 3182
Headteacher: Mr M Jones BSC Hons, PGCE
Age range: 2–11
Fees: Day £800–£8,586

St Mary's College
Everest Road, Crosby, Liverpool, Merseyside L23 5TW
Tel: 0151 924 3926
Principal: Mr Michael Kennedy Bsc, MA
No. of pupils: 880 VIth132
Fees: Day £7,573–£11,161

The Belvedere Preparatory School
23 Belvidere Road, Princes Park, Aigburth, Liverpool, Merseyside L8 3TF
Tel: 0151 471 1137
Head of School: Ms Clare Burnham
Age range: 3–11
No. of pupils: 180

Tower College
Mill Lane, Rainhill, Prescot, Merseyside L35 6NE
Tel: 0151 426 4333
Principal: Miss R J Oxley NNEB, RSH
Age range: 3–16

South-East

Berkshire **D194**
Buckinghamshire **D195**
East Sussex **D195**
Hampshire **D196**
Isle of Wight **D198**
Kent **D198**
Surrey **D200**
West Sussex **D202**

*See also Greater London (D169) for schools in Kent and Surrey

KEY TO SYMBOLS
- Boys' school
- Girls' school
- International school
- Tutorial or sixth form college
- A levels
- Boarding accommodation
- Bursaries
- International Baccalaureate
- Learning support
- Entrance at 16+
- Vocational qualifications
- (IAPS) Independent Association of Prep Schools
- (HMC) The Headmasters' & Headmistresses' Conference
- (ISA) Independent Schools Association
- (GSA) Girls' School Association
- (BSA) Boarding Schools' Association
- (S) Society of Heads

Unless otherwise indicated, all schools are coeducational day schools. Single-sex and boarding schools will be indicated by the relevant icon.

England – South-East

Berkshire

Alder Bridge Steiner-Waldorf School
Bridge House, Mill Lane, Padworth, Reading, Berkshire RG7 4JU
Tel: 0118 971 4471
Head of School: Lucia Dimarco
Age range: 3–14 years

Caversham Preparatory School
16 Peppard Road, Caversham, Reading, Berkshire RG4 8JZ
Tel: 01189 478 684
Head of School: Mrs Naomi Williams
Age range: 3–11 years

Claires Court Junior Boys
Ridgeway, The Thicket, Maidenhead, Berkshire SL6 3QE
Tel: 01628 327400
Head of School: Mr Dean Richards
Age range: B4–11 years

Claires Court Nursery, Girls and Sixth Form
1 College Avenue, Maidenhead, Berkshire SL6 6AW
Tel: 01628 327500
Head of Junior Girls: Ms Lindsay King
Age range: B16–18 years G3–18 years

Crosfields School
Shinfield Road, Reading, Berkshire RG2 9BL
Tel: 0118 987 1810
Headmaster: Mr Craig Watson
Age range: 3–16 years

Deenway Montessori School & Unicity College
3-5 Sidmouth Street, Reading, Berkshire RG1 4QX
Tel: 0118 9574737
Headmaster: Mr Munawar Karim LL.B (Hons), M.A, Mont. Dip.
Age range: 3–18+ years

Dolphin School
Waltham Road, Hurst, Reading, Berkshire RG10 0FR
Tel: 0118 934 1277
Headmaster: Mr Adam Hurst
Age range: 3–13 years

EAGLE HOUSE SCHOOL
For further details see p. 102
Sandhurst, Berkshire GU47 8PH
Tel: 01344 772134
Email: info@eaglehouseschool.com
Website: www.eaglehouseschool.com
Headmaster: Mr A P N Barnard BA(Hons), PGCE
Age range: 3–13 years
No. of pupils: 394
Fees: Day £18,615 FB £25,905

Elstree School
Woolhampton Hill, Woolhampton, Reading, Berkshire RG7 5TD
Tel: 01189 713302
Headmaster: Mr Sid Inglis B.A. (Hons), P.G.C.E.
Age range: 3–13 years
No. of pupils: 270

ETON END SCHOOL
For further details see p. 101
35 Eton Road, Datchet, Slough, Berkshire SL3 9AX
Tel: 01753 541075
Email: admin@etonend.org
Website: www.etonend.org
Head of School: Mrs Sophie Banks MEd
Age range: 3–11 years
No. of pupils: 244
Fees: Day £10,266–£13,119

Hemdean House School
Hemdean Road, Caversham, Reading, Berkshire RG4 7SD
Tel: 0118 947 2590
Head Teacher: Mrs H Chalmers BSc
Age range: 2–11 years

Herries Preparatory School
Dean Lane, Cookham Dean, Berkshire SL6 9BD
Tel: 01628 483350
Headteacher: Mr Robert Grosse
Age range: 3–11 years

HIGHFIELD PREPARATORY SCHOOL
For further details see p. 106
2 West Road, Maidenhead, Berkshire SL6 1PD
Tel: 01628 624918
Email: office@highfieldprep.org
Website: www.highfieldprep.org
Headteacher: Mrs Joanna Leach
Age range: B2–7 years G2–11 years

Holme Grange School
Heathlands Road, Wokingham, Berkshire RG40 3AL
Tel: 0118 978 1566
Headteacher: Mrs Claire Robinson BA (Open) PGCE NPQH
Age range: 3–16 years
No. of pupils: 660
Fees: Day £10,665–£16,140

Lambrook School
Winkfield Row, Nr Ascot, Berkshire RG42 6LU
Tel: 01344 882717
Headmaster: Mr Jonathan Perry
Age range: 3–13 years
No. of pupils: 600

Long Close School
Upton Court Road, Upton, Slough, Berkshire SL3 7LU
Tel: 01753 520095
Headteacher: Miss K Nijjar BA (Hons), Med, MA
Age range: 2–16 years
No. of pupils: 329

Ludgrove
Wokingham, Berkshire RG40 3AB
Tel: 0118 978 9881
Head of School: Mr Simon Barber
Age range: B8–13 years

LVS Ascot
London Road, Ascot, Berkshire SL5 8DR
Tel: 01344 882770
Principal: Mrs Christine Cunniffe BA (Hons), MMus, MBA
Age range: 4–18 years
No. of pupils: 800
Fees: Day £10,785–£19,335 FB £27,585–£33,975

Meadowbrook Montessori School
Malt Hill, Warfield, Berkshire RG42 6JQ
Tel: 01344 890869
Director of Education: Ms Serena Gunn
Age range: 18 months–11 years

Newbold School
Popeswood Road, Binfield, Bracknell, Berkshire RG42 4AH
Tel: 01344 421088
Headteacher: Mrs Jaki Crissey MA, BA, PGCE Primary
Age range: 3–11 years

OneSchool Global UK Reading Campus (Primary)
401 Old Whitley Wood Lane, Reading, Berkshire RG2 8QA
Tel: 0118 931 2938
Age range: 7–11 years

Our Lady's Preparatory School
The Avenue, Crowthorne, Wokingham, Berkshire RG45 6PB
Tel: 01344 773394
Headmaster: Mr Michael Stone
Age range: 3 months–11 years

Papplewick School
Windsor Road, Ascot, Berkshire SL5 7LH
Tel: 01344 621488
Headmaster: Mr Tom Bunbury
Age range: B6–13 years

Reddam House Berkshire
Bearwood Road, Sindlesham, Wokingham, Berkshire RG41 5BG
Tel: 0118 467 8731
Head of School: Mr Rick Cross
Age range: 3 months–18 years
No. of pupils: 650
Fees: Day £11,490–£18,330 WB £27,981–£32,244 FB £29,526–£33,789

St Andrew's School
Buckhold, Pangbourne, Reading, Berkshire RG8 8QA
Tel: 0118 974 4276
Head Master: Ed Graham
Age range: 3–13 years
Fees: Day £3,890–£6,525

St Bernard's Preparatory School
Hawtrey Close, Slough, Berkshire SL1 1TB
Tel: 01753 521821
Headteacher: Mrs A Verma
Age range: 2.5–11 years

St Edward's Prep
64 Tilehurst Road, Reading, Berkshire RG30 2JH
Tel: 0118 957 4342
Headmaster: Mr Jonathan Parsons
Age range: 4–11 years

St George's School Windsor Castle
Windsor Castle, Windsor, Berkshire SL4 1QF
Tel: 01753 865553
Head Master: Mr W Goldsmith BA (Hons), FRSA, FCCT
Age range: 3–13 years

St John's Beaumont Preparatory School
Priest Hill, Old Windsor, Berkshire SL4 2JN
Tel: 01784 432428
Headmaster: Mr G E F Delaney BA(Hons), PGCE, MSc
Age range: B3–13 years
No. of pupils: 250
Fees: Day £3,410–£6,525 FB £7,647–£10,005

St Joseph's College
Upper Redlands Road, Reading, Berkshire RG1 5JT
Tel: 0118 966 1000
Head of School: Mrs Laura Stotesbury
Age range: 3–18 years

St Piran's School
Gringer Hill, Maidenhead, Berkshire SL6 7LZ
Tel: 01628 594300
Headmaster: Mr Sebastian Sales
Age range: 2–11 years

England – South-East

Sunningdale School
Dry Arch Road, Sunningdale,
Berkshire SL5 9PY
Tel: 01344 620159
Headmaster: Tom Dawson MA, PGCE
Age range: B7–13 years

The Abbey School
Kendrick Road, Reading,
Berkshire RG1 5DZ
Tel: 0118 987 2256
Head: Mr Will le Fleming
Age range: G3–18 years
No. of pupils: 1000
Fees: Day £11,025–£18,885

The Marist Preparatory School
King's Road, Sunninghill,
Ascot, Berkshire SL5 7PS
Tel: 01344 624291
Vice Principal Prep Phase: Mrs Jane Gow
Age range: G2.5–11 years

The Oratory Preparatory School
Great Oaks, Goring Heath,
Reading, Berkshire RG8 7SF
Tel: 0118 984 4511
Headmaster: Mr Rob Stewart
Age range: 2–13 years

The Vine Christian School
Three Mile Cross Church,
Basingstoke Road, Three Mile
Cross, Reading, Berkshire RG7 1HF
Tel: 0118 988 6464
Head of School: Mrs René Esterhuizen
Age range: 3–18 years

Upton House School
115 St Leonard's Road,
Windsor, Berkshire SL4 3DF
Tel: 01753 862610
Head: Mrs Rhian Thornton BA (Hons) NPQH LLE PGCE
Age range: 2–11 years
No. of pupils: 287
Fees: Day £3,230–£5,400

Waverley Preparatory School & Day Nursery
Waverley Way, Finchampstead,
Wokingham, Berkshire RG40 4YD
Tel: 0118 973 1121
Principal: Mr Guy Shore
Age range: 3 months–11 years

Buckinghamshire

Gayhurst School
Bull Lane, Gerrards Cross,
Buckinghamshire SL9 8RJ
Tel: 01753 882690
Headmaster: Gareth R A Davies
Age range: 3–11 years

Maltman's Green School
Maltmans Lane, Gerrards Cross,
Buckinghamshire SL9 8RR
Tel: 01753 883022
Headmistress: Mrs Jill Walker BSc (Hons), MA Ed, PGCE
Age range: G2–11 years
No. of pupils: 320
Fees: Day £2,075–£5,370

St Mary's School
94 Packhorse Road, Gerrards
Cross, Buckinghamshire SL9 8JQ
Tel: 01753 883370
Head of School: Mrs Patricia Adams
Age range: G3–18 years

Thorpe House School
Oval Way, Gerrards Cross,
Buckinghamshire SL9 8QA
Tel: 01753 882474
Headmaster: Mr Nicholas Pietrek
Age range: B4–16 years

East Sussex

Battle Abbey School
Battle, East Sussex TN33 0AD
Tel: 01424 772385
Headmaster: Mr D Clark BA(Hons)
Age range: 2–18
No. of pupils: 286 VIth48
Fees: Day £6,939–£16,914
FB £26,649–£31,932

Brighton & Hove Montessori School
67 Stanford Avenue, Brighton,
East Sussex BN1 6FB
Tel: 01273 702485
Headteacher: Mrs Daisy Cockburn AMI, MontDip
Age range: 2–11

Brighton College Nursery, Pre-Prep & Prep School
Walpole Lodge, Walpole Road,
Brighton, East Sussex BN2 0EU
Tel: +44 (0)1273 704210
Head of School: Mr John Weeks BA
Age range: 3–13
No. of pupils: 505
Fees: Day £3,520–£6,780

Brighton Girls GDST
Montpelier Road, Brighton,
East Sussex BN1 3AT
Tel: 01273 280280
Head: Jennifer Smith
Age range: G3–18
No. of pupils: 680 VIth70
Fees: Day £7,191–£14,421

Brighton Steiner School
John Howard House, Roedean
Road, Brighton, East Sussex BN2 5RA
Tel: 01273 386300
Chair of the College of Teachers: Carrie Rawle
Age range: 3–16
Fees: Day £7,800–£8,100

Charters Ancaster
Woodsgate Place, Gunters Lane,
Bexhill-on-Sea, East Sussex TN39 4EB
Tel: 01424 216670
Nursery Manager: Susannah Crump
Age range: 6 months–5
No. of pupils: 125

Claremont Preparatory & Nursery School
Ebdens Hill, Baldslow, St Leonards-
on-Sea, East Sussex TN37 7PW
Tel: 01424 751555
Headmistress: Abra Stoakley
Age range: 1–13
Fees: Day £6,900–£12,600

Darvell School
Darvell, Brightling Road,
Robertsbridge, East
Sussex TN32 5DR
Tel: 01580 883300
Head of School: Mr Timothy Maas
Age range: 4–16

Deepdene School
195 New Church Road, Hove,
East Sussex BN3 4ED
Tel: 01273 418984
Heads: Mrs Nicola Gane & Miss Elizabeth Brown
Age range: 6 months–11 years
Fees: Day £8,349

Greenfields Independent Day & Boarding School
Priory Road, Forest Row,
East Sussex RH18 5JD
Tel: +44 (0)1342 822189
Executive Head: Mr. Jeff Smith
Age range: 2–19

JeMs Nursery
15 The Upper Drive, Hove,
East Sussex BN3 6GR
Tel: 01273 328 675
Head of School: Ms. Penina Efune
Age range: 1–4

Lancing Prep Hove
The Droveway, Hove,
East Sussex BN3 6LU
Tel: 01273 503452
Headmistress: Mrs Kirsty Keep BEd
Age range: 3–13 years

Lewes Old Grammar School
High Street, Lewes, East
Sussex BN7 1XS
Tel: 01273 472634
Headmaster: Mr Robert Blewitt
Age range: 3–18
No. of pupils: 463 VIth50
Fees: Day £8,760–£14,625

Michael Hall School
Kidbrooke Park, Priory Road,
Forest Row, East Sussex RH18 5JA
Tel: 01342 822275
Age range: 0 years–18 years
No. of pupils: VIth102
Fees: Day £9,245–£12,670

Roedean Moira House
Upper Carlisle Road, Eastbourne,
East Sussex BN20 7TE
Tel: 01323 644144
Headmaster: Mr Andrew Wood
Age range: G0–18
No. of pupils: 289

Sacred Heart School
Mayfield Lane, Durgates,
Wadhurst, East Sussex TN5 6DQ
Tel: 01892 783414
Headteacher: Mrs H Blake BA(Hons), PGCE
Age range: 2–11
No. of pupils: 121
Fees: Day £8,355

England – South-East

Skippers Hill Manor Preparatory School
Five Ashes, Mayfield,
East Sussex TN20 6HR
Tel: 01825 830234
Headmaster: Mr Phillip Makhouli
Age range: 2–13
Fees: Day £2,660–£4,615

ST ANDREW'S PREP
For further details see p. 112
Meads Street, Eastbourne,
East Sussex BN20 7RP
Tel: 01323 733203
Email: admissions@standrewsprep.co.uk
Website: www.standrewsprep.co.uk
Headmaster: Tom Gregory BA(Hons), PGCE
Age range: 9 months–13 years
No. of pupils: 374

St Bede's Preparatory School
Duke's Drive, Eastbourne,
East Sussex BN20 7XL
Tel: +44 (0)1323 734222
Age range: 3 months–13 years

St Christopher's School
33 New Church Road, Hove,
East Sussex BN3 4AD
Tel: 01273 735404
Head of School: Ms Elizabeth Lyle
Age range: 4–13 years

The Drive Prep School
101 The Drive, Hove, East Sussex BN3 6GE
Tel: 01273 738444
Head Teacher: Mrs S Parkinson CertEd, CertPerfArts
Age range: 7–16 years

Vinehall
Robertsbridge, East Sussex TN32 5JL
Tel: 01580 880413
Headmaster: Joff Powis
Age range: 2–13 years
No. of pupils: 220
Fees: Day £10,350–£19,290 WB £22,575–£23,100 FB £24,525–£25,125

Windlesham School
190 Dyke Road, Brighton,
East Sussex BN1 5AA
Tel: 01273 553645
Headmaster: Mr John Ingrassia
Age range: 3–11
No. of pupils: 195
Fees: Day £6,015–£8,955

Hampshire

Alton School
Anstey Lane, Alton,
Hampshire GU34 2NG
Tel: 01420 82070
Head: Karl Guest
Age range: 0–18 years
No. of pupils: 400

BALLARD SCHOOL
For further details see p. 98
Fernhill Lane, New Milton,
Hampshire BH25 5SU
Tel: 01425 626900
Email: registrar@ballardschool.co.uk
Website: www.ballardschool.co.uk
Headmaster: Mr Andrew McCleave
Age range: 2–16 years
No. of pupils: 451
Fees: Day £3,015–£5,550

Bedales Prep School, Dunhurst
Petersfield, Hampshire GU32 2DP
Tel: 01730 300200
Head of School: Colin Baty
Age range: 8–13
No. of pupils: 200
Fees: Day £16,920–£18,765 FB £22,215–£24,930

Boundary Oak School
Roche Court, Wickham Road,
Fareham, Hampshire PO17 5BL
Tel: 01329 280955
Executive Headmaster: Mr James Polansky MA (Cantab) PGCE
Age range: 2–16 years
No. of pupils: 348
Fees: Day £9,195–£14,886 WB £16,155–£21,078 FB £18,144–£23,067

Brockwood Park & Inwoods School
Brockwood Park, Bramdean,
Hampshire SO24 0LQ
Tel: +44 (0)1962 771744
Principal: Mr Antonio Autor
Age range: 14–19
No. of pupils: 112 VIth39
Fees: Day £5,630–£6,400 FB £21,400

Churcher's College
Petersfield, Hampshire GU31 4AS
Tel: 01730 263033
Headmaster: Mr Simon Williams, MA, BSc
Age range: 3–18 years
Fees: Day £10,830–£16,440

Daneshill School
Stratfield Turgis, Basingstoke,
Hampshire RG27 0AR
Tel: 01256 882707
Head of School: Jim Massey
Age range: 3–13 years
No. of pupils: 303
Fees: Day £11,550–£15,615

Ditcham Park School
Ditcham Park, Petersfield,
Hampshire GU31 5RN
Tel: 01730 825659
Headmaster: Mr Graham Spawforth MA, MEd
Age range: 2.5–16
No. of pupils: 379
Fees: Day £2,835–£4,753

Durlston Court
Becton Lane, Barton-on-Sea, New Milton, Hampshire BH25 7AQ
Tel: 01425 610010
Head of School: Mr Richard May
Age range: 2–13 years
No. of pupils: 260

Embley
Embley Park, Romsey,
Hampshire SO51 6ZE
Tel: 01794 512206
Headteacher: Mr Cliff Canning
Age range: 2–18
No. of pupils: 500
Fees: Day £8,754–£31,338

Farleigh School
Red Rice, Andover,
Hampshire SP11 7PW
Tel: 01264 710766
Headmaster: Fr Simon Everson
Age range: 3–13 years
No. of pupils: 460

Forres Sandle Manor
Fordingbridge, Hampshire SP6 1NS
Tel: 01425 653181
Head of School: Mr Robert Tasker
Age range: 2–13 years
No. of pupils: 145

Glenhurst School
16 Beechworth Road, Havant,
Hampshire PO9 1AX
Tel: 023 9248 4054
Principal: Mrs E M Haines
Age range: 3 months–5 years

Grantham Farm Montessori School & The Children's House
Grantham Farm, Baughurst,
Tadley, Hampshire RG26 5JS
Tel: 0118 981 5821
Head Teacher: Ms Emma Wetherley
Age range: 3–8

HIGHFIELD AND BROOKHAM SCHOOLS
For further details see p. 105
Highfield Lane, Liphook,
Hampshire GU30 7LQ
Tel: 01428 728000
Email: admissions@highfieldandbrookham.co.uk
Website: www.highfieldandbrookham.co.uk
Headteachers: Mr Phillip Evitt MA (Hons), PGCE & Mrs Sophie Baber BA (Hons), PGCE, PG Cert
Age range: 2–13 years
No. of pupils: 448

Kingscourt School
182 Five Heads Road,
Catherington, Hampshire PO8 9NJ
Tel: 023 9259 3251
Head of School: Amanda Bembridge
Age range: 3–11 years
No. of pupils: 158
Fees: Day £2,856

Mayville High School
35/37 St Simon's Road, Southsea,
Portsmouth, Hampshire PO5 2PE
Tel: 023 9273 4847
Headteacher: Mrs Rebecca Parkyn
Age range: 6 months–16 years
No. of pupils: 479
Fees: Day £7,635–£11,235

Meoncross School
Burnt House Lane, Stubbington,
Fareham, Hampshire PO14 2EF
Tel: 01329 662182
Headmaster: Mr Mark Cripps
Age range: 2–16 years
No. of pupils: 405
Fees: Day £8,736–£12,576

England – South-East

Moyles Court School
Moyles Court, Ringwood,
Hampshire BH24 3NF
Tel: 01425 472856
Headmaster: Mr Richard Milner-Smith
Age range: 3–16
No. of pupils: 195
Fees: Day £6,885–£14,655
FB £21,246–£26,805

Norman Court
West Tytherley, Stockbridge,
Hampshire SP5 1NH
Tel: 01980 322 322

Portsmouth High School GDST
Kent Road, Southsea, Portsmouth,
Hampshire PO5 3EQ
Tel: 023 9282 6714
Headmistress: Mrs Jane Prescott BSc NPQH
Age range: G3–18 years
No. of pupils: 500
Fees: Day £2,574–£4,800

Prince's Mead School
Worthy Park House, Kings Worthy,
Winchester, Hampshire SO21 1AN
Tel: 01962 888000
Headmaster: Peter Thacker
Age range: 4–11

Ringwood Waldorf School
Folly Farm Lane, Ashley,
Ringwood, Hampshire BH24 2NN
Tel: 01425 472664
Age range: 3–18
No. of pupils: 235
Fees: Day £6,240–£9,000

Rookwood School
Weyhill Road, Andover,
Hampshire SP10 3AL
Tel: 01264 325900
Headmaster: Mr A Kirk-Burgess BSc, PGCE, MSc (Oxon)
Age range: 2–16
Fees: Day £9,360–£15,600
FB £23,250–£27,465

Sherborne House School
Lakewood Road, Chandlers Ford,
Eastleigh, Hampshire SO53 1EU
Tel: 023 8025 2440
Head Teacher: Mr Mark Beach
Age range: 3–11
No. of pupils: 293
Fees: Day £8,295–£9,675

Sherfield School
South Drive, Sherfield-on-Loddon,
Hook, Hampshire RG27 0HU
Tel: 01256 884800
Headmaster: Mr Nick Brain BA(Hons), PGCE, MA, NPQH
Age range: 3 months–18 years
No. of pupils: 450
Fees: Day £10,320–£17,085 WB £18,960–£26,130 FB £22,125–£30,495

St John's College
Grove Road South, Southsea,
Portsmouth, Hampshire PO5 3QW
Tel: 023 9281 5118
Head of School: Mrs Mary Maguire
Age range: 4–18
No. of pupils: 560 VIth86
Fees: Day £9,975–£13,125
FB £28,500–£32,250

St Neot's School
St Neot's Road, Eversley,
Hampshire RG27 0PN
Tel: 0118 9739650
Head of School: Deborah Henderson
Age range: 2–13 years
No. of pupils: 248
Fees: Day £3,931–£5,624

St Nicholas' School
Redfields House, Redfields Lane, Church Crookham,
Fleet, Hampshire GU52 0RF
Tel: 01252 850121
Headmistress: Dr O Wright PhD, MA, BA Hons, PGCE
Age range: B3–7 G3–16
No. of pupils: 325

ST SWITHUN'S PREP
For further details see p. 114
Alresford Road, Winchester,
Hampshire SO21 1HA
Tel: 01962 835750
Email: prepoffice@stswithuns.com
Website: www.stswithuns.com
Head of School: Mr Jonathan Brough
Age range: B3–4 years G3–11 years
No. of pupils: 186

Stockton House School
Stockton Avenue, Fleet,
Hampshire GU51 4NS
Tel: 01252 616323
Early Years Manager: Mrs Jenny Bounds BA EYPS
Age range: 2–5

Stroud School, King Edward VI Preparatory School
Highwood House, Highwood Lane,
Romsey, Hampshire SO51 9ZH
Tel: 01794 513231
Headmistress: Mrs Rebecca Smith
Age range: 3–13 years
Fees: Day £3,838–£6,159

The Gregg Prep School
17-19 Winn Road, Southampton,
Hampshire SO17 1EJ
Tel: 023 8055 7352
Head Teacher: Mrs J Caddy
Age range: 3–11
Fees: Day £8,295

The King's School
Lakesmere House, Allington Lane,
Fair Oak, Eastleigh, Southampton,
Hampshire SO50 7DB
Tel: 023 8060 0986
Headteacher: Mrs Heather Bowden
Age range: 4–16 years

The New Forest Small School
1 Southampton Road, Lyndhurst,
Hampshire SO43 7BU
Tel: 02380 284415
Headteacher: Maz Wilberforce
Age range: 3–16 years

The Pilgrims' School
3 The Close, Winchester,
Hampshire SO23 9LT
Tel: 01962 854189
Head: Dr Sarah Essex
Age range: B4–13 years

The Portsmouth Grammar Junior School
High Street, Portsmouth,
Hampshire PO1 2LN
Tel: +44 (0)23 9268 1336
Headmaster: Peter Hopkinson BA, PGCE
Age range: 4–11
No. of pupils: 398
Fees: Day £8,127–£9,012

Thorngrove School
The Mount, Highclere, Newbury,
Hampshire RG20 9PS
Tel: 01635 253172
Headmaster: Mr Adam King
Age range: 2–13
Fees: Day £14,070–£17,595

Twyford School
Twyford, Winchester,
Hampshire SO21 1NW
Tel: 01962 712269
Headmaster: Mr Andrew Harvey
Age range: 3–13 years

Walhampton
Walhampton, Lymington,
Hampshire SO41 5ZG
Tel: 01590 613 300
Headmaster: Mr Titus Mills
Age range: 2–13
No. of pupils: 353
Fees: Day £9,000–£17,625
FB £20,250–£24,750

West Hill Park Preparatory School
Titchfield, Fareham,
Hampshire PO14 4BS
Tel: 01329 842356
Headmaster: A P Ramsay BEd(Hons), MSc
Age range: 2–13
No. of pupils: 288
Fees: Day £10,800–£18,300
FB £19,500–£22,650

Yateley Manor School
51 Reading Road, Yateley,
Hampshire GU46 7UQ
Tel: 01252 405500
Headmaster: Mr Robert Upton
Age range: 3–13
No. of pupils: 453
Fees: Day £11,160–£15,300

England – South-East

Isle of Wight

PRIORY SCHOOL OF OUR LADY OF WALSINGHAM
For further details see p. 110
Beatrice Avenue, Whippingham,
Isle of Wight PO32 6LP
Tel: 01983 861222
Email: mail@prioryschool.org.uk
Website: www.prioryschool.org.uk
Headmaster: Mr Edmund Matyjaszek
Age range: 4–18 years
No. of pupils: 170
Fees: Day £6,900–£9,990

Ryde School with Upper Chine
Queen's Road, Ryde, Isle of Wight PO33 3BE
Tel: 01983 562229
Headmaster: Mr Mark Waldron MA (Cantab)
Age range: 2 1/2–18 years
No. of pupils: 800
Fees: Day £7,935–£14,190 WB £27,420–£27,885 FB £30,795–£31,260

Kent

Ashford Prep School
Great Chart, Ashford, Kent TN23 3DJ
Tel: 01233 620493
Head: Nick Tiley-Nunn
Age range: 3–11

Ashford School
East Hill, Ashford, Kent TN24 8PB
Tel: 01233 739030
Head: Mr Michael Hall
Age range: 3 months–18 years
No. of pupils: 916 VIth127
Fees: Day £10,815–£18,294 WB £26,775 FB £38,778

Beech Grove School
Forest Drive, Nonington, Dover, Kent CT15 4FB
Tel: 01304 842980
Head of School: Mr Timothy Maas
Age range: 4–19

Beechwood Sacred Heart
12 Pembury Road, Tunbridge Wells, Kent TN2 3QD
Tel: 01892 532747
Acting Head: Mrs Helen Rowe
Age range: 3–18
No. of pupils: 400 VIth70
Fees: Day £8,685–£17,385 WB £26,850 FB £29,850

Bronte School
Mayfield, 7 Pelham Road, Gravesend, Kent DA11 0HN
Tel: 01474 533805
Headmistress: Ms Emma Wood
Age range: 3–11
No. of pupils: 120
Fees: Day £9,330

Bryony School
Marshall Road, Rainham, Gillingham, Kent ME8 0AJ
Tel: 01634 231511
Head of School: Mrs N Gee
Age range: 2–11 years

Chartfield School
45 Minster Road, Westgate on Sea, Kent CT8 8DA
Tel: 01843 831716
Head & Proprietor: Miss L P Shipley
Age range: 4–11

Dover College
Effingham Crescent, Dover, Kent CT17 9RH
Tel: 01304 205969
Headmaster: Mr Gareth Doodes MA (Hons)
Age range: 3–18
No. of pupils: 301
Fees: Day £7,725–£16,050 WB £21,000–£25,500 FB £24,750–£31,500

Dulwich Prep Cranbrook
Coursehorn, Cranbrook, Kent TN17 3NP
Tel: 01580 712179
Headmaster: Mr Paul David BEd(Hons)
Age range: 3–13
No. of pupils: 535
Fees: Day £5,970–£18,390

Elliott Park School
18-20 Marina Drive, Minster, Sheerness, Kent ME12 2DP
Tel: 01795 873372
Head: Ms Colleen Hiller
Age range: 3–11

Fosse Bank School
Mountains, Noble Tree Road, Hildenborough, Tonbridge, Kent TN11 8ND
Tel: 01732 834212
Headmistress: Miss Alison Cordingley
Age range: 2–11
No. of pupils: 124
Fees: Day £10,605–£13,185

Gad's Hill School
Higham, Rochester, Medway, Kent ME3 7PA
Tel: 01474 822366
Headmaster: Mr Paul Savage
Age range: 3–16
No. of pupils: 370
Fees: Day £8,988–£12,504

Haddon Dene School
57 Gladstone Road, Broadstairs, Kent CT10 2HY
Tel: 01843 861176
Head: Miss Alison Hatch
Age range: 3–11
No. of pupils: 200
Fees: Day £5,700–£7,230

Hilden Grange School
62 Dry Hill Park Road, Tonbridge, Kent TN10 3BX
Tel: 01732 352706
Headmaster: Mr J Withers BA(Hons)
Age range: 3–13
No. of pupils: 311

Hilden Oaks Preparatory School & Nursery
38 Dry Hill Park Road, Tonbridge, Kent TN10 3BU
Tel: 01732 353941
Head of School: Mrs. K Joiner
Age range: 3 months–11 years

Holmewood House School
Barrow Lane, Langton Green, Tunbridge Wells, Kent TN3 0EA
Tel: 01892 860000
Headmaster: Mr Scott Carnochan
Age range: 3–13 years
No. of pupils: 450

KENT COLLEGE JUNIOR SCHOOL
For further details see p. 108
Harbledown, Canterbury, Kent CT2 9AQ
Tel: 01227 762436
Email: admissions@kentcollege.co.uk
Website: kentcollege.com/junior-index.php
Head: Mr Simon James
Age range: 0–11 years
No. of pupils: 200
Fees: Day £10,587–£16,473 FB £26,901

Kent College Pembury
Old Church Road, Pembury, Tunbridge Wells, Kent TN2 4AX
Tel: +44 (0)1892 822006
Head of School: Miss Katrina Handford
Age range: G3–18 years
No. of pupils: 500
Fees: Day £22,575 WB £28,200 FB £35,700

King's Preparatory School, Rochester
King Edward Road, Rochester, Medway, Kent ME1 1UB
Tel: 01634 888577
Headmaster: Mr Tom Morgan
Age range: 8–13 years

King's Pre-Preparatory School, Rochester
Chadlington House, Lockington Grove, Rochester, Kent ME1 1RH
Tel: 01634 888566
Headmistress: Mrs C Openshaw
Age range: 3–8
No. of pupils: 149
Fees: Day £10,155–£11,010

England – South-East

Lorenden Preparatory School
Painter's Forstal, Faversham, Kent ME13 0EN
Tel: 01795 590030
Head of School: Mr Richard McIntosh
Age range: 3–11 years
No. of pupils: 122
Fees: Day £3,085–£4,485

Marlborough House School
High Street, Hawkhurst, Kent TN18 4PY
Tel: 01580 753555
Head: Mr Eddy Newton
Age range: 3–13 years
No. of pupils: 250
Fees: Day £9,165–£18,690

Northbourne Park School
Betteshanger, Deal, Kent CT14 0NW
Tel: 01304 611215/218
Headmaster: Mr Sebastian Rees BA(Hons), PGCE, NPQH
Age range: 2–13 years
No. of pupils: 195
Fees: Day £9,105–£17,346 WB £21,834 FB £25,281

OneSchool Global UK Maidstone Campus
Heath Road, Maidstone, Kent ME17 4HT
Tel: 03000 700 507
Age range: 7–18 years

Radnor House, Sevenoaks
Combe Bank Drive, Sevenoaks, Kent TN14 6AE
Tel: 01959 563720
Head: Mr David Paton BComm (Hons) PGCE MA
Age range: 2.5–18
No. of pupils: 250

Rose Hill School
Coniston Avenue, Tunbridge Wells, Kent TN4 9SY
Tel: 01892 525591
Head: Emma Neville
Age range: 3–13
Fees: Day £11,325–£15,225

Russell House School
Station Road, Otford, Sevenoaks, Kent TN14 5QU
Tel: 01959 522352
Headmaster: Mr Craig McCarthy
Age range: 2–11

Saint Ronan's School
Water Lane, Hawkhurst, Kent TN18 5DJ
Tel: 01580 752271
Headmaster: William Trelawny-Vernon BSc(Hons)
Age range: 3–13 years

Sevenoaks Preparatory School
Godden Green, Sevenoaks, Kent TN15 0JU
Tel: 01732 762336
Headmaster: Mr Luke Harrison
Age range: 2–13 years

Shernold School
Hill Place, Queens Avenue, Maidstone, Kent ME16 0ER
Tel: 01622 752868
Head Teacher: Ms. Sandra Dinsmore BA Hons. PGCE
Age range: 3–11
No. of pupils: 142
Fees: Day £7,245–£8,190

Solefield School
Solefields Road, Sevenoaks, Kent TN13 1PH
Tel: 01732 452142
Headmistress: Ms Helen McClure
Age range: B4–13 years

Somerhill
Tonbridge, Kent TN11 0NJ
Tel: 01732 352124
Principal: Mr Duncan Sinclair
Age range: 2–13 years

SPRING GROVE SCHOOL
For further details see p. 111
Harville Road, Wye, Kent TN25 5EZ
Tel: 01233 812337
Email: office@springgroveschool.co.uk
Website: www.springgroveschool.co.uk
Head of School: Mrs Therésa Jaggard
Age range: 2–11 years
No. of pupils: 226
Fees: Day £9,459–£13,290

St Andrew's School
24-28 Watts Avenue, Rochester, Medway, Kent ME1 1SA
Tel: 01634 843479
Principal: Mrs E Steinmann-Gilbert
Age range: 2–11
No. of pupils: 367
Fees: Day £7,725–£8,178

St Edmund's Junior School
St Thomas Hill, Canterbury, Kent CT2 8HU
Tel: 01227 475600
Head: Edward O'Connor
Age range: 3–13
No. of pupils: 230
Fees: Day £9,696–£16,101 WB £25,455 FB £27,933

St Faith's at Ash School
5 The Street, Ash, Canterbury, Kent CT3 2HH
Tel: 01304 813409
Headmaster: Mr Lawrence Groves
Age range: 2–11
No. of pupils: 225
Fees: Day £5,415–£9,885

St Lawrence College
Ramsgate, Kent CT11 7AE
Tel: 01843 572931
Head of College: Mr Barney Durrant
Age range: 3–18 years
No. of pupils: 585
Fees: Day £7,995–£17,025 FB £27,765–£37,455

St Michael's Preparatory School
Otford Court, Row Dow, Otford, Sevenoaks, Kent TN14 5RY
Tel: 01959 522137
Head: Mr Nik Pears
Age range: 2–13 years

Steephill School
Off Castle Hill, Fawkham, Longfield, Kent DA3 7BG
Tel: 01474 702107
Head: Mrs Caroline Birtwell BSc, MBA, PGCE
Age range: 3–11
No. of pupils: 131
Fees: Day £9,750

Sutton Valence Preparatory School
Chart Sutton, Maidstone, Kent ME17 3RF
Tel: 01622 842117
Head: Miss C Corkran
Age range: 3–11
No. of pupils: 320
Fees: Day £3,000–£4,610

The Granville School
2 Bradbourne Park Road, Sevenoaks, Kent TN13 3LJ
Tel: 01732 453039
Headmistress: Mrs Louise Lawrance B. Prim. Ed. (Hons)
Age range: B3–4 G3–11

The Junior King's School, Canterbury
Milner Court, Sturry, Canterbury, Kent CT2 0AY
Tel: 01227 714000
Head: Emma Károlyi
Age range: 3–13
Fees: Day £11,475–£19,290 FB £26,475

The Mead School
16 Frant Road, Tunbridge Wells, Kent TN2 5SN
Tel: 01892 525837
Headmaster: Mr Andrew Webster
Age range: 3–11
No. of pupils: 188
Fees: Day £4,536–£11,625

The New Beacon School
Brittains Lane, Sevenoaks, Kent TN13 2PB
Tel: 01732 452131
Headmaster: Mr M Piercy BA(Hons)
Age range: B4–13 years

Walthamstow Hall Pre-Prep and Junior School
Sevenoaks, Kent TN13 3LD
Tel: 01732 451334
Headmistress: Miss S Ferro
Age range: G2–11
No. of pupils: 218
Fees: Day £12,135–£15,300

Wellesley House
114 Ramsgate Road, Broadstairs, Kent CT10 2DG
Tel: 01843 862991
Headmaster: Mr G D Franklin
Age range: 7–13
No. of pupils: 133
Fees: Day £12,231–£19,917 FB £26,331

England – South-East

Surrey

ABERDOUR SCHOOL
For further details see p. 96
Brighton Road, Burgh Heath,
Tadworth, Surrey KT20 6AJ
Tel: +44 (0)1737 354119
Email: enquiries@
aberdourschool.co.uk
Website:
www.aberdourschool.co.uk
Headmaster: Mr S. D. Collins
Age range: 2–11 years
No. of pupils: 343
Fees: Day £4,710–£16,272

ACS Cobham International School
Heywood, Portsmouth Road,
Cobham, Surrey KT11 1BL
Tel: +44 (0) 1932 867251
Head of School: Mr
Barnaby Sandow
Age range: 2–18

ACS Egham International School
Woodlee, London Road,
Egham, Surrey TW20 0HS
Tel: +44 (0) 1784 430 800
Head of School: Mr Jeremy Lewis
Age range: 4–18
Fees: Day £11,090–£25,870

Aldro School
Lombard Street, Shackleford,
Godalming, Surrey GU8 6AS
Tel: 01483 810266
Headmaster: Mr Chris Carlier
Age range: 7–13 years

Amesbury School
Hazel Grove, Hindhead,
Surrey GU26 6BL
Tel: 01428 604322
Head of School: Mr
Jonathan Whybrow
Age range: 2–13 years
No. of pupils: 360

Banstead Preparatory School
Sutton Lane, Banstead,
Surrey SM7 3RA
Tel: 01737 363601
Headteacher: Miss Vicky Ellis
Age range: 2–11
No. of pupils: 225

Barfield School
Guildford Road, Runfold,
Farnham, Surrey GU10 1PB
Tel: 01252 782271
Headmaster: Mr Andy Boyle
Age range: 2–11 years

BARROW HILLS SCHOOL
For further details see p. 97
Roke Lane, Witley, Godalming,
Surrey GU8 5NY
Tel: +44 (0)1428 683639
Email: info@barrowhills.org
Website: www.barrowhills.org
Headmaster: Mr Philip Oldroyd
Age range: 2–13 years
No. of pupils: 216
Fees: Day £16,785

Belmont School
Feldemore, Holmbury St Mary,
Dorking, Surrey RH5 6LQ
Tel: 01306 730852
Headmistress: Mrs Helen Skrine
BA, PGCE, NPQH, FRSA
Age range: 2–16 years
Fees: Day £9,660–£16,740
WB £20,430–£21,300

Bishopsgate School
Bishopsgate Road, Englefield
Green, Egham, Surrey TW20 0YJ
Tel: 01784 432109
Headmaster: Mr R Williams
Age range: 3–13 years

Caterham School
Harestone Valley, Caterham,
Surrey CR3 6YA
Tel: 01883 343028
Head: Mr C. W. Jones MA(Cantab)
Age range: 11–18
No. of pupils: VIth321
Fees: Day £18,735–£19,620 WB
£30,936–£33,270 FB £36,795–£38,760

Chinthurst School
52 Tadworth Street, Tadworth,
Surrey KT20 5QZ
Tel: 01737 812011
Head: Miss Catherine Trundle
Age range: B3–11 years

City of London Freemen's School
Ashtead Park, Ashtead,
Surrey KT21 1ET
Tel: 01372 277933
Headmaster: Mr R Martin
Age range: 7–18
No. of pupils: 877 VIth213
Fees: Day £14,067–£19,194 WB
£29,784–£29,841 FB £30,780–£30,816

Claremont Fan Court School
Claremont Drive, Esher,
Surrey KT10 9LY
Tel: 01372 473780
Head: Mr William Brierly
Age range: 2 1/2–18 years
No. of pupils: 1010

COWORTH FLEXLANDS SCHOOL
For further details see p. 100
Valley End, Chobham,
Surrey GU24 8TE
Tel: 01276 855707
Email: secretary@
coworthflexlands.co.uk
Website:
www.coworthflexlands.co.uk
Head of School: Miss
Nicola Cowell
Age range: B2.5–7 years
G2.5–11 years
No. of pupils: 120

Cranleigh Preparatory School
Horseshoe Lane, Cranleigh,
Surrey GU6 8QH
Tel: 01483 542058
Headmaster: Mr Neil
Brooks BA(Hons) (QTS)
Age range: 7–13 years

Cranmore School
Epsom Road, West Horsley,
Surrey KT24 6AT
Tel: 01483 280340
Headmaster: Mr Barry Everitt
Age range: 2–13 years

Danes Hill School
Leatherhead Road, Oxshott,
Surrey KT22 0JG
Tel: 01372 842509
Age range: 3–13 years
No. of pupils: 725
Fees: Day £6,981–£20,340

Danesfield Manor School
Rydens Avenue, Walton-on-
Thames, Surrey KT12 3JB
Tel: 01932 220930
Principal: Mrs Jo Smith
Age range: 2–11
No. of pupils: 170
Fees: Day £9,456–£10,098

Downsend School
1 Leatherhead Road,
Leatherhead, Surrey KT22 8TJ
Tel: 01372 372197
Headmaster: Mr Ian Thorpe
Age range: 2–16 years
No. of pupils: 792
Fees: Day £11,970–£17,985

Downsend School (Ashtead Pre-Prep)
Ashtead Lodge, 22 Oakfield
Road, Ashtead, Surrey KT21 2RE
Tel: 01372 385439
Head Teacher: Tessa Roberts
Age range: 2–6
No. of pupils: 66
Fees: Day £11,535

Downsend School (Epsom Pre-Prep)
Epsom Lodge, 6 Norman Avenue,
Epsom, Surrey KT17 3AB
Tel: 01372 385438
Head Teacher: Vanessa Conlan
Age range: 2–6
No. of pupils: 110
Fees: Day £11,535

Downsend School (Leatherhead Pre-Prep)
Leatherhead Lodge, Epsom Road,
Leatherhead, Surrey KT22 8ST
Tel: 01372 385437
Headteacher: Mrs Gill Brooks
Age range: 2–6
No. of pupils: 106
Fees: Day £11,535

Drayton House Pre-School and Nursery
35 Austen Road, Guildford,
Surrey GU1 3NP
Tel: 01483 504707
Headmistress: Mrs J Tyson-Jones
Froebel Cert.Ed. London University
Age range: 6 months–5 years
No. of pupils: 65
Fees: Day £4,420–£12,500

Duke of Kent School
Peaslake Road, Ewhurst,
Surrey GU6 7NS
Tel: 01483 277113
Head: Mrs Sue Knox
BA(Hons) MBA MEd
Age range: 3–16 years
No. of pupils: 316
Fees: Day £2,740–£6,540

Dunottar School
High Trees Road, Reigate,
Surrey RH2 7EL
Tel: 01737 761945
Head of School: Mr Mark Tottman
Age range: 11–18
No. of pupils: 460
Fees: Day £18,621

Edgeborough
84 Frensham Road, Frensham,
Farnham, Surrey GU10 3AH
Tel: 01252 792495
Headmaster: Mr Dan Thornburn
Age range: 2–13 years
No. of pupils: 370

Emberhurst School
94 Ember Lane, Esher,
Surrey KT10 8EN
Tel: 020 8398 2933
Headmistress: Mrs P Chadwick BEd
Age range: 2–7
No. of pupils: 70

England – South-East

Essendene Lodge School
Essendene Road, Caterham, Surrey CR3 5PB
Tel: 01883 348349
Head Teacher: Mrs K Ali
Age range: 2–11
No. of pupils: 153
Fees: Day £3,315–£7,305

Ewell Castle School
Church Street, Ewell, Epsom, Surrey KT17 2AW
Tel: 020 8393 1413
Principal: Mr Silas Edmonds
Age range: 3–18 years
No. of pupils: 670
Fees: Day £5,382–£18,141

Feltonfleet School
Cobham, Surrey KT11 1DR
Tel: 01932 862264
Head of School: Mrs S Lance
Age range: 3–13 years
No. of pupils: 492

Frensham Heights
Rowledge, Farnham, Surrey GU10 4EA
Tel: 01252 792561
Head: Mr Rick Clarke
Age range: 3–18
No. of pupils: 497 VIth105
Fees: Day £7,110–£21,060 FB £27,450–£32,070

Glenesk School
Ockham Road North, East Horsley, Surrey KT24 6NS
Tel: 01483 282329
Headmistress: Mrs Sarah Bradley
Age range: 2–7 years
No. of pupils: 100
Fees: Day £11,658–£13,176

GREENFIELD SCHOOL
For further details see p. 104
Old Woking Road, Woking, Surrey GU22 8HY
Tel: 01483 772525
Email: schooloffice@greenfield.surrey.sch.uk
Website: www.greenfield.surrey.sch.uk
Headmistress: Mrs Tania Botting MEd
Age range: 6 months–11 years
No. of pupils: 335

Guildford High School
London Road, Guildford, Surrey GU1 1SJ
Tel: 01483 561440
Headmistress: Mrs F J Boulton BSc, MA
Age range: G4–18
No. of pupils: 985
Fees: Day £11,400–£18,300

Hall Grove School
London Road, Bagshot, Surrey GU19 5HZ
Tel: 01276 473059
Headmaster: Mr Alastair Graham
Age range: 3–13
No. of pupils: 410
Fees: Day £10,800–£15,450

Halstead Preparatory School
Woodham Rise, Woking, Surrey GU21 4EE
Tel: 01483 772682
Headmistress: Mrs P Austin
Age range: G3–11
No. of pupils: 220
Fees: Day £10,800–£15,210

Hampton Court House
Hampton Court Road, East Molesey, Surrey KT8 9BS
Tel: 020 8943 0889
Headmaster: Mr Guy Holloway
Age range: 3–18 years

Hazelwood School
Wolf's Hill, Limpsfield, Oxted, Surrey RH8 0QU
Tel: 01883 712194
Head: Mrs Lindie Louw
Age range: 2–13
No. of pupils: 399
Fees: Day £10,275–£16,380

Hoe Bridge School
Hoe Place, Old Woking Road, Woking, Surrey GU22 8JE
Tel: 01483 760018
Headmaster: Mr C Webster MA BSc (Hons) PGCE
Age range: 2–13 years

Kingswood House School
56 West Hill, Epsom, Surrey KT19 8LG
Tel: 01372 723590
Headmaster: Mr Duncan Murphy BA (Hons), MEd, FRSA
Age range: 4–16 years
No. of pupils: 250

Lingfield College
Racecourse Road, Lingfield, Surrey RH7 6PH
Tel: 01342 832407
Headmaster: Mr R Bool B.A. Hons, MBA
Age range: 2–18
No. of pupils: 935
Fees: Day £11,250–£21,801

Longacre School
Hullbrook Lane, Shamley Green, Guildford, Surrey GU5 0NQ
Tel: 01483 893225
Head of School: Mr Matthew Bryan MA(Cantab.), MA(Oxon.), MSc, FRSA
Age range: 2–11 years
No. of pupils: 267
Fees: Day £11,355–£17,250

Lyndhurst School
36 The Avenue, Camberley, Surrey GU15 3NE
Tel: 01276 22895
Head: Mr A Rudkin BEd(Hons)
Age range: 3–11
No. of pupils: 126

Manor House School, Bookham
Manor House Lane, Little Bookham, Leatherhead, Surrey KT23 4EN
Tel: 01372 457077
Headteacher: Ms Tracey Fantham BA (Hons) MA NPQH
Age range: B2–4 years G2–16 years
No. of pupils: 300
Fees: Day £9,747–£18,315

Micklefield School
10 Somers Road, Reigate, Surrey RH2 9DU
Tel: 01737 224212
Head: Mr R Ardé
Age range: 3–11 years
No. of pupils: 210
Fees: Day £10,965–£13,935

MILBOURNE LODGE SCHOOL
For further details see p. 109
Arbrook Lane, Esher, Surrey KT10 9EG
Tel: 01372 462737
Email: registrar@milbournelodge.co.uk
Website: www.milbournelodge.co.uk
Head: Mrs Judy Waite
Age range: 4–13 years
No. of pupils: 276
Fees: Day £13,695–£17,205

Notre Dame School
Cobham, Surrey KT11 1HA
Tel: 01932 869990
Head of Seniors: Mrs Anna King MEd, MA (Cantab), PGCE
Age range: 2–18
No. of pupils: 600

Oakhyrst Grange School
160 Stanstead Road, Caterham, Surrey CR3 6AF
Tel: 01883 343344
Headmaster: Mr Alex Gear
Age range: 4–11 years
No. of pupils: 152
Fees: Day £1,472–£3,414

OneSchool Global UK Hindhead Campus
Tilford Road, Hindhead, Surrey GU26 6SJ
Tel: 01428 601800
Age range: 7–18 years

OneSchool Global UK Kenley Campus
Victor Beamish Avenue, Kenley, Surrey CR3 5FX
Tel: 01883 338634
Age range: 7–18 years

Parkside School
The Manor, Stoke d'Abernon, Cobham, Surrey KT11 3PX
Tel: 01932 862749
Headteacher: Ms Nicole Janssen
Age range: B2–13 years G2–4 years
No. of pupils: 270

Reigate St Mary's Prep & Choir School
Chart Lane, Reigate, Surrey RH2 7RN
Tel: 01737 244880
Headmaster: Mr Marcus Culverwell MA
Age range: 2–11 years

RGS Prep
Maori Road, Guildford, Surrey GU1 2EL
Tel: 01483 880650
Head of School: Mr Toby Freeman-Day
Age range: B3–11 years
Fees: Day £15,999

Ripley Court School
Rose Lane, Ripley, Surrey GU23 6NE
Tel: 01483 225217
Headmistress: Ms Aislinn Clarke
Age range: 3–13

Rowan Preparatory School
6 Fitzalan Road, Claygate, Surrey KT10 0LX
Tel: 01372 462627
Headmistress: Mrs Susan Clarke BEd, NPQH
Age range: G2–11
No. of pupils: 317
Fees: Day £11,526–£15,294

Rydes Hill Preparatory School
Rydes Hill House, Aldershot Road, Guildford, Surrey GU2 8BP
Tel: 01483 563160
Headmistress: Mrs Sarah Norville
Age range: B3–7 G3–11
No. of pupils: 180
Fees: Day £3,006–£4,565

Shrewsbury House Pre-Preparatory School
22 Milbourne Lane, Esher, Surrey KT10 9EA
Tel: 01372 462781
Head: Mr Jon Akhurst BA (Hons) PGCE
Age range: 3–7
Fees: Day £6,225–£13,740

St Catherine's, Bramley
Station Road, Bramley, Guildford, Surrey GU5 0DF
Tel: 01483 899609
Headmistress: Alice Phillips
Age range: G4–18
Fees: Day £9,240–£18,885 FB £31,125

England – South-East

St Christopher's School
6 Downs Road, Epsom,
Surrey KT18 5HE
Tel: 01372 721807
Headteacher: Mrs A C
Thackray MA, BA(Hons)
Age range: 3–7
No. of pupils: 137
Fees: Day £10,485

St Edmund's School
Portsmouth Road, Hindhead,
Surrey GU26 6BH
Tel: 01428 604808
Headmaster: Mr A J Walliker
MA(Cantab), MBA, PGCE
Age range: 2–16 years

St George's Junior School
Thames Street, Weybridge,
Surrey KT13 8NL
Tel: 01932 839400
Head Master: Mr Antony Hudson
MA (CANTAB), MBA, PGCE, NPQH
Age range: 3–11 years
No. of pupils: 644
Fees: Day £5,640–£14,640

St Hilary's School
Holloway Hill, Godalming,
Surrey GU7 1RZ
Tel: 01483 416551
Headmistress: Mrs Jane
Whittingham BEdCert,
ProfPracSpLD
Age range: B2–11 G2–11
No. of pupils: 250
Fees: Day £10,092–£14,850

St Ives School
Three Gates Lane, Haslemere,
Surrey GU27 2ES
Tel: 01428 643734
Headteacher: Kay Goldsworthy
Age range: 2–11
No. of pupils: 149
Fees: Day £9,900–£13,950

**St Teresa's Effingham
(Preparatory School)**
Effingham, Surrey RH5 6ST
Tel: 01372 453456
Headmaster: Mr. Mike Farmer
Age range: B2–4 G2–11
No. of pupils: 100
Fees: Day £1,185–£14,685
WB £25,515 FB £28,665

St. Andrew's School
Church Hill House, Horsell,
Woking, Surrey GU21 4QW
Tel: 01483 760943
Headmaster: Mr D Fitzgerald
Age range: 3–13 years
No. of pupils: 300
Fees: Day £4,203–£16,545

**Surbiton Preparatory
School**
3 Avenue Elmers, Surbiton,
Surrey KT6 4SP
Tel: 020 8390 6640
Principal: Mrs Rebecca Glover
Age range: B4–11 G4–11
No. of pupils: 135
Fees: Day £10,857–£13,974

**TASIS The American
School in England**
Coldharbour Lane, Thorpe,
Surrey TW20 8TE
Tel: +44 (0)1932 582316
Head of School: Mr Bryan Nixon
Age range: 3–18
No. of pupils: 620
Fees: Day £12,280–
£26,375 FB £48,900

The Hawthorns School
Pendell Court, Bletchingley,
Redhill, Surrey RH1 4QJ
Tel: 01883 743048
Head of School: Mr Adrian Floyd
Age range: 2–13 years

The Royal Junior School
Portsmouth Road, Hindhead,
Surrey GU26 6BW
Tel: 01428 607977
Principal: Mrs Anne J P Lynch
Age range: 6 weeks–11 years
Fees: Day £10,200–£11,955

Tormead School
27 Cranley Road, Guildford,
Surrey GU1 2JD
Tel: 01483 575101
Headmistress: Mrs Christina Foord
Age range: G4–18
No. of pupils: 760 VIth120
Fees: Day £8,385–£15,915

Warlingham Park School
Chelsham Common,
Warlingham, Surrey CR6 9PB
Tel: 01883 626844
Headmaster: Mrs S S Buist
Age range: 2–11
No. of pupils: 96
Fees: Day £4,230–£8,565

Weston Green School
Weston Green Road, Thames
Ditton, Surrey KT7 0JN
Tel: 020 8398 2778
Headteacher: Mrs Sarah Evans
Age range: 2–11
No. of pupils: 200
Fees: Day £3,389–£3,809

Westward School
47 Hersham Road, Walton-
on-Thames, Surrey KT12 1LE
Tel: 01932 220911
Headmistress: Mrs
Shelley Stevenson
Age range: 3–12
No. of pupils: 140
Fees: Day £7,380–£8,235

Woodcote House School
Snows Ride, Windlesham,
Surrey GU20 6PF
Tel: 01276 472115
Headmaster: Mr D.M.K. Paterson
Age range: B7–13 years

Yehudi Menuhin School
Stoke Road, Stoke d'Abernon,
Cobham, Surrey KT11 3QQ
Tel: 01932 864739
Interim Head: Richard Tanner
Age range: 7–19
No. of pupils: 80 VIth36
Fees: FB £34,299

West Sussex

**Ardingly College
Preparatory School**
Haywards Heath, West
Sussex RH17 6SQ
Tel: 01444 893200
Head of Prep School:
Mr Harry Hastings
Age range: 2 1/2–13 years

Brambletye
Brambletye, East Grinstead,
West Sussex RH19 3PD
Tel: 01342 321004
Headmaster: Will Brooks
Age range: 2–13 years

Burgess Hill Girls
Keymer Road, Burgess Hill,
West Sussex RH15 0EG
Tel: 01444 241050
Head of School: Liz Laybourn
Age range: B2.5–4 years
G2.5–18 years
No. of pupils: 505 VIth70
Fees: Day £9,150–£20,850
FB £31,800–£36,750

Conifers School
Egmont Road, Midhurst,
West Sussex GU29 9BG
Tel: 01730 813243
Headmistress: Mrs Emma Smyth
Age range: 2–13
No. of pupils: 104
Fees: Day £7,350–£9,750

Copthorne Prep School
Effingham Lane, Copthorne,
West Sussex RH10 3HR
Tel: 01342 712311
Headmaster: Mr Chris Jones
Age range: 2–13
No. of pupils: 340
Fees: Day £9,750–£16,740
WB £20,400 FB £25,500

Cottesmore School
Buchan Hill, Pease Pottage,
West Sussex RH11 9AU
Tel: 01293 520648
Head: T F Rogerson
Age range: 4–13
No. of pupils: 170
Fees: Day £3,199–£4,267 FB £9,095

Cumnor House Sussex
London Road, Danehill, Haywards
Heath, West Sussex RH17 7HT
Tel: 01825 792 006
Head of School: Mr Fergus Llewellyn
Age range: 2–13
No. of pupils: 385
Fees: Day £8,985–£19,530
WB £22,635 FB £23,250

Dorset House School
The Manor, Church Lane, Bury,
Pulborough, West Sussex RH20 1PB
Tel: 01798 831456
Headmaster: Mr Matt Thomas
Med BA Ed (Hons) (Exeter) FRGS
Age range: 4–13 years
No. of pupils: 140
Fees: Day £9,315–£18,945
WB £1,258–£4,488

England – South-East

Great Ballard School
Eartham House, Eartham, Nr
Chichester, West Sussex PO18 0LR
Tel: 01243 814236
Head of School: Mr Matt King
Age range: 2.5–16 years
No. of pupils: 136
Fees: Day £8,580–£16,200

Great Walstead School
East Mascalls Lane,
Lindfield, Haywards Heath,
West Sussex RH16 2QL
Tel: 01444 483528
Headmaster: Mr Chris Calvey
Age range: 2.5–13 years
No. of pupils: 345
Fees: Day £2,895–£5,550

Handcross Park School
Handcross, Haywards Heath,
West Sussex RH17 6HF
Tel: 01444 400526
Headmaster: Mr Richard Brown
Age range: 2–13
No. of pupils: 339
Fees: Day £3,230–£6,360 WB
£5,370–£7,480 FB £6,030–£8,130

Hurstpierpoint College Prep School
Hurstpierpoint, West Sussex BN6 9JS
Tel: 01273 834975
Head: Mr I D Pattison BSc
Age range: 4–13
No. of pupils: 360

Lancing Prep Worthing
Broadwater Road, Worthing,
West Sussex BN14 8HU
Tel: 01903 201123
Head: Mrs Heather Beeby
Age range: 2–13 years

Oakwood Preparatory School
Chichester, West Sussex PO18 9AN
Tel: 01243 575209
Headteacher: Mrs Clare Bradbury
Age range: 2.5–11 years
No. of pupils: 275
Fees: Day £3,170–£5,110

Our Lady of Sion School
Gratwicke Road, Worthing,
West Sussex BN11 4BL
Tel: 01903 204063
Headmaster: Mr Steven Jeffery
Age range: 3–18
No. of pupils: 410
Fees: Day £8,640–£13,575

Pennthorpe School
Church Street, Horsham,
West Sussex RH12 3HJ
Tel: 01403 822391
Headmistress: Alexia Bolton
Age range: 2–13
No. of pupils: 362
Fees: Day £2,070–£16,605

Seaford College
Lavington Park, Petworth,
West Sussex GU28 0NB
Tel: 01798 867392
Headmaster: J P Green MA BA
Age range: 6–18 years
No. of pupils: 903 VIth235
Fees: Day £3,665–£7,595 WB
£7,635–£10,290 FB £11,750

Shoreham College
St Julians Lane, Shoreham-by-
Sea, West Sussex BN43 6YW
Tel: 01273 592681
Headmaster: Mr R Taylor-West
Age range: 3–16 years
No. of pupils: 375
Fees: Day £9,750–£15,150

Sompting Abbotts Preparatory School
Church Lane, Sompting,
West Sussex BN15 0AZ
Tel: 01903 235960
Principal: Mrs P M Sinclair
Age range: 2–13 years

The Prebendal School
52-55 West Street, Chichester,
West Sussex PO19 1RT
Tel: 01243 772220
Headteacher: Mrs L Salmond Smith
Age range: 3–13
No. of pupils: 181
Fees: Day £8,160–£15,495 WB
£18,975–£20,100 FB £22,290

Westbourne House School
Coach Road, Chichester,
West Sussex PO20 2BH
Tel: 01243 782739
Headmaster: Mr Martin Barker
Age range: 2.5–13 years

Windlesham House School
London Road, Washington,
Pulborough, West Sussex RH20 4AY
Tel: 01903 874701
Head of School: Ben Evans
Age range: 4–13
No. of pupils: 280

South-West

Bath & North-East Somerset D206
Bristol D206
Cornwall D206
Devon D207
Dorset D208
Somerset D208

KEY TO SYMBOLS
- Boys' school
- Girls' school
- International school
- Tutorial or sixth form college
- A levels
- Boarding accommodation
- Bursaries
- International Baccalaureate
- Learning support
- Entrance at 16+
- Vocational qualifications
- Independent Association of Prep Schools
- The Headmasters' & Headmistresses' Conference
- Independent Schools Association
- Girls' School Association
- Boarding Schools' Association
- Society of Heads

Unless otherwise indicated, all schools are coeducational day schools. Single-sex and boarding schools will be indicated by the relevant icon.

England – South-West

Bath & North-East Somerset

King Edward's Junior School
North Road, Bath, Bath & North-East Somerset BA2 6JA
Tel: 01225 464218
Head of School: Mr Greg Taylor
Age range: 7–11 years

King Edward's Pre-Prep & Nursery School
Weston Lane, Bath, Bath & North-East Somerset BA1 4AQ
Tel: 01225 421681
Head of School: Ms Jayne Gilbert
Age range: 3–7 years

Kingswood School
Lansdown Road, Bath, Bath & North-East Somerset BA1 5RG
Tel: 01225 734200
Headmaster: Mr Andrew Gordon-Brown
Age range: 9 months–18 years
No. of pupils: 772 VIth189
Fees: Day £10,463–£15,884 WB £20,723–£30,932 FB £24,671–£34,235

MONKTON PREP SCHOOL
For further details see p. 119
Church Road, Combe Down, Bath, Bath & North-East Somerset BA2 7ET
Tel: 01225 831200
Email: mpsadmissions@monkton.org.uk
Website: www.monktoncombeschool.com
Head: Mrs Catherine Winchcombe
Age range: 2–13 years (boarding from 8)
No. of pupils: 305

Royal High School Bath, GDST
Lansdown Road, Bath, Bath & North-East Somerset BA1 5SZ
Tel: +44 (0)1225 313877
Head: Mrs Kate Reynolds
Age range: G3–18 years
No. of pupils: 640
Fees: Day £4,865 WB £9,674 FB £10,762

The Paragon School
Lyncombe House, Lyncombe Vale, Bath, Bath & North-East Somerset BA2 4LT
Tel: 01225 310837
Head of School: Ms Rosie Allen
Age range: 3–11 years

Bristol

Badminton Junior School
Westbury Road, Westbury-on-Trym, Bristol BS9 3BA
Tel: 0117 905 5200
Head of Junior School: Ms Heidi Welch
Age range: G3–11 years

Bristol Grammar School
University Road, Bristol BS8 1SR
Tel: 0117 973 6006
Headmaster: Mr Jaideep Barot
Age range: 4–18 years

Bristol Steiner School
Redland Hill House, Redland, Bristol BS6 6UX
Tel: 0117 933 9990
Head Teacher: Nicola Forder
Age range: 3–11 years
No. of pupils: 128
Fees: Day £7,977

Carmel Christian School
817a Bath Road, Brislington, Bristol BS4 5NL
Tel: 0117 977 5678
Head of School: Ms Joanne Collins
Age range: 3–5 years

Cleve House School
254 Wells Road, Knowle, Bristol BS4 2PN
Tel: 0117 9777218
Head of School: Ms Clare Fraser
Age range: 2–11 years

Clifton College Preparatory School
The Avenue, Clifton, Bristol BS8 3HE
Tel: +44 (0)117 315 7502
Head of Preparatory School: Mr Jim Walton
Age range: 2–13 years
No. of pupils: 440
Fees: Day £10,680–£18,600 WB £17,460–£22,035 FB £25,905–£30,690

Clifton High School
College Road, Clifton, Bristol BS8 3JD
Tel: 0117 973 0201
Head of School: Mr Matthew Bennett
Age range: 3–18 years

Colston's School
Stapleton, Bristol BS16 1BJ
Tel: 0117 965 5207
Headmaster: Mr Jeremy McCullough
Age range: 3–18 years
No. of pupils: 816
Fees: Day £8,055–£14,625

Fairfield School
Fairfield Way, Backwell, Bristol BS48 3PD
Tel: 01275 462743
Headmistress: Mrs Lesley Barton
Age range: 2–11 years

Gracefield Preparatory School
266 Overndale Road, Fishponds, Bristol BS16 2RG
Tel: 0117 956 7977
Headteacher: Mr J Gunter
Age range: 4–11 years

Queen Elizabeth's Hospital
Berkeley Place, Clifton, Bristol BS8 1JX
Tel: 0117 930 3040
Head: Mr Rupert Heathcote
Age range: B7–18 years G16–18 years

Redmaids' High Junior School
Grange Court Road, Westbury-on-Trym, Bristol BS9 4DP
Tel: 0117 962 9451
Headteacher: Mrs Lisa Brown BSc (Hons)
Age range: G7–11 years

The Downs Preparatory School
Wraxall, Bristol BS48 1PF
Tel: 01275 852008
Head: Ms Debbie Isaachsen
Age range: 4–13 years

Tockington Manor School
Washingpool Hill Road, Tockington, Bristol BS32 4NY
Tel: 01454 613229
Headmaster: Mr Stephen Symonds
Age range: 2–13 years

Torwood House School
8 Durdham Park, Redland, Bristol BS6 6XA
Tel: 01179 736620
Head Teacher: Mrs Dionne Seagrove B.Ed, M.Ed
Age range: 0–11 years

Cornwall

Polwhele House School
Truro, Cornwall TR4 9AE
Tel: 01872 273011
Headmaster: Mr Alex McCullough
Age range: 3–13
No. of pupils: 100
Fees: Day £8,820–£13,620

St Joseph's School
15 St Stephen's Hill, Launceston, Cornwall PL15 8HN
Tel: 01566 772580
Head Teacher: Mr Oliver Scott
Age range: 4–16
No. of pupils: 215
Fees: Day £5,490–£13,875

St Petroc's School
Ocean View Road, Bude, Cornwall EX23 8NJ
Tel: 01288 352876
Headmaster: Mr Hilton
Age range: 0–11
Fees: Day £5,850–£8,850

St. Piran's School
14 Trelissick Road, Hayle, Cornwall TR27 4HY
Tel: 01736 752612
Headteacher: Mrs Carol de Labat BEd(Hons), CertEd
Age range: 4–16
Fees: Day £2,775–£7,080

England – South-West

Truro High School for Girls
Falmouth Road, Truro,
Cornwall TR1 2HU
Tel: 01872 272830
Headmaster: Glenn Moodie
Age range: B3–5 G3–18
No. of pupils: 432 VIth60
Fees: Day £8,001–£13,896 WB £25,185–£26,040 FB £27,261–£28,182

Truro School
Trennick Lane, Truro,
Cornwall TR1 1TH
Tel: 01872 272763
Headmaster: Mr A S Gordon-Brown BCom, MSc, CA (SA)
Age range: 3–18
No. of pupils: 780 VIth210

Devon

Abbey School
Hampton Court, St Marychurch,
Torquay, Devon TQ1 4PR
Tel: 01803 327868
Principal: Mrs Sylvia Greinig
Age range: 0–11 years
No. of pupils: 78

Blundell's Preparatory School
Milestones House, Blundell's Road, Tiverton, Devon EX16 4NA
Tel: 01884 252393
Head Master: Mr Andrew Southgate BA Ed (Hons)
Age range: 3–11
No. of pupils: 220
Fees: Day £5,880–£12,195

EXETER CATHEDRAL SCHOOL
For further details see p. 115
The Chantry, Palace Gate, Exeter, Devon EX1 1HX
Tel: 01392 255298
Email: admissions@exetercs.org
Website: www.exetercathedralschool.co.uk
Headmaster: James Featherstone
Age range: 3–13 years
No. of pupils: 266
Fees: Day £2,823–£4,623 FB £2,722

Exeter School
Victoria Park Road, Exeter,
Devon EX2 4NS
Tel: 01392 307080
Head: Ms Louise Simpson
Age range: 7–18 years
No. of pupils: 944
Fees: Day £12,120–£14,700

Fletewood School
88 North Road East,
Plymouth, Devon PL4 6AN
Tel: 01752 663782
Headteacher: Mrs R Gray
Age range: 3–11
No. of pupils: 70
Fees: Day £4,425

King's School
Hartley Road, Mannamead,
Plymouth, Devon PL3 5LW
Tel: 01752 771789
Head of School: Mrs Clare Page
Age range: 8 months–11 years
No. of pupils: 230
Fees: Day £2,165–£2,720

Kingsley School
Northdown Road, Bideford,
Devon EX39 3LY
Tel: 01237 426200
Headteacher: Mr Alastair Ramsay
Age range: 0–18
No. of pupils: 395
Fees: Day £2,055 WB £5,785 FB £8,275

Magdalen Court School
Mulberry House, Victoria Park Road, Exeter, Devon EX2 4NU
Tel: 01392 494919
Head: Mrs Sarah Wrightson
Age range: 0–18+
No. of pupils: 150 VIth20
Fees: Day £5,670–£10,200

OneSchool Global UK Plymouth Campus
Foulston Avenue, Plymouth,
Devon PL5 1HL
Tel: 01752 363290
Age range: 7–18 years

Park School
Park Road, Dartington,
Totnes, Devon TQ9 6EQ
Tel: 01803 864588
Teacher-in-charge: Amanda Bellamy
Age range: 3–12
Fees: Day £6,147–£9,654

Plymouth College Preparatory School
St Dunstan's Abbey, The Millfields, Plymouth, Devon PL1 3JL
Tel: 01752 201352
Headmaster: Mrs Jo Hayward
Age range: 3–11 years

Shebbear College
Shebbear, Beaworthy,
Devon EX21 5HJ
Tel: 01409 282000
Headmaster: Mr S. D. Weale MA (Oxon)
Age range: 3–18
No. of pupils: 350 VIth78
Fees: Day £5,235–£12,975 WB £14,250–£14,985 FB £18,750–£26,325

South Devon Steiner School
Hood Manor, Buckfastleigh Road, Dartington, Totnes, Devon TQ9 6AB
Tel: 01803 897 377
Education Manager: Jeff van Zyl
Age range: 3–19
No. of pupils: 307

St Christopher's Preparatory School
Mount Barton, Staverton,
Devon TQ9 6PF
Tel: 01803 762202
Headmistress: Alexandra Cottell
Age range: 3–11
No. of pupils: 100
Fees: Day £7,350–£9,900

St Peter's School
Harefield, Lympstone,
Exmouth, Devon EX8 5AU
Tel: 01395 272148
Headmistress: Mrs Charlotte Johnston
Age range: 3–13
No. of pupils: 275
Fees: Day £7,650–£13,065 WB £19,935

St Wilfrid's School
25-29 St David's Hill, Exeter,
Devon EX4 4DA
Tel: 01392 276171
Headmistress: Mrs Alexandra E M MacDonald-Dent DPhyEd
Age range: 5–16

St. John's School
Broadway, Sidmouth,
Devon EX10 8RG
Tel: 01395 513984
Head of School: Bryan Kane
Age range: 2 1/2–16 years
No. of pupils: 200
Fees: Day £6,906–£11,403 FB £19,422–£21,291

Stover School
Stover, Newton Abbot,
Devon TQ12 6QG
Tel: +44 (0)1626 354505
Headmaster: Mr R W D Notman
Age range: 3–18

The Maynard School
Denmark Road, Exeter,
Devon EX1 1SJ
Tel: 01392 273417
Headmistress: Miss Sarah Dunn BSc (Hons) PGCE and NPQH
Age range: G4–18
No. of pupils: VIth80
Fees: Day £6,285–£13,248

The New School
The Avenue, Exminster,
Exeter, Devon EX6 8AT
Tel: 01392 496122
Head: Mr Daniel Ayling
Age range: 3–7 years
No. of pupils: 71
Fees: Day £8,676–£8,934

Trinity School
Buckeridge Road, Teignmouth,
Devon TQ14 8LY
Tel: 01626 774138
Headmaster: Mr Lawrence Coen
Age range: 3–18
No. of pupils: 110
Fees: Day £7,755–£12,300 WB £18,945–£25,590 FB £20,550–£27,750

West Buckland School
Barnstaple, Devon EX32 0SX
Tel: 01598 760281
Headmaster: Mr Phillip Stapleton
Age range: 3–18
No. of pupils: VIth135
Fees: Day £8,070–£15,060 FB £24,345–£30,720

England – South-West

Dorset

Bournemouth Collegiate School (BCS Prep)
40 St Osmund's Road, Lower Parkstone, Poole, Dorset BH14 9JY
Tel: 01202 714110
Head of School: Miss Kay Smith
Age range: 2–11 years
No. of pupils: 267
Fees: Day £7,365–£12,075

Castle Court School
Knoll Lane, Corfe Mullen, Wimborne, Dorset BH21 3RF
Tel: 01202 694438
Headmaster: Mr Luke Gollings
Age range: 2–13
No. of pupils: 307
Fees: Day £8,790–£15,825

Clayesmore Preparatory School
Iwerne Minster, Blandford Forum, Dorset DT11 8PH
Tel: 01747 813155
Head of School: Mr William Dunlop
Age range: 3–13
No. of pupils: 230
Fees: Day £13,230–£18,750 FB £17,670–£25,110

Dumpton School
Deans Grove House, Deans Grove, Wimborne, Dorset BH21 7AF
Tel: 01202 883818
Headmaster: Mr Christian Saenger
Age range: 2–13 years

Hanford School
Child Okeford, Blandford, Dorset DT11 8HN
Tel: 01258 860219
Headmaster: Mr Rory Johnston
Age range: G7–13
No. of pupils: 100
Fees: Day £6,250 FB £7,500

Knighton House School and The Orchard Pre-prep
Durweston, Blandford, Dorset DT11 0PY
Tel: 01258 452065
Headmaster: Mr Robin Gainher
Age range: B3–7 G3–13
No. of pupils: 90
Fees: Day £2,325–£4,950 FB £5,800–£7,600

Leweston Prep School
Sherborne, Dorset DT9 6EN
Tel: 01963 210790
Head of School: Miss Alanda Phillips
Age range: 0–11
No. of pupils: 227

Park School
45-49 Queens Park, South Drive, Bournemouth, Dorset BH8 9BJ
Tel: 01202 396640
Head of School: Mrs Melanie Dowler
Age range: 2–11
No. of pupils: 387
Fees: Day £7,275–£8,805

Port Regis
Motcombe Park, Shaftesbury, Dorset SP7 9QA
Tel: 01747 857800
Head of School: S L Ilett
Age range: 2–13
No. of pupils: 324

Sherborne Preparatory School
Acreman Street, Sherborne, Dorset DT9 3NY
Tel: 01935 812097
Headmaster: Mr Nick Folland Bsc (Hons), MIAPS, MISI
Age range: 2–13
No. of pupils: 258
Fees: Day £9,060–£17,130 WB £23,445–£24,540 FB £23,445–£24,540

St Martin's School
15 Stokewood Road, Bournemouth, Dorset BH3 7NA
Tel: 01202 292011
Headteacher: Laura Richards
Age range: 4–11 years
No. of pupils: 100
Fees: Day £5,835–£7,533

Sunninghill Preparatory School
South Court, South Walks, Dorchester, Dorset DT1 1EB
Tel: 01305 262306
Headmaster: Mr John Thorpe BSc (Hons), PGCE
Age range: 3–13
No. of pupils: 184
Fees: Day £8,850–£15,450

Talbot Heath
Rothesay Road, Bournemouth, Dorset BH4 9NJ
Tel: 01202 761881
Head: Mrs A Holloway MA, PGCE
Age range: G3–18
No. of pupils: 582
Fees: Day £2,201–£4,801 WB £3,305 FB £3,704

Talbot House Preparatory School
8 Firs Glen Road, Bournemouth, Dorset BH9 2LR
Tel: 01202 510348
Headteacher: Mrs Emma Haworth
Age range: 3–11
Fees: Day £4,320–£8,097

Yarrells Preparatory School
Yarrells House, Upton, Poole, Dorset BH16 5EU
Tel: 01202 622229
Headteacher: Mrs Sally Weber-Spokes BA (Hons), PGCE, IAPS, ISI
Age range: 2–13
No. of pupils: 253
Fees: Day £2,395–£4,250

Somerset

All Hallows Preparatory School
Cranmore Hall, Shepton Mallet, Somerset BA4 4SF
Tel: 01749 881600
Head of School: Dr Trevor Richards
Age range: 3–13
No. of pupils: 265

Ashbrooke House School & Pre-School
9 Ellenborough Park North, Weston-Super-Mare, Somerset BS23 1XH
Tel: 01934 629515
Headteacher & Director: Miss Karen Wallington
Age range: 3–11

Chard School
Fore Street, Chard, Somerset TA20 1QA
Tel: 01460 63234
Head of School: Katie Hill
Age range: 0–11
No. of pupils: 100
Fees: Day £6,450–£7,650

HAZLEGROVE PREP SCHOOL
For further details see p. 116
Hazlegrove House. Sparkford, Somerset BA22 7JA
Tel: +44 (0)1963 442606
Email: admissions@hazlegrove.co.uk
Website: www.hazlegrove.co.uk
Headmaster: Mr Mark White MA (Hons)
Age range: 2–13 years
No. of pupils: 364
Fees: Day £3,076–£6,237 FB £7,235–£9,232

KING'S HALL SCHOOL
For further details see p. 117
Kingston Road, Taunton, Somerset TA2 8AA
Tel: 01823 285920
Email: admissions@kings-taunton.co.uk
Website: www.kingshalltaunton.co.uk
Head: Mr Justin Chippendale
Age range: 2–13 years
No. of pupils: 320
Fees: Day £8,265–£17,670

MILLFIELD PREPARATORY SCHOOL
For further details see p. 118
Edgarley Hall, Glastonbury, Somerset BA6 8LD
Tel: 01458 832446
Email: admissions@millfieldprep.com
Website: www.millfieldschool.com/prep
Headmaster: Dan Thornburn
Age range: 2–13 years
No. of pupils: 434

Perrott Hill
North Perrott, Crewkerne, Somerset TA18 7SL
Tel: 01460 72051
Joint Acting Headteachers: Mr Bryan Kane & Mr Will Silk
Age range: 3–13
No. of pupils: 183
Fees: Day £6,450–£15,750 WB £19,200 FB £22,740

England – South-West

Queen's College
Trull Road, Taunton,
Somerset TA1 4QS
Tel: 01823 272559
Headmistress: Dr Lorraine Earps
Age range: 3–18
No. of pupils: 784 VIth150
Fees: Day £6,450–£18,450
FB £14,655–£31,980

Sidcot School
Oakridge Lane, Winscombe,
Somerset BS25 1PD
Tel: 01934 843102
Headmaster: Iain Kilpatrick
BA MEd FRSA
Age range: 3–18 years
No. of pupils: 603
Fees: Day £2,900–£6,510
FB £9,830–£12,030

Springmead Preparatory School & Nursery
13 Castle Corner, Beckington,
Frome, Somerset BA11 6TA
Tel: 01373 831555
Principal: Ms Madeleine Taylor
Age range: 3–11 years

Sunny Hill Prep School
Sunny Hill, Bruton,
Somerset BA10 0NT
Tel: 01749 814 427
Head: Mrs Helen Snow BEd
Age range: B2–7 G2–11
No. of pupils: 68
Fees: Day £8,505–£13,116 WB
£21,300–£21,651 FB £23,529–£23,880

Taunton Preparatory School
Staplegrove Road, Taunton,
Somerset TA2 6AD
Tel: 01823 703307
Headmaster: Andrew Edwards
Age range: 0–13 years

TAUNTON SCHOOL
For further details see p. 120
Staplegrove Road, Taunton,
Somerset TA2 6AD
Tel: +44 (0)1823 703703
Head of School: Mr. Lee Glaser
Age range: 0–18
No. of pupils: 1000
Fees: Day £3,020–£14,260

Wellington Prep School
South Street, Wellington,
Somerset TA21 8NT
Tel: 01823 668700
Headmaster: Adam Gibson
Age range: 3–11
Fees: Day £6,330–£11,520

Wellington School
South Street, Wellington,
Somerset TA21 8NT
Tel: 01823 668800
Headmaster: Henry
Price MA (Oxon)
Age range: 3–18
No. of pupils: VIth165
Fees: Day £6,330–£15,225 WB
£23,130–£24,105 FB £28,890–£30,810

Wells Cathedral Junior School
8 New Street, Wells,
Somerset BA5 2LQ
Tel: 01749 834400
Headteacher: Julie Barrow
Age range: 3–11
No. of pupils: 150
Fees: Day £7,641–£15,375
WB £20,322–£22,900 FB
£23,458–£26,036

Wells Cathedral School
The Liberty, Wells, Somerset BA5 2ST
Tel: 01749 834200
Head: Mr Alastair Tighe
Age range: 3–18
No. of pupils: 750 VIth194
Fees: Day £7,641–£18,801 WB
£20,322–£27,843 FB £23,458–£31,464

West Midlands

Herefordshire D212
Shropshire D212
Staffordshire D212
Warwickshire D213
West Midlands D213
Worcestershire D214

KEY TO SYMBOLS
- Boys' school
- Girls' school
- International school
- Tutorial or sixth form college
- A levels
- Boarding accommodation
- Bursaries
- International Baccalaureate
- Learning support
- Entrance at 16+
- Vocational qualifications
- Independent Association of Prep Schools
- The Headmasters' & Headmistresses' Conference
- Independent Schools Association
- Girls' School Association
- Boarding Schools' Association
- Society of Heads

Unless otherwise indicated, all schools are coeducational day schools. Single-sex and boarding schools will be indicated by the relevant icon.

England – West Midlands

Herefordshire

Hereford Cathedral Junior School
28 Castle Street, Hereford, Herefordshire HR1 2NW
Tel: 01432 363511
Headmaster: Mr Chris Wright
Age range: 3–11 years

Lucton School
Lucton, Herefordshire HR6 9PN
Tel: 01568 782000
Headmaster: Mr Jon Tyler
Age range: 1–18 years (Boarding from 7)
No. of pupils: 300
Fees: Day £7,500–£14,250 WB £24,345–£28,695 FB £35,130

Shropshire

Adcote School for Girls
Little Ness, Shrewsbury, Shropshire SY4 2JY
Tel: 01939 260202
Headmistress: Mrs Diane Browne
Age range: G7–18
Fees: Day £9,141–£14,838 FB £19,618–£38,100

Bedstone College
Bedstone, Bucknell, Shropshire SY7 0BG
Tel: 01547 530303
Headmaster: Mr David Gajadharsingh
Age range: 4–18
No. of pupils: 230
Fees: Day £5,025–£14,655 FB £17,475–£26,520

BIRCHFIELD SCHOOL
For further details see p. 122
Albrighton, Wolverhampton, Shropshire WV7 3AF
Tel: 01902 372534
Email: admissions@birchfieldschool.co.uk
Website: www.birchfieldschool.co.uk
Headmistress: Sarah Morris
Age range: 4–16 years
No. of pupils: 142
Fees: Day £7,500–£11,000

Castle House School
Chetwynd End, Newport, Shropshire TF10 7JE
Tel: 01952 567600
Headmaster: Mr Ian Sterling
Age range: 2–11 years

Ellesmere College
Ellesmere, Shropshire SY12 9AB
Tel: 01691 622321
Head of School: Mr Brendan Wignall MA, FRSA, MCMI
Age range: 7–18 years
No. of pupils: 550
Fees: Day £6,520 WB £8,465 FB £11,855

MOOR PARK
For further details see p. 123
Richards Castle, Ludlow, Shropshire SY8 4DZ
Tel: 01584 876 061
Email: head@moorpark.org.uk
Website: www.moorpark.org.uk
Headmaster: Mr Charles G O'B Minogue
Age range: 0–13 years
No. of pupils: 214
Fees: Day £2,225–£6,215 FB £7,700–£9,225

MORETON HALL
For further details see p. 124
Weston Rhyn, Oswestry, Shropshire SY11 3EW
Tel: 01691 776028
Email: moretonhallprep@moretonhall.com
Website: www.moretonhall.org/moreton-prep
Head: Mr John Bond
Age range: 6 months–11 years
No. of pupils: 150
Fees: Day £10,650–£15,135 FB £24,570

Oswestry School
Upper Brook Street, Oswestry, Shropshire SY11 2TL
Tel: 01691 655711
Headmaster: Mr Julian Noad BEng
Age range: 4–18
No. of pupils: VIth92
Fees: Day £8,700–£15,690 WB £23,610 FB £26,850–£31,200

Packwood Haugh School
Ruyton XI Towns, Shrewsbury, Shropshire SY4 1HX
Tel: 01939 260217
Headmaster: Clive Smith-Langridge BA(Hons), PGCE
Age range: 4–13
No. of pupils: 212
Fees: Day £8,805–£18,330 FB £23,430–£26,430

Prestfelde Preparatory School
London Road, Shrewsbury, Shropshire SY2 6NZ
Tel: 01743 245400
Head of School: Mrs F Orchard
Age range: 3–13 years

Shrewsbury High School GDST
32 Town Walls, Shrewsbury, Shropshire SY1 1TN
Tel: 01743 494000
Head: Ms J Sharrock
Age range: B3–13 G3–18
No. of pupils: VIth120
Fees: Day £7,686–£14,481

St Winefride's Convent School
Belmont, Shrewsbury, Shropshire SY1 1TE
Tel: 01743 369883
Headmistress: Sister M Felicity CertEd, BA(Hons)
Age range: 3–11
No. of pupils: 179
Fees: Day £4,355–£4,380

THE OLD HALL SCHOOL
For further details see p. 128
Stanley Road, Wellington, Shropshire TF1 3LB
Tel: 01952 223117
Email: admissions@oldhall.co.uk
Website: www.oldhall.co.uk
Headmaster: Mr Martin Stott
Age range: 4–11
No. of pupils: 232
Fees: Day £8,850–£13,920

White House School
Heath Road, Whitchurch, Shropshire SY13 2AA
Tel: 01948 662730
Headmistress: Mrs H M Clarke
Age range: 3–11
Fees: Day £4,950

Staffordshire

Abbotsholme School
Rocester, Uttoxeter, Staffordshire ST14 5BS
Tel: 01889 590217
Head of School: Mr Simon Ruscoe-Price
Age range: 2–18
No. of pupils: 285
Fees: Day £8,985–£22,485 WB £18,525–£27,450 FB £24,585–£33,750

Chase Grammar School
Lyncroft House, St John's Road, Cannock, Staffordshire WS11 0UR
Tel: 01543 501800
Principal: Mr Michael Hartland
Age range: 2–19

Denstone College Preparatory School
Smallwood Manor, Uttoxeter, Staffordshire ST14 8NS
Tel: 01889 562083
Head of School: Mrs Tracey Davies
Age range: 4–11 years
No. of pupils: 100
Fees: Day £3,669–£4,719

Edenhurst Preparatory School
Westlands Avenue, Newcastle-under-Lyme, Staffordshire ST5 2PU
Tel: 01782 619348
Headteacher: Mr Michael Hibbert
Age range: 3 months–11 years
Fees: Day £3,019–£3,655

England – West Midlands

Lichfield Cathedral School
The Palace, The Close, Lichfield, Staffordshire WS13 7LH
Tel: 01543 306170
Head: Mrs Susan E Hannam BA (Hons) MA PGCE
Age range: 3–18 years
No. of pupils: 426
Fees: Day £8,805–£13,815

Newcastle under Lyme School
Mount Pleasant, Newcastle-under-Lyme, Staffordshire ST5 1DB
Tel: 01782 631197
Headmaster: Mr Michael Getty BA, NPQH
Age range: 3–18 years
No. of pupils: 879 VIth152
Fees: Day £3,152–£4,330

St Dominic's Priory School Stone
21 Station Road, Stone, Staffordshire ST15 8EN
Tel: +44 (0)1785 814181
Head of School: Mrs Rebecca Harrison
Age range: 3–16
No. of pupils: 163
Fees: Day £7,560–£11,508

St Joseph's Preparatory School
London Road, Trent Vale, Stoke-on-Trent, Staffordshire ST4 5NT
Tel: 01782 417533
Head: Mrs S D Hutchinson
Age range: 3–11
Fees: Day £7,605–£8,040

St. Dominic's Grammar School
32 Bargate Street, Brewood, Staffordshire ST19 9BA
Tel: 01902 850248
Headteacher: Mr Peter McNabb BSc Hons, PGCE
Age range: 2–18 years
No. of pupils: 198 VIth31
Fees: Day £6,834–£13,212

Yarlet School
Yarlet, Stafford, Staffordshire ST18 9SU
Tel: 01785 286568
Headmaster: Mr I Raybould BEd(Hons)
Age range: 2–13 years

Warwickshire

Arnold Lodge School
15-17 Kenilworth Road, Leamington Spa, Warwickshire CV32 5TW
Tel: 01926 778050
Headmaster: David Preston
Age range: 4–18
No. of pupils: 300
Fees: Day £11,124–£13,887

Bilton Grange Preparatory School
Dunchurch, Rugby, Warwickshire CV22 6QU
Tel: 01788 810217
Headmaster: Mr Alex Osiatynski MA Oxon PGCE
Age range: 3–13 years

Crackley Hall School
St Joseph's Park, Kenilworth, Warwickshire CV8 2FT
Tel: 01926 514444
Headmaster: Mr R Duigan
Age range: 4–11
No. of pupils: 214
Fees: Day £9,720–£10,821

OneSchool Global UK Atherstone Campus
Long Street, Atherstone, Warwickshire CV9 1AE
Tel: 01827 721751
Age range: 7–18 years

Stratford Preparatory School
Church House, Old Town, Stratford-upon-Avon, Warwickshire CV37 6BG
Tel: 01789 297993
Headmaster: Mr N Musk MA, BA(Jt Hons), PGCE
Age range: 2–11
Fees: Day £9,600–£11,280

The Crescent School
Bawnmore Road, Bilton, Rugby, Warwickshire CV22 7QH
Tel: 01788 521595
Headmaster: Mr J.P. Thackway B.A.Hons, P.G.C.E.
Age range: 4–11
No. of pupils: 156
Fees: Day £9,342–£10,191

The Croft Preparatory School
Alveston Hill, Loxley Road, Stratford-upon-Avon, Warwickshire CV37 7RL
Tel: 01789 293795
Headmaster: Mr Marcus Cook
Age range: 2–11
No. of pupils: 425
Fees: Day £7,962–£12,213

The Kingsley School
Beauchamp Avenue, Leamington Spa, Warwickshire CV32 5RD
Tel: 01926 425127
Headteacher: Ms Heather Owens
Age range: B3–11 G3–18
No. of pupils: 333 VIth61
Fees: Day £10,599–£13,254

Twycross House Pre-Preparatory School (The Hollies)
The Green, Twycross (Near Atherstone), Warwickshire CV9 3PQ
Tel: 01827 880725
Joint Heads: Mr S D Assinder & Mrs R T Assinder
Age range: 4–8

Twycross House School
Main Road, Twycross, Atherstone, Warwickshire CV9 3QA
Tel: 01827 880651
Headmaster: Mr S D Assinder
Age range: 8–18
Fees: Day £9,270–£10,485

Warwick Preparatory School
Bridge Field, Banbury Road, Warwick, Warwickshire CV34 6PL
Tel: 01926 491545
Headmistress: Hellen Dodsworth
Age range: B3–7 G3–11
No. of pupils: 438
Fees: Day £7,767–£12,666

Warwick School
Myton Road, Warwick, Warwickshire CV34 6PP
Tel: 01926 776400
Head Master: Dr D Smith
Age range: B7–18
No. of pupils: 1214 VIth249
Fees: Day £11,181–£13,194 WB £26,883 FB £28,758

West Midlands

Al Ameen Primary School
Stanfield House, 447 Warwick Way, Birmingham, West Midlands B11 2JR
Tel: 0121 706 3322
Head Teacher: Maulana Mohammed Aminur Rahman
Age range: 3–11
No. of pupils: 22

Bablake Junior School
Coundon Road, Coventry, West Midlands CV1 4AU
Tel: 024 7627 1260
Headmaster: Mr L Holder
Age range: 7–11 years

Bablake PrePrep
The Grange, Brownshill Green Road, Coventry, West Midlands CV6 3EG
Tel: 024 7622 1677
Head of Pre Prep: Mrs T Horton
Age range: 3–7
Fees: Day £8,097

Edgbaston High School for Girls
Westbourne Road, Edgbaston, Birmingham, West Midlands B15 3TS
Tel: 0121 454 5831
Head of School: Mrs Clare Macro
Age range: G2.5–18 years
No. of pupils: 880
Fees: Day £3,106–£4,695

Elmfield Rudolf Steiner School
14 Love Lane, Stourbridge, West Midlands DY8 2EA
Tel: 01384 394633
College of Teachers: Education Admin
Age range: 3–17
No. of pupils: VIth100
Fees: Day £5,220–£8,034

Emmanuel School (Walsall)
36 Wolverhampton Road, Walsall, West Midlands WS2 8PR
Tel: 01922 635810
Head Teacher: Mr Jonathan Swain BA PGCE
Age range: 3–16
No. of pupils: 82
Fees: Day £4,044

England – West Midlands

Eversfield Preparatory School
Warwick Road, Solihull,
West Midlands B91 1AT
Tel: 0121 705 0354
Headmaster: Mr R A Yates
BA, PGCE, LPSH
Age range: 3–11 years
No. of pupils: 335
Fees: Day £8,410–£12,300
£

Greenfields Primary School
472 Coventry Road, Birmingham,
West Midlands B10 0UG
Tel: 0121 7724567
Headteacher: P. Sa'eed Alam
Age range: 5–11

Hallfield School
48 Church Road, Edgbaston,
Birmingham, West Midlands B15 3SJ
Tel: 0121 454 1496
Head Master: Mr Keith Morrow
Age range: 3 months–13 years

Hamd House Preparatory School
730 Bordesley Green, Birmingham,
West Midlands B9 5PQ
Tel: +44 (0) 121 771 3030
Headteacher: Mr S Ali
Age range: 3–11
No. of pupils: 206

Highclare School
10 Sutton Road, Erdington,
Birmingham, West Midlands B23 6QL
Tel: 0121 373 7400
Head: Dr Richard Luker
Age range: B1–12 G1–18
No. of pupils: 638 VIth28
Fees: Day £5,420–£12,645
A £

Hydesville Tower School
25 Broadway North, Walsall,
West Midlands WS1 2QG
Tel: 01922 624374
Headmaster: Mr Warren Honey
BSc (Hons), PGCE Durham
University, MEd Open Univ+
Age range: 3–16 years
No. of pupils: 289
Fees: Day £9,738–£13,758
£

King Henry VIII Preparatory School
Kenilworth Road, Coventry,
West Midlands CV3 6PT
Tel: 024 7627 1307
Headteacher: Miss Caroline Soan
Age range: 3–11 years

Kingswood School
St James Place, Shirley, Solihull,
West Midlands B90 2BA
Tel: 0121 744 7883
Headmaster: Mr Rob
Luckham BSc(Hons), PGCE
Age range: 3–11
No. of pupils: 89
£

Lambs Christian School
113 Soho Hill, Hockley, Birmingham,
West Midlands B19 1AY
Tel: 0121 5543790
Headteacher: Mrs
Patricia Ekhuenelo
Age range: 3–11

Lote Tree Primary
643 Foleshill Road, Coventry,
West Midlands CV6 5JQ
Tel: 024 7626 1803
Head: Mrs Ashique
Age range: 2–11

Mayfield Preparatory School
Sutton Road, Walsall, West
Midlands WS1 2PD
Tel: 01922 624107
Headmaster: Mr Matthew Draper
Age range: 2–11
No. of pupils: 212
Fees: Day £5,220–£8,700

Newbridge Preparatory School
51 Newbridge Crescent,
Tettenhall, Wolverhampton,
West Midlands WV6 0LH
Tel: 01902 751088
Headmistress: Mrs Sarah Fisher
Age range: B3–4 G3–11
No. of pupils: 148

Norfolk House School
4 Norfolk Road, Edgbaston,
Birmingham, West Midlands B15 3PS
Tel: 0121 454 7021
Head of School: Ms
Susannah Palmer
Age range: 3–11 years
Fees: Day £2,539–£3,672

PATTISON SCHOOL
For further details see p. 126
86-90 Binley Road, Coventry,
West Midlands CV3 1FQ
Tel: 024 7645 5031
Email: office@pattisons.co.uk
Website: www.pattisons.co.uk
Head of School: Mr
Graeme Delaney
Age range: 2–18 years

PRIORY SCHOOL
For further details see p. 125
39 Sir Harry's Road,
Edgbaston, Birmingham,
West Midlands B15 2UR
Tel: 0121 440 4103
Email: enquiries@
prioryschool.net
Website: www.prioryschool.net
Headteacher: Mr J Cramb
Age range: 6 months–18 years
A £

Rosslyn School
1597 Stratford Road, Hall Green,
Birmingham, West Midlands B28 9JB
Tel: 0121 744 2743
Head of School: Mrs Irina Jones
Age range: 2–11

Ruckleigh School
17 Lode Lane, Solihull, West
Midlands B91 2AB
Tel: 0121 705 2773
Headmistress: Mrs Barbara Forster
Age range: 3–11
Fees: Day £8,640–£9,120

Solihull Preparatory School
Malvern Hall, Brueton Avenue,
Solihull, West Midlands B91 3EN
Tel: 0121 705 1265
Head of School: Mr Mark Penney
Age range: G3–18
No. of pupils: 430 VIth40
Fees: Day £9,900–£12,750
A £

Solihull School
Warwick Road, Solihull,
West Midlands B91 3DJ
Tel: 0121 705 0958
Headmaster: Mr David E J J Lloyd
Age range: 7–18
No. of pupils: 1013 VIth279
Fees: Day £10,491–£12,897
A £

St George's School, Edgbaston
31 Calthorpe Road, Birmingham,
West Midlands B15 1RX
Tel: 0121 625 0398
Head of School: Mr Gary
Neal BEd (Hons)
Age range: 3–18
No. of pupils: 368 VIth48
Fees: Day £6,060–£9,765
A £

Tettenhall College
Wood Road, Tettenhall,
Wolverhampton, West
Midlands WV6 8QX
Tel: 01902 751119
Headteacher: Mr
Christopher McAllister
Age range: 2–18 years
No. of pupils: 410
A £

The Blue Coat School
Somerset Road, Edgbaston,
Birmingham, West Midlands B17 0HR
Tel: 0121 410 6800
Headmaster: Mr N G Neeson
Age range: 2–11
Fees: Day £4,059–£12,714
£

The Shrubbery School
Walmley Ash Road, Walmley, Sutton
Coldfield, West Midlands B76 1HY
Tel: 0121 351 1582
Head Teacher: Hilary Atkins
Age range: 3–11
Fees: Day £3,765–£8,808

WEST HOUSE SCHOOL
For further details see p. 129
24 St James's Road,
Edgbaston, Birmingham,
West Midlands B15 2NX
Tel: 0121 440 4097
Email: secretary@
westhouseprep.com
Website:
www.westhouseprep.com
Headmaster: Mr Alistair M J
Lyttle BA(Hons), PGCE, NPQH
Age range: B1–11
years G1–4 years
No. of pupils: 350
Fees: Day £2,200–£4,226

Worcestershire

Abberley Hall School
Abberley Hall, Worcester,
Worcestershire WR6 6DD
Tel: 01299 896275
Headmaster: Mr Jonnie Besley
Age range: 2–13 years

Bowbrook House School
Peopleton, Pershore,
Worcestershire WR10 2EE
Tel: 01905 841242
Headteacher: Mr C D
Allen BSc(Hons)
Age range: 3–16
Fees: Day £5,775–£11,388
£

England – West Midlands

Bromsgrove Preparatory School
Old Station Road, Bromsgrove, Worcestershire B60 2BU
Tel: 01527 579600
Headmistress: Jacqui Deval-Reed
Age range: 7–13
Fees: Day £11,640–£15,105 WB £17,685–£21,390 FB £24,240–£29,895

Bromsgrove Pre-preparatory & Nursery School
Avoncroft House, Hanbury Road, Bromsgrove, Worcestershire B60 4JS
Tel: 01527 579679 (Ext:204)
Age range: 2–7

Cambian New Elizabethan School
Quarry Bank, Hartlebury, Kidderminster, Worcestershire DY11 7TE
Tel: 01299 250258
Head of School: Sara Ferguson
Age range: 7–19
No. of pupils: 45

Heathfield Knoll School
Wolverley, Kidderminster, Worcestershire DY10 3QE
Tel: 01562 850204
Head of School: Mr. L. G. Collins B.Sc.(Hons), M.A.,P.G.C.E.
Age range: 3 months–16 years
No. of pupils: 223
Fees: Day £9,045–£14,283

King's Hawford
Lock Lane, Claines, Worcester, Worcestershire WR3 7SD
Tel: 01905 451292
Head of School: Ms Jennie Phillips
Age range: 2–11 years
No. of pupils: 270
Fees: Day £2,661–£4,789

King's St Alban's
Mill Street, Worcester, Worcestershire WR1 2NJ
Tel: 01905 354906
Head of School: Mr Richard Chapman
Age range: 2–11 years
No. of pupils: 182
Fees: Day £2,538–£4,593

Madresfield Early Years Centre
Hayswood Farm, Madresfield, Malvern, Worcestershire WR13 5AA
Tel: 01684 574378
Head: Mrs A Bennett M.B.E.
Age range: 1–5
No. of pupils: 216
Fees: Day £5,800–£6,500

RGS Dodderhill
Crutch Lane, Droitwich, Worcestershire WR9 0BE
Tel: 01905 778290
Headmistress: Mrs Sarah Atkinson
Age range: G4–16
No. of pupils: 190
Fees: Day £6,870–£11,700

RGS Springfield
Springfield, Britannia Square, Worcester, Worcestershire WR1 3DL
Tel: 01905 24999
Headmistress: Mrs Laura Brown
Age range: 2–11
No. of pupils: 140
Fees: Day £8,160–£12,546

RGS The Grange
Grange Lane, Claines, Worcester, Worcestershire WR3 7RR
Tel: 01905 451205
Headmaster: Mr Gareth Hughes
Age range: 2–11
No. of pupils: 350
Fees: Day £8,160–£12,546

River School
Oakfield House, Droitwich Road, Worcester, Worcestershire WR3 7ST
Tel: 01905 457047
Principal: Mr Adrian Parsonage
Age range: 2–16

The Downs Malvern
Colwall, Malvern, Worcestershire WR13 6EY
Tel: 01684 544100
Headmaster: Mr Alastair Cook
Age range: 3–13
Fees: Day £7,107–£17,076 WB £12,882–£19,890 FB £14,640–£22,602

The Elms
Colwall, Malvern, Worcestershire WR13 6EF
Tel: 01684 540344
Headmaster: Mr Chris Hattam
Age range: 3–13
No. of pupils: 200
Fees: Day £8,085–£19,500 FB £24,000–£24,480

Winterfold House
Chaddesley Corbett, Kidderminster, Worcestershire DY10 4PW
Tel: 01562 777234
Headmistress: Mrs Denise Toms BA (Hons) QTS, NPQH
Age range: 3 months–13 years

Yorkshire & Humberside

East Riding of Yorkshire D218
North Yorkshire D218
North-East Lincolnshire D219
South Yorkshire D219
West Yorkshire D219

KEY TO SYMBOLS
- Boys' school
- Girls' school
- International school
- Tutorial or sixth form college
- A levels
- Boarding accommodation
- Bursaries
- International Baccalaureate
- Learning support
- Entrance at 16+
- Vocational qualifications
- (IAPS) Independent Association of Prep Schools
- (HMC) The Headmasters' & Headmistresses' Conference
- (ISA) Independent Schools Association
- (GSA) Girls' School Association
- (BSA) Boarding Schools' Association
- (S) Society of Heads

Unless otherwise indicated, all schools are coeducational day schools. Single-sex and boarding schools will be indicated by the relevant icon.

England – Yorkshire & Humberside

East Riding of Yorkshire

Froebel House School
5 Marlborough Avenue,
Kingston upon Hull, East
Riding of Yorkshire HU5 3JP
Tel: 01482 342272
Headmaster: Mr A Roberts
M.Ed BA Hons PGCE
Age range: 4–11
No. of pupils: 131
Fees: Day £4,398–£4,623

Hessle Mount School
Jenny Brough Lane, Hessle, East
Riding of Yorkshire HU13 0JZ
Tel: 01482 643371
Headmistress: Miss Sarah Cutting
Age range: 3–8
No. of pupils: 155
Fees: Day £6,000–£6,300

Hull Collegiate School
Tranby Croft, Anlaby, Kingston
upon Hull, East Riding of
Yorkshire HU10 7EH
Tel: 01482 657016
Headteacher: Mrs Alex Wilson
Age range: 3–18
No. of pupils: 650
Fees: Day £5,013–£11,796
(A)(£)

Hymers College
Hymers Avenue, Kingston upon Hull,
East Riding of Yorkshire HU3 1LW
Tel: 01482 343555
Headmaster: Mr D Elstone
Age range: 8–18
No. of pupils: 977 VIth215
Fees: Day £9,459–£11,358
(A)(£)

North Yorkshire

Ashville College
Green Lane, Harrogate,
North Yorkshire HG2 9JP
Tel: 01423 566358
Headmaster: Mr Richard Marshall
Age range: 3–18
No. of pupils: 870
Fees: Day £8,430–£14,640
FB £18,390–£27,780

Aysgarth School
Newton le Willows, Bedale,
North Yorkshire DL8 1TF
Tel: 01677 450240
Head of School: Mr Rob Morse
Age range: B3–13 years

Belmont Grosvenor School
Swarcliffe Hall, Birstwith, Harrogate,
North Yorkshire HG3 2JG
Tel: 01423 771029
Headmistress: Mrs Sophia
Ashworth Jones
Age range: 3 months–11 years
No. of pupils: 144
Fees: Day £9,888–£11,712

**BOOTHAM JUNIOR
SCHOOL**
For further details see p. 131
Rawcliffe Lane, York, North
Yorkshire YO30 6NP
Tel: 01904 655021
Email: junior@
boothamschool.com
Website:
www.boothamschool.com
Head: Mrs Helen Todd
Age range: 3–11 years
Fees: Day £2,430–£3,630

Brackenfield School
128 Duchy Road, Harrogate,
North Yorkshire HG1 2HE
Tel: 01423 508558
Headteacher: Ms Patricia Sowa
Age range: 2–11
No. of pupils: 179
Fees: Day £8,235–£8,850

**Chapter House
Preparatory School**
Thorpe Underwood Hall, Ouseburn,
York, North Yorkshire YO26 9SZ
Tel: 01423 333330
Head Teacher: Mrs
Karen Kilkenny BSc
Age range: 3–10

Cundall Manor School
Helperby, York, North
Yorkshire YO61 2RW
Tel: 01423 360200
Head of School: Mrs Amanda
Kirby BA (Hons), PGCE, NPQH
Age range: 2–16 years
Fees: Day £10,380–£16,800
WB £21,765–£22,110

Fyling Hall School
Robin Hood's Bay, Whitby,
North Yorkshire YO22 4QD
Tel: 01947 880353
Headmaster: Mr. Steven Allen
Age range: 4–18
No. of pupils: VIth54
Fees: Day £6,684–£9,177 WB
£9,207–£11,778 FB £16,230–£19,995

Giggleswick Junior School
Mill Lane, Giggleswick, Settle,
North Yorkshire BD24 0DG
Tel: 01729 893100
Headmaster: Mr. James Mundell
Age range: 3–11 (boarding from 9)
No. of pupils: 75
Fees: Day £7,965–£12,765 FB £21,240

Highfield Prep School
Clarence Drive, Harrogate,
North Yorkshire HG1 2QG
Tel: 01423 504 543
Head: James Savile
Age range: 4–11
No. of pupils: 216
Fees: Day £9,420–£10,740 FB £23,820

**Queen Ethelburga's
Collegiate**
Thorpe Underwood Hall, Ouseburn,
York, North Yorkshire YO26 9SS
Tel: 01423 33 33 30
Principal: Dan Machin
Age range: 3–19 years
No. of pupils: 1400

Queen Mary's School
Baldersby Park, Topcliffe, Thirsk,
North Yorkshire YO7 3BZ
Tel: 01845 575000
Head: Carole Cameron
Age range: B3–8 G3–16
No. of pupils: 235
Fees: Day £8,265–£18,420
FB £20,475–£24,165

**SCARBOROUGH
COLLEGE**
For further details see p. 134
Filey Road, Scarborough,
North Yorkshire YO11 3BA
Tel: +44 (0)1723 360620

Email: admin@
scarboroughcollege.co.uk
Website: www.
scarboroughcollege.co.uk
Headmaster: Mr Guy Emmett
Age range: 3–18 years
No. of pupils: 484
Fees: Day £8,022–£15,741
FB £24,528–£32,277

St Olave's School
Clifton, York, North
Yorkshire YO30 6AB
Tel: 01904 527416
The Master: Mr A Falconer
Age range: 8–13
No. of pupils: 355
Fees: Day £12,345–£14,955
FB £23,160–£25,560

St Peter's School 2-8
Clifton, York, North
Yorkshire YO30 6AB
Tel: 01904 527361
Head of School: Mr Phil Hardy
Age range: 2–8

Terrington Hall
Terrington, York, North
Yorkshire YO60 6PR
Tel: 01653 648227
Headmaster: Mr. Simon Kibler
Age range: 3–13
No. of pupils: 150

The Mount Junior School
Dalton Terrace, York, North
Yorkshire YO24 4DD
Tel: 01904 667513
Head: Mr Martyn Andrews
BSc(Hons), PGCE
Age range: 3–11
Fees: Day £1,710–£2,280

The Read School
Drax, Selby, North Yorkshire YO8 8NL
Tel: 01757 618248
Acting Head: M A Voisey
Age range: 3–18
No. of pupils: VIth36
Fees: Day £8,457–£11,970 WB
£21,279–£24,429 FB £22,743–£26,019

**Wharfedale
Montessori School**
Bolton Abbey, Skipton, North
Yorkshire BD23 6AN
Tel: 01756 710452
Headmistress/Principal:
Mrs Jane Lord
Age range: 2–12
Fees: Day £7,350

York Steiner School
Danesmead, Fulford Cross, York,
North Yorkshire YO10 4PB
Tel: 01904 654983
Administrator: Maurice Dobie
Age range: 3–14
No. of pupils: 197
Fees: Day £6,750

England – Yorkshire & Humberside

North-East Lincolnshire

OneSchool Global UK Ridgeway Campus
Ridge Way, Scunthorpe, North-East Lincolnshire DN17 1BS
Tel: 03300 552611
Age range: 7–18 years

St James' School
22 Bargate, Grimsby, North-East Lincolnshire DN34 4SY
Tel: 01472 503260
Headmaster: Dr J Price
Age range: 2–18
No. of pupils: 238 VIth25

St Martin's Preparatory School
63 Bargate, Grimsby, North-East Lincolnshire DN34 5AA
Tel: 01472 878907
Headmaster: Mr S Thompson BEd
Age range: 2–11
Fees: Day £5,580–£6,780

The Children's House
Station Road, Stallingborough, North-East Lincolnshire DN41 8AJ
Tel: 01472 886000
Headteacher: Ms Theresa Ellerby
Age range: 4–11

South Yorkshire

Bethany School
Finlay Street, Sheffield, South Yorkshire S3 7PS
Tel: 0114 272 6994
Head of School: Mr David Charles B.Eng. (Hons) (Sheffield) PGCE
Age range: 4–16 years

Birkdale School
4 Oakholme Road, Sheffield, South Yorkshire S10 3DH
Tel: 0114 266 8408
Head of School: Mr Peter Harris
Age range: 4–18 years

Hill House School
6th Avenue, Auckley, Doncaster, South Yorkshire DN9 3GG
Tel: +44 (0)1302 776300
Principal: David Holland
Age range: 3–18
Fees: Day £8,700–£13,200

Mylnhurst Preparatory School & Nursery
Button Hill, Woodholm Road, Ecclesall, Sheffield, South Yorkshire S11 9HJ
Tel: 0114 2361411
Headmistress: Hannah Cunningham
Age range: 3–11

Sheffield High School GDST
10 Rutland Park, Sheffield, South Yorkshire S10 2PE
Tel: 0114 266 0324
Headmistress: Nina Gunson
Age range: G4–18
No. of pupils: 1020
Fees: Day £9,216–£12,975

Sycamore Hall Preparatory School
1 Hall Flat Lane, Balby, Doncaster, South Yorkshire DN4 8PT
Tel: 01302 856800
Headmistress: Miss J Spencer
Age range: 3–11
Fees: Day £4,890

Westbourne School
Westbourne Road, Sheffield, South Yorkshire S10 2QT
Tel: 0114 2660374
Headmaster: Mr John B Hicks MEd
Age range: 3–16 years

West Yorkshire

ACKWORTH SCHOOL
For further details see p. 130
Pontefract Road, Ackworth, Pontefract, West Yorkshire WF7 7LT
Tel: 01977 233 600
Email: admissions@ackworthschool.com
Website: www.ackworthschool.com
Headteacher: Mr. Anton Maree BA Rhodes (HDE)
Age range: 2.5–18 years
No. of pupils: 510
Fees: Day £3,000–£4,935 FB £8,436–£10,692

Al Mu'min Primary School
Clifton St, Bradford, West Yorkshire BD8 7DA
Tel: 01274 488593
Headteacher: Mr M M Azam
Age range: 4–11
No. of pupils: 102

Al-Furqaan Preparatory School
Drill Hall House, Bath Street, Dewsbury, West Yorkshire WF13 2JR
Tel: 01924 453 661
Head of School: Ms Shaheda Ughratdar
Age range: 2–11

Bradford Christian School
Livingstone Road, Bolton Woods, Bradford, West Yorkshire BD2 1BT
Tel: 01274 532649
Headmaster: P J Moon BEd(Hons)
Age range: 4–16
Fees: Day £2,460–£4,440

Bradford Grammar School
Keighley Road, Bradford, West Yorkshire BD9 4JP
Tel: 01274 542492
Headmaster: Dr Simon Hinchliffe
Age range: 6–18
No. of pupils: VIth266

BRONTË HOUSE SCHOOL
For further details see p. 132
Apperley Bridge, Bradford, West Yorkshire BD10 0NR
Tel: 0113 250 2811
Email: admissions@woodhousegrove.co.uk
Website: www.woodhousegrove.co.uk
Head: Mrs Sarah Chatterton
Age range: 2–11 years
No. of pupils: 312
Fees: Day £9,765–£12,978

Crystal Gardens
38-40 Greaves Street, Bradford, West Yorkshire BD5 7PE
Tel: 01274 575400
Headteacher: Rashta Bibi
Age range: 4–11

Dale House Independent School & Nursery
Ruby Street, Carlinghow, Batley, West Yorkshire WF17 8HL
Tel: 01924 422215
Headmistress: Mrs S M G Fletcher BA, CertEd
Age range: 2–11 years

Darul Uloom Dawatul Imaan
Harry Street, Off Wakefield Road, Bradford, West Yorkshire BD4 9PH
Tel: 01274 402233
Headteacher: Moulana Abdurrahman Kayat Sahib

Fulneck Junior School
Fulneck, Pudsey, Leeds, West Yorkshire LS28 8DS
Tel: 0113 257 0235
Head of Junior School: Mr Chris Bouckley
Age range: 3–11 (boarding from age 9)
No. of pupils: 128

Gateways School
Leeds Road, Harewood, Leeds, West Yorkshire LS17 9LE
Tel: 0113 2886345
Headmistress: Dr Tracy Johnson
Age range: B2–15 years G2–18 years
No. of pupils: 430
Fees: Day £9,270–£14,865

Ghyll Royd School and Pre-School
Greystone Manor, Ilkley Road, Burley in Wharfedale, West Yorkshire LS29 7HW
Tel: 01943 865575
Headteacher: Mr David Martin BA MA PGCE
Age range: 2–11 years
No. of pupils: 100
Fees: Day £3,200

Heathfield Junior School
Oldham Road, Rishworth, West Yorkshire HX6 4QF
Tel: +44 (0)1422 823564
Head of School: Mr A. M. Wilkins
Age range: 3–11

Hipperholme Grammar School
Bramley Lane, Hipperholme, Halifax, West Yorkshire HX3 8JE
Tel: 01422 202256
Head: Mrs Jackie Griffiths
Age range: 3–18
No. of pupils: VIth30
Fees: Day £8,799–£10,995

England – Yorkshire & Humberside

Huddersfield Grammar School
Royds Mount, Luck Lane, Marsh, Huddersfield, West Yorkshire HD1 4QX
Tel: 01484 424549
Headmistress: Mrs Donna Holmes
Age range: 3–16 years
No. of pupils: 546
Fees: Day £9,009–£11,103

Islamic Tarbiyah Preparatory School
Ambler Street, Bradford, West Yorkshire BD8 8AW
Tel: 01274 490462
Headteacher: Mr S A Nawaz
Age range: 5–10

Lady Lane Park School
Lady Lane, Bingley, West Yorkshire BD16 4AP
Tel: 01274 551168
Headmaster: Mr Nigel Saunders
Age range: 2–11
No. of pupils: 150
Fees: Day £8,016

Leeds Menorah School
399 Street Lane, Leeds, West Yorkshire LS17 6JQ
Tel: 0113 2697709
Age range: 3–16

Madni Academy
40-42 Scarborough Street, Savile Town, Dewsbury, West Yorkshire WF12 9AY
Tel: 01924 500335
Headmistress: Mrs S A Mirza
Age range: G3–18

Mill Cottage Montessori School
Wakefield Road, Brighouse, West Yorkshire HD6 4HA
Tel: 01484 400500
Principal: Ailsa Nevile
Age range: 0–11

Moorfield School
Wharfedale Lodge, 11 Ben Rhydding Road, Ilkley, West Yorkshire LS29 8RL
Tel: 01943 607285
Headmistress: Mrs Tina Herbert
Age range: 2–11 years
No. of pupils: 110
Fees: Day £10,395

Moorlands School
Foxhill, Weetwood Lane, Leeds, West Yorkshire LS16 5PF
Tel: 0113 2785286
Headmaster: Miss J Atkinson
Age range: 2–11
No. of pupils: 149
Fees: Day £8,985–£10,566

Netherleigh & Rossefield School
Parsons Road, Heaton, Bradford, West Yorkshire BD9 4AY
Tel: 01274 543162
Headteacher: Miss A Leary
Age range: 2–11

OneSchool Global UK York Campus
Bishopthorpe Road, York, West Yorkshire YO23 2QA
Tel: 01904 663300
Age range: 7–18 years

Paradise Primary School
1 Bretton Street, Dewsbury, West Yorkshire WF12 9BB
Tel: 01924 439803
Headteacher: Mrs Hafsa Patel
Age range: 2–11
No. of pupils: 217

Queen Elizabeth Grammar School (Junior School)
158 Northgate, Wakefield, West Yorkshire WF1 3QY
Tel: 01924 373821
Acting Head: Mr M Shevill BEd MSc FCCT
Age range: B4–11 years

Queenswood School
Queen Street, Morley, Leeds, West Yorkshire LS27 9EB
Tel: 0113 2534033
Headteacher: Mrs J A Tanner MMus, BA, FTCL, ARCO
Age range: 4–11
Fees: Day £6,000–£6,447

Richmond House School
170 Otley Road, Leeds, West Yorkshire LS16 5LG
Tel: 0113 2752670
Headteacher: Mrs Helen Stiles
Age range: 3–11
No. of pupils: 219
Fees: Day £5,850–£9,150

Silcoates School
Wrenthorpe, Wakefield, West Yorkshire WF2 0PD
Tel: 01924 291614
Headmaster: Chris Wainman MA
Age range: 4–18

The Branch Christian School
Dewsbury Revival Centre, West Park Street, Dewsbury, West Yorkshire WF13 4LA
Tel: +44 (0)1924 452511
Head of School: Jo Holt
Age range: 3–16
No. of pupils: 26

THE FROEBELIAN SCHOOL
For further details see p. 133
Clarence Road, Horsforth, Leeds, West Yorkshire LS18 4LB
Tel: 0113 2583047
Email: office@froebelian.co.uk
Website: www.froebelian.com
Head Teacher: Mrs Catherine Dodds BEd (Hons), PGCE
Age range: 3–11 years
No. of pupils: 181
Fees: Day £5,535–£8,250

The Gleddings School
Birdcage Lane, Savile Park, Halifax, West Yorkshire HX3 0JB
Tel: 01422 354605
School Director: Mrs Jill Wilson CBE
Age range: 3–11
No. of pupils: 191
Fees: Day £3,555–£5,910

The Grammar School at Leeds
Alwoodley Gates, Harrogate Road, Leeds, West Yorkshire LS17 8GS
Tel: 0113 2291552
Principal: Mrs Sue Woodroofe
Age range: 3–18
No. of pupils: 2120 VIth418
Fees: Day £9,441–£13,788

The Mount School
3 Binham Road, Edgerton, Huddersfield, West Yorkshire HD2 2AP
Tel: 01484 426432
Head of School: Mr Euan Burton-Smith
Age range: 3–11
No. of pupils: 115
Fees: Day £8,070

Wakefield Girls' High School (Junior School)
2 St John's Square, Wakefield, West Yorkshire WF1 2QX
Tel: 01924 374577
Head: Ms Heidi-Jayne Boyes BSc (Hons)
Age range: G4–11 years

Wakefield Grammar Pre-Preparatory School
Margaret Street, Wakefield, West Yorkshire WF1 2DG
Tel: 01924 231627
Age range: 3–7 years

Wakefield Independent School
The Nostell Centre, Doncaster Road, Nostell, Wakefield, West Yorkshire WF4 1QG
Tel: 01924 865757
Headmistress: Mrs K E Caryl
Age range: 2.5–16
No. of pupils: 190
Fees: Day £5,100–£7,050

Westville House School
Carter's Lane, Middleton, Ilkley, West Yorkshire LS29 0DQ
Tel: 01943 608053
Headteacher: Mrs Nikki Hammond BA(Hons) PGCE
Age range: 3–11

WOODHOUSE GROVE SCHOOL
For further details see p. 136
Apperley Bridge, Bradford, West Yorkshire BD10 0NR
Tel: 0113 250 2477
Headmaster: Mr James Lockwood MA
Age range: 11–18
No. of pupils: 751
Fees: Day £14,490–£14,694 FB £30,555–£30,720

Northern Ireland

County Antrim D222
County Down D222
County Londonderry D222

KEY TO SYMBOLS
- Boys' school
- Girls' school
- International school
- Tutorial or sixth form college
- A levels
- Boarding accommodation
- Bursaries
- International Baccalaureate
- Learning support
- Entrance at 16+
- Vocational qualifications
- (IAPS) Independent Association of Prep Schools
- (HMC) The Headmasters' & Headmistresses' Conference
- (ISA) Independent Schools Association
- (GSA) Girls' School Association
- (BSA) Boarding Schools' Association
- Society of Heads

Unless otherwise indicated, all schools are coeducational day schools. Single-sex and boarding schools will be indicated by the relevant icon.

NORTHERN IRELAND

County Antrim

Campbell College Junior School
Belmont Road, Belfast,
County Antrim BT4 2ND
Tel: 028 9076 3076
Head of Junior School: Miss Andrea Brown
Age range: B3–11 years G3–4 years

Inchmarlo
Cranmore Park, Belfast,
County Antrim BT9 6JR
Tel: 028 9038 1454
Head of School: Mr A Smyth

Methodist College
1 Malone Road, Belfast,
County Antrim BT9 6BY
Tel: 028 9020 5205
Principal: Mr J Scott W Naismith
Age range: 4–19
No. of pupils: 2307 VIth548

Victoria College Belfast
Cranmore Park, Belfast,
County Antrim BT9 6JA
Tel: 028 9066 1506
Principal: Ms Patricia Slevin
Age range: G2–18
No. of pupils: 1070 VIth224
Fees: Day £4,825–£7,550
FB £11,100–£18,650

County Down

Holywood Steiner School
34 Croft Road, Holywood,
County Down BT18 0PR
Tel: 028 9042 8029
Chairperson of the School Management Team: Julie Higgins
Age range: 3–17 years
No. of pupils: 110
Fees: Day £4,008–£4,512

OneSchool Global UK Newry Campus
22 Rampart Road, Newry,
County Down BT34 2QU
Tel: 02830 260777
Age range: 7–18 years

Rockport School
Craigavad, Holywood,
County Down BT18 0DD
Tel: 028 9042 8372
Headmaster: Mr George Vance
Age range: 3–18
No. of pupils: 200
Fees: Day £6,540–£15,810 WB £17,970–£22,770 FB £21,450–£26,160

County Londonderry

OneSchool Global UK Knockloughrim Campus
23 Rocktown Road, Knockloughrim,
County Londonderry BT45 8QE
Tel: 02879 645191
Age range: 7–18 years

Scotland

Aberdeen D224
Aberdeenshire D224
Angus D224
Argyll & Bute D224
Borders D224
Clackmannanshire D224
Dundee D224
East Lothian D224
Edinburgh D224
Fife D225
Glasgow D225
Moray D225
Perth & Kinross D225
Renfrewshire D225
South Ayrshire D225
South Lanarkshire D225
Stirling D225

KEY TO SYMBOLS
- Boys' school
- Girls' school
- International school
- Tutorial or sixth form college
- A levels
- Boarding accommodation
- Bursaries
- International Baccalaureate
- Learning support
- Entrance at 16+
- Vocational qualifications
- (IAPS) Independent Association of Prep Schools
- (HMC) The Headmasters' & Headmistresses' Conference
- (ISA) Independent Schools Association
- (GSA) Girls' School Association
- (BSA) Boarding Schools' Association
- (S) Society of Heads

Unless otherwise indicated, all schools are coeducational day schools. Single-sex and boarding schools will be indicated by the relevant icon.

SCOTLAND

Aberdeen

Albyn School
17-23 Queen's Road,
Aberdeen AB15 4PB
Tel: 01224 322408
Headmaster: Mr Stefan Horsman
Age range: 2–18 years

International School of Aberdeen
Pitfodels House, North
Deeside Road, Pitfodels,
Cults, Aberdeen AB15 9PN
Tel: 01224 730300
Head of School: Mr Nick Little
Age range: 3–18 years

Robert Gordon's College
Schoolhill, Aberdeen AB10 1FE
Tel: 01224 646346
Head of College: Mr Robin Macpherson
Age range: 3–18 years

St Margaret's School for Girls
17 Albyn Place, Aberdeen AB10 1RU
Tel: +44 (0)1224 584466
Headmistress: Miss Anna Tomlinson
Age range: B3–5 years G3–18 years

Aberdeenshire

OneSchool Global UK Caledonia (North) Campus
Millden, Balmedie,
Aberdeenshire AB23 8YY
Tel: 01259 303030
Age range: 7–18 years

Angus

Lathallan School
Brotherton Castle, Johnshaven,
Montrose, Angus DD10 0HN
Tel: 01561 362220
Headmaster: Mr Richard Toley
Age range: 6 months–18 years

Argyll & Bute

Lomond School
10 Stafford Street, Helensburgh,
Argyll & Bute G84 9JX
Tel: +44 (0)1436 672476
Principal: Mrs Johanna Urquhart
Age range: 3–18 years
No. of pupils: 320
Fees: Day £9,200–£12,750
WB £22,150 FB £29,650

Borders

St. Mary's School
Abbey Park, Melrose,
Borders TD6 9LN
Tel: 01896 822517
Headmaster: Mr Liam Harvey
Age range: 2–13 years

Clackmannan-shire

Dollar Academy
Dollar, Clackmannanshire FK14 7DU
Tel: 01259 742511
Rector: Mr Ian Munro
Age range: 5–18 years
No. of pupils: 1340
Fees: Day £10,899–£14,571 WB £28,197–£31,869 FB £30,051–£33,723

OneSchool Global UK Caledonia (South) Campus
The Pavillions, Stirling Road, Alloa,
Clackmannanshire FK10 1TA
Tel: 01259 303030
Age range: 7–18 years

Dundee

High School of Dundee
Euclid Crescent, Dundee DD1 1HU
Tel: 01382 202921
Rector: Mrs Lise Hudson
Age range: 3–18 years
No. of pupils: 1000
Fees: Day £9,618–£13,650

East Lothian

Belhaven Hill School
Belhaven Road, Dunbar,
East Lothian EH42 1NN
Tel: 01368 862785
Headmaster: Mr. Olly Langton
Age range: 5–13 years

Loretto Junior School
North Esk Lodge, 1 North
High Street, Musselburgh,
East Lothian EH21 6JA
Tel: 0131 653 4570
Headmaster: Mr Andrew Dickenson
Age range: 3–12 years

The Compass School
West Road, Haddington,
East Lothian EH41 3RD
Tel: 01620 822642
Headmaster: Mr Mark Becher MA(Hons), PGCE
Age range: 3–12 years

Edinburgh

Cargilfield School
45 Gamekeeper's Road,
Edinburgh EH4 6HU
Tel: 0131 336 2207
Headmaster: Mr. Robert Taylor
Age range: 3–13 years

Clifton Hall School
Newbridge, Edinburgh EH28 8LQ
Tel: 0131 333 1359
Headmaster: Mr R Grant
Age range: 3–18 years

Edinburgh Montessori Arts School
18N Liberton Brae,
Edinburgh EH16 6AE
Tel: 0131 600 0123
Principal: Ms Emma Rattigan
Age range: 1–18 years

Edinburgh Steiner School
60-64 Spylaw Road,
Edinburgh EH10 5BR
Tel: 0131 337 3410
Age range: 3.5–18 years
No. of pupils: 360

ESMS Junior School
11 Queensferry Terrace,
Edinburgh EH4 3EQ
Tel: +44 (0)131 311 1111
Head of School: Mr Mike Kane
Age range: 3–11 years

Fettes College Preparatory School
East Fettes Avenue,
Edinburgh EH4 1DL
Tel: +44 (0)131 332 2976
Headmaster: Mr A A Edwards
Age range: 7–13 years

George Heriot's School
Lauriston Place, Edinburgh EH3 9EQ
Tel: 0131 229 7263
Principal: Mr Gareth Warren
Age range: 3–18 years

George Watson's College
69-71 Colinton Road,
Edinburgh EH10 5EG
Tel: 0131 446 6000
Principal: Mr Melvyn Roffe
Age range: 3–18 years

Mannafields Christian School
Unit B12, St Margaret's House, 151
London Road, Edinburgh EH7 6AE
Tel: 131516 3221
Age range: 5–14 years

MERCHISTON CASTLE SCHOOL
For further details see p. 138
294 Colinton Road,
Edinburgh EH13 0PU
Tel: 0131 312 2200
Email: admissions@merchiston.co.uk
Website: www.merchiston.co.uk
Headmaster: Mr Jonathan Anderson
Age range: B7–18 years
No. of pupils: 400
Fees: Day £15,330–£26,040
FB £22,080–£35,880

Regius School
69a Whitehill Street, Newcraighall,
Edinburgh EH21 8QZ
Tel: 0131 669 2913
Age range: 5–14 years

St George's School for Girls
Garscube Terrace,
Edinburgh EH12 6BG
Tel: 0131 311 8000
Head: Mrs Alex Hems
Age range: B2–5 years G2–18 years

St Mary's Music School
Coates Hall, 25 Grosvenor
Crescent, Edinburgh EH12 5EL
Tel: 0131 538 7766
Headteacher: Dr Kenneth Taylor
BSc Hons, PhD, PGCE, PG Dip
Age range: 9–19 years

The Edinburgh Academy
42 Henderson Row,
Edinburgh EH3 5BL
Tel: 0131 556 4603
Rector: Barry Welsh
Age range: 2–18 years

SCOTLAND

Fife

ST LEONARDS SCHOOL
For further details see p. 140
The Pends, St Andrews,
Fife KY16 9QJ
Tel: 01334 472126
Email: registrar@
stleonards-fife.org
Website: stleonards-fife.org
Head: Mr Simon Brian
Age range: 5–18 years
No. of pupils: 577
Fees: Day £9,840–£15,939
FB £24,342–£37,920

Glasgow

Belmont House School
Sandringham Avenue, Newton
Mearns, Glasgow G77 5DU
Tel: 0141 639 2922
Principal: Mr Melvyn D Shanks
BSc, DipEd, MInstP, CPhys, SQH
Age range: 3–18 years

Fernhill School
Fernbrae Avenue, Burnside,
Rutherglen, Glasgow G73 4SG
Tel: 0141 634 2674
Head Teacher: Mr Mark Donnelly
Age range: 2–18 years

**Hutchesons'
Grammar School**
21 Beaton Road, Glasgow G41 4NW
Tel: 0141 423 2933
Rector: Mr Colin Gambles
BSc (Hons) PGCE
Age range: 3–18 years

Kelvinside Academy
33 Kirklee Road, Glasgow G12 0SW
Tel: 0141 357 3376
Rector: Mr Daniel J
Wyatt BA (Ed) Hons
Age range: 3–18 years

Olivewood Primary School
81 Lister Street, Glasgow G4 0BZ
Age range: 5–11 years

St Aloysius' College
45 Hill Street, Glasgow G3 6RJ
Tel: 0141 332 3190
Head Master: Mr Matthew Bartlett
MA (Cantab), PGCE, NLE, NPQH
Age range: 3–18 years

**The Glasgow Academy,
Kelvinbridge**
Colebrooke Street, Kelvinbridge,
Glasgow G12 8HE
Tel: 0141 334 8558
Rector: Mr Matthew K
Pearce BA (Dunelm)
Age range: 3–18 years

**The Glasgow Academy,
Milngavie**
Mugdock Road, Milngavie,
Glasgow G62 8NP
Tel: 0141 956 3758
Rector: Mr Matthew K
Pearce BA (Dunelm)
Age range: 3–8 years

**The Glasgow Academy,
Newlands**
54 Newlands Road, Newlands,
Glasgow G43 2JG
Tel: 0141 632 0736
Rector: Mr Matthew K
Pearce BA (Dunelm)
Age range: 3–8 years

**The High School
of Glasgow**
637 Crow Road, Glasgow G13 1PL
Tel: 0141 954 9628
Rector: Mr John O'Neill
Age range: 3–18 years

Moray

Drumduan School
Clovenside Road, Forres,
Moray IV36 2RD
Tel: + 44 (0)1309 676300
Principal Teacher:
Krzysztof Zajaczkowski
Age range: 3–18 years

Gordonstoun
Elgin, Moray IV30 5RF
Tel: 01343 837829
Principal: Ms Lisa Kerr BA
Age range: 4.5–18 years

Perth & Kinross

Ardvreck School
Crieff, Perth & Kinross PH7 4EX
Tel: 01764 653112
Headmistress: Mrs Ali Kinge
Age range: 3–13 years

**CRAIGCLOWAN
PREPARATORY SCHOOL**
For further details see p. 142
Edinburgh Road, Perth,
Perth & Kinross PH2 8PS
Tel: 01738 626310
Email: headspa@
craigclowan-school.co.uk
Website:
www.craigclowan-school.co.uk
Head of School: John Gilmour
Age range: 3–13 years
No. of pupils: 212
Fees: Day £4,950

Kilgraston School
Bridge of Earn, Perth, Perth
& Kinross PH2 9BQ
Tel: 01738 812257
Head: Mrs Dorothy MacGinty
Age range: G5–18 years

Morrison's Academy
Ferntower Road, Crieff,
Perth & Kinross PH7 3AN
Tel: 01764 653885
Rector: Mr A J McGarva
Age range: 2–18 years

Renfrewshire

**Al-Qalam Primary
& High School**
Ben Nevis Road, Paisley,
Renfrewshire PA2 7LA
Tel: 014123 72236
Executive Head: Mr
Shoeb Sarguroh

**Cedars School of
Excellence**
31 Ardgowan Square, Greenock,
Renfrewshire PA16 8NJ
Tel: 01475 723905
Age range: 5–18 years

St Columba's School
Duchal Road, Kilmacolm,
Renfrewshire PA13 4AU
Tel: 01505 872238
Rector: Ms Victoria J. Reilly
Age range: 3–18 years

South Ayrshire

Wellington School
Carleton Turrets, 1 Craigweil Road,
Ayr, South Ayrshire KA7 2XH
Tel: 01292 269321
Head: Mr S Johnson MA
(Cantab) PGCE
Age range: 3–18 years

South Lanarkshire

Hamilton College
Bothwell Road, Hamilton,
South Lanarkshire ML3 0AY
Tel: 01698 282700
Headteacher: Mr Richard Charman
Age range: 2–18 years
No. of pupils: 400
Fees: Day £8,985–£12,588

Stirling

**Fairview International
School, Bridge of Allan**
52 Kenilworth Road, Bridge
of Allan, Stirling FK9 4RY
Tel: +44 (0)1786 231952
Headteacher: Mr David Hicks
Age range: 5–18 years

Wales

Carmarthenshire D228
Clwyd D228
Denbighshire D228
Glamorgan D228
Gwynedd D228
Monmouthshire D229
Pembrokeshire D229
Powys D229

KEY TO SYMBOLS
- Boys' school
- Girls' school
- International school
- Tutorial or sixth form college
- A levels
- Boarding accommodation
- Bursaries
- International Baccalaureate
- Learning support
- Entrance at 16+
- Vocational qualifications
- Independent Association of Prep Schools
- The Headmasters' & Headmistresses' Conference
- Independent Schools Association
- Girls' School Association
- Boarding Schools' Association
- Society of Heads

Unless otherwise indicated, all schools are coeducational day schools. Single-sex and boarding schools will be indicated by the relevant icon.

WALES

Carmarthenshire

Llandovery College
Queensway, Llandovery,
Carmarthenshire SA20 0EE
Tel: +44(0)1550 723000
Warden: Mr Dominic Findlay
Age range: 4–18 years

St. Michael's School
Bryn, Llanelli, Carmarthenshire
SA14 9TU
Tel: 01554 820325
Headmaster: Mr Benson Ferrari
Age range: 3–18 years

Clwyd

Rydal Penrhos Preparatory School
Pwllycrochan Avenue, Colwyn
Bay, Clwyd LL29 7BT
Tel: +44 (0)1492 530 381
Head of School: Mrs Lucy Davies
Age range: 2–11 years

Denbighshire

Fairholme Preparatory School
The Mount, Mount Road, St.
Asaph, Denbighshire LL17 0DH
Tel: 01745 583 505
Principal: Mrs E Perkins MA(Oxon)
Age range: 3–11 years

Myddelton College
Peakes Lane, Denbigh,
Denbighshire LL16 3EN
Tel: +44 174 547 2201
Head Teacher: Mr Andrew Allman
Age range: 4–18 years

Glamorgan

Cardiff Montessori School
Golden Gate, 73 Ty Glas
Avenue, Llanishen, Cardiff,
Glamorgan CF14 5DX
Tel: 02920 567311
Head of School: Ms Esma Izzidien
Age range: 2–12 years

Cardiff Muslim Primary School
Merthyr Street, Cathays,
Cardiff, Glamorgan CF24 4JL
Tel: 029 2034 2040
Headteacher: Sakhawat Ali

Cardiff Steiner School
Hawthorn Road West, Llandaff
North, Cardiff, Glamorgan CF14 2FL
Tel: 029 2056 7986
Age range: 3–18 years

Ely Presbyterian Church School
4-6 Archer Road, Cardiff,
Glamorgan CF5 4FR
Tel: 02920 596410
Headteachers: Mrs Julia
Haines & Stephanie Williams
Age range: 3–16 years

Howell's School, Llandaff GDST
Cardiff Road, Llandaff, Cardiff,
Glamorgan CF5 2YD
Tel: 029 2056 2019
Principal: Mrs Sally Davis BSc
Age range: B16–18
years G3–18 years

Kings Monkton School
6 West Grove, Cardiff,
Glamorgan CF24 3XL
Tel: 02920 482854
Principal: Mr Paul Norton
Age range: 3–18 years

Oakleigh House School
38 Penlan Crescent, Uplands,
Swansea, Glamorgan SA2 0RL
Tel: 01792 298537
Headmistress: Mrs Rhian
Ferriman BA(Hons)Ed, MEd
Age range: 2.5–11 years

OneSchool Global UK Swansea Campus
Sway Road, Morriston, Swansea,
Glamorgan SA6 6JA
Tel: 01792 581221
Age range: 7–18 years

St Clare's School
Newton, Porthcawl,
Glamorgan CF36 5NR
Tel: 01656 782509
Head of School: Helen Hier
Age range: 2.5–18 years
No. of pupils: 250
Fees: Day £6,753–£11,799

St John's College, Cardiff
College Green, Old St Mellons,
Cardiff, Glamorgan CF3 5YX
Tel: 029 2077 8936
Headteacher: Mr Shaun
Moody BA (Hons) PGCE
Age range: 3–18 years

The Cathedral School, Llandaff
Cardiff Road, Llandaff, Cardiff,
Glamorgan CF5 2YH
Tel: 029 2056 3179
Head: Ms Clare Sherwood
Age range: 3–18 years

Ummul Mumineen Academy
142 Penarth Road, Grangetown,
Cardiff, Glamorgan CF11 6NJ
Tel: 02920 220 383
Age range: 8–16 years

Westbourne School
Hickman Road, Penarth,
Glamorgan CF64 2AJ
Tel: 029 2070 5705
Headteacher: Dr GW Griffiths
BSc, PhD, ARCS, PGCE
Age range: 2–18 years
No. of pupils: 351
Fees: Day £8,520–£14,975
FB £35,850–£37,950

Gwynedd

Bangor Independent School
The Old Canonry, 39
Ffordd Gwynedd, Bangor,
Gwynedd LL57 1DT
Tel: 01248 354635
Headteacher: Mr Paul Gash
Age range: 3–11 years

ST GERARD'S SCHOOL
For further details see p. 144
Ffriddoedd Road, Bangor,
Gwynedd LL57 2EL
Tel: 01248 351656
Email: sgadmin@st-gerards.org
Website: www.st-gerards.org
Head Teacher: Mr
Campbell Harrison
Age range: 4–18 years
No. of pupils: 143
Fees: Day £7,695–£11,655

Treffos School
Llansadwrn, Nr. Menai Bridge, Isle
of Anglesey, Gwynedd LL59 5SD
Tel: 01248 712322
Headmaster: Dr S. Humphreys
Age range: 3–11 years

WALES

Monmouthshire

Llangattock School Monmouth
Llangattock-Vibon-Avel, Monmouth, Monmouthshire NP25 5NG
Tel: 01600 772 213
Principal: Ms Rosemary Whaley
Age range: 2–19 years

Monmouth Prep School
Hadnock Road, Monmouth, Monmouthshire NP25 3NG
Tel: 01600 715930
Age range: 3–11 years

Monmouth School for Boys
Almshouse Street, Monmouth, Monmouthshire NP25 3XP
Tel: 01600 713143
Age range: B11–18 years

Monmouth School for Girls
Hereford Road, Monmouth, Monmouthshire NP25 5XT
Tel: 01600 711100
Age range: G11–18 years

Rougemont School
Llantarnam Hall, Malpas Road, Newport, Monmouthshire NP20 6QB
Tel: 01633 820800
Headmaster: Mr Robert Carnevale
Age range: 3–18 years

Pembrokeshire

Castle School Pembrokeshire
Glenover House, Scarrowscant Lane, Haverfordwest, Pembrokeshire SA61 1ES
Tel: 01437 558010
Director: Ms Harriet Harrison
Age range: 3–18 years

Nant-y-Cwm Steiner School
Llanycefn, Clunderwen, Pembrokeshire SA66 7QJ
Tel: +44 (0)1437 563640
Age range: 3–14 years

Redhill Preparatory School
The Garth, St David's Road, Haverfordwest, Pembrokeshire SA61 2UR
Tel: 01437 762472
Head Teacher: Mr Adrian Thomas
Age range: 0–11 years

Powys

OneSchool Global UK Newtown Campus
Sarn, Newtown, Powys SY16 4EJ
Tel: 01686 670152
Age range: 7–18 years

Index

Index

A

Abberley Hall School **Worcestershire** ... D214
Abbey Gate College **Cheshire** ... D188
Abbey School **Devon** ... D207
Abbot's Hill School **Hertfordshire** ... 55, D160
Abbotsford Preparatory School **Greater Manchester** ... D189
Abbotsholme School **Staffordshire** ... D212
Abercorn School **London** ... D182
Aberdour School **Surrey** ... 96, D200
Abingdon Preparatory School **Oxfordshire** ... D153
Ackworth School **West Yorkshire** ... 130, D219
ACS Cobham International School **Surrey** ... D200
ACS Egham International School **Surrey** ... D200
ACS Hillingdon International School **Middlesex** ... D171
Adcote School for Girls **Shropshire** ... D212
Airthrie School **Gloucestershire** ... D152
Akeley Wood School **Buckinghamshire** ... D152
AKS Lytham **Lancashire** ... D190
Al Ameen Primary School **West Midlands** ... D213
Al Mu'min Primary School **West Yorkshire** ... D219
Al-Aqsa Schools Trust **Leicestershire** ... D166
Al-Falah Primary School **London** ... D176
Al-Furqaan Preparatory School **West Yorkshire** ... D219
Al-Khair School **Surrey** ... D172
Al-Mizan School **London** ... D176
Al-Noor Primary School **Essex** ... D170
Al-Qalam Primary & High School **Renfrewshire** ... D225
Al-Risalah Secondary School **London** ... D180
Al-Sadiq & Al-Zahra Schools **London** ... D177
Albyn School **Aberdeen** ... D224
Aldenham School **Hertfordshire** ... D160
Alder Bridge Steiner-Waldorf School **Berkshire** ... D194
Alderley Edge School for Girls **Cheshire** ... D188
Aldro School **Surrey** ... D200
Aldwickbury School **Hertfordshire** ... D160
All Hallows Preparatory School **Somerset** ... D208
All Saints School **Norfolk** ... D161
Alleyn Court School **Essex** ... D159
Alleyn's School **London** ... D179
Alpha Preparatory School **Middlesex** ... D171
Alton School **Hampshire** ... D196
Altrincham Preparatory School **Greater Manchester** ... D189
Amesbury School **Surrey** ... D200
Annemount School **London** ... D176
Ardingly College Preparatory School **West Sussex** ... D202
Ardvreck School **Perth & Kinross** ... D225
Argyle House School **Tyne & Wear** ... D186
Arnold House School **London** ... D177
Arnold Lodge School **Warwickshire** ... D213
Ashbridge Independent School **Lancashire** ... D190
Ashbrooke House School & Pre-School **Somerset** ... D208
Ashfold School **Buckinghamshire** ... D152
Ashford Prep School **Kent** ... D198
Ashford School **Kent** ... D198
Ashgrove School **Kent** ... D171
Ashton House School **Middlesex** ... D171
Ashville College **North Yorkshire** ... D218
Austin Friars School **Cumbria** ... D188
Avalon Preparatory School **Merseyside** ... D191
Avenue House School **London** ... D182
Avenue Pre-Prep & Nursery School **London** ... D176
Avon House Preparatory School **Essex** ... D170
Avondale School **Wiltshire** ... D155
Ayscoughfee Hall School **Lincolnshire** ... D167
Aysgarth School **North Yorkshire** ... D218

B

Babington House School **Kent** ... D171
Bablake Junior School **West Midlands** ... D213
Bablake PrePrep **West Midlands** ... D213
Badminton Junior School **Bristol** ... D206
Ballard School **Hampshire** ... 98, D196
Bancroft's School **Essex** ... D170
Bangor Independent School **Gwynedd** ... D228
Banstead Preparatory School **Surrey** ... D200
Barfield School **Surrey** ... D200
Barlborough Hall School **Derbyshire** ... D166
Barnard Castle Preparatory School **Durham** ... D186
Barnardiston Hall Preparatory School **Suffolk** ... D162
Barrow Hills School **Surrey** ... 97, D200
Bassett House School **London** ... D182
Battle Abbey School **East Sussex** ... D195
Beachborough School **Northamptonshire** ... D167
Beaudesert Park School **Gloucestershire** ... D152
Beaulieu Convent School **Jersey** ... D150
Bedales Prep School, Dunhurst **Hampshire** ... D196
Bedford Girls' School **Bedfordshire** ... D158
Bedford Greenacre Independent School **Bedfordshire** ... D158
Bedford Modern School **Bedfordshire** ... D158
Bedford Preparatory School **Bedfordshire** ... D158
Bedstone College **Shropshire** ... D212
Beech Grove School **Kent** ... D198
Beech Hall School **Cheshire** ... D188
Beech House School **Greater Manchester** ... D189
Beechwood Nursery School **London** ... D180
Beechwood Park School **Hertfordshire** ... D160
Beechwood Sacred Heart **Kent** ... D198
Beehive Preparatory School **Essex** ... D170
Beeston Hall School **Norfolk** ... D161
Beis Chinuch Lebonos Girls School **London** ... D176
Beis Malka Girls School **London** ... D176
Beis Rochel D'Satmar Girls School **London** ... D176
Beis Ruchel Girls School **Greater Manchester** ... D189
Beis Soroh Schneirer **London** ... D177
Beis Trana Girls' School **London** ... D176
Belhaven Hill School **East Lothian** ... D224
Belmont Grosvenor School **North Yorkshire** ... D218
Belmont House School **Glasgow** ... D225
Belmont School **Surrey** ... D200
Belmont, Mill Hill Preparatory School **London** ... D177
Benedict House Preparatory School **Kent** ... 74, D171
Berkhampstead School **Gloucestershire** ... 46, D153
Berkhamsted School **Hertfordshire** ... D160
Bertrum House Nursery **London** ... D180
Bethany School **South Yorkshire** ... D219
Bicker Preparatory School & Early Years **Lincolnshire** ... D167
Bickley Park School **Kent** ... D171
Bilton Grange Preparatory School **Warwickshire** ... D213
Birchfield School **Shropshire** ... 122, D212
Birkdale School **South Yorkshire** ... D219
Birkenhead School **Merseyside** ... D191
Bishop Challoner School **Kent** ... D171
Bishop's Stortford College Prep School **Hertfordshire** ... D160
Bishopsgate School **Surrey** ... D200
Blackheath High School GDST **London** ... D179
Blackheath Prep **London** ... 80, D179
Blundell's Preparatory School **Devon** ... D207
Bnois Jerusalem School **London** ... D176
Bnos Yisroel School **Greater Manchester** ... D189
Bobov Primary School **London** ... D176
Bolton School **Greater Manchester** ... D189
Bootham Junior School **North Yorkshire** ... 131, D218
Boundary Oak School **Hampshire** ... D196
Bournemouth Collegiate School (BCS Prep) **Dorset** ... D208
Bow, Durham School **Durham** ... D186
Bowbrook House School **Worcestershire** ... D214
Bowdon Preparatory School for Girls **Cheshire** ... D188
Brabyns Preparatory School **Cheshire** ... D188
Brackenfield School **North Yorkshire** ... D218
Bradford Christian School **West Yorkshire** ... D219
Bradford Grammar School **West Yorkshire** ... D219
Braeside School **Essex** ... D170
Brambletye **West Sussex** ... D202

Index

Branwood Preparatory School **Greater Manchester** D189
Breaside Preparatory School **Kent**..D171
Bredon School **Gloucestershire**..D153
Brentwood Preparatory School **Essex**..56, D159
Bridgewater School **Greater Manchester** 94, D189
Brighton & Hove Montessori School **East Sussex**...............................D195
Brighton College Nursery, Pre-Prep & Prep School **East Sussex**............D195
Brighton Girls GDST **East Sussex**..D195
Brighton Steiner School **East Sussex**..D195
Bristol Grammar School **Bristol**...D206
Bristol Steiner School **Bristol**..D206
Brockhurst & Marlston House Schools **West Berkshire**......................D154
Brockwood Park & Inwoods School **Hampshire**...............................D196
Bromley High School GDST **Kent**..D171
Bromsgrove Pre-preparatory & Nursery School **Worcestershire**............D215
Bromsgrove Preparatory School **Worcestershire**..............................D215
Brontë House School **West Yorkshire**....................................132, D219
Bronte School **Kent**..D198
Brooke House Day School **Leicestershire**.....................................D166
Brooke Priory School **Rutland**...D168
Brookes UK **Suffolk**..D162
Broomfield House School **Surrey**..D172
Broomwood Hall Lower School **London**.......................................D180
Broughton Manor Preparatory School **Buckinghamshire**...................D152
Bryony School **Kent**..D198
Buckingham Preparatory School **Middlesex**..................................D171
Burgess Hill Girls **West Sussex**..D202
Bury Catholic Preparatory School **Greater Manchester** D189
Bury Grammar Schools **Greater Manchester** D189
Bute House Preparatory School for Girls **London** D182
Buxlow Preparatory School **Middlesex**...D171

C

Caldicott **Buckinghamshire**..D152
Cambian New Elizabethan School **Worcestershire**..........................D215
Cambridge Steiner School **Cambridgeshire**...................................D158
Cameron Vale School **London**...D180
Campbell College Junior School **County Antrim** D222
Cardiff Montessori School **Glamorgan**...D228
Cardiff Muslim Primary School **Glamorgan**...................................D228
Cardiff Steiner School **Glamorgan**..D228
Cargilfield School **Edinburgh**..D224
Carleton House Preparatory School **Merseyside** D191
Carmel Christian School **Bristol**...D206
Carrdus School **Oxfordshire**..D153
Casterton, Sedbergh Preparatory School **Cumbria** D188
Castle Court School **Dorset**..D208
Castle House School **Shropshire**..D212
Castle School Pembrokeshire **Pembrokeshire**.................................D229
Caterham School **Surrey**..D200
Caversham Preparatory School **Berkshire**.....................................D194
Cedars School of Excellence **Renfrewshire**...................................D225
Chafyn Grove School **Wiltshire**..D155
Chandlings **Oxfordshire**...D153
Channing School **London** D176
Chapter House Preparatory School **North Yorkshire**........................D218
Chard School **Somerset**..D208
Charlotte House Preparatory School **Hertfordshire**..........................D160
Charterhouse Square School **London** D176
Charters Ancaster **East Sussex**..D195
Chartfield School **Kent** D198
Chase Grammar School **Staffordshire**..D212
Cheadle Hulme School **Greater Manchester** D189
Cheam School **West Berkshire**..D154
Cheltenham College Preparatory School **Gloucestershire**.................D153
Chepstow House School **London**...D182
Chesham Preparatory School **Buckinghamshire**.............................D152
Chetham's School of Music **Greater Manchester** D189
Chigwell School **Essex**..D170
Child First Aylesbury Pre-School **Buckinghamshire**.........................D152
Chinthurst School **Surrey** D200

Chiswick & Bedford Park Prep School **London**...............................D182
Christ Church Cathedral School **Oxfordshire**.................................D153
Christian Fellowship School **Merseyside** D191
Churcher's College **Hampshire**..D196
City of London Freemen's School **Surrey** D200
City of London School for Girls **London**.......................................D176
Claires Court Junior Boys **Berkshire** D194
Claires Court Nursery, Girls and Sixth Form **Berkshire**......................D194
Claremont Fan Court School **Surrey** D200
Claremont Preparatory & Nursery School **East Sussex**......................D195
Clarendon Cottage School **Greater Manchester** D189
Claysmore Preparatory School **Dorset**...D208
Cleve House School **Bristol** D206
Clevelands Preparatory School **Greater Manchester** D189
Clifton College Preparatory School **Bristol**....................................D206
Clifton Hall School **Edinburgh**..D224
Clifton High School **Bristol**..D206
Clifton Lodge School **London**...D182
Cokethorpe School **Oxfordshire**..D153
Colchester High School **Essex**..D159
Colfe's Junior School **London**...D179
Collingwood School **Surrey**..D172
Colston Bassett Preparatory School **Nottinghamshire**......................D168
Colston's School **Bristol**..D206
Conifers School **West Sussex** D202
Connaught House School **London** D182
Coopersale Hall School **Essex** D159
Copthill Independent Day School **Lincolnshire**..............................D167
Copthorne Prep School **West Sussex** D202
Coteswood House Pre-school & Day Nursery **Nottinghamshire**..........D168
Cothill House **Oxfordshire** D153
Cottesmore School **West Sussex** D202
Covenant Christian School **Greater Manchester** D189
Coworth Flexlands School **Surrey** 100, D200
Crackley Hall School **Warwickshire**..D213
Craigclowan Preparatory School **Perth & Kinross**.....................142, D225
Cranford House School **Oxfordshire** 47, D153
Cranleigh Preparatory School **Surrey** D200
Cranmore School **Surrey**...D200
Cransley School **Cheshire**..D188
Crosfields School **Berkshire** D194
Crown House Preparatory School **Buckinghamshire** 48, D152
Croydon High School GDST **Surrey** D172
Crystal Gardens **West Yorkshire**..D219
Culford Pre-Preparatory School **Suffolk** D162
Culford Preparatory School **Suffolk** D162
Cumnor House Kindergarten & PreSchool, South Croydon **Surrey**.....D172
Cumnor House School for Boys **Surrey** D172
Cumnor House School for Girls **Surrey** D172
Cumnor House Sussex **West Sussex**..D202
Cundall Manor School **North Yorkshire**......................................D218

D

Daiglen School **Essex**..D170
Dair House School **Buckinghamshire** D152
Dale House Independent School & Nursery **West Yorkshire**..............D219
Dallington School **London** D176
Dame Allan Junior School **Tyne & Wear**......................................D186
Dame Catherine Harpur's School **Derbyshire**.................................D166
Danes Hill School **Surrey** D200
Danesfield Manor School **Surrey** D200
Daneshill School **Hampshire**..D196
Darul Uloom Dawatul Imaan **West Yorkshire**................................D219
Darvell School **East Sussex**..D195
Date Valley School Trust **Surrey** D172
Davenies School **Buckinghamshire** D152
De La Salle College **Jersey**..D150
Dean Close Pre-Preparatory & Preparatory School **Gloucestershire**...D153
Dean Close St John's **Gloucestershire** D153
Deenway Montessori School & Unicity College **Berkshire** D194
Deepdene School **East Sussex**..D195

233

Index

Denstone College Preparatory School **Staffordshire** D212
Derby Grammar School **Derbyshire**..................D166
Derby High School **Derbyshire**..................D166
Devonshire House Preparatory School **London**..................81, D177
Ditcham Park School **Hampshire**..................D196
Dollar Academy **Clackmannanshire**..................D224
Dolphin School **London**..................D180
Dolphin School **Berkshire**..................D194
Donhead Preparatory School **London**..................D180
Dorset House School **West Sussex**..................D202
Dover College **Kent**..................D198
Downham Preparatory School & Montessori Nursery **Norfolk**..................D161
Downsend School **Surrey**..................D200
Downsend School (Ashtead Pre-Prep) **Surrey**..................D200
Downsend School (Epsom Pre-Prep) **Surrey**..................D200
Downsend School (Leatherhead Pre-Prep) **Surrey**..................D200
Dragon School **Oxfordshire**..................D154
Drayton House Pre-School and Nursery **Surrey**..................D200
Drumduan School **Moray**..................D225
Dudley House School **Lincolnshire**..................D167
Duke of Kent School **Surrey**..................D200
Dulwich College **London**..................D179
Dulwich College Kindergarten & Infants School **London**..................D179
Dulwich Prep Cranbrook **Kent**..................D198
Dulwich Prep London **London**..................D179
Dumpton School **Dorset**..................D208
Duncombe School **Hertfordshire**..................D160
Dunottar School **Surrey**..................D200
Durham High School for Girls **Durham**..................D186
Durlston Court **Hampshire**..................D196
Durston House **London**..................D182
Dwight School London **London**..................D176

E

Eagle House School **Berkshire**..................102, D194
Eastcourt Independent School **Essex**..................D170
Eaton House Belgravia **London**..................D180
Eaton House The Manor **London**..................D180
Eaton House The Manor Pre Prep and Nursery **London**..................D180
Eaton House The Manor Prep School **London**..................D180
Eaton Square School Belgravia **London**..................D180
Eaton Square School Kensington **London**..................D180
Ecole Francaise Jacques Prevert **London**..................D182
Edenhurst Preparatory School **Staffordshire**..................D212
Edgbaston High School for Girls **West Midlands**..................D213
Edge Grove School **Hertfordshire**..................D160
Edgeborough **Surrey**..................D200
Edinburgh Montessori Arts School **Edinburgh**..................D224
Edinburgh Steiner School **Edinburgh**..................D224
Educare Small School **Surrey**..................D172
Egerton Rothesay School **Hertfordshire**..................D160
Elizabeth College Junior School **Guernsey**..................D150
Ellesmere College **Shropshire**..................D212
Elliott Park School **Kent**..................D198
Elm Green Preparatory School **Essex**..................D159
Elmfield Rudolf Steiner School **West Midlands**..................D213
Elmhurst School **Surrey**..................D172
Elstree School **Berkshire**..................D194
Eltham College **London**..................D179
Eltham College Junior School **London**..................D179
Ely Presbyterian Church School **Glamorgan**..................D228
Emberhurst School **Surrey**..................D200
Embley **Hampshire**..................D196
Emmanuel Christian School **Oxfordshire**..................D154
Emmanuel School **Derbyshire**..................D166
Emmanuel School (Walsall) **West Midlands**..................D213
Emmaus School **Wiltshire**..................D155
ESMS Junior School **Edinburgh**..................D224
Essendene Lodge School **Surrey**..................D201
Eton End School **Berkshire**..................101, D194
Eveline Day & Nursery Schools **London**..................D180

Eversfield Preparatory School **West Midlands**..................D214
Ewell Castle School **Surrey**..................D201
Exeter Cathedral School **Devon**..................115, D207
Exeter School **Devon**..................D207

F

Fairfield Prep School **Leicestershire**..................D166
Fairfield School **Bristol**..................D206
Fairholme Preparatory School **Denbighshire**..................D228
Fairstead House School **Suffolk**..................57, D162
Fairview International School, Bridge of Allan **Stirling**..................D225
Falcons Prep Richmond **Surrey**..................D172
Falcons School for Girls **London**..................D180
Falkner House **London**..................D180
Faraday Prep School **London**..................D176
Farleigh School **Hampshire**..................D196
Farringtons Junior School **Kent**..................D171
Farrowdale House Preparatory School **Greater Manchester**..................D189
FCJ Primary School **Jersey**..................D150
Felsted Preparatory School **Essex**..................D159
Feltonfleet School **Surrey**..................D201
Fernhill School **Glasgow**..................D225
Fettes College Preparatory School **Edinburgh**..................D224
Fig Tree Primary School **Nottinghamshire**..................D168
Finborough School **Suffolk**..................D162
Finchley & Acton Yochien School **London**..................D176
Finton House School **London**..................D180
Fletewood School **Devon**..................D207
Forest Park Preparatory School **Greater Manchester**..................D189
Forest Preparatory School **Greater Manchester**..................D189
Forest School **London**..................D176
Forres Sandle Manor **Hampshire**..................D196
Fosse Bank School **Kent**..................D198
Framlingham College **Suffolk**..................D162
Framlingham College Prep School **Suffolk**..................D162
Francis Holland School, Sloane Square, SW1 **London**..................D180
Frensham Heights **Surrey**..................D201
Froebel House School **East Riding of Yorkshire**..................D218
Fulham Prep School **London**..................D182
Fulneck Junior School **West Yorkshire**..................D219
Fyling Hall School **North Yorkshire**..................D218

G

Gad's Hill School **Kent**..................D198
Garden House School **London**..................D180
Gatehouse School **London**..................D176
Gateshead Jewish Primary School **Tyne & Wear**..................D186
Gateway School **Buckinghamshire**..................D152
Gateways School **West Yorkshire**..................D219
Gayhurst School **Buckinghamshire**..................D195
George Heriot's School **Edinburgh**..................D224
George Watson's College **Edinburgh**..................D224
Ghyll Royd School and Pre-School **West Yorkshire**..................D219
Gidea Park Preparatory School & Nursery **Essex**..................D170
Giggleswick Junior School **North Yorkshire**..................D218
Glebe House School **Norfolk**..................D161
Glendower School **London**..................D180
Glenesk School **Surrey**..................D201
Glenhurst School **Hampshire**..................D196
Godolphin Preparatory School **Wiltshire**..................D155
Godstowe Preparatory School **Buckinghamshire**..................52, D152
Golders Hill School **London**..................D177
Goodwyn School **London**..................D177
Gordonstoun **Moray**..................D225
Gosfield School **Essex**..................D159
Gracefield Preparatory School **Bristol**..................D206
Grange Park Preparatory School **London**..................D176
Grangewood Independent School **London**..................D176
Grantham Farm Montessori School & The Children's House **Hampshire**..................D196
Grantham Preparatory International School **Lincolnshire**..................D167

Index

Great Ballard School **West Sussex** ... D203
Great Beginnings Montessori Nursery **London** ... D182
Great Walstead School **West Sussex** ... D203
Greater Grace Christian School **Cheshire** ... D188
Greek Primary School of London **London** ... D182
Green Meadow Independent Primary School **Cheshire** ... D188
Greenbank Preparatory School **Cheshire** ... D188
Greenfield School **Surrey** ... 104, D201
Greenfields Independent Day & Boarding School **East Sussex** ... D195
Greenfields Primary School **West Midlands** ... D214
Greenwich House School **Lincolnshire** ... D167
Greenwich Steiner School **London** ... D179
Gresham's Nursery and Pre-Prep School **Norfolk** ... D162
Gresham's Prep School **Norfolk** ... D162
Griffin House Preparatory School **Buckinghamshire** ... 50, D152
Grimsdell, Mill Hill Pre-Preparatory School **London** ... D177
Guildford High School **Surrey** ... D201
Guru Gobind Singh Khalsa College **Essex** ... D170
Gurukula - The Hare Krishna Primary School **Hertfordshire** ... D160

H

Haberdashers' Aske's School for Girls **Hertfordshire** ... D160
Haddon Dene School **Kent** ... D198
Hale Preparatory School **Cheshire** ... D188
Hall Grove School **Surrey** ... D201
Hall School Wimbledon Junior School **London** ... D180
Hallfield School **West Midlands** ... D214
Halstead Preparatory School **Surrey** ... D201
Hamd House Preparatory School **West Midlands** ... D214
Hamilton College **South Lanarkshire** ... D225
Hampstead Hill Pre-Prep & Nursery School **London** ... D177
Hampton Court House **Surrey** ... D201
Hampton Prep and Pre-Prep School **Middlesex** ... D171
Handcross Park School **West Sussex** ... D203
Handel House Preparatory School **Lincolnshire** ... D167
Hanford School **Dorset** ... D208
Harrodian **London** ... D180
Harvington School **London** ... D182
Hatherop Castle School **Gloucestershire** ... D153
Hawkesdown House School Kensington **London** ... 82, D182
Hazelwood School **Surrey** ... D201
Hazlegrove Prep School **Somerset** ... 116, D208
Headington Preparatory School **Oxfordshire** ... D154
Heath House Preparatory School **London** ... D179
Heath Mount School **Hertfordshire** ... D160
Heathcote School **Essex** ... 58, D159
Heatherton School **Buckinghamshire** ... D152
Heathfield House School **London** ... D182
Heathfield Junior School **West Yorkshire** ... D219
Heathfield Knoll School **Worcestershire** ... D215
Heathland School **Lancashire** ... D190
Heathside School Hampstead **London** ... D177
Helvetia House School **Jersey** ... D150
Hemdean House School **Berkshire** ... D194
Hendon Prep School **London** ... D178
Hereford Cathedral Junior School **Herefordshire** ... D212
Hereward House School **London** ... D178
Herington House School **Essex** ... D159
Herne Hill School **London** ... D179
Herries Preparatory School **Berkshire** ... D194
Hessle Mount School **East Riding of Yorkshire** ... D218
Heywood Prep **Wiltshire** ... D155
High Elms Manor School **Hertfordshire** ... D160
High March **Buckinghamshire** ... 53, D152
High School of Dundee **Dundee** ... D224
Highclare School **West Midlands** ... D214
Highfield and Brookham Schools **Hampshire** ... 105, D196
Highfield Prep School **North Yorkshire** ... D218
Highfield Preparatory School **Berkshire** ... 106, D194
Highfield Priory School **Lancashire** ... D190
Highfields School **Nottinghamshire** ... D168

Highgate **London** ... D176
Highgate Junior School **London** ... D177
Highgate Pre-Preparatory School **London** ... D177
Hilden Grange School **Kent** ... D198
Hilden Oaks Preparatory School & Nursery **Kent** ... D198
Hill House **London** ... D180
Hill House School **South Yorkshire** ... D219
Hipperholme Grammar School **West Yorkshire** ... D219
Hoe Bridge School **Surrey** ... D201
Holland House School **Middlesex** ... D171
Holland Park Pre Prep School and Day Nursery **London** ... D182
Hollygirt School **Nottinghamshire** ... D168
Holme Grange School **Berkshire** ... D194
Holmewood House School **Kent** ... D198
Holmwood House Preparatory School **Essex** ... D159
Holy Cross Preparatory School **Surrey** ... 73, D172
Holywood Steiner School **County Down** ... D222
Homefield Preparatory School **Surrey** ... D172
Hopelands Preparatory School **Gloucestershire** ... D153
Hornsby House School **London** ... D180
Horris Hill **West Berkshire** ... D154
Howe Green House School **Hertfordshire** ... 59, D160
Howell's School, Llandaff GDST **Glamorgan** ... D228
Huddersfield Grammar School **West Yorkshire** ... D220
Hull Collegiate School **East Riding of Yorkshire** ... D218
Hulme Hall Grammar School **Greater Manchester** ... D189
Hunter Hall School **Cumbria** ... D188
Hurlingham Nursery School **London** ... D180
Hurlingham School **London** ... D180
Hurstpierpoint College Prep School **West Sussex** ... D203
Hutchesons' Grammar School **Glasgow** ... D225
Hydesville Tower School **West Midlands** ... D214
Hyland House School **London** ... D176
Hymers College **East Riding of Yorkshire** ... D218

I

Ibstock Place School **London** ... D180
ICS London **London** ... D178
Immanuel School **Essex** ... D170
Inchmarlo **County Antrim** ... D222
Instituto Español Vicente Cañada Blanch **London** ... D182
International School of Aberdeen **Aberdeen** ... D224
International School of London (ISL) **London** ... D182
Iona School **Nottinghamshire** ... D168
Ipswich High School **Suffolk** ... D162
Ipswich Prep School **Suffolk** ... 60, D162
IRIS School **London** ... D178
Islamic Tarbiyah Preparatory School **West Yorkshire** ... D220

J

Jack and Jill School **Middlesex** ... D171
Jameah Girls Academy **Leicestershire** ... D166
James Allen's Girls' School **London** ... D179
Jamia Al-Hudaa Residential College **Nottinghamshire** ... D168
JeMs Nursery **East Sussex** ... D195

K

Keble Prep **London** ... D177
Kelvinside Academy **Glasgow** ... D225
Kensington Prep School **London** ... D180
Kent College Junior School **Kent** ... 108, D198
Kent College Pembury **Kent** ... D198
Kerem School **London** ... D177
Kew College **Surrey** ... D173
Kew Green Preparatory School **Surrey** ... D173
Kilgraston School **Perth & Kinross** ... D225
Kimbolton School **Cambridgeshire** ... D158
King Edward's Junior School **Bath & North-East Somerset** ... D206

Index

King Edward's Pre-Prep & Nursery School **Bath & North-East Somerset**..D206
King Fahad Academy **London**..D182
King Henry VIII Preparatory School **West Midlands**..D214
King of Kings School **Greater Manchester**..D189
King's College School **Cambridgeshire**..D158
King's Ely Acremont & Nursery **Cambridgeshire**..D158
King's Ely Junior **Cambridgeshire**..61, D158
King's Hall School **Somerset**..117, D208
King's Hawford **Worcestershire**..D215
King's House School **Bedfordshire**..D158
King's House School **Surrey**..D173
King's Pre-Preparatory School, Rochester **Kent**..D198
King's Preparatory School, Rochester **Kent**..D198
King's School **Devon**..D207
King's St Alban's **Worcestershire**..D215
Kings Kids Christian School **London**..D179
Kings Monkton School **Glamorgan**..D228
Kingscourt School **Hampshire**..D196
Kingshott **Hertfordshire**..62, D160
Kingsley School **Devon**..D207
Kingswood House School **Surrey**..D201
Kingswood School **West Midlands**..D214
Kingswood School **Bath & North-East Somerset**..D206
Kirkham Grammar School **Lancashire**..D190
Kirkstone House School **Lincolnshire**..D167
Kitebrook Preparatory School **Gloucestershire**..D153
Knighton House School and The Orchard Pre-prep **Dorset**..D208
Knightsbridge School **London**..D180

L

L'Ecole Bilingue **London**..D182
L'Ecole de Battersea **London**..D180
L'Ecole des Petits **London**..D180
La Petite Ecole Francaise **London**..D182
Lady Barn House School **Cheshire**..D188
Lady Eleanor Holles (Junior Department) **Middlesex**..D171
Lady Lane Park School **West Yorkshire**..D220
Laleham Lea School **Surrey**..D173
Lambrook School **Berkshire**..D194
Lambs Christian School **West Midlands**..D214
Lancaster Steiner School **Lancashire**..D190
Lancing Prep Hove **East Sussex**..D195
Lancing Prep Worthing **West Sussex**..D203
Langley Preparatory School at Taverham Hall **Norfolk**..D162
Lathallan School **Angus**..D224
Latymer Prep School **London**..D182
Laxton Junior School **Northamptonshire**..D167
Le Herisson **London**..D182
Leeds Menorah School **West Yorkshire**..D220
Leehurst Swan School **Wiltshire**..D155
Leicester Grammar Junior School **Leicestershire**..D166
Leicester High School for Girls **Leicestershire**..D166
Leicester Islamic Academy **Leicestershire**..D166
Leicester Prep School **Leicestershire**..D166
Lewes Old Grammar School **East Sussex**..D195
Leweston Prep School **Dorset**..D208
Lichfield Cathedral School **Staffordshire**..D213
Lime House School **Cumbria**..D188
Lincoln Minster School **Lincolnshire**..D167
Lingfield College **Surrey**..D201
Little Acorns Montessori School **Hertfordshire**..D160
Littlegarth School **Essex**..D159
Llandovery College **Carmarthenshire**..D228
Llangattock School Monmouth **Monmouthshire**..D229
Lloyd Williamson School Foundation **London**..D182
Lochinver House School **Hertfordshire**..D160
Lockers Park **Hertfordshire**..D160
Lomond School **Argyll & Bute**..D224
London Christian School **London**..D179
London Steiner School **London**..D180
London Welsh School Ysgol Gymraeg Llundain **London**..D182

Long Close School **Berkshire**..D194
Longacre School **Surrey**..D201
Longridge Towers School **Northumberland**..D186
Longwood School **Hertfordshire**..D160
Lorenden Preparatory School **Kent**..D199
Loreto Preparatory School **Greater Manchester**..D189
Loretto Junior School **East Lothian**..D224
Lote Tree Primary **West Midlands**..D214
Loughborough Amherst School **Leicestershire**..D166
Loyola Preparatory School **Essex**..D170
Lubavitch House School (Junior Boys) **London**..D176
Lucton School **Herefordshire**..D212
Ludgrove **Berkshire**..D194
LVS Ascot **Berkshire**..D194
Lycée Français Charles de Gaulle de Londres **London**..D181
Lyndhurst House Prep School **London**..83, D178
Lyndhurst School **Surrey**..D201
Lyonsdown School **Hertfordshire**..D170

M

Madni Academy **West Yorkshire**..D220
Madresfield Early Years Centre **Worcestershire**..D215
Magdalen College School **Oxfordshire**..D154
Magdalen Court School **Devon**..D207
Magdalene House Preparatory School **Cambridgeshire**..D158
Maidwell Hall **Northamptonshire**..D167
Maldon Court Preparatory School **Essex**..D159
Maltman's Green School **Buckinghamshire**..D195
Manchester High School for Girls **Greater Manchester**..D189
Manchester Junior Girls School **Greater Manchester**..D189
Manchester Muslim Preparatory School **Greater Manchester**..D189
Mannafields Christian School **Edinburgh**..D224
Manor House School, Bookham **Surrey**..D201
Manor Lodge School **Hertfordshire**..D160
Maple Walk Prep School **London**..D178
Maranatha Christian School **Wiltshire**..D155
Maria Montessori School - Hampstead **London**..D178
Marlborough House School **Kent**..D199
Mayfield Preparatory School **West Midlands**..D214
Maytime Montessori Nursery - Cranbrook Road **Essex**..D170
Maytime Montessori Nursery - Eastwood Road **Essex**..D170
Maytime Montessori Nursery - Wanstead Road **Essex**..D170
Mayville High School **Hampshire**..D196
Meadowbrook Montessori School **Berkshire**..D194
Meadowpark School & Nursery **Wiltshire**..D155
Meoncross School **Hampshire**..D196
Merchant Taylors' Prep **Hertfordshire**..D160
Merchiston Castle School **Edinburgh**..138, D224
Merton Court Preparatory School **Kent**..78, D171
Methodist College **County Antrim**..D222
Michael Hall School **East Sussex**..D195
Micklefield School **Surrey**..D201
Milbourne Lodge School **Surrey**..109, D201
Mill Cottage Montessori School **West Yorkshire**..D220
Millfield Preparatory School **Somerset**..118, D208
Milton Keynes Preparatory School **Buckinghamshire**..D152
Monkton Prep School **Bath & North-East Somerset**..119, D206
Monmouth Prep School **Monmouthshire**..D229
Monmouth School for Boys **Monmouthshire**..D229
Monmouth School for Girls **Monmouthshire**..D229
Monton Village Nursery & Forest School **Greater Manchester**..D190
Moor Allerton Preparatory School **Greater Manchester**..D190
Moor Park **Shropshire**..123, D212
Moorfield School **West Yorkshire**..D220
Moorland School **Lancashire**..D190
Moorlands School **West Yorkshire**..D220
Moreton Hall **Shropshire**..124, D212
Morrison's Academy **Perth & Kinross**..D225
Moulsford Preparatory School **Oxfordshire**..54, D154
Mowden Hall School **Northumberland**..D186
Moyles Court School **Hampshire**..D197

236

Index

Myddelton College **Denbighshire** D228
Mylnhurst Preparatory School & Nursery **South Yorkshire** D219

N

Naima Jewish Preparatory School **London** D178
Nancy Reuben Primary School **London** D178
Nant-y-Cwm Steiner School **Pembrokeshire** D229
Netherleigh & Rossefield School **West Yorkshire** D220
New College School **Oxfordshire** D154
New Hall School **Essex** D159
Newbold School **Berkshire** D194
Newbridge Preparatory School **West Midlands** D214
Newcastle High School for Girls GDST **Tyne & Wear** D186
Newcastle Preparatory School **Tyne & Wear** D186
Newcastle School for Boys **Tyne & Wear** D186
Newcastle under Lyme School **Staffordshire** D213
Newland House School **Middlesex** D171
Newton Prep **London** D181
Norfolk House School **London** D177
Norfolk House School **West Midlands** D214
Norland Place School **London** D183
Norman Court **Hampshire** D197
Normanhurst School **London** D176
Normanton House School **Derbyshire** D166
North Bridge House Nursery and Pre-Prep Hampstead **London** D178
North Bridge House Nursery and Pre-Prep West Hampstead **London** D178
North Bridge House Prep School Regent's Park **London** 84, D178
North London Collegiate School **Middlesex** D171
North London Rudolf Steiner School **London** D177
Northampton High School GDST **Northamptonshire** D167
Northbourne Park School **Kent** D199
Northcote Lodge **London** D181
Northwood College for Girls GDST **Middlesex** D171
Norwich High School for Girls GDST **Norfolk** D162
Norwich School **Norfolk** D162
Norwich Steiner School **Norfolk** D162
Notre Dame Preparatory School **Norfolk** 63, D162
Notre Dame School **Surrey** D201
Notting Hill & Ealing High School GDST **London** D183
Notting Hill Preparatory School **London** D183
Nottingham Girls' High School GDST **Nottinghamshire** D168
Nottingham High Infant and Junior School **Nottinghamshire** D168

O

Oakfield Preparatory School **London** D179
Oakfields Preparatory School **Essex** D170
Oakhill School & Nursery **Lancashire** D190
Oakhyrst Grange School **Surrey** D201
Oaklands School **Essex** D170
Oakleigh House School **Glamorgan** D228
Oaks International School **Cambridgeshire** D158
Oakwood Independent School **Surrey** D173
Oakwood Preparatory School **West Sussex** D203
Ockbrook School **Derbyshire** D166
Octavia House School, Vauxhall **London** D179
Octavia House School, Walworth **London** D179
Old Buckenham Hall School **Suffolk** 64, D163
Old Palace of John Whitgift School **Surrey** D173
Old Vicarage School **Surrey** D173
Old Vicarage School **Derbyshire** D166
Oldham Hulme Grammar School **Greater Manchester** D190
Oliver House Preparatory School **London** D181
OneSchool Global UK Atherstone Campus **Warwickshire** D213
OneSchool Global UK Biggleswade Campus **Bedfordshire** D158
OneSchool Global UK Bristol Campus **Gloucestershire** D153
OneSchool Global UK Caledonia (North) Campus **Aberdeenshire** D224
OneSchool Global UK Caledonia (South) Campus **Clackmannanshire** D224
OneSchool Global UK Colchester Campus **Essex** D159
OneSchool Global UK Dunstable Campus **Bedfordshire** D158
OneSchool Global UK Gloucester Campus **Gloucestershire** D153
OneSchool Global UK Hindhead Campus **Surrey** D201
OneSchool Global UK Kenley Campus **Surrey** D201
OneSchool Global UK Knockloughrim Campus **County Londonderry** ... D222
OneSchool Global UK Lancaster Campus **Lancashire** D190
OneSchool Global UK Maidstone Campus **Kent** D199
OneSchool Global UK Newry Campus **County Down** D222
OneSchool Global UK Newtown Campus **Powys** D229
OneSchool Global UK Northampton Campus **Northamptonshire** D167
OneSchool Global UK Northwich Campus **Cheshire** D188
OneSchool Global UK Nottingham Campus **Nottinghamshire** D168
OneSchool Global UK Plymouth Campus **Devon** D207
OneSchool Global UK Reading Campus (Primary) **Berkshire** D194
OneSchool Global UK Ridgeway Campus **North-East Lincolnshire** D219
OneSchool Global UK Salisbury Campus **Wiltshire** D155
OneSchool Global UK Swaffham Campus **Norfolk** D162
OneSchool Global UK Swansea Campus **Glamorgan** D228
OneSchool Global UK York (Springwell) Campus **Tyne & Wear** D186
OneSchool Global UK York Campus **West Yorkshire** D220
Orchard House School **London** D183
Orchard School & Nursery **Bedfordshire** D158
Orley Farm School **Middlesex** D171
Orwell Park School **Suffolk** D163
Oswestry School **Shropshire** D212
Our Lady of Sion School **West Sussex** D203
Our Lady's Abingdon School **Oxfordshire** D154
Our Lady's Preparatory School **Berkshire** D194
Overstone Park School **Northamptonshire** D167
Oxford High School GDST **Oxfordshire** D154
Oxford House School **Essex** D159
Oxford Montessori School **Oxfordshire** D154
OYY Lubavitch Girls School **Greater Manchester** D190

P

Packwood Haugh School **Shropshire** D212
Palmers Green High School **London** D177
Papplewick School **Berkshire** D194
Paradise Primary School **West Yorkshire** D220
Pardes House Primary School **London** D177
Park Hill School **Surrey** D173
Park School **Dorset** D208
Park School **Devon** D207
Park School for Girls **Essex** D170
Parkgate House School **London** D181
Parkside School **Surrey** D201
Parsons Green Prep School **London** D181
Pattison School **West Midlands** 126, D214
Pembridge Hall School **London** D183
Pennthorpe School **West Sussex** D203
Perrott Hill **Somerset** D208
Pilgrims Pre-Preparatory School **Bedfordshire** D158
Pillar Box Montessori Nursery & Pre-Prep School **London** D176
Pinewood School **Wiltshire** D155
Pipers Corner School **Buckinghamshire** D152
Pitsford School **Northamptonshire** D167
Plumtree School **Nottinghamshire** D168
Plymouth College Preparatory School **Devon** D207
Polam School **Bedfordshire** D158
Polwhele House School **Cornwall** D206
Port Regis **Dorset** D208
Portsmouth High School GDST **Hampshire** D197
Pownall Hall School **Cheshire** D188
Prenton Preparatory School **Merseyside** D191
Prestfelde Preparatory School **Shropshire** D212
Prestwich Preparatory School **Greater Manchester** D190
Prince's Gardens Preparatory School **London** D181
Prince's Mead School **Hampshire** D197
Prior Park Preparatory School **Wiltshire** D155
Priory School **West Midlands** 125, D214
Priory School of Our Lady of Walsingham **Isle of Wight** 110, D198
Prospect House School **London** D181
Putney High School GDST **London** D181

Index

Q

Quainton Hall School & Nursery **Middlesex** D171
Queen Elizabeth Grammar School (Junior School) **West Yorkshire** D220
Queen Elizabeth's Hospital **Bristol**..................D206
Queen Ethelburga's Collegiate **North Yorkshire** D218
Queen Mary's School **North Yorkshire** D218
Queen's College **Somerset** D209
Queen's College Preparatory School **London** D183
Queen's Gate School **London** D181
Queenswood School **West Yorkshire** D220
Quinton House School **Northamptonshire** D167
Quwwat-ul Islam Girls School **London** D176

R

Radlett Preparatory School **Hertfordshire** D161
Radnor House **Middlesex** D172
Radnor House, Sevenoaks **Kent** D199
Rainbow Montessori School **London** D178
Ratcliffe College **Leicestershire** D166
Ravenscourt Park Preparatory School **London** D183
Red House School **Stockton-on-Tees** D186
Redcliffe School Trust Ltd **London** D181
Reddam House Berkshire **Berkshire** D194
Reddiford School **Middlesex** D172
Redhill Preparatory School **Pembrokeshire** D229
Redmaids' High Junior School **Bristol** D206
Regius School **Edinburgh** D224
Reigate St Mary's Prep & Choir School **Surrey** D201
Rendcomb College **Gloucestershire** D153
Repton Prep **Derbyshire** D166
RGS Dodderhill **Worcestershire** D215
RGS Prep **Surrey** D201
RGS Springfield **Worcestershire** D215
RGS The Grange **Worcestershire** D215
Richmond House School **West Yorkshire** D220
Riddlesworth Hall Preparatory School **Norfolk** D162
Ringwood Waldorf School **Hampshire** D197
Ripley Court School **Surrey** D201
River House Montessori School **London** D176
River School **Worcestershire** D215
Riverston School **London** D179
Robert Gordon's College **Aberdeen** D224
Rockport School **County Down** D222
Roedean Moira House **East Sussex** D195
Rokeby School **Surrey** D173
Rookwood School **Hampshire** D197
Rose Hill School **Kent** D199
Rosemary Works Independent School **London** D177
Rosemead Preparatory School & Nursery, Dulwich **London** D179
Rossall School **Lancashire** D190
Rosslyn School **West Midlands** D214
Rougemont School **Monmouthshire** D229
Rowan Preparatory School **Surrey** D201
Roxeth Mead School **Middlesex** D172
Royal Grammar School **Tyne & Wear** D186
Royal High School Bath, GDST **Bath & North-East Somerset** D206
Royal Russell Junior School **Surrey** D173
Ruckleigh School **West Midlands** D214
Rupert House School **Oxfordshire** D154
Russell House School **Kent** D199
Rydal Penrhos Preparatory School **Clwyd** D228
Ryde School with Upper Chine **Isle of Wight** D198
Rydes Hill Preparatory School **Surrey** D201
Rye St Antony **Oxfordshire** D154

S

S. Anselm's School **Derbyshire** D166
Sacred Heart School **East Sussex** D195
Saint Christina's School **London** D178
Saint Felix School **Suffolk** D163
Saint Nicholas School **Essex** D159
Saint Pierre School **Essex** D159
Saint Ronan's School **Kent** D199
Salcombe Preparatory School **London** D177
Salisbury Cathedral School **Wiltshire** D155
Salterford House School **Nottinghamshire** D168
Sancton Wood School **Cambridgeshire** D158
Sandroyd School **Wiltshire** D155
Sarum Hall School **London** D178
Saville House School **Nottinghamshire** D168
Scarborough College **North Yorkshire** 134, D218
Scarisbrick Hall School **Lancashire** D190
Seaford College **West Sussex** D203
Seaton House School **Surrey** D173
Sevenoaks Preparatory School **Kent** D199
Shebbear College **Devon** D207
Sheffield High School GDST **South Yorkshire** D219
Sherborne House School **Hampshire** D197
Sherborne Preparatory School **Dorset** D208
Sherfield School **Hampshire** D197
Shernold School **Kent** D199
Sherrardswood School **Hertfordshire** D161
Shoreham College **West Sussex** D203
Shrewsbury High School GDST **Shropshire** D212
Shrewsbury House Pre-Preparatory School **Surrey** D201
Shrewsbury House School **Surrey** D173
Sibford School **Oxfordshire** D154
Sidcot School **Somerset** D209
Silcoates School **West Yorkshire** D220
Sinclair House Montessori Nursery **London** D181
Sinclair House Preparatory School **London** D181
Skippers Hill Manor Preparatory School **East Sussex** D196
Snaresbrook Preparatory School **London** D176
Solefield School **Kent** D199
Solihull Preparatory School **West Midlands** D214
Solihull School **West Midlands** D214
Somerhill **Kent** D199
Sompting Abbotts Preparatory School **West Sussex** D203
South Devon Steiner School **Devon** D207
South Hampstead High School GDST **London** D178
South Lee Preparatory School **Suffolk** D163
Southbank International School - Hampstead **London** D178
Southbank International School - Kensington **London** D183
Spratton Hall **Northamptonshire** 72, D167
Spring Grove School **Kent** 111, D199
Springmead Preparatory School & Nursery **Somerset** D209
St Albans High School for Girls **Hertfordshire** D161
St Aloysius' College **Glasgow** D225
St Ambrose Preparatory School **Greater Manchester** D190
St Andrew's Prep **East Sussex** 112, D196
St Andrew's School **Berkshire** D194
St Andrew's School **Kent** D199
St. Andrew's School **Surrey** D202
St Anne's College Grammar School **Lancashire** D191
St. Anne's Preparatory School **Essex** D159
St. Anthony's School for Boys **London** 90, D178
St. Anthony's School for Girls **London** 88, D178
St Aubyn's School **Essex** D170
St Augustine's Priory **London** D183
St Bede's College **Greater Manchester** D190
St Bede's Preparatory School **East Sussex** D196
St Benedict's Junior School and Nursery **London** D183
St Benedict's School **London** 86, D183
St Bernard's Preparatory School **Berkshire** D194
St Catherine's Prep **Middlesex** 76, D172
St Catherine's, Bramley **Surrey** D201
St Catherine's School **Middlesex** D172
St Cedd's School **Essex** 65, D159
St Christopher School **Hertfordshire** D161
St Christopher's Preparatory School **Devon** D207
St Christopher's School **East Sussex** D196

238

Index

St Christopher's School **Middlesex**	D172
St Christopher's School **Surrey**	D202
St Christopher's School **London**	D178
St Christopher's The Hall School **Kent**	D171
St Clare's School **Glamorgan**	D228
St Columba's School **Renfrewshire**	D225
St Crispin's School **Leicestershire**	D166
St. David's Prep **Kent**	D171
St David's School **Surrey**	D173
St. Dominic's Grammar School **Staffordshire**	D213
St. Dominic's Priory School Stone **Staffordshire**	D213
St Dunstan's College **London**	D179
St Edmund's College & Prep School **Hertfordshire**	D161
St Edmund's Junior School **Kent**	D199
St Edmund's Prep **Hertfordshire**	D161
St Edmund's School **Surrey**	D202
St Edward's Prep **Berkshire**	D194
St Edward's Preparatory School **Gloucestershire**	D153
St Faith's **Cambridgeshire**	D158
St Faith's at Ash School **Kent**	D199
St Francis School **Wiltshire**	D155
St Francis' College **Hertfordshire**	D161
St Gabriel's **West Berkshire**	D154
St George's Junior School **Surrey**	D202
St George's Preparatory School **Jersey**	D150
St George's Preparatory School & Little Dragons Nursery **Lincolnshire**	D167
St George's School **Bedfordshire**	D158
St George's School for Girls **Edinburgh**	D224
St George's School Windsor Castle **Berkshire**	D194
St George's School, Edgbaston **West Midlands**	D214
St Gerard's School **Gwynedd**	144, D228
St Helen and St Katharine **Oxfordshire**	D154
St Helen's College **Middlesex**	D172
St Helen's School **Middlesex**	D172
St Hilary's School **Surrey**	D202
St Hilda's **Hertfordshire**	D161
St Hilda's School **Hertfordshire**	D161
St Hugh's School **Lincolnshire**	D167
St Hugh's School **Oxfordshire**	D154
St Ives School **Surrey**	D202
St James Preparatory School **London**	D183
St James' School **North-East Lincolnshire**	D219
St John's Beaumont Preparatory School **Berkshire**	D194
St John's College **Hampshire**	D197
St John's College School **Cambridgeshire**	66, D158
St John's College, Cardiff **Glamorgan**	D228
St. John's Prep. School **Hertfordshire**	D161
St John's Priory School **Oxfordshire**	D154
St. John's School **Devon**	D207
St John's School **Middlesex**	D172
St John's School **Essex**	D159
St John's Wood Pre-Preparatory School **London**	D178
St Joseph's College **Suffolk**	D163
St Joseph's College **Berkshire**	D194
St Joseph's In The Park **Hertfordshire**	D161
St Joseph's Preparatory School **Staffordshire**	D213
St Joseph's School **Nottinghamshire**	D168
St Joseph's School **Cornwall**	D206
St Joseph's School, Park Hill **Lancashire**	D191
St Lawrence College **Kent**	D199
St Leonards School **Fife**	140, D225
St Margaret's Preparatory School **Wiltshire**	D155
St Margaret's Preparatory School **Essex**	D159
St Margaret's School **London**	D178
St Margaret's School for Girls **Aberdeen**	D224
St Margaret's School, Bushey **Hertfordshire**	D161
St Martin's Preparatory School **North-East Lincolnshire**	D219
St Martin's School **Middlesex**	D172
St Martin's School **London**	D178
St Martin's School **Dorset**	D208
St Mary's College **Merseyside**	D191
St Mary's Hare Park School & Nursery **Essex**	D170
St Mary's Music School **Edinburgh**	D224
St Mary's Preparatory School **Oxfordshire**	D154
St. Mary's School **Borders**	D224
St Mary's School **Cambridgeshire**	D158
St Mary's School **Buckinghamshire**	D195
St Mary's School **Essex**	D159
St Mary's School Hampstead **London**	D178
St Michael's Church Of England Preparatory School **Essex**	D159
St Michael's Preparatory School **Kent**	D199
St Michael's Preparatory School **Jersey**	D150
St. Michael's School **Carmarthenshire**	D228
St Michael's School **West Berkshire**	D154
St Neot's School **Hampshire**	D197
St Nicholas School **London**	D178
St Nicholas' School **Hampshire**	D197
St Olave's Preparatory School **London**	D179
St Olave's School **North Yorkshire**	D218
St Paul's Cathedral School **London**	85, D176
St Paul's Juniors **London**	D181
St Paul's Steiner School **London**	D177
St Peter & St Paul School **Derbyshire**	D166
St Peter's School **Devon**	D207
St Peter's School **Northamptonshire**	D167
St Peter's School 2-8 **North Yorkshire**	D218
St Petroc's School **Cornwall**	D206
St Philip's School **London**	D181
St Philomena's Catholic School **Essex**	D159
St Piran's School **Berkshire**	D194
St. Piran's School **Cornwall**	D206
St Pius X Preparatory School **Lancashire**	D191
St Swithun's Prep **Hampshire**	114, D197
St Teresa's Effingham (Preparatory School) **Surrey**	D202
St Wilfrid's School **Devon**	D207
St Winefride's Convent School **Shropshire**	D212
St Wystan's School **Derbyshire**	D166
Staines Preparatory School **Surrey**	D173
Stamford Junior School **Lincolnshire**	D167
Stanborough School **Hertfordshire**	D161
Steephill School **Kent**	D199
Stella Maris Junior School **Greater Manchester**	D190
Stephen Perse Junior School, Dame Bradbury's School **Essex**	D159
Stephen Perse Junior School, Fitzwilliam Building **Cambridgeshire**	D158
Stephen Perse Nurseries & Early Years **Cambridgeshire**	D158
Stockport Grammar School **Greater Manchester**	D190
Stockton House School **Hampshire**	D197
Stoke College **Suffolk**	D163
Stonar School **Wiltshire**	D155
Stoneygate School **Leicestershire**	D166
Stonyhurst St Mary's Hall **Lancashire**	D191
Stormont **Hertfordshire**	D161
Stover School **Devon**	D207
Stratford Preparatory School **Warwickshire**	D213
Streatham & Clapham High School GDST **London**	D181
Stroud School, King Edward VI Preparatory School **Hampshire**	D197
Summer Fields **Oxfordshire**	D154
Summerhill School **Suffolk**	D163
Sunningdale School **Berkshire**	D195
Sunninghill Preparatory School **Dorset**	D208
Sunny Hill Prep School **Somerset**	D209
Sunrise Nursery, Stoke Newington **London**	D177
Sunrise Primary School **London**	D177
Surbiton High School **Surrey**	D173
Surbiton Preparatory School **Surrey**	D202
Sussex House School **London**	D181
Sutton High School GDST **Surrey**	D173
Sutton Valence Preparatory School **Kent**	D199
Swanbourne House School **Buckinghamshire**	D152
Swedish School **London**	D181
Sycamore Hall Preparatory School **South Yorkshire**	D219
Sydenham High School GDST **London**	D179

Index

T

Tabernacle School **London**	D183
Talbot Heath **Dorset**	D208
Talbot House Preparatory School **Dorset**	D208
Talmud Torah Chaim Meirim School **London**	D177
Talmud Torah Machzikei Hadass School **London**	D176
Talmud Torah Yetev Lev School **London**	D177
Tashbar of Manchester **Greater Manchester**	D190
TASIS The American School in England **Surrey**	D202
Taunton Preparatory School **Somerset**	D209
Taunton School **Somerset**	120, D209
Tayyibah Girls School **London**	D177
Teesside High School **Stockton-on-Tees**	D186
Terra Nova School **Cheshire**	D188
Terrington Hall **North Yorkshire**	D218
Tettenhall College **West Midlands**	D214
The Abbey School **Berkshire**	D195
The Academy School **London**	D178
The Acorn School **Gloucestershire**	D153
The American School in London **London**	D178
The Beacon School **Buckinghamshire**	D152
The Belvedere Preparatory School **Merseyside**	D191
The Blue Coat School **West Midlands**	D214
The Branch Christian School **West Yorkshire**	D220
The Buchan School **Isle of Man**	D190
The Cathedral School, Llandaff **Glamorgan**	D228
The Cavendish School **London**	D178
The Chadderton Preparatory Grammar School **Greater Manchester**	D190
The Children's House **North-East Lincolnshire**	D219
The Children's House Upper School **London**	D177
The Chorister School **Durham**	D186
The Christian School (Takeley) **Essex**	D159
The Compass School **East Lothian**	D224
The Crescent School **Warwickshire**	D213
The Croft Preparatory School **Warwickshire**	D213
The Dixie Grammar School **Leicestershire**	D166
The Downs Malvern **Worcestershire**	D215
The Downs Preparatory School **Bristol**	D206
The Drive Prep School **East Sussex**	D196
The Edinburgh Academy **Edinburgh**	D224
The Elms **Worcestershire**	D215
The Falcons Pre-Preparatory School for Boys **London**	D183
The Firs School **Cheshire**	D188
The Froebelian School **West Yorkshire**	133, D220
The Glasgow Academy, Kelvinbridge **Glasgow**	D225
The Glasgow Academy, Milngavie **Glasgow**	D225
The Glasgow Academy, Newlands **Glasgow**	D225
The Gleddings School **West Yorkshire**	D220
The Gower School Montessori Nursery **London**	D177
The Gower School Montessori Primary **London**	D177
The Grammar School at Leeds **West Yorkshire**	D220
The Grange School **Cheshire**	D188
The Granville School **Kent**	D199
The Gregg Prep School **Hampshire**	D197
The Grove Independent School **Buckinghamshire**	D152
The Haberdashers' Aske's Boys' School **Hertfordshire**	D161
The Hall Pre-Preparatory School & Nursery **Middlesex**	D172
The Hall School **London**	D179
The Hammond School **Cheshire**	D188
The Hampshire School, Chelsea **London**	D181
The Hawthorns School **Surrey**	D202
The High School of Glasgow **Glasgow**	D225
The Japanese School **London**	D183
The Junior King's School, Canterbury **Kent**	D199
The King Alfred School **London**	D179
The King's School **Gloucestershire**	D153
The King's School **Hampshire**	D197
The King's School **Hertfordshire**	D161
The King's School Chester **Cheshire**	D188
The King's School in Macclesfield **Cheshire**	D188
The King's School, Witney **Oxfordshire**	D154
The Kingsley School **Warwickshire**	D213
The Ladies' College **Guernsey**	D150
The Lyceum School **London**	D176
The Mall School **Middlesex**	D172
The Manchester Grammar School **Greater Manchester**	D190
The Manor Preparatory School **Oxfordshire**	D154
The Marist Preparatory School **Berkshire**	D195
The Maynard School **Devon**	D207
The Mead School **Kent**	D199
The Merlin School **London**	D181
The Montessori Pavilion - The Kindergarten School **London**	D181
The Mount Junior School **North Yorkshire**	D218
The Mount School **West Yorkshire**	D220
The Mulberry House School **London**	D179
The New Beacon School **Kent**	D199
The New Forest Small School **Hampshire**	D197
The New School **Devon**	D207
The Norwegian School **London**	D181
The Old Hall School **Shropshire**	128, D212
The Old School Henstead **Suffolk**	D163
The Oratory Preparatory School **Berkshire**	D195
The Orchard School **Nottinghamshire**	D168
The Paragon School **Bath & North-East Somerset**	D206
The Perse Pelican Pre-Prep & Nursery **Cambridgeshire**	D158
The Perse Prep School **Cambridgeshire**	D158
The Peterborough School **Cambridgeshire**	D158
The Pilgrims' School **Hampshire**	D197
The Pointer School **London**	D180
The Portsmouth Grammar Junior School **Hampshire**	D197
The Prebendal School **West Sussex**	D203
The Purcell School, London **Hertfordshire**	D161
The Queen's School **Cheshire**	95, D188
The Read School **North Yorkshire**	D218
The Richard Pate School **Gloucestershire**	D153
The Roche School **London**	D181
The Rowans School **London**	D181
The Royal Junior School **Surrey**	D202
The Royal Masonic School for Girls **Hertfordshire**	D170
The Ryleys School **Cheshire**	D188
The Shrubbery School **West Midlands**	D214
The St Michael Steiner School **Middlesex**	D172
The Study Preparatory School **London**	D181
The Study School **Surrey**	D173
The Ursuline Preparatory School Ilford **Essex**	D170
The Villa School & Nursery **London**	D180
The Village Prep School **London**	92, D179
The Vine Christian School **Berkshire**	D195
The Webber Independent School **Buckinghamshire**	D152
The White House Preparatory School & Woodentops Kindergarten **London**	D181
Thetford Grammar School **Norfolk**	D162
Thomas's Preparatory School - Battersea **London**	D181
Thomas's Preparatory School - Clapham **London**	D181
Thomas's Preparatory School - Fulham **London**	D181
Thomas's Preparatory School - Kensington **London**	D183
Thorngrove School **Hampshire**	D197
Thornton College **Buckinghamshire**	D152
Thorpe Hall School **Essex**	D159
Thorpe House School **Buckinghamshire**	D195
Tockington Manor School **Bristol**	D206
Torah Vodaas **London**	D179
Tormead School **Surrey**	D202
Torwood House School **Bristol**	D206
Tower College **Merseyside**	D191
Tower House School **London**	D181
Town Close School **Norfolk**	D162
Treffos School **Gwynedd**	D228
Trevor-Roberts School **London**	D179
Tring Park School for the Performing Arts **Hertfordshire**	D161
Trinity Christian School **Greater Manchester**	D190
Trinity School **Devon**	D207
Truro High School for Girls **Cornwall**	D207
Truro School **Cornwall**	D207

Index

TTTYY School **London** D177
Twickenham Preparatory School **Middlesex** D172
Twycross House Pre-Preparatory School (The Hollies) **Warwickshire** D213
Twycross House School **Warwickshire** D213
Twyford School **Hampshire** D197

U

Ummul Mumineen Academy **Glamorgan** D228
Unicorn School **Surrey** D173
University College School Hampstead (UCS) Junior **London** D179
University College School Hampstead (UCS) Pre-Prep **London** D179
Upton House School **Berkshire** D195
Ursuline Preparatory School **London** D181
Ursuline Preparatory School **Essex** D159

V

Victoria College Belfast **County Antrim** D222
Victoria College Preparatory School **Jersey** D150
Viking School **Lincolnshire** D167
Vinehall **East Sussex** D196
Vita et Pax School **London** D177

W

Wakefield Girls' High School (Junior School) **West Yorkshire** D220
Wakefield Grammar Pre-Preparatory School **West Yorkshire** D220
Wakefield Independent School **West Yorkshire** D220
Walhampton **Hampshire** D197
Walthamstow Hall Pre-Prep and Junior School **Kent** D199
Walton Pre-Preparatory School & Nursery **Buckinghamshire** D152
Wandsworth Preparatory School **London** D181
Warlingham Park School **Surrey** D202
Warminster School **Wiltshire** D155
Warwick Preparatory School **Warwickshire** D213
Warwick School **Warwickshire** D213
Watchorn Christian School **Derbyshire** D166
Waverley Preparatory School & Day Nursery **Berkshire** D195
Wellesley House **Kent** D199
Wellingborough School **Northamptonshire** D167
Wellington Prep School **Somerset** D209
Wellington School **Somerset** D209
Wellington School **South Ayrshire** D225
Wellow House School **Nottinghamshire** D168
Wells Cathedral Junior School **Somerset** D209
Wells Cathedral School **Somerset** D209
West Buckland School **Devon** D207
West Hill Park Preparatory School **Hampshire** D197
West House School **West Midlands** 129, D214
West Lodge School **Kent** D171
Westbourne House School **West Sussex** D203
Westbourne School **South Yorkshire** D219
Westbourne School **Glamorgan** D228
Westbrook Hay Prep School **Hertfordshire** D161

Westbury House **Surrey** D173
Westfield School **Tyne & Wear** D186
Westholme School **Lancashire** D191
Westminster Abbey Choir School **London** D181
Westminster Cathedral Choir School **London** D182
Westminster Under School **London** D182
Weston Green School **Surrey** D202
Westonbirt Prep School **Gloucestershire** D153
Westville House School **West Yorkshire** D220
Westward School **Surrey** D202
Wetherby Pre-Preparatory School **London** D183
Wetherby Preparatory School **London** D183
Wharfedale Montessori School **North Yorkshire** D218
White House School **Shropshire** D212
Whitehall School **Cambridgeshire** D158
Wickham Court School **Kent** D171
Widford Lodge Preparatory School **Essex** D160
Willington Prep **London** D182
Wilmslow Preparatory School **Cheshire** D188
Wimbledon Common Preparatory **London** D182
Wimbledon High School GDST **London** D182
Winchester House School **Northamptonshire** D167
Windermere School, Elleray Campus **Cumbria** D189
Windlesham House School **West Sussex** D203
Windlesham School **East Sussex** D196
Windrush Valley School **Oxfordshire** D154
Winston House Preparatory School **London** D176
Winterfold House **Worcestershire** D215
Witham Hall Preparatory School **Lincolnshire** D167
Withington Girls' School **Greater Manchester** D190
Woodbridge School **Suffolk** D163
Woodbridge School Prep **Suffolk** D163
Woodcote House School **Surrey** D202
Woodford Green Preparatory School **Essex** 79, D170
Woodhouse Grove School **West Yorkshire** 136, D220
Woodlands School, Great Warley **Essex** D160
Woodlands School, Hutton Manor **Essex** D160
Worksop College Preparatory School, Ranby House **Nottinghamshire** ... D168
Wycliffe College **Gloucestershire** D153
Wymondham College Prep School **Norfolk** 68, D162
Wynstones School **Gloucestershire** D153

Y

Yarlet School **Staffordshire** D213
Yarm Preparatory School **Stockton-on-Tees** D186
Yarrells Preparatory School **Dorset** D208
Yateley Manor School **Hampshire** D197
Yehudi Menuhin School **Surrey** D202
Yesodey Hatorah Senior Girls' School **London** D177
York House School **Hertfordshire** 70, D161
York Steiner School **North Yorkshire** D218
Yorston Lodge School **Cheshire** D188